CONCEPTUAL COORDINATION

How the Mind Orders Experience in Time

CONCEPTUAL COORDINATION

How the Mind Orders Experience in Time

William J. Clancey

Institute for Human and Machine Cognition
University of West Florida, Pensacola
and
NASA Ames Research Center
Moffett Field, CA

LEA LAWRENCE ERLBAUM ASSOCIATES, PUBLISHERS
1999 Mahwah, New Jersey   London

The final camera copy for this work was prepared by the author, and therefore the publisher takes no responsibility for
consistency or correctness of typographical style. However,
this arrangement helps to make publication of this kind of
scholarship possible.

Lawrence Erlbaum Associates, Inc., Publishers
10 Industrial Avenue
Mahwah, NJ 07430

Cover design by Kathryn Houghtaling Lacey

Library of Congress Cataloging-in-Publication Data

Conceptual Coordination : how the mind orders experience in
time / by William J. Clancey.
        p.   cm.
   Includes bibliographical references and index.
   ISBN 0-8058-3143-6 (c : alk. paper).
   1. Cognitive science.   2. Cognition.   3. Knowledge, Theory of.
   4. Artificial Intelligence I. Title.
   BF311.C5395   1999
   153—dc21
                                              99-28055
                                              CIP
Books published by Lawrence Erlbaum Associates are printed on
acid-free paper, and their bindings are chosen for strength and durabil-
ity.

Printed in the United States of America
10 9 8 7 6 5 4 3 2 1

*Dedicated to my hosts and friends in 18 countries
who have provided a forum for these ideas*

Contents

Preface

Contrasting human knowledge and computer systems is essential for anyone seeking to apply computer technology, to understand human cognition by modeling it, or to build machines that are as intelligent as people. This is because, in some ways, conventional computational methods exceed what the human brain can do. In other areas, however, the brain is far more capable than today's computer programs. My objective in this book is to tease apart these two aspects so we know what to build on and what requires improvement in our past inventions.

At the core of my inquiry is a broader view of conceptualization, admitting especially nonverbal organizers, and an approach for tying conceptualization to physical behavior and perception. Throughout I pursue the hypothesis that neurobiological memory is not a place where descriptions or indeed any kinds of things are stored; rather, conceptual memory is in essence a memory for processes. This book reconsiders from scratch what human process memory can do and develops a kind of specification for building a machine that has the same capability.

CONCEPTUAL COORDINATION

Our everyday experience is ordered by an ongoing understanding of what we are doing, where we are, and what role we are playing in larger social enterprises. I call this *conceptual coordination*. Our thought and behavior is inherently temporal; coordination entails a relation of ideas and actions in time. Two kinds of temporal relations are illustrated and compared in this book: *sequential ordering* (one categorization of experience follows another) and *simultaneous ordering* (two or more categorizations mutually define each other). When categorizing operates on its own results, higher-order categorizations may be formed, producing the varieties of hierarchical composition, object classification, and proceduralization familiar to cognitive psychologists. Conventional computer models contain a complex repository of stored rules, pattern descriptions, and procedures designed to replicate observed human behavior. In this book I show how relatively simple neural processes of activation, working on themselves, can produce complex behaviors by combinations of categorization, coupling, and sequencing.

Thus, traditional models serve as a kind of *specification* for producing a scientific *explanation* of how the brain physically works. In short, the map is not the territory—pattern descriptions are not literally stored in the brain like recipes and conventional computer programs. Taxonomic models of knowledge roughly characterize what people know, but inadequately represent how categories form and how they relate structurally and temporally to constitute a conceptual *system*. Philosophical debates argue about the relation of symbols to what is in the brain. However, not enough attention is paid to how *relations between symbols* are dynamically operating in different modalities (verbal, visual, gestural, etc.) within perceptual-motor circuits. Dewey (1939) pioneered this argument, as in this excerpt where he said that Bertrand Russell equated all knowledge and reasoning with the manipulation of descriptions, here called *propositions*:

> The exclusive devotion of Mr. Russell to discourse is manifested in his assumption that *propositions* are the subject matter of inquiry, a view assumed so unconsciously it is taken for granted that Pierce and I likewise assume it. But according to our view—and according to any thoroughgoing empiricist—*things and events* are the material objects of inquiry, and propositions are a *means* of inquiry, so that as conclusions of a given inquiry they become means of carrying on further inquiries. Like other means they are modified and improved in the course of use. (p. 573)

In this respect, descriptive cognitive models are a means, a tool, for investigating the brain. Propositions about the world, whether stated by a problem solver or a scientist about the problem solver's knowledge, reveal how the person has experienced things and events. It remains to explain how the world comes to be experienced in this way, which I argue can only be accomplished by moving from propositions—descriptions of knowledge—to the neural bases for cognition. This is not to discount the importance of language or social analyses, but to emphasize that the neural level also constrains and shapes experience.

In *Situated Cognition* (Clancey, 1997c) I introduced the idea that categories might be coupled, arising together and mutually constraining each other. I contrasted *coupling* with *reasoning*, and showed that much of descriptive cognitive modeling research has attempted to read complex notions of describing, indexing, matching, search, and inference—all aspects of higher-order conscious behavior of a person—into the simpler neural processes of perception and physical coordination. This theoretical ploy, called *historical revisionism* by Schön, has produced a great variety of useful computer techniques and systems, but such methods do not measure up to what the brain can do and seriously misconstrue the nature of knowledge, memory, and thinking.

I have suggested instead that conceptualization might operate in a way similar to perception, with concepts being coupled (simultaneous), rather than only inferred (sequential). I have also stressed that concepts are not only verbal.

Categorizing relations across modalities is an important foundation for creative thought, and indeed a major source for articulated theories.

In this book, I aim to answer the question I raised in *Situated Cognition*:: If knowledge is not stored descriptions, in the manner claimed by most cognitive models, then how does memory work? Such an investigation must necessarily look at different kinds of phenomena, for I am not questioning the accuracy or validity of existing experiments and models per se. Instead, I move down a level of detail. Specifically, suppose that A is associated with B in a subject's behavior. Rather than modeling this as a rule, "A => B," which is stored in memory, I pursue the hypothesis that the relation between A and B is a physical neural activation—neural process A activates neural process B. The idea that meaningful relations are physically connected in the brain ("connectionism") is the basis for inventing a new kind of *process memory* architecture, which is my objective here.

Another idea I have emphasized is that speaking is not translating what has already been verbalized inside. We must therefore elucidate the nature of concepts such that they can work together to organize speech. Especially, we should explore multimodal forms of conceptualization—gesture, image, and sound. Can we build up from a kind of subatomic (subsymbolic) theory of categorization memory how referential and intentional behavior is possible? This strategy leads to the hypothesis that conceiving of objects and referring to them in our thought is not part of the neural architecture (e.g., like pointers and variable bindings as in a programming language), but a semantic, learned notion that then acts as a fundamental component of reasoning.

Some capabilities that we get for free in higher-level programming languages, especially sequential memory, are "implemented" in a different way in neural memory. Significantly, other features of programming languages that are an essential aspect of higher-order consciousness, such as the ability to hold multiple ideas active and compare them, are perhaps only found in nature in primates (although ravens show some potential here). Rather than treating all intelligence as based on a universal, mathematically defined computer, we need to understand the variety of conceptual coordination architectures that occur in nature. Perhaps the simpler varieties will be easier to understand and replicate in a machine.

A key idea of my analysis is that some features of intelligent behavior, such as the ability to give a name to an object or an idea and the ability to count, are based on fundamental aspects of neural activation, such as the ability to categorize a relation between a percept and another categorization. The experience of knowing that you "have an idea" requires categorizing that categorizing is occurring. But such *conceptual coordinations* are learned, not built into the architecture. By virtue of how the architecture is activated in place, memory and "controlling" processes are indistinguishable. Consequently, many organizers that some researchers have thought to be innate or built in, such as grammar, logical thought, or goal-directed behavior, may actually be learned processing capabilities constituting a kind of "virtual machine" (see chapters **5** and **9**).

Computer science, psychology, and neurobiology provide many of the pieces we need to understand how the brain works—a memory mechanism that is quite different from most computer systems. To invent this new kind of memory machine, a process memory, we need to break with familiar ideas about computation. This requires resisting a conservative pull, the belief that we already understand intelligence, that our models fit human behavior perfectly well, and that nothing more remains to be discovered but implementation details. I claim that in those details, we will find that the very foundation of modern cognitive psychology has been wrong, that concepts are not symbolic descriptions stored in a repository, that understanding is not a graphic parse describing meaning, that behaving does not proceed by packing up a plan or procedure and executing it. To support these claims, I closely examine existing models of memory, showing how all our diagrams assume a kind of static, whole, connected form that is not necessary. Then closely examining human experience from this new perspective, I show how ordered behavior in time might be constructed and composed dynamically from simple processes of sequential and synchronous activation of categories.

Equally important, I stress how experience in time is organized by a person's ongoing reconceptualization of "what I am doing now" (WIDN). In terms of *mechanism*, this aspect of higher-order consciousness involves a capability to hold and relate multiple categorizations on different levels (as in planning errands while remaining focused on this afternoon's activities and what I will do downtown by car), which most programming languages take for granted. Consequently, the differences between this aspect of conceptual coordination in people and data structures and processes in computer systems has not been critically examined. Moreover, in terms of *content*, ongoing conceptualization of WIDN constructs a persona—a constellation of role, norms, and expectations—that constrains what constitutes a problematic situation and how it is pursued. This social aspect of knowledge is very often viewed as a distraction from or distortion of "real" task knowledge, as in favoritism, cliques, and knowing how to get ahead in an organization. However, as a conceptualization of activity, such social understanding constitutes an embracing, contextual grasp of values—often called *motivation*—that drives and shapes problem solving, affecting the quality of everything we do.

READER'S GUIDE

This book has three parts, consisting of a computational background, an analysis of human experience, and a reconsideration of past models:

Part I: Computational Models of Process Memory
Part II: Serial Learning as Physical Coordination
Part III: Speaking as Creating Knowledge

In Part I well-known representational ideas, such as graphs and production rules, are reexamined in terms of the assumption that memories are stored, matched, and copied as if they were things. Two key examples—the duck-rabbit ambiguous figure and a perceptual color illusion—illustrate the distinction between simultaneous and synchronous activation and how they work together. I present a simple notation for how categories are activated in time, called *activation trace diagrams*. New ideas for building a neural process memory are introduced.

Part II examines four examples of behavior that occur within at most a few minutes, including repetition in a skill, navigation, slips, and creative invention by analogy. These behaviors reveal how perceptual details and actions are related in time. We look closely at what people experience, especially momentary transformations from one idea or action to another. Our psychological analysis shifts from viewing behavior in terms of goals and descriptive states—a kind of blueprint or template view of knowledge—to viewing how one categorization activates another—a temporal view of how internal neural constructions develop and build on one another.

Part III reconsiders a variety of memory mechanisms—ranging from Bartlett to Piaget and Chomsky to computational models—that purport to explain how human coordination is physical, conceptual, and reconstructive. I show how reasoning is unwittingly incorporated in "librarian" and "investigative" models of memory, such that what happens within a single activation process and over cycles of articulate conception are conflated. With the constraints of activation trace diagrams in mind, I provide a novel analysis of the neural basis of grammatical speaking, explaining limitations in comprehension on the basis of very simple properties of activation in time.

I conclude Part III by reconsidering conventional problem-solving models of knowledge, showing that the patterns found in such models—which do fit human behavior well—may have an underlying basis in how multiple conceptual systems in the brain may impose organizations on one another.

The final chapter summarizes what my investigation reveals about the neural basis of consciousness and suggests how the philosophically and perennially challenging questions of intentionality and reference might now be resolved. This book does not describe how to build a human brain, but I believe it suggests the right angle of attack, which builds on what we have learned but seriously addresses the shortcomings in what we know.

ACKNOWLEDGMENTS

Many people have inspired and supported the ideas presented here. I am especially grateful to Jeanne Bamberger and Donald Schön for showing me how to look more carefully at experience, especially to appreciate the work people are doing as they create their own representations of the world. The work of Lucy Suchman and Jean Lave in cognitive anthropology and Phil Agre and David Chapman in artificial intelligence (AI) showed especially how "using" representations might be reconstrued as transactions, mutual transformations of physical materials and internal constructions, rather than information-processing tasks of digesting and regurgitating somebody else's problem descriptions and procedures. These ideas were later elaborated for me in the Dewey reading group at the Institute for Research on Learning (IRL) (with Jeremy Roschelle, Erik Bredo, Jim Greeno, and Ray McDermott). Israel Rosenfield has also shared and strongly supported this historical approach to cognitive science.

Beyond the direction and inspiration of the seminal studies I have mentioned already, I am indebted to my friends and colleagues in AI and cognitive science who have patiently read and commented on earlier versions of this material: Peter Benda, Mike Bickhard, Patrick Brezillon, Jim Greeno, Bob Howard, John Kolen, Rick Lewis, John McDermott, Stellan Ohlsson, John O'Neill, Rolf Pfeifer, Jeremy Roschelle, Valerie Shalin, Maarten Sierhuis, Steve Smoliar, Luc Steels, Kurt VanLehn, Erik Vinkhuyzen, David Zager, Stephane Zrehen, and the students and researchers at Zurich University. Joseph Toth deserves special mention for his detailed reading, intellectually incisive comments, and unwavering support over several years of an e-mail friendship.

Probably my most important experience during this investigation has been the broadening of my researcher identity as I have met and talked to people in the international AI and cognitive science communities. I have found many people around the world who have enthusiastically supported this work. I especially thank my hosts: Stefano Cerri, Jennie Clothier, Paul Compton, Ernesto Costa, Pierre Dillenbourg, Brian Gaines, Brian Gardner, Heinz Mandl, Patrick Mendelsohn, Bob McKay, Fumio Mizoguchi, Jean-François Nicaud, John O'Neill, Steve Regoczi, John Self, Mario Stefanelli, Chan Tak-Wai, Mario

Tokoro, Axel van Lamsweerde, Xin Yao, and Christina Zucchermaglio. The openness and thoughtful response I received confirmed my intuition that cognitive science could be more broadly defined to integrate the phenomena I study here. It is to these people and those who have come up to me after my talks and sent related materials to read that I dedicate this book.

Closer to home, I am especially grateful to IRL for encouraging my work on neuropsychological aspects of learning during 1991-1997, when most of this material was prepared. Funding was provided in part by the Xerox Foundation and Nynex Science and Technology, Inc. The book was completed during my initial year at the NASA/Ames Research Center, in the Computational Sciences Division, where I have sought to apply these ideas within the rubric of human-centered computing. I am grateful to Jeanette Johnson for so quickly providing reprints. Judy Amsel's enthusiastic support at LEA has been a godsend; I also am deeply appreciative of the copyeditor's detailing of the manuscript (especially for correcting to "ROM" my many fervent italicizations). My other distant collaborator at LEA, Sara Scudder, helped make my preparation of camera-ready copy a smooth and almost enjoyable process.

In practice, most work of this kind is done on weekends and on vacations; I thank my wife, Danielle Fafchamps, for allowing me to pursue my intellectual demons.

William J. Clancey

PART I

COMPUTATIONAL MODELS OF PROCESS MEMORY

1

Introduction: The Temporal Relations of Conceptualization

All the psychological schools and trends overlook the cardinal point that every thought is a generalization; and they all study word and meaning without any reference to development.

—Lev Vygotsky, *Thought and Language*, 1934, p. 217

Metaphors strongly influence scientific inquiry, biasing our models and the questions we ask. Historically, metaphors for the human brain have ranged from "mechanical like a clock" to telephone switchboards and digital computer systems. Recently, some computer scientists have suggested that we study human–computer interaction in terms of how the "wet computer" (the human brain) is related to the "dry computer" (programs and hardware). Although such talk may have a place, it is scientifically a questionable guide for either appropriately using today's computer programs or inventing more intelligent machines. In particular, to move beyond present-day programs to replicate human capability in artificial intelligence, we must begin by acknowledging how people and today's computers are *different*. We must ground and direct our inquiry by the frank realization that today's programs are incapable of conceiving ideas—not just *new* ideas—they cannot conceive at all. The nature of conceptualization is perhaps the most poorly grasped of all cognitive phenomena we seek to explain and replicate in computer systems.

At least since the 1980s, an increasing number of cognitive scientists have concluded that if we are to understand the variety of behavior in people and other animals, and indeed how complex reasoning is possible at all, we must reformulate the computational metaphor that has been the basis of our very successful models of human knowledge and problem solving. We must reformulate the very idea that knowledge consists of stored data and programs.

1

We need a theory of memory and learning that respects what we know about neural processes. Rather than the idea that the brain is a wet computer, we need another metaphor, less like a clock or calculator and more like how biological systems actually work.

Most present-day computer models of human thinking suggest that conceptualizing involves manipulating descriptions of the world and behavior in a deductive argument. In these models, concepts are like defined words in a dictionary and behaving like following recipes in a cookbook. In this book I explore the idea that conceptualizing is more akin to physical coordination. For conceptualizing to serve reasoning, it cannot be made up of the products of thought—words, definitions, and reasonable arguments—but must be of a different character. *Conceptual coordination* refers to how higher-order neural processes (categories of categories) form and combine, and especially how they relate in time.

In this introductory chapter, I argue that fundamental ideas about what memory is and how it works are at issue. I illustrate the idea of conceptualization as coordination in terms of a distinction between *simultaneous* and *sequential* processes. Subsequent chapters in Part I reveal how conventional programming languages have biased psychological theories of memory, to the point that what the brain accomplishes is both taken for granted and under-appreciated.

1.1 THE ESSENTIAL IDEA: MATCHING AND COPYING VERSUS ACTIVATING IN PLACE

In this book I explore the hypothesis that so-called procedural memory (often called *serial learning* in the psychological literature) is at the neural level quite unlike stored procedures in a computer's memory. By a procedure, I mean any ordered sequence of behaviors, including habits; carrying out mathematical algorithms such as long division; and speaking in regular, grammatical sentences. In the theory I develop, such procedures are always reconstructed and never just rotely followed.

According to prevalent scientific models,[1] human memory is something like a library. When a particular memory is needed, an internal librarian goes off to the right shelf and brings out the book for you to read. By the conventional model of memory, you get the whole book delivered at once, as a piece—it was stored intact, unchanged from the last time you put it away. In this conventional account of memory, procedural knowledge is like a recipe, with the steps written out in advance and stored off to the side until they are needed (Fig. 1.1).

---

[1]There are indeed several scientific models of memory in contention. By the prevalent or conventional model, I mean the model that dominated cognitive psychology and artificial intelligence from the 1950s through the 1980s, described here as the storage view. This book is about other views, too, which arguably are becoming more prevalent.

In the example shown in Fig. 1.1 a "production rule" in long-term memory, "A implies B," matches the current contents of short-term memory (A). In the "remembering" process, B is copied into short-term memory, which is a special place for storing copies of information so that it can be read and modified (this place is called a *buffer* or set of *registers*). By copying from long-term memory, the rule that "A follows B" can be attended to and followed by a computer program. The memory librarian, a special program inside the computer, finds information by several methods: by the *location* where it is stored (e.g., like the Dewey decimal system), by the *name* associated with the memory (e.g., the title of the information), or by the *contents* of the memory (e.g., as indexed by a subject catalog). By this view, knowledge consists of structures stored in long-term memory, which are indexed, retrieved and copied by the librarian when needed.

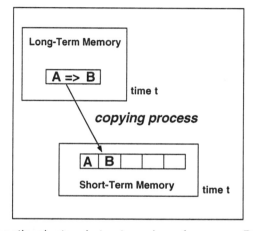

Fig. 1.1. Conventional, stored structure view of memory. Remembering is retrieving by matching and copying text into a "buffer" or "register."

In general, symbolic cognitive modeling of the 1950s through the 1980s assumed that this computational process is literally what happens in the brain: Human remembering is copying descriptions into short-term memory. Human thinking consists of manipulating the copy, not the long-term memory. When a person formulates a new idea or learns a new procedure, a description is copied back to long-term memory. By this view, remembering, thinking, learning, and memorizing are different processes, occurring at different times, using different structures located in different places. Indeed, many scientists have believed that, when we reason, these memory operations repeatedly search, copy, and revise a memory store. Thinking is a process of manipulating copies of structures retrieved from memory; learning is a process of selectively writing associations back into long-term memory. Consequently, the terms *search, retrieve,* and *match* are prevalent throughout the cognitive psychology and artificial intelligence literature (e.g., see Shapiro, 1992).

In the theory of memory I develop in this book, each "step" in our behavior physically activates the next step (Fig. 1.2). I call this a *process memory*. In the simplest case, process memory consists of only one thing being active at a time (A at Time *t*, B at the next point in time, *t'*). That is, the working memory has only one element at a time (compare to the buffer in Fig. 1.1). (I hope the reader is skeptical about terms like *thing* and *point in time*, as these are terms that we must become precise about.) For working memory to contain multiple ideas (both A and B, or more generally 7 ± 2 ideas, as descriptive models suggest), there must be an additional capability to hold A active while B is active. We often take this capability for granted. How is it possible that more than one idea can be active in a neural system at one time? As I show, questioning how memory actually works leads to additional important questions about the evolution of neural architecture and a better understanding of what consciousness accomplishes.

By the view I am developing, supported by recent research in cognitive neuroscience, working memory is a series of activations becoming active again, wherever they might be located in the brain. Instead of copying the "contents" of memory, a physical process is simply reactivated *in place*. A is associated with B not because a descriptive statement like "A implies B" is stored in memory, but because the structure constituting the categorization, A, physically activates the structure constituting the categorization, B. This is the essence of the connectionist or neural network approach. (Chapter 3 provides details about how categorizations may be formed as neural maps.)

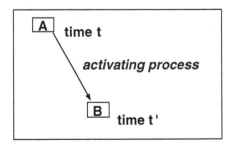

Fig. 1.2. Association by sequential activation in time.

In this simplest form of activation (Fig. 1.2), A (designating some categorizing process) is active at Time *t*, but not at Time *t'*. The relation "A activates B" is not logical in the sense of the meaning ("A implies B" or "if A then B"), but strictly temporal in the sense of sequential events—the activation of B follows the activation of A. At a lower level, some neurons involved in A's activation are contributing to B's activation at Time t'. But in an important sense, in the simplest forms of sequential activation the physical structure called A only exists as a coherent structure at Time t.

Metaphorically, activation of a structure is something like a meeting of people: The group only exists as a unit when the meeting is occurring. Individuals might potentially belong to many groups and hence participate in other kinds of meetings at other times. But (in this metaphor) a given group structure only acts as a physical unit when a meeting is occurring. In this simple view, A and B are two groups of neurons, such that A only exists as a physical structure when group A is "meeting" (i.e., activated together) and B does not exist at this time. But the activation of A at Time t tends to activate B next, at Time t', as if one meeting is followed by another.

I said that the relation "A activates B" is not logical. Logical relations are *higher-order categorizations,* or *learned* relations, not part of the neural mechanism of memory. By assuming that the units of memory are logical associations ("if A then B," "A causes B," "A is a kind of B," "A contains B," "B follows A," etc.) many symbolic theories of memory impose the content and organization of higher-order, conscious behavior (called *reasoning*) onto all levels of knowledge. Paraphrasing Bertrand Russell, they suggest that "it is logic all the way down." By this view, logical associations are stored as whole "if–then" structures (Fig. 1.1), called *production rule memory*.

I am suggesting that when we think "A implies B" we are constructing a higher-order categorization involving the idea of implication itself (just as causes, kind of, and next step are higher-order ideas). That is, the relations of logic are *categorizations* that indicate how other categorizations (ideas) are related. More fundamental, simpler associations form on the basis of temporal relation alone; namely, Categorization A activates Categorization B (Fig. 1.2).

Now that we are considering temporal relations, another possibility becomes apparent: Structures may exist together by virtue of activating each other at the same time. Fig. 1.3 shows that A and B activate each other simultaneously; this is called a *coupling* relation.

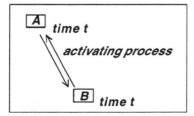

Fig. 1.3. Simultaneous activation. Association by activation at the same point in time (coupling).

1.1.1 Activation Trace Diagrams

The nature of networks in computer programs and how network diagrams are interpreted provides another way of understanding the distinction between conventional stored memory and a process memory. Consider how a diagram representing a conventional cognitive model depicts a network with concepts and relations (Fig. 1.4). Mathematically, the network is a special kind of graph. By this view, a memory is a network that exists independently, off by itself, stored in a repository, like a note on a piece of paper or a diagram in a book. For example, in the representation of the sentence, "John hit Bill with his hand," the categorizations "John," "Bill," and "hand" all exist as physical structures at the same point in time and are related by other, primitive, categorizations: PROPEL, MOVE, "object," "instrumental," and so forth. To remember that "John hit Bill with his hand," this theory of memory claims that you must store such a structure in your long-term memory. Again, the conventional view is that the structure is stored as a whole, connected thing and is retrieved as a unit unchanged from its form when put away. (With rare exception, forgetting is not incorporated into symbolic models of memory, just as learning is not inherent—occurring at every step—in most symbolic models of behavior.)

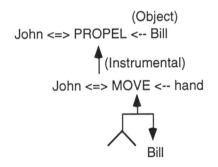

Fig. 1.4. Conventional view of memory as a static network. *Conceptual dependency* representation of "John hit Bill with his hand." PROPEL and MOVE are conceptual primitives with an actor designated by a double arrow (⇔). (Adapted from *Encyclopedia of Artificial Intelligence*, Shapiro, 1992, p. 261. Copyright ©1992. Reprinted by permission of John Wiley & Sons, Inc.).

Less commonly in the computational modeling literature, one finds diagrams that show a "trace" of processing events occurring in time. This is the kind of diagram I frequently use in this book (Fig. 1.5). In this *activation trace diagram*, three time periods are represented, designated t, t', and t''. Each letter in the diagram designates a categorization, a physical neural structure. In the example, categorizations X and A are active and activating each other (a coupling). X activates Y, such that at the next point in time, t', Y is active. Also at t', B is active and coupled to Y. Most important, at Time t', as shown here, structures associated with X and A are no longer active; in some important sense they do not exist. If they are reactivated, they will have a different physical form. Only Y and B exist at Time t'. Finally, at Time t'' Z becomes active and Y and B do not exist. In chapter 10, I show how such diagrams better explain grammatical behavior than the static, nonsequential view of conceptual relations in a parse graph (Fig. 1.4).

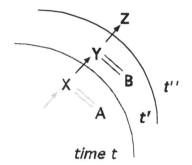

Fig. 1.5. Activation trace diagram—neural processes activating each other sequentially in time (X → Y → Z) and coupled neural processes (X = A, Y = B). Shading suggests that Time t is in the past, so connections are weakening or no longer active.

1.1.2 Categorized Sequences

In considering the neural basis of procedural memory, we need one more activation relationship, namely the idea of a *categorized sequence*, more commonly called a *chunk* (Fig. 1.6). C is a higher-order categorization, subsuming the sequence X → Y → Z. In physical neural terms, C is a neural map that in some way activates and is activated by X, Y, and Z. In semantic terms, C is a kind of *conceptualization*. Exactly how the neurons are related in categorizations X, Y, Z, and C is not clear. I present various possibilities in this book. By the meeting metaphor, C is a group in a meeting that contains or influences a sequence of other meetings (X, Y, and Z). The point of the diagram is to show how categorizations may be related temporally by a kind of physical inclusion process called *subsumption*. That is, C physically exists as an active structure starting at Time t and persists through Time t'', X, Y, and Z are activating at the points in Time t, t', and t'', respectively. C physically contains (subsumes) X, Y, and Z. In Part II, I reexamine a variety of cognitive phenomena to tease apart how this physical activation relation works, especially how hierarchical sequencing with substitutions produces what we view as serial behavior.

From the neural perspective, a central claim about memory is that activations in time are prone to recur. This is the fundamental *reconstructive* aspect of memory: If A becomes active again (Fig. 1.6), A will bias the activation of X at the same point in time, which will bias the activation of Y at the next point in time, and so forth. Similarly, if C becomes active, this will bias the production of the sequence, $X \rightarrow Y \rightarrow Z$.[2]

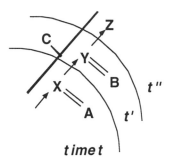

Fig. 1.6. Higher-order (conceptual) categorization of a sequence (C).

The point of using activation trace diagrams (Fig. 1.6) is to raise issues about how the structures are physically related, that is, to develop a structural-causal model of neural systems at the level of detail of how categorizing occurs in time. For example, if a sequence consists of categorizations activating in time, then how can a categorization be repeated? For instance, when we spell the word *book* is there a "pointer" from *o* to itself? Why do not we keep repeating, so we spell out, "boooooo..."? The activation perspective forces reconsideration of how conceptual control works, which conventional "symbolic" models based on programming languages take for granted (see Fig. 6.6 for further consideration of the *book* example).

1.1.3 Research Program

Given that the title of this book is *Conceptual Coordination*, I need to stress that how I talk and think about conceptualization and coordination is nonconventional. To start, conceptualizations, as I develop the idea, are *higher-order categorizations*, that is, categorizations of other categorizations. I consider two kinds of higher-order categorizations: sequential and simultaneous categorizations. A *sequential* higher-order categorization, as in a practiced procedure that satisfies a goal, is a categorization of an ordered sequence of activations (designated by C in Fig. 1.6). A *simultaneous* higher-order categorization, as in face recognition or learned (chunked) arrangements on a chessboard, relates multiple couplings at the same point in time (such as X = A).

---

[2]Reconstruction at this level should not be confused with a person's deliberate attempt to reconstruct a story, such as by relating categorizations in different modalities (images, names, sounds) and reasoning about the causal relations of events. The reconstruction here is merely reactivation of neural relations.

Subsequent sections in this chapter illustrate and further contrast sequential and simultaneous (also called *successive* and *synchronous*) categorizations.

To this point, I have introduced what may appear to be a lot of abstract terminology, but really that is all there is to it. Using just the ideas given here, I provide new analyses of a wide variety of human behavior, including a person interacting with a graphical computer interface, a child learning to swim, typing errors, and previously unexplained patterns in universal grammar. My technical ploy is to adopt a simple way of interpreting behavior—in terms of how categorizations are activating each other in time. This approach is quite constrained compared to the library model of memory deriving from conventional programming ("the brain is a wet computer") and forces us to question aspects of behavior that we would never have even observed before. We shift from describing what people are doing in terms of stored recipes to wondering more basically, "How could the brain do this at all?"

As I have indicated, cognitive scientists are now starting to call into question how computational models work. Schneider (1999) nicely summarized the reconsideration of biological processes:

> Biology provides not only rich concepts that suggest different and powerful metaphors but also excellent models for processing with a different style of computing than often present in computational optimization constraints. For example, the computer model provided the concepts of a general Short-Term-Store (STS) and a Long-Term-Store (LTS) which is based on computer RAM and disk storage . . . . This suggested a false independence of content in STS and LTS. (p. 342)

> Over the years, working memory has transitioned from the concept of a temporary buffer of information (as in the STS of Atkinson and Shriffin) to multiple processors (Baddeley) and distributed networks of processing (Rumelhart and McClelland). (p. 342)

To repeat the central hypothesis of this version of cognitive neuroscience, *neurobiological memory* is a mechanism by which categorizations activate each other in time. In contrast, the conventional diagram of "knowledge" stored in a computer memory suggests that human memory is a place where symbol networks (with symbols like "John" and PROPEL) are stored intact, as wholes, in a timeless way (like text in a book). The reconstructive process of biological memory involves activation in time of physically connected structures—hence the term *connectionism*—not storage, copying, and assembly in a new space. When a new categorization forms, it physically relates the structures that are part of the present functional, perceptual-motor circuit. Thus, memory is a capability of reusing categorization structures that have been active together in the past.

Several points about my analytic approach need to be stressed. First, I do not provide a simulation model of a new memory system, but rather a specification for how categorizations (which are neural processes) relate in time. The typical approach of simulation modeling, if pursued unreflectively by adopting conventional programming metaphors, would miss the very points I am trying to develop. Nevertheless, I strongly agree that a "lower level" simulation that attempts to capture some of the processes described here is valuable, and I discuss efforts in that direction (especially chapter 10).

Second, I hypothesize that once we have better analyzed human experience and existing models, we will be able to build mechanisms that transcend what the human brain can do. In particular, this study suggests that human long-term memory has different characteristics than a computer database. On the one hand, memory in computational systems is more literal (and hence reliable) and on the other hand it is more rigid (and hence less adaptable). These differences are visible when we spend less time shoe-horning observations into an architecture that makes the same old assumptions about storage and indexing, and more time analyzing human experience and theorizing about the fundamental processes of forming, sequencing, chunking, and substituting categories in time. That is, we must stop viewing the brain as a wet computer and try to understand what it is actually doing.

The next section provides examples of synchronous and sequential activation, illustrating how they interact in apparently simple visual processing. I then provide a brief historical perspective to this approach, which predates conventional computer models. I conclude this chapter by summarizing the theoretical components again so they are more easily referenced.

1.2 SYNCHRONOUS VERSUS SEQUENTIAL ACTIVATION

The idea of *synchronous association* (ideas combined simultaneously) and *successive association* (ideas following each other in time) was fundamental to early British associationism of the 19th century (Anderson and Bower, 1973/1980). According to this distinction, associations form synchronously and simultaneously, and reactivate in the same way in learned behavior. But the distinction has not been an essential consideration in the study of memory architectures. For example, Anderson and Bower said that the idea has been "of little interest in our present concern with human memory" (p. 22). Associations in semantic network models, knowledge-based systems, and logic systems alike are viewed as statically stored in memory (all elements of memory coexist, as in Fig. 1.1 and Fig. 1.4).

In this book I stress that some associations are formed and reactivated sequentially (Fig. 1.2). By hypothesis, sequential associations do not coexist in the brain unless or until they are held active and associated in a larger, higher-order construct (a *categorized sequence,* Fig. 1.6). Furthermore, simultaneous associations consist of constituents physically activating each other, quite unlike the impression given of diagrams like Fig. 1.4 that parts are merely linked by name or address pointers (in the manner that information on an envelope links the sender and a recipient).

In effect, in a simultaneous activation if you extinguish one part, you lose the other. So if B and C are coupled (Fig. 1.4), erasing C would erase B. But this is not how a conventional stored program memory works. In short, conventional stored program memory replicates neither sequential nor simultaneous memory, because it is based on "stuff residing in a place," not a process activating in time.[3] To make this point clear, I present examples of simultaneous and sequential associations and then proceed to analyze basic, alternative architectures for memory that have been explored in cognitive science.

In large part, the distinction between synchronous and successive activation has been disguised by the distinction between data and program. In conventional computer programming, both data and program are statically and often independently stored in long-term memory. This leads to the idea in descriptive cognitive modeling that short- and long-term memory are different structures in different places in the brain. Indeed, the same assumption underlies the view that facts and procedures are separate kinds of memory (like the dichotomy between theoretical knowledge in math and science and the physical skills of a laborer).

The distinction between program and data is reminiscent of the separation of mind (mental process) and body (physical stuff). In many descriptive cognitive models, as we will see for example in the discussion of EPAM (chapter 11), facts and procedures are stored in different ways: Facts are often stored as propositions (sentences in some language, statements) and indexed by their meaning; procedures are stored as ordered steps. We should remain open to the grain of truth in this distinction, but I would like to pursue with some skepticism the idea that knowledge of "facts" exists separately from the procedures that create and act on them.

The more fundamental question is whether knowledge can be viewed as stored things at all. I claim that the synchronous versus successive activation distinction is more powerful than the storage metaphor for understanding the origin of procedural knowledge, especially how it relates to different sensory modalities (rhythm, image, posture). My goal is to invent a new "computational" architecture (i.e., an artificial mechanism). The point of bringing the analysis down to the level of data structures, memory, and activation is to show that we need a broader view of computation (which does not take variables, buffers, and copying for granted) and hence a broader view of what a mechanism could be (in which the parts are not fixed in relation but coming into being and changing their relations dynamically). My broader claim is that human consciousness, intentionality, and judgment will not be understood until such lower-level aspects of the human brain are understood. Neural architecture is not a mere

---

[3]This is not to say that a conventional programming language cannot be used to build an activation memory of the kind I am describing, just that the conventional stored programming architecture does not replicate the temporal and coupling effects.

"implementation" choice for symbolic calculators; it accomplishes something that present-day machines cannot.

The following two examples begin to deliver on these claims. By examining experience in terms of how categorizations are activated and relate in time, and not making conventional assumptions about storage and working memory, we see that fundamental neural processes are capable of organizing and reconstructing our experience in ways that today's symbol processing machines do not replicate.

1.2.1 Synchronous Activation: The Duck–Rabbit Ambiguous Figure

Figures with multiple visual interpretations provide a simple example of synchronous activation. The familiar "duck–rabbit" ambiguous drawing (Fig. 1.7) may be seen as either a duck (facing to the left) or a rabbit (facing a bit oddly to the right). The same marks on the page participate in different ways in these two interpretations: The lines to the left constitute a beak or ears, just as the bump on the right delineates the head of the duck and the mouth of the rabbit. In both perceptions, the dot and rounded central area are viewed as being an eye in a head. In shifting interpretations, these various elements come as a package; they change their relations together, simultaneously. That is, perceived features of the drawing are constructed and related synchronously to each other and to the conception of the object.

Fig. 1.7. Duck-rabbit ambiguity. (From Wittgenstein, 1953/1958, p. 194; derived from Jastrow, FACT AND FABLE IN PSYCHOLOGY.).

At a neural level, which we do not consciously experience, the visual elements are being regrouped, such that the whole is "seen as" a particular *figure*. We conceive of the figure as being a duck or a rabbit, and simultaneously are *perceptually categorizing* aspects of the figure in different ways. For example, when you conceive of the figure as a duck, you perceptually categorize the indentation as a boundary marker at the back of the head. When you conceive of the figure as a rabbit, the same black line area is perceptually categorized as a mouth region. That is, multiple categorizations are arising simultaneously and constraining the overall conceptualization (duck or rabbit). Such an overall organization is often called a *schema*. In some way, which we do not understand neurally, visual aspects of the figure are being individually categorized and related to form a particular kind of figure, a conceptualization—not just an assemblage of discordant parts, but a recognized thing.

Most important, we cannot categorize visual aspects in different ways at the same time. If you are seeing the rabbit and start to look at the ears as being a beak pointing left, you will see the duck (or perhaps feel confused). The individual visual aspects of the drawing can only be one thing at a time; a line cannot be both a mouth and the space between two ears. Moreover, when you see the duck, you are drawn to see the beak—the categorizations are coupled, so they activate and reinforce each other. Thus, there is a kind of "all or nothing" process by which we quickly, and apparently all at once, see the image as either a duck or a rabbit. We may also deliberately switch back and forth, shifting focal attention within the figure. In our experience we do not know how this reorganization occurs in the brain, nor can we control its particulars; the recognition process is said to be *cognitively impenetrable* (Pylyshyn, 1984, pp. 133ff.).

In other ambiguous figures, some visual elements may be disregarded in one interpretation and play an important part in another. That is, a perceptual categorization may not occur at all, even although the same marks are present on the page. In Fig. 1.8, we may view A and B as similar because they each have three fingers, or say that B and C are similar because they each have three indentations. In the first case, the small "prong" on the right side of B is not perceived as a finger. Indeed, categorization is not an absolute process of parsing the world (finding out the "truth"), but participates within higher-order, logical-conceptual organizations that coordinate "the parts." Chapter 7 explores how levels of categorization constrain each other in analogical reasoning. In particular, the finger-indentation example illustrates how *conceptualization of similarity* coordinates what perceptual categorizations are formed and related.

A   B   C

Fig. 1.8. Which are more similar, A and B or B and C? (From Medin, Goldstone, and Gentner,1993, p. 262. Copyright ©1993 by the American Psychological Association. Reprinted with permission.).

To summarize, the duck–rabbit example illustrates basic processes of the visual conceptualization process:

• Categorization of visual forms.

- Interaction of categorizations on different "levels."
- Mutual (coupled) activation.
- Exclusive relations (one interpretation at a time).

Many of these ideas have been studied and described by psychologists over the years (e.g., Gregory, 1970). My point here is that how such coupling works—physically in time—now appears to be fundamental for understanding more complex phenomena, such as habit formation and even reasoning.

To carry this analysis further, let us consider how it is possible to conceive multiple objects *of the same kind*. If we recognize a duck by activating a schema, what is neurally activating when we see multiple ducks (Fig. 1.9)? Why cannot we see this figure as a duck next to a rabbit? This example shows that the "copy and post" model of working memory (Fig. 1.1) is inappropriate—neural operations in the brain cannot simply copy and reuse categorizations in this way.[4]

Fig. 1.9. "I'm seeing two ducks" or "I'm seeing two rabbits." Why is it difficult to see one duck and one rabbit?

Arbib (1981) provided a mixed storage and activation model of the general case, which I show does not work. In Arbib's explanation, working memory, where our experience is "posted," is a neural level of *schema assemblages* that represent multiple instantiations of schemas (Fig. 1.10). For example, if we see a scene with two ducks, we would instantiate the "duck schema" in long-term memory once for each duck we see in the scene. In the middle section of Fig. 1.10, each instantiation, called an *episode*, is represented as a copy of the schema, posted spatially, as on a kind of working memory "blackboard." Features (the bottom layer) create schema episodes (middle layer). The different features detected at the lowest sensory level (e.g., a bump feature) compete with each other to produce a schema interpretation. Projected down from the schema level are inhibitory relations that prevent certain combinations of features or lead some marks to be disregarded. Thus, a given set of marks on the page cannot be interpreted as both a duck and a rabbit simultaneously. The schemas are "building blocks" from long-term memory; the episode assemblage

---

[4]Of course, the person can copy and post representations, either in the external environment, as in writing or diagrams, or in imagination. My overall claim is that operations of a conscious person have been imported into the lower-level machinery, so what the brain can do and the higher-order, sequential aspects of consciousness are confused.

represents a *scene* at this moment. The construction of an episode synchronously relates visual features and a long-term memory schema.

Referring to the discrete manner in which we see the duck–rabbit forms (Fig. 1.7) as one thing and can shift back and forth, Arbib (1981) suggested,

> The inhibition between duck schema and rabbit schema that would seem to underlie our perception of the duck–rabbit is not so much "wired in" as it is based on the restriction of the low-level features to activate only one of several schemas. (p. 33)

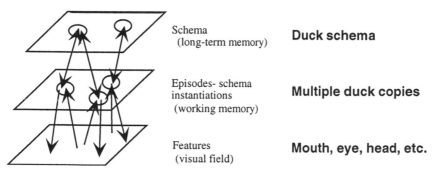

Schema (long-term memory)	**Duck schema**
Episodes- schema instantiations (working memory)	**Multiple duck copies**
Features (visual field)	**Mouth, eye, head, etc.**

Fig. 1.10. A visual scene is an assembly of spatially configured copies of schemas, copied from long-term memory and constrained by features in the visual field. (Adapted from Arbib, 1981, p. 32. Copyright ©1981. Reprinted by permission of Lawrence Erlbaum Associates, Inc.).

Arbib's notion of features and schemas with a dynamic relation between levels is appealing, but the idea of an assemblage as an instantiation or copy is not intuitively obvious. Surely it is possible that if I see one duck, I might produce a copy, in the manner a conventional computer program copies data to produce another data structure (cf. Fig. 1.1). But why cannot I see a duck and a rabbit at the same time when there are two sets of features to be mapped onto two different schemas in long-term memory? Something about the activation process is not properly modeled here.

Consider Fig. 1.11, where the figures have been arranged to suggest that the duck is biting the rabbit's nose. Here it is clear that in seeing two objects we visually scan from one to the other, sequentially in time. Although we might tell ourselves that the right figure is a duck and say that the left is a rabbit, there is a strong pull to repeat the previous categorization. Even when distorted, so the figures are no longer identical, the activation effect dominates over our deliberate attempt to control what categorization occurs. So if you start on the left seeing a rabbit, you might jump to the right to say it is a duck. But as soon as you pull back to view the whole, you see two rabbits. The effect is more than a competition of higher-order categorizations for perceptual features—there is plainly a bias to reactivate the immediately previous higher-order interpretation. (See Chapter 4 for an example of impulsive repetition.) In contrast, in Arbib's model it is possible to post a combination of ducks and rabbits together in the working memory. The copy and post mechanism (Fig. 1.10) is therefore too general (more powerful than neural processes), because it suggests a capability that people do not have and does not explain the bias to see a repeated figure of the same type.

Fig. 1.11. A duck biting the rabbit's nose?

To push the copying model to absurdity, what if I walk into a room with wallpaper depicting thousands of duck–rabbits (Fig. 1.12)? Is it plausible that my brain literally makes a physically distinct neural copy to represent each duck–rabbit in the room?

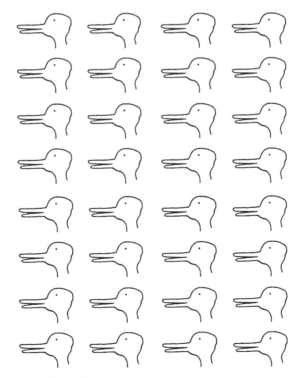

Fig. 1.12. Duck-rabbit wallpaper.

An alternative approach is to consider the viewer's experience over time (Fig. 1.13). By this view, rather than posting or copying, the duck schema is simply activated again. Each activation is part of a conceptualization ("I am seeing a duck now"), corresponding to episodes or schema instantiations in Fig. 1.10. Instead of imagining these schemas as necessarily all *posted* (physically copied) at the same time, conceptualizing is occurring over time: First a duck is seen; attention shifts, and another duck is seen. Rather than a structured representation that is isomorphic to the actual visual scene, the internal process involves the *repeated activation* of the duck schema (which I prefer to simply call a categorization). Moreover, the activation is not a "duck" categorization in isolation, but a broader conceptualization of what I am doing now ("I am seeing a duck", designated Ai).

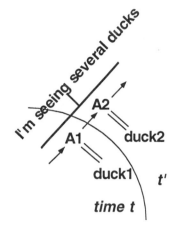

Fig. 1.13. Categorization of a sequence ("I am seeing several ducks") consisting of a single "duck schema" ("duck") activated sequentially in time. Each duck$_i$ is a perceptual categorization of features on the wall. Each Ai is a conceptualization of a scene incorporating a duck categorization ("I am seeing a duck").

Categorizing the sequence (A1 → A2) is a still broader, generalized conceptualization of "what I am doing now" (WIDN)— "I am seeing several ducks." That is, rather than a structure that holds assembled copies of duck schemas, we have a *conceptualization* of the experience of seeing multiple objects of the same kind. Rather than a data structure that locates categories spatially (Fig. 1.10), we have a higher-order *categorization of experience over time*.

In the case of the wallpaper, one might see only a few duck–rabbits at a time and peripherally perceive many similar shapes. Together, this leads to categorizing the whole as being "a continuous pattern of duck–rabbits."[5] I stress

---

[5]Here I am paraphrasing a related analysis by Pessoa et al. (1998, section 9.2).

that this is a person's experience, and thus higher-order categorizations of WIDN are continuously occurring. In some respects, the incorporation of higher-order *categorizations of patterns* provides for a simpler, less-cluttered view of how neural structures are related. Specifically, rather than endless copying (or any copying at all) one can posit higher-order categorizations that are *about* the experienced simultaneous and sequential patterning. Of course, on the other hand, one must also now explain how a categorization that has occurred in the past (e.g., the first duck–rabbit categorization) is available a moment later so the person can say, "I am seeing another duck rabbit." That is, how can we know that an experience is repeating? What prevents it from repeating endlessly, like a loop? Indeed, many of the detailed analyses I make in this book focus precisely on how repetition of categorization is detected and controlled.

The shift in perspective from a static history to how neural processes relate by activation in time builds on Hebb's (1949) observation that "perception of a simple pattern is not a single lasting state, terminated by an external event, but a sequence of states or processes" (p. 99). The schema assemblage is not necessarily a representational structure existing at one moment, but in the simplest case is a *sequence of activity*. That is, the pattern is not a thing in memory, but a categorization of a sequence of activation relations.

Consider how attention shifts such that the whole and the parts are experienced over time, as when we are looking at the rabbit and next see the ears as being a beak and then are looking at the duck. Assuming that t represents an organized assembly of parts a, b, and c, Hebb (1949) claimed that the psychological evidence suggests a sequence of categorizing, something like this: a—b—t—a—c—t—c—b— (p. 99). He called this series of "ideational" events and motor elements a *phase sequence*.[6] The hypothesis I am exploring is that such serial activation should be considered first as a fundamental aspect of the memory mechanism, before positing a copying process and intermediate data structures.

The duck–rabbit wallpaper example illustrates a combination of synchronous and successive activation, plus higher-order categorization that makes sense of the experience, encapsulating what is happening. This view leads us to question what we might take for granted if we assume a memory architecture that is like a conventional program with variables and copies of data. For example, how is it possible to count duck–rabbits? Do we count the number of instantiations in a neural buffer (Fig. 1.10) or do we need only to hold active the last number counted and say the next number while referring to something in the world? What is "referring"? The neural coordination of pointing, categorizing a kind of object, and relating the categorization to the next physical thing in space is a complex, fundamental example of conceptual coordination. Rather than starting

---

[6]For a modern, highly technical treatment of Hebbian learning, see Montague and Sejnowski (1994).

with a modeling language that allows us to say "For I = 1 to N," I am suggesting that we need to move down a level to examine what is actually occurring in the person's experience. What categorizations are actually occurring and how are they related temporally and on different levels? Shifting from a spatial to a temporal representation reveals that these questions need to be asked.

1.2.2 Sequential Activation:
Explanation of Kolers' Color Phi Phenomenon

Kolers' color phi phenomenon[7] is another famous example of conceptual coordination. This is a complex manifestation of the "phi" phenomenon, the illusion of apparent motion, "such as the experiencing of motion pictures when there is only the rapid succession of stills shown" (Sahakian, 1976, p. 264). At first, the phenomenon appears to be strictly an issue of sequential experiences with some kind of "filling in" process. However, like the duck–rabbit wallpaper, the experience can be understood only when synchronous relations are taken into account.

Wertheimer (1912/1961) described the general phi phenomenon:

Two objects were successively given as stimuli. These were perceived. First a was seen, then b; between, a "motion from a to b was seen," without the corresponding motion or the spatially and temporally continuous positions between a and b actually being exposed as stimuli.

The psychic state of affairs can be called—without prejudice—$a \, \Phi \, b$. Φ designates something that exists outside the perceptions of a and b; what happens between a and b, in the space interval between a and b; what is added to a and b . . .

Φ is something that uniformly concerns a and b, something which is built on them, which embraces and unites them. (pp. 1049–1050)

Sahakian (1976) indicated the significance of the phi phenomenon in psychological theory:

[It] established facts that were perceptual and that were not independent local sensations. Perceptual fields really exist despite their not being sense elements . . . . Learning consists of grasping the structured whole and is not just a mechanical response to a stimulus. Learning is the *insight* gained when one appreciates the *situation as a totality* by seeing how its relations are *structured as a whole*. (p. 265)

---

[7]Paul A. Kolers is not to be confused with Wolfgang Köhler, who investigated the phi phenomenon with Max Wertheimer.

In Kolers' (1972) color phi phenomenon[8] (Dennett, 1992; Dennett & Kinsbourne, 1992), two color spots—one red, one green—are flashed sequentially, a short distance apart (Fig. 1.14). But subjects report seeing a single moving spot, the color of which changes midway:

> When conditions are right the visual system creates a perceptual object in the intervening space where physically there is none. The perceptual object, moreover, resolves differences in appearance between the two physical objects, such as differences in color and shape. Hence the perceptual construction is not a mere redundant filling in of the space between flashes with copies of the flashes themselves; it is an active resolution of their difference. Any satisfactory theory therefore must account, first, for the perception of motion itself from discrete sequences flashes; second, for the perception and resolution of figural disparities; and third, for the relation of illusory to veridical motion. (Kolers, 1972, p. 18)

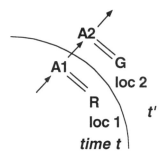

Fig. 1.14. Experimenter's initial view of Kolers' color phi phenomenon. Two flashes (Red and Green) occur in sequence a short distance apart (locations 1 and 2). Neural activation sequence at the time of the Green flash (t') relates two scenes A1 and A2, with coupled perceptual categorizations Red and Green. Why does the subject perceive a single object changing color in midtrajectory?

---

[8]Kolers' (1972) phenomenon actually refers to "Beta" or "optimal" motion, which he distinguished from phi phenomenon:

> The term 'phi phenomenon' or 'phi movement' is sometimes used generically for illusory motion. This is misleading usage, for phi motion correctly refers only to global 'figureless' or 'objectless' apparent motion, analogous to the very rapid passage of a real object across the field of view too quickly for its contours to be made out. Beta motion, on the other hand, refers to the perception of a well-defined object moving smoothly and continuously from one location to another, analogous to the slow passage of a real object across the field of view. (pp. 9–10)

The distinction is important, for it justifies my analysis of the phenomenon as a *conceptual* coordination, involving conception of an object. However, in this section I adopt the term "color phi" used by Dennett and others.

By my interpretation (Fig. 1.15), a higher-order categorization that "an object changed color" is, in Wertheimer's terms, "something that uniformly concerns" R and G, and "embraces and unites them." According to Dennett, the subjective experience has a temporally distinctive character, not fixed by the discriminations of the two flashes. The higher-order categorization I postulate is a *relation* "structured as a whole" that constitutes the understanding (a conception) of perceptual change.

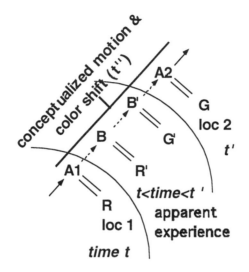

Fig. 1.15. Kolers' color phi phenomenon shown as a conceptualization of motion based on a perceived flow. A categorized sequence (schema) constructed at Time *t'''* (> *t'*, after the red and green flashes) includes perceptual categorizations (R' and G'), driven at the lowest levels by adjacent activity on the V1 cortical surface. B and B' represent postulated global maps that are part of a conceptualization of an object in motion. Time is from the experimenter's perspective.

What is the neural process by which an object appears to change color? How especially could this apparent change occur in subjective experience before the second color flash occurs? Wertheimer's earlier analysis suggests that the puzzle arises in postulating two prior, independently existing experiences (*a* and *b*), plus a later experience of motion derived from them. As Dennett (1992) summarized this paradoxical position, the independent experiences would have to be edited by a Stalinesque delay that allows modifying the stimuli before they arrive as a "product" or by an Orwellian postexperiential modification that revises the timing of the sensations. He suggested instead that the perceived effect (what I refer to as the higher-order conceptualization of motion) is just one of several "drafts" the brain created during the experience (by Time t'').[9]

> The Multiple Drafts model goes on to claim that the brain does not bother "constructing" any representations that go to the trouble of "filling in" the blanks. That would be a waste of time and (shall we say?) *paint*. The judgment is *already in*, so the brain can get on with other tasks! (p. 128)

Dennett postulated that the "judgment" of intervening motion and color shift could occur before "filling in." The paradox arises when we assume that there are intermediate *steps* by which independent experiences (R and G) are revised:

> The difference I am after is the difference between jumping to a conclusion and stepping to a conclusion by making some bogus steps on which to rest the conclusion (e.g., paint in the region, and then use that painted-in region as one's "evidence" for the conclusion subsequently drawn). (Dennett, 1993, p. 208)

Here Dennett argued for a move from a "traditional" view of "filling in" (painting and evidence) to a dynamic effect "treating input from one area as if it came from another" (p. 209). That is, what is "added" is not necessarily a set of discrete steps, but *categorizing* that something more structured ("more of the same") occurred.

At this point, more detailed consideration of the neural evidence is helpful. Churchland and Ramachandran (1993) provided the following analysis:

> The basic facts are these: on the cortical surface at V1 there exists a 2-D, retinotopically organized representation of the visual field: it is as close to being a literal picture as one could possibly wish, save that no one is literally looking at it. Certain small areas of that 2-D surface fail to receive information from one or other retina, information that is received by the rest of the surface. The failure is chronic in the case of the blind spot, and temporary in the case of "artificial scotoma." But in both cases, *the deprived areas regularly show vigorous representational activity*, activity of the very same kind displayed elsewhere on that surface, activity driven by the activity of the cells immediately adjacent to the stimulus-deprived area. *Such interpolated activity has a measurable time course*, and it can even survive for some seconds the cessation of the surrounding activation. (p. 50, italics added)

> The assumption that assorted cases must be psychophysically and neurobiologically uniform is fallacious. The basic neurobiological point is that there may be many different kinds of perceptual completion, at many different stages of processing, employing different mechanisms. Some probably operate early in the system, such as blind spot filling in, others may kick in later. Some cases may be very like perceiving a whole object, others may not. There may be a wide range of kinds of completion—kinds that are distinct psychophysically, computationally, and neurobiologically . . .

> If, as it seems, that brain does sometimes fill in, the reason may be because the filled-in representation is used in some subsequent stage of processing . . . .

---

[9]See citations in chapters 2 and 6 for additional explanation of the multiple drafts theory.

> Obviously, it is fallacious to conclude from the absence of a homunculus that no
> such intermediate level representation *could* be needed. (p. 50–51)

By my interpretation of Kolers' color phi phenomenon, "interpolated" neural activity is not just a matter of adjacent visual processing, but the formation of a higher-order categorization constituting the conceptualization of an object changing color (Fig. 1.15). "An object changed colors" is a conceptualization, not just a sequence of sensations or a single perception. This fits Churchland and Ramachandran's (1993) claim that there are different "kinds of completion." The experience of coherence may be predominantly perceptual, as in the case of a neon sign, with apparently smoothly moving lines and arrows. Or a higher-order categorization may involve intermediate neural activations that show spatial relations are conceived as a single object in motion. Such "interpolated" activation is not a "mechanical response" to preexisting, located perceptual categorizations (R and G). Rather, the conceptual categorization of the sequence, "one thing has moved and its color has changed" is a dynamic characterization of a *flow*, the spatial activation of neural maps in time (represented by R' and G' between Time t and t''). The character of this "filling in" depends on the duration of the flashes and the space and time between them (Sahakian, 1976).

The persistence of "interpolated" activity in V1 for some seconds easily accounts for the phi phenomenon of apparent motion within a 60-msec period. Quickly juxtaposed in time (as in the 1/24-sec separation of motion picture frames), the dynamic relations at lower levels enable an activity of higher-level relating, conceived as an object moving and changing colors. Separated further in time, the impression is of distinct objects in different places at different times. Furthermore, the resultant, constructed sequence derives from a topological relation between the first and second flashes, and there are intermediate categorizations (R', G') consistent with this topology.

The topological aspect is important. Kolers did not claim that such "filling in" occurred for all sensory processes:

> In particular, he did not extend the principle of isomorphism to sensory qualities,
> such as brightness and color . . . . The principle was restricted to "structural
> properties" of the perceptual field, that is, to characteristics of perceptual
> organization, such as grouping and part–whole relationships. (Pessoa, Thompson, &
> Noë, 1998, p. 727)

That is, topological higher-order categorizations of perceptual phenomena (grouping, moving, shrinking) bear a structural relation to topological aspects of the visual field. To be clear, the intermediate scenes shown as B and B' in Fig. 1.15 are categorizations with activation relations that are spatial (adjacent), not only temporal.

In interpreting Fig. 1.15, we must avoid "analytical isomorphism" (Pessoa et al., 1998, p. 742), which views discrete objects in the diagram as corresponding to discrete structures and events in the brain. What intermediate categorization and global mapping activity (B, B') lies between the visual neural processing and the conceptualization of motion? In this respect, Rosenfield (1992) cautioned against analyzing temporal experience in terms of categories that independently exist in time. The *categorization of a flow* does not necessarily require discrete, intermediate states. In drawing such diagrams, we neatly place B and B' to fill in the gaps in our analysis, but the categorization of a higher-order relation does not necessarily involve such intermediate steps. In Rosenfield's terms, experience

> cannot be accounted for by the neuroscientists' claim that specific parts of the brain are responding to the presence of particular stimuli at a particular moment . . . . [T]heir categories of color, say, or smell, or sound, or motion are discrete entities independent of time. But more importantly, . . . a sense of consciousness comes precisely from the flow of perceptions, from relations among them (both spatial and temporal), from the dynamic, but constant relation to them as governed by one unique personal perspective sustained throughout a conscious life; the *dynamic* sense of consciousness eludes the neuroscientists' analyses. (p. 6)

This underscores that the relations between the higher-order categorization and the other categorizations (B, B') in Fig. 1.15 is not only sequential, but synchronous—the conception of an object moving is a continuous, dynamic relation, with a coupling between lower and higher-order activity:

> [T}he impression of motion is a consequence of the brain's processing the relation between the one image and the next and the next. To put it more precisely, the consciousness of motion comes from the brain's relating one set of stimuli to the next set . . . . It is this relating, this connecting between moments—not the moments themselves—that is consciousness. Conscious perception is temporal: the continuity of consciousness derives from the correspondence which the brain establishes from moment to moment. Without this activity of connecting, we would merely perceive a sequence of unrelated stimuli from moment to unrelated moment, and we would be unable to transform this experience into knowledge and understanding of the world. This is why conscious human knowledge is so different from the "knowledge" that can be stored in a machine or in a computer. (pp. 6–7)

The conceptualization of a single object moving and changing color is "grasping the structured whole" (Sahakian, 1976) and "an activity of relating" (Rosenfield, 1992). Nevertheless, this "insight" has a physical manifestation. The conventional analysis, driven especially by symbolic computer modeling, is to postulate independently existing entities, states, and transformations, such that the physical neural system is characterized as discretely changing at moments in time. But understanding the temporal paradox of Kolers' color phi phenomenon forces us to acknowledge that the experience of motion is not composed incrementally from a set of independent *experiences*. Consciousness of time is complex, involving coordination of multiple sensory systems within a conceptual framework of objects and events. The conceptualization of a *single object* changing colors is enabled by a variety of lower-level filling in and dynamic change in visual processing. At a lower level, this filling in constitutes the awareness of motion; a higher level it constitutes an act of comprehension and interpretation. This higher-order conceptualization—the conscious experience of a world of temporal events—is a characterization of a dynamic process, and not assembled like *things* into a more complex object.

The neural relations of sequential activation, synchronous activation, scene coupling, and higher-order categorization allow us to abstractly describe the color phi phenomena. But diagrams like Fig. 1.15 all too easily fit familiar assumptions that experiences are "time stamped" and higher-order organizations are deduced in a building-block way from independently existing components. In Wertheimer's (1912/1961) terms, the higher-level categorization of motion both includes and unifies stimuli—"something that uniformly concerns *a* and *b*, something which is built on them, which embraces and unites them" (p. 1050). The very essence of my inquiry is to better formulate such structural relations so that we may understand their realization as physical processes in the brain. Throughout, we must be aware of the tendency to view processes in terms of discrete components and states. Higher-order organizations are not merely names for a succession of steps, but themselves dynamic, temporal relations of neural processes.

1.3 HISTORICAL BACKGROUND: THE SCIENTIFIC STUDY OF EVERYDAY PHENOMENA

At the conclusion of their reappraisal of the "filling in" phenomena, Pessoa Pessoa et al. (1998) concluded:

> We advocate careful studies of perceptual experience at the personal level as a complement to experimental research. Whenever we attempt to understand and explain our perception, we do so on the basis of our own perceptual experience of the world. Unless this experience has been conceptually clarified and systematically described, our scientific explanations will always be incomplete. (p. 747)

The examples I have given so far and those that follow exemplify this effort to articulate the person's point of view (WIDN), as well as the "subpersonal" neural processes, without confusing the two. That is, I attempt to relate the internal organizing mechanism to the person's larger conception of WIDN and the environmental task structure. So although this book is primarily about neural architecture, the examples are necessarily about people, who are always actively engaged in making sense of their experience. Rather than talking about "sense making" as if it were just a kind of puzzle solving (i.e., just a logical problem), I emphasize that the overarching conceptualization of the person, which takes the form of WIDN (often equivalently, "Who am I being now?"), is essential. That is, to understand how and why neural processes are changing, we need to consider what the person conceives he or she is doing.

As the color phi phenomenon illustrates, "experience" is not necessarily what an outside observer would say has occurred. There is therefore an anecdotal component to many of the examples we consider: The person's story of what *apparently* happened is a key source of information (Dennett, 1992). Such experience can be reported, but not directly observed. Nevertheless, by systematically collecting many such reports, as in the data of slips in speaking (chapter 6), or narrowing the investigation to phenomena that can be directly measured, as in the study of typing errors, a study can approach the precision of a laboratory experiment. Indeed, for the reader impatient with "anecdotal" evidence, I wish to stress that all the analysis in Part II preceded, motivated, and set the foundation for my analysis of transformational grammar in Part III. This latter study involves systematic data collected about natural language comprehension difficulties. I might have placed this material first, in the manner of a proof, but then all the finer points of how we need to look at everyday experience in a new way, exemplified by Part II, would have been lost.

The distinction between experimental data and everyday phenomena is less in the number of subjects or the use of controls, and more about the unexpected character of what can happen in an everyday, natural setting. Naturalistic settings have a special value for my present purpose, which is to reveal flexibility of neural processes. Experiments designed to fit stored program assumptions, such as the common approach of providing text in some form as "input" to a subject, makes it difficult to see where such assumptions might be faulty.[10] My analysis attempts to reveal the assumptions that any given architecture based on stored program mechanisms might make about memory (see the discussions of Soar in section 2.2 and EPAM in chapter 11).

The consideration of "bottom up," subjective phenomena relates to several trends in cognitive research:

- Situated cognition studies of people in everyday settings (Hutchins, 1995; Lave, 1988; Lave & Wenger, 1991).
- The shift from viewing categories as necessary and sufficient feature descriptions to prototypical, contextual relations (Bransford, McCarrell, Franks, & Nitsch, 1977; Jenkins, 1974; Rosch, 1978).
- Reformulation of intelligence in terms of multiple competencies in different modalities (linguistic, musical, kinesthetic, etc.; Gardner, 1985);
- The study of the grounding of verbal concepts in body experience (Johnson, 1987; Lakoff, 1987).
- Explanation of autism in terms of coordination across sensory modalities, leading to difficulty conceiving of reference and intentionality (e.g., see Barresi and Moore, 1996).
- Reconsideration of animal cognition (that it might exist; Griffin, 1984, 1992) and social behavior (Tomasello, Kruger, & Ratner, 1993).

---

[10]See the extended discussion of Bransford et al.'s memory experiments in Clancey (1997c).

- Anthropological studies of neurological dysfunctions (Clancey, 1997a, Rosenfield, 1988, 1992; Sacks, 1987).

To systematically describe naturalistic data, I use the well-known method in cognitive science of describing processes qualitatively. I use a semiformal notation, activation trace diagrams (Fig. 1.13), which provide a way of simplifying and generalizing examples of experienced behavior. I stress that these diagrams are descriptions of interactive behavior and experience, not mechanisms. They are intended to reveal patterns in neural processes, specifically relations between categorizations occurring in time.

In particular, I break from the dominant approach in cognitive psychology of equating models with descriptions of knowledge. On this basis, relating categorization temporally and compositionally, we can begin to unpack what consciousness does. By describing phenomenological experience over time in terms of attention shifts and recategorizing, we shift from studying and formalizing the semantic, logical relations of inference and judgment (a matter of conceptual content) to the neural processes coordinating human behavior and experiences (a matter of mechanism). As illustrated in the analysis of the duck–rabbit and Kolers' color phi phenomenon, activation trace diagrams relate perceptual categorizations to the categorized sequence conceptualization of WIDN. Such coordinating processes are inherently interactive, by virtue of coming into play as the agent is behaving and through their relations to other processes already active or mutually activating. The discussion of self-organizing strings (chapter 9) illustrates how such a mechanism might be simultaneously a memory, a pattern representation, and an organizing process.

Many cognitive neuroscientists have argued for such an analysis and notation. For example, Arbib (1981) described the need for an intermediate, graphic notation for describing learned organizers of coordinated action:

> a language in which we can talk about the coordination and control of multiple activations of different motor schemas and thus begin to analyze complex feats of motor coordination in terms of units (schemas) whose implementation we can explore in terms of neural circuitry. (p . 37)

> We are at a level of analysis somewhere between pure artificial intelligence and an attempt at setting forth the "style of the brain," but we are still far away from an analysis of detailed neural circuitry. (p. 35)

Vygotsky (1934/1986) attempted to reunify the elements of psychological analysis by focusing on children's learning in everyday context. He claimed that in analyzing meaning descriptively, we separated thought and words, losing track of their systemic relations:

> The living union of sound and meaning that we call the word is broken up into two parts, which are assumed to be held together merely by mechanical associative connections . . . . This type of analysis provides no adequate basis for the study of the multiform concrete relations between thought and language that arise in the

course of development and functioning of verbal thought in its various aspects. Instead of enabling us to examine and explain specific instances and phases, and to determine concrete regularities in the course of events, this method produces generalities pertaining to all speech and all thought. It leads us, moreover, into serious errors by ignoring the unitary nature of the process under study. (p. 5)

That is, conventional analysis splits sound and meaning as experiences ("the living union") into parts that are presumed to be linked mechanically (cf. Fig. 1.1 and Fig. 1.4). This analysis indeed finds general patterns that describe language and thought. However, the concrete relations of verbal thought (such as simultaneous activation, a unitary relation, Fig. 1.3) are ignored and developmental processes are subsequently misunderstood.

Shannon (1992), who explicated many of the same issues about stored symbol network models that I emphasize, summarizes Vygotsky's claim that a special kind of *biological* unit is required:

Psychology should define units as the basis for any explanation it offers...following the example of the cell in biology . . . . Such units should exhibit internal structure, be readily integrated with the organism's real action in the world, tie together different faculties of mental function and manifest distinct patterns of development. (p. 247)

By choosing categorization within a sequence of behavior as the unit to study, the conceptual coordination perspective fits Vygotsky's suggestion.

Following Dennett (1992, in his support for Minsky's [1985] *Society of Mind),* and of course Hebb, whose work and approach directly bears on the present inquiry, I view my analysis as an "imaginative exploration," a necessary theoretical stage:

All the testable theories so far concocted are demonstrably false, and it is foolish to think that the breakthroughs of vision required to compose new testable theories will come out of the blue without a good deal of imaginative exploration of the kind Minsky indulges in (I have been playing the same game, of course). (Dennett, 1992, p. 263)

Elman (1989) presented a similar point of view:

It is not that we have no sense of what the machinery is; the problem is much more a matter of lacking a computational model of what the machinery does, and how. Here we are still at the metaphor and hand-waving stage, but that is not a stage to shun; it is a stage to pass through on our way to more explicit models. (p. 18; cf. Servan-Schreiber, Cleeremans, & McClelland, 1988, p. 4, 1991).

I have cited these remarks to emphasize that an important theoretical stage in the progression of science involves a representational shift, with new terms and notations. That is the point of my analyses and the role of the diagrams—to relate descriptive cognitive models to neurobiology in a new way. Some researchers might believe that we cannot evaluate progress without having a new computational model in hand that works better than the conventional approach. But I believe it is equally valid to survey and reconsider a wide variety of phenomena and existing models before proceeding to program a new model. That is my choice and what I have done.

1.4 THEORY IN A NUTSHELL

With respect to the broad concerns of cognitive science, I pursue the hypothesis that consciousness can be understood and artificially constructed. However, I claim that to understand notions such as intentionality and reference, which have been the focus of studies of human intelligence, we must first understand the limitations of descriptive cognitive models: We have not elucidated or explained how categorizing processes are related and reconstructed in conceptual systems. As I said at the onset, today's program's cannot conceive at all. The very idea of memory in the best cognitive models is inadequate; both the structure and process of remembering must be taken apart and redeveloped. In so doing, we will find that the processes of perception, conception, and physical coordinating are not related in the simple ways suggested by conventional block diagrams of cognitive systems, by which sensory data are input to a reasoner that sends motor commands to a physical movement device.

In this section, I summarize the two basic claims of my inquiry: First, we should look for the neural correlates of primitive programming operations. Second, we should study human experience more closely to understand how categorizing occurs in time—fundamental operations that are not part of conventional programming languages.

1.4.1 Reconsidering What Programming Languages Take for Granted

By building on the constructs of higher-order programming languages—sequential memory, categorization of sequences as procedures, composition of procedures, binding of world data to variables, and so forth—that became commonly available in the late 1960s (e.g., Fortran IV, Algol68), most cognitive science research of the 1970s jumped over the more fundamental issues of how all these basic operations were possible and whether they in fact operated in the same way in the human brain as in a programmed digital computer. The primitive constructs of programming languages are basically the operations and notations of a reasoning person—named places, conditional actions, registers with stored values, counting, looping iteratively, qualitative comparisons. By getting these for free, memory and learning researchers did not consider that such operations and notational systems might be higher-level accomplishments that not every conceptualizing animal can do. What allows the human brain to accomplish what other mammalian brains cannot?

At another level, but very important to the understanding of neural systems, activation trace diagrams raise fundamental questions about whether categorizations are structures or processes. Is it better to talk about a categorizing process rather than a categorization *thing*? Specifically, a higher-order categorization, C (Fig. 1.6), might be better viewed as a categorizing process, which in some sense constrains the activation of X, Y, and Z so they become active in that order. Again, we might view C as a physical neural map (a structure-thing) that literally contains the neural maps X, Y, and Z.

The example of Kolers' color phi phenomenon illustrated how such a mechanism could account for why we experience Y when only X and Z have occurred. Related questions involve whether there is a special relation between C and X, the first categorization in the sequence. As a simple example, consider how you may remember the first letter of someone's name, but not recollect the name itself. Typing errors and other slips (chapter 6) suggest that there is an inner structure to categorized sequences that biases what kind of substitutions may occur (or equivalently why errors do not occur). Similarly, study of basic serial learning in children and animals (called *path finding;* chapter 5) suggests an ability to "return to the beginning and start over" and an inability to enact behaviors backward. Going backward may be trivial in a conventional computer model, but in a mechanism based on activation in time, a special, higher-order coordination might be required.

If the brains of all mammalian species do not have the same processing characteristics, understanding what is common or fundamental to memory (such as sequence and scene categorization) is essential for neuroscience, cognitive psychology, and artificial intelligence (AI) research. This understanding would on the one hand help us to be sure that our computational systems are as complex as they might be, and on the other hand provide a basis for understanding what additional capabilities higher-order consciousness confers on people, which other animals lack. Such an investigation complements past work on designing a program–model framework to perform certain kinds of computations of association, storage, and symbolic processing. Ultimately, my goal as an AI researcher is to relate descriptive models, connectionism, and neurobiology to build more capable machines. Progress requires articulating the differences between the best models and naturally occurring cognitive experience.

1.4.2 Summary: Categorizing in Time

Cognitive models have traditionally treated procedural memory, including inference rules ("if X then Y"), as if human memory is just like computer random-access memory: Associations are indexed in some way (either by location or content), they are retrieved unchanged from their form when stored (an essential characteristic of "memory"), and like programs reapplied in some new setting. A procedure is a thing and it can be brought out whole.

In this book, I explore the hypothesis that a sequential association, such as an inference rule or steps in a procedure, is a temporal relation of activation, such that if X implies Y, memory does not store the description "(IF X THEN Y)." Rather, the relation is one of temporal activation, such that when X is presently active, Y is a categorization that is potentially active next. I present examples, analyze computer models, and argue that every "next step" in serial behavior fits a relatively simple pattern by which categorizations are formed and related to each other. The mechanism of serial behavior involves:

- Reactivation of categorizing processes.
- Categorizing processes are physically constrained (activated) by recently active categorizations, including lower-order perceptual-motor processes and higher-order organizers (scenes and sequences).
- Every categorization is a generalization of how the categorization was previously active (moments or years ago) in coordinated behavior.

These conjectures are driven by two observations about memory made more than 50 years ago (showing the memory value of books after all): First, Bartlett described new conceptions as being manufactured out of previously active coordinations. How ways of seeing, moving, talking, and so forth. have worked together in the past will bias their future coordination, in the sense that they are physically connected again by the same relations. Second, Vygotsky observed that every coordinated action (or descriptive claim, image, conception) is a *generalization* of what we are already doing (saying, seeing, categorizing). Putting these together, we need a mechanism that resequences and recomposes categorizations in time, such that every reconstruction is a kind of generalization (or adaptation) of a previously created construction.

The basic building block of this theory is the notion of *categorization* which may be *simple* (*perceptual categorizations* such as the classification of a feature of an object, e.g., color or texture) or *higher-order* (categorizations of other categorizations).

I explore the idea that higher-order categorizations are of two types: a categorization of a *scene* (simultaneous relation in time) or a categorization of a *sequence of categorizations* (sequential relation in time). Categorization of sequences corresponds to the notion of a "chunk" in conventional models of memory. But note that there are two kinds of chunks: *temporally simultaneous* (e.g., the layout of a chess board at some point in a game) and *temporally sequential* (e.g., an idiomatic spoken phrase in a language). Both scenes and categorized sequences may serve as higher-order organizers to influence future experience.

Furthermore, in higher-order conscious behavior, as in people, an ongoing categorization of a scene is occurring that characterizes WIDN (e.g., C in Fig. 1.6):

- The categorization of WIDN subsumes most recent previous "steps", such that, barring impasses and sharp transitions (which do occur) the present categorization of WIDN is broadened to retrospectively include WIDN a moment ago (longitudinal aspect; Y subsumes X in Fig. 1.6).
- The categorization of WIDN is coupled to perceptual categorizations occurring at the same time (latitudinal aspect; A and B in Fig. 1.6).

The intuition behind this theory is that a variety of manifestations that have been described and separated in different theories of memory, going by names such as *declarative memory, episodic memory, skills, chunking* and so on, are all aspects of a few fundamental processes by which categories are activated, subsumed, and related in time. Furthermore, understanding human behavior requires bringing all the various processes of learning and reasoning under the conceptual purview of a person sustaining a sense of self, a role in a setting—the social perspective.

The fundamental activation relations among categories are represented by the notation given in Table 1.1. Features become perceptual categories; categories may be then simultaneously, sequentially, or compositionally related.

Table 1.1

Notation for How Categorizations are Related

C	C ⇔ C	C → C	C—I C1 → C2
Any categorization, simplest is perceptual categorization (classification relation)	Coupling, part of a scene (simultaneous relation)	Procedure (sequential relation)	Categorization of a sequence (compositional relation)

Although four building blocks are shown in this table, these are formed from just two basic processes of synchronous and sequential activation:

- A perceptual categorization is itself a coupling (or *classification couple*, chapter 3)
- A categorization of a sequence is a kind of coupling relation such that C1 and C2 are held active to form a unit.

That is, the chunking of scenes and sequences are the result of coupling and sequential activation operating on their own formations. However, the mechanism by which higher-order constructs form is not to be taken for granted—holding active a categorization that previously occurred (C1) and relating it now to an active categorization (C2) was evidently a tremendous evolutionary advance. That is, the ability to relate categorizations activating now as part of interaction with the world to categorizations in the imagination ("deliberately" reactivated) is at the heart of intentionality, referential meaning, and consciousness (Clancey, in preparation).

1.5 ORGANIZATION OF THE BOOK

The remaining chapters in Part I provide background, first, to be more specific about what I am questioning in existing computational models of memory and, second, to ground my claims in specific neurobiological theories of coupling and sequence learning. Chapter 2 considers conventional memory architectures in more detail, and relates my analysis to connectionism and other subsymbolic accounts. Chapter 3 pieces together existing "neural network" theories to show how the temporal sequencing, coupling, and higher-order composition I describe are neurobiologically plausible.

In Part II, I explore sequential phenomena on different levels of organization, ranging from reactive behavior to problem solving:

- Coupling of perceptual-motor activity and conception.
- Extending a *felt path*, as in rat navigation.
- Slips and composed parallel binding of categories.
- Seeing-as and reasoning by analogy.

These phenomena are selected because they are examples of how people organize their own experience, revealing how we are everyday investigators and creative improvisers. The examples all involve simple acts of repetition, generalization, ordering, and substitution. A person is engaging in some interactive behavior that changes the world. These changes are categorized and fed back into the ongoing behavior to form a coordinated transaction: doing, reperceiving, reconceiving WIDN, and doing again. Each perceptual-conceptual-motor coordination is itself involved in processes of repetition, generalization, ordering, and substitution. When the coordination is momentarily lost, a breakdown occurs, producing a slip. Slips then reveal for us how categorization works (by virtue of showing incommensurate pieces that were produced) and what higher-order organizing processes accomplish (by virtue of showing repetitions, generalizations, orderings, and substitutions that are not allowed to occur).

In Part III I reexamine and synthesize previous reconstructive models of verbal memory: Bartlett's view of schema reactivation, Piaget's approach to knowledge construction, Chomsky's theory of Universal Grammar, Feigenbaum and Simon's model of discrimination learning (EPAM), Schank's model of case-based memory (MOPs), and Kauffman's string theory. I show that most conventional theory has unwittingly placed higher-order conceptualization work within the basic memory and learning mechanism. By adhering to the foundational concerns of Bartlett, Piaget, Chomsky, and Kauffman, the implicit assumptions of computational storage architectures become visible. Teasing apart conventional models involves questioning claims many researchers take for granted (e.g., that expectations are verbal expressions), so the going is not always easy.

The central chapter in Part III is a detailed analysis of comprehension difficulties in natural language understanding due to interference in short-term memory (chapter 10). By adhering to simple ideas of how categorizations are related in time, we are able to explain patterns in transformational grammar, previously called movement and interference in terms of more basic operations of neural activation, anchoring, and composition. This analysis will be complicated for some researchers by confusion or biases against Chomsky's work; but I insist that wrestling with difficult and controversial areas is essential for making progress. In the concluding chapter, I provide a broader view of conceptual coordination and consider methodological issues in pursuing these topics.

2

Computational Memory Architectures

Schema theorists talk of schemata for rooms, stories, restaurants, birthday parties, and many other high-level concepts. In our parallel distributed processing models, units do not tend to represent such complex concepts . . . . If we are to do justice to the concept of the schema, we are going to have to look beyond the individual unit. We are going to have to look for schemata as properties of entire networks rather than single units or small circuits.

—David E. Rumelhart, Paul Smolensky, James L. McClelland, and Geoffrey E. Hinton, *Schemata and sequential thought processes in PDP models*, 1986, Vol. 2, p. 8

Computer scientists have invented many different ways to store and retrieve data in computer memory. These architectures range from the most basic random access storage to complex activation mechanisms introduced in chapter 1. As further background, I summarize in this chapter how a variety of well-known computational memory architectures—arrays, linked lists, semantic graphs of various sorts, procedures expressed in a logic calculus, and probabilistic graphs—have been used to represent sequential concepts (e.g., words, sentences, and mathematical functions). In examining these various memory systems, we rediscover why computational modeling is so valuable for understanding how the brain works. By contrasting models, we can elucidate aspects of programming languages that people take for granted or that are neurobiologically implausible.

Very simple computational ideas, such as arrays, pointers, and markers, raise fundamental questions about how sequential memory might be "implemented" in the brain. For example, a common issue is how a given memory element can be "reused" so that it may participate in more than one internal structure at a time, without making copies of the element. Copying is one of the most basic operations in conventional programming, but as the examples of chapter 1 indicate, it is not the only possible mechanism, nor is it obviously operating in the simplest cases of pattern recognition (the duck–rabbit wallpaper example) or temporal experience (Kolers' color phi phenomenon).

The common idea that sequential behavior depends on a memory of a procedure assumes that recognizing or enacting a sequence—whether it be a habit, a grammatical sentence, or a complex business office procedure—involves a procedure-thing, such that all patterned behavior involves *remembering* (cf. Fig. 1.1) and remembering involves things called *memories*.[1] From a conventional computational perspective, memories are assumed to be objects of some kind, which mathematically are *graphs*, by which conditional steps or events are ordered. That is, all models of memory based on the stored program approach assume that "knowledge of a sequence" involves a kind of graph stored in memory; models differ only in the details of how this graph is represented and how it is used to affect behavior.

Furthermore, the operations used in conventional programming of manipulating data structures have promoted two basic assumptions about procedural knowledge and reasoning about procedures:

- *Parsimony:* The memory architecture should represent sequential behaviors and experience (such as phonemic parts of a word) in the same manner that facts are represented; that is, as units that can be indexed and independently retrieved.
- *Transparency*: All purposeful (goal-driven) behavior requires deductively reasoning about procedures, which therefore must be represented in memory in a structured way, so their parts can be manipulated and independently revised.

This idea of procedural memory has been developed in the descriptive cognitive modeling paradigm in a variety of representational and processing architectures. A graph object or *unit* representing a sequence of events has been called an *event schema* (Anderson, 1990, p. 140), a *frame* (Minsky, 1977), or in the case of stereotypical events, a *script* (Schank & Abelson, 1977). The same idea has also been applied to representing knowledge of story structure and themes in graphs called *story schemas*. The common idea is that memory of sequential patterns is an abstraction of experience that describes stereotypic sequences of actions in words. For example, Schank's well-known restaurant script includes steps such as order meal, sit down, eat food, and pay. These scripts may be hierarchically organized (e.g., a separate procedure for paying), as well as organized into taxonomies (e.g., kinds of restaurants).

The intuition behind the idea of an "event schema" captures part of the sequential aspect of memory that I am exploring in this book. However, a neurobiological and social view of experience suggests that we delve into more detail about *how activation processes work* (how is any memory of ordered

---

[1]See *Situated Cognition* (Clancey, 1997c, chapter 3, "Remembering Controversies") for a discussion of the history of computational modeling of memory.

"steps" possible?) and *how compositional processes work* (how is any relation between previously unrelated ideas possible?). Here are the mechanisms to have in the back of your mind as we critically reexamine common computational models:

- An activation sequence is an interactive behavior organizer (not a kind of log or story about what happened), but an aspect of physical coordination.
- A sequence may be attentively reconstructed in a bottom-up way, rather than enacted as a whole (like a recipe or a fixed, stored program).
- Each "step" involves both *actions* (e.g., sit, eat, pay) and *categorizations* (e.g., table, food, money).
- Steps may be either particular incidents, a generalized recategorization of a "step," or an embedded sequence.
- In human behavior, "steps" are subsumed by conceptualizations of "What I'm doing now"—part of the nature and function of consciousness.
- In human problem solving specifically, an additional mechanism allows holding multiple, possibly nonsequential categorizations active, so they can be compared, reordered, or their relation otherwise locally categorized.

After surveying conventional, elementary approaches for storing sequential memories, I describe in some detail how episodic memory is represented in Soar, one of the best cognitive models. I use the activation trace perspective to elucidate assumptions made in Soar's architecture about explicit representation of goals and states. Finally, I briefly discuss connectionist approaches and the "subsymbolic" controversy.

In this review, I return to the roots of the computational modeling of memory. A variety of computer programming metaphors have been applied: replaying fixed sequences (executive model), moving pointers through fixed networks (interpretive model), reactivating sequences (data-driven model), searching problem-solving paths (goal-driven model). I reexamine these mechanisms, aiming to tease apart what aspects do and do not fit what we know about human cognition. This effort is crucial if we are to appreciate how programming languages have in some respects gone beyond what the brain can do, and in other respects lack the generative and associative capabilities of the neural system.

2.1 COMPUTER LANGUAGE APPROACHES

In conventional computer languages, data are separated from programs within a random access memory (RAM). The idea of random access means that any element can be accessed at any time. In practice the memory is partitioned according to various "process owners" (so my program cannot access your memory area). In fact memory access is often sequential, such that the next element accessed immediately follows the one accessed before. The simplest form of sequential memory is an indexed memory array. Variations allow the next element to be specified by name or a pointer and for this association to be probabilistic. I consider how these storage architectures relate to the activation trace perspective.

2.1.1 Indexed Memory Array

An indexed memory array is the simplest way to store a sequential memory in computer programming languages (Fig. 2.1). The array has a name (here "A"), and the elements of the array are stored in physically contiguous locations in RAM. Thus, if the first element is stored at RAM address 9000, the second element will be stored at location 9001. In fact, if the programming language uses a base 0 counting scheme for indexing arrays, it is trivial to compute the location of any element: Let A be the address of the first element, designated A(0), then the location of the array element A(N) is the address A + N.

Address	*Value*
9000	b
9001	o
9002	o
9003	k

Fig. 2.1. Indexed data array in a conventional programming language.

As the example indicates, if data are repeated so the same value appears in multiple cells (e.g., the letter "o" appears in A(1) and A(2)), then the value is simply copied. If we want to know "Where are the locations where the letters 'ook' appear?" we must search the entire memory. Given that people can answer questions like "Name three words that rhyme with 'book' very quickly, it seems unlikely that the brain is searching memory sequentially. This leads to the idea that another kind of link is required, called an *associative link*, which represents more than sequential relationships. (Of course, the rhyming example is my clever way of signaling that other modalities, such as sound and image are involved, not just letters.)

But there is another problem with indexed memory arrays—they are simply too reliable. Again from the viewpoint of human behavior, if the only kind of sequential memory were like an indexed array, it would be difficult to explain why when you are typing "book" you type "boat" instead. In conventional computer memory, when a program is reading out the values of an array, we are guaranteed that if "book" is stored in array A, then when we execute a command such as "PRINT A," the proper letters will appear in sequence. But in human memory, when we begin one sequence of behavior, it is possible that another one will be "captured" and take over. Again, the implication is that a link of some kind exists that relates the "bo" in one array to the "bo" in another array. When a program is manipulating direct addresses, this cannot happen; 9002 will always be processed after 9001. But in human remembering it is as if the instruction to "PRINT A" becomes lost in the details: The handle on array A is lost and the association between the values of different arrays becomes more important. In short, sequential human memory has a probabilistic, recombinatorial aspect, something like chromosomes crossing over, rather than letters being stored and retrieved from post boxes.

Finally, it is important to note that computer programs are conventionally stored in RAM, just like data, in contiguous locations. Fig. 2.2 shows a portion of a program in a hypothetical language, which prints the elements of the A array.

Address	Operation
1000	I<- address(A)
1001	PRINT value(I)
1002	INCREMENT I
1003	IF(I-N, 1000, 1004, 1004)
1004	. . . .

Fig. 2.2. Portion of a conventional program stored in memory.

The details of this program, such as the use of variables, are not important here;[2] the point is that the instructions, determining what happens next, are stored in contiguous locations like data. Storing programs like data is of course one of the powerful ideas of digital computer systems. The issue for our purposes is not so much the use of contiguous locations or storing instructions per se, but that the instructions are isolated, noninteracting elements. When the instruction at location 1001 is executed, "PRINT value(I)," it never happens that a similar instruction somewhere else in memory gets executed instead (such as "PRINT value(J)"). Starting to execute one procedure does not lead to a similar procedure being run instead.

But once again, in human experience we find an apparently different kind of memory. We find that people pour orange juice into their coffee cup, they blow on ice cream (as if it were hot soup), they call one friend when they meant to call another, they walk into a room for a pen and come out with a book but no pen, and so on. The evidence suggests that sequential behaviors are not just rotely replayed like programs, but are in some sense reconstructed. The reconstructive process is *associative*, in the sense that elements in procedures that are meaningfully related, sound alike, look alike, and so on, can substitute

---

[2]The IF operator jumps to the next address, depending on the value of the expression, here "I minus N"; jumping to 1000 if I < N, and 1004 otherwise.

for each other. A procedure in human memory is not necessarily activated or applied as a whole, but instead the memory architecture and reconstruction process allows variations by associations. It is as if applying the instruction "PRINT value (I)" has the side effect of potentially starting up other procedures that use the same instruction (PRINT), of doing something else to I (READ I), or grabbing J instead (PRINT J).

In conclusion, in conventional computer systems, data and programs are stored as sequential arrays in memory in numbered locations. Human memory appears to be less rigid, such that "what comes next" is dependent on the contents of what is happening now. This is called an *associative memory* and is partly the inspiration for the linked list approach, which I consider next.

2.1.2 Linked List Memory

From a conventional programming view, one of the limitations of an indexed memory array is that it forces the programmer to store all elements in sequential locations and to always keep track of the length of the array. For example, if I am using an array to store words, I must decide when I am writing the program how many words can be stored (in today's languages I might also use a dynamic array, whereby my program keeps track of the count and varies the allocation at runtime as required).

But what happens when I want to insert an element in the array? If the array stores a single word, this is not an expected event. The spelling of words usually does not change at runtime. However, if the array is storing an ordered list, such as a plan for things to do tomorrow morning, insertion and reordering will be common. This leads to the idea of a linked list, which became part of AI programming languages as early as the 1950s. Fig. 2.3 shows the element of a linked list, called a *cell*. Unlike an element in an indexed array, a cell in a linked list contains (at least) two parts, a value and a pointer to the next cell in the list. Both the value and the pointer are usually addresses to other cells. This allows the value to be an *atom* (a primitive value, such as a letter) or another list.

Address X:

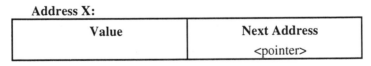

Value	Next Address <pointer>

Fig. 2.3. Cell in a linked list.

The linked list memory approach has several advantages for implementing an associative memory: It allows faster insertion, changing the length of the sequence at runtime, and nesting of sequences. It is unnecessary to record the length of the array if the last element is indicated by a pointer, called *null* (designated by the symbol ∅). Because elements may be noncontiguous, the use of storage is potentially more efficient (although if the number of cells available is relatively limited, bookkeeping will be required to reuse cells—called "garbage-collecting" in the 1960s, but perhaps more aptly named "recycling" today).

The most well-known programming language with built-in features for creating and manipulating linked lists is Lisp (LISt Processing). Lisp programs are also stored as lists, in a special list designated by the first value, PROG. In practice, although a Lisp program may manipulate another Lisp program as a list, the PROG list is compiled into a conventional memory array like that shown in Fig. 2.2.

Researchers have used Lisp to implement a variety of memory architectures with very different properties. In particular, any of the memory architectures described in subsequent sections might be implemented in Lisp (just as the linked list architecture of Lisp itself can be emulated by ordinary procedural languages such as C++). This leads to the distinction between a given *implementation* (such as Lisp running on a particular kind of digital computer such as an Intel™ PC) and a *virtual machine*, the memory architecture of storage structures and search-copying processes designed by the researcher, which is viewed as a cognitive model of human memory. Such level distinctions still hold when we consider neural architectures (such as the distinction between individual neurons and groups of neurons constituting a neural map). But very often this ability to emulate one architecture using another has led researchers to wrongly conclude that the actual implementation of cognitive architecture is not relevant—today's digital computers are all general-purpose "universal" machines, which can emulate any computational memory architecture.

The claim that a digital computer is a universal machine is mathematically grounded in the theory of computing, and hence valid in a mathematical sense. But the claim of universality necessarily ignores practical considerations, such as the implications for learning, timing, and creativity. Most arguments about universal machines assume that learning will occur at a higher-level of operation, as acts of deliberation, reflection, and memory revision, in the manner that a person reflects on a life experience and learns from it. In one sense, this approach is appropriate, insofar as learning of this kind is a conscious act. But what about learning at a lower level, within the construction of memory itself? Are all memory architectures equivalent for learning procedures and categorizing scenes?

As I have indicated, aspects of conventional programming language implementations have become assumptions or taken-for-granted capabilities that a cognitive model of consciousness needs to ultimately explain. To repeat, these taken-for-granted aspects include the idea that structures actually exist in long-term memory when they are not being used, the idea that programs can be retrieved as whole pieces and held in hand like recipes or printouts of computer programs, the idea that viewing an object as a variable comes for free (that all creatures with brains have something like variables), and the idea that multiple ideas can be held active in a working memory (that all creatures with brains have a working memory).

It should now be evident that my interest in explicating computational notations such as linked lists has three aspects. First, my analysis includes the traditional concern about how such architectures can be used to model human behavior (Does such a model of memory fit what people do and experience?). Second, my analysis considers how such an architecture might be neurally realized (Does the architecture have a plausible realization in terms of neural activation?). Third, does the neural activation perspective explain previously unexplored or puzzling phenomena in human experience?

The linked list notation provides an opportunity to discuss a key question about how categorizations are included in a sequence—are they directly included (as "types") or are they indirectly included by a pointer ("tokens")? To understand how this question arises, consider first a straightforward linked list implementation of a categorized sequence (Fig. 2.4), showing a possible realization for the activation trace shown in Fig. 1.6 .

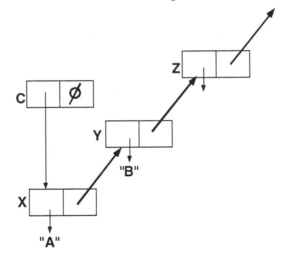

Fig. 2.4. Conventional linked list data structure representing the list C, whose value is (A B . . .).

Such a data structure stored in long-term memory (LTM) could be used to generate the sequence "A, B, ..." But again, this is not like human associative memory; the values A, B, and so on, do not point back into the list. For example, given A, the list head, C, is not accessible. The association represented here is that C contains A, but A is not associated with the list. On the plus side, C's value is a list, which is like a categorized sequence (C is a "higher-order" element). But the path designated by C has the opposite problem of an indexed memory array—it is too fragile—all the steps must be traversed in sequence.

So let's adjust the representation a bit by allowing multiple links (Fig. 2.5). Rather than having C's next element be null, let it point to each of the elements of the list X, Y, and Z. Further, assume that the list does not exist as one thing in memory, but rather the "next pointers" (X → Y, Y → Z) only activate in time, as the sequence is reenacted.

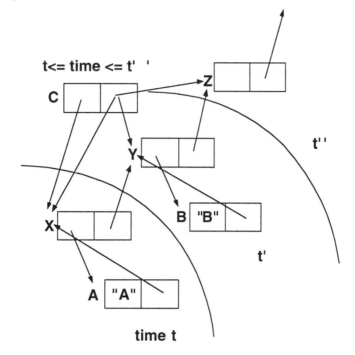

Fig. 2.5. Modified linked list representation of categorization relations.

The figure shows a list, corresponding to a categorized sequence, with three elements, labeled X, Y, and Z, which activate in this order in time. C is active throughout this time, *partially* activating each of the three elements simultaneously. Already we see the value of this notation, for it reveals that C must not actually activate Y and Z, but only contribute to their activation. When C is activated, X becomes active, too. Then Y and Z become partially activated at the next points in time. Thus, if X were to activate other elements besides Y, the presence of C would further bias Y to be activated next. X becomes active with C at Time *t* because it receives two activation "energies" from C. Y becomes active next because it receives activation from C and X. If C is active, then X remains active, so at Time *t''* all elements are active. Of course a list structure may only point to one next element, so the idea of "activates" is not a standard pointer (address or memory location), but a multiple set of connections (in the way a neural map may activate multiple maps; see chapter 3).

A and B are shown to be list elements whose values are atomic (e.g., perceptual categorizations). Notice that the simpler notation, in which the value of X points to "A" directly would not work, because the categorization of "A" must activate X also—a coupling. Hence, "A" is shown as being part of another list element, activated by X and activating X at the same time. In this case, the pointer relation from A is not "the next point in time" but the same time. This requires that the cells designating lower-level categorizations, such as A and B, must be different from the cells designating higher-order categorizations, such as X, Y, and Z. Activation in lower-order cells is "now"; activation in higher-order cells is "next." That is, different kinds of activations are represented.

To summarize, a list notation could be used to represent activation trace diagrams with the following revisions:

1. The elements of the list do not originally exist together; the "next" pointer (the pointer from the right-hand side, called CDR in Lisp) of higher-order elements activates another element at the next point in time (e.g., X activates Y).
2. The right-hand side is not literally an address as in Lisp, which would restrict it to point to one element, but an activation relation. Thus, a given element may activate multiple elements at the next point in time (C activates X, Y, and Z).
3. The "value" of a list element (the pointer from the left-hand side, called CAR in Lisp) designates *a categorization that is simultaneously active* (e.g., C's activation immediately activates X).
4. In the case of a value that is itself a list (a categorized sequence, C), the next pointer points to all the elements in the list simultaneously (consequently, there is not sufficient strength to activate any element).
5. The "value" of a categorized sequence is the first element ("head") of the sequence (the value of C is X).
6. Primitive values (*atoms*, such as "A" and "B") are not encoded numbers or letters (as in a binary representation), but themselves constructed units (*perceptual categorizations*, as shown in chapter 3).

The discussion of "higher-order" and "lower-order" cells illustrates how the discipline of implementing a process in a computer representation forces distinctions to be discovered and brings into question consistency of the theory. For example, there is good reason to suppose that elements of a sequence, such as X, Y, and, Z, should activate the composition itself, C. But my diagram does not show this. Does it make sense that a single neural group, represented by the pointer to A could also activate C at the same time? My purpose here is not to specify a complete neural activation model in Lisp (see Pfeifer, Schreter, Fogelman-Soulié, & Steels, 1989, for examples), but to demonstrate that conventional languages, such as Lisp, do not replicate the kinds of units or relationships between units that a neurobiological memory entails (cf. the opening quote from Rumelhart et al., 1986).

The use of another list to represent a primitive element (A) deserves more discussion. The difference between a value that is a pointer to the categorization itself (a *type*, such as "A") and a pointer that indirectly points to the categorization (a *token*, such as A) is called the *type–token distinction* in cognitive modeling research. In this case, X points to the token, A, rather than the type "A" itself. Building associations out of tokens allows a categorization (type) to be included in different ways in different sequences. Otherwise, "if we have many associations leading to an idea and many associations leading from the idea, then the representation must have some way to determine which predecessors go with which successors" (Anderson & Bower, 1980, p. 20). Fig. 2.6 illustrates this problem and different resolutions.

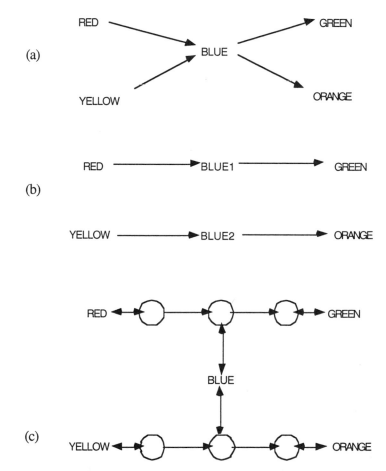

Fig. 2.6. "Alternative associative structures. (a) the British conception; (b) with multiple copies of ideas; and (c) with the type–token distinction." (From HUMAN ASSOCIATIVE MEMORY, Anderson & Bower, 1980, p. 21. Copyright © 1980. Reprinted by permission of Lawrence Erlbaum Associates, Inc.).

In the original British conception of associationism involving only types, if memory contains an association from Red to Blue and Blue to Orange (Fig. 2.6a), "it is likely that the subject may recollect the sequence Red-Blue-Orange, but this sequence never in fact occurred" (p. 20). That is, a memory sequence consisting only of unique symbols leads to reconstructing sequences from memory that were never experienced. Such memory sequences are not produced by the subject when asked to recall what sequences were presented; therefore, this is a poor model of human memory.

On the other hand, always copying the type (Fig. 2.6b) leads to two problems: Much more storage is required, and we would not be reminded of old associations at all "if every time we thought of the idea we found ourselves with a new, virgin copy of that idea" (p. 20).

By introducing the type–token distinction (Fig. 2.6c), a new association or sequence is constructed from tokens (represented by circles in this diagram) that are associated with types (designated by words). An internal construct, called a *token* is created and used to form new associations. At the same time, these tokens are coupled to basic, more primitive ideas, called types (e.g., "BLUE" in (c)). This is precisely the relation between the list subelement A (a token) and the primitive categorization "A" (a type) in the list diagrams. The problem of redundancy is reduced and the possibility of association is enabled. This is a better model of human memory.

The type–token idea appears in conventional programming language in different forms, such as variable–value and object–instance. Use of tokens is prevalent in descriptive cognitive modeling. In the next section I consider how the type–token idea can be extended to represent roles that data plays in a computation, such that procedures can be represented by a kind of linked list.

2.1.3 Actors in Dataflow Graphs

Sowa (1984) presents a formal graph language, called *conceptual structures*, that combines predicate logic with graphic structures to represent conceptual relations, including facts and procedures. Fig. 2.7 shows a definition of the factorial function by a conceptual graph called an *actor*.

The example illustrates how the conceptual graph language formally combines programmatic operations (such as "add 1") with declarative specification of the roles and types of data. For example, the input, n, is declared to be of type NUMBER. Two other types (rectangles) are indicated as ranges corresponding to a number that is zero and a number greater than zero. Binding operations are designated by "*" such that the result of multiplying is bound to the output, x.

The boxes in this diagram that do not contain a reference to a NUMBER are other actors. Thus, ADD1 is an actor, as are IDENT (whose output is identical to its input) and FACTORIAL. These names are types, too. So the node FACTORIAL is an instance of the type FACTORIAL, a type that is defined by this entire graph. The presence of a FACTORIAL instance in the definition of the FACTORIAL type makes the definition recursive.

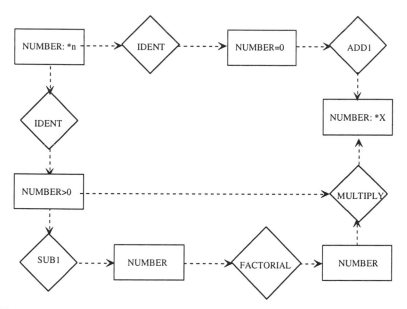

Fig. 2.7. A recursively defined actor, FACTORIAL (input n; output x). (From CONCEPTUAL STRUCTURES, Sowa,1984, Figure 4.18, p. 191. Copyright ©1984 Addison Wesley Longman. Reprinted by permission of Addison Wesley Longman.).

The actual process of computation involves flow of data through the graph, with special "marks" indicating the direction of flow, the asserted (given) data nodes, and the requested (goal) node. Without going into details here, the essential idea is that such a graphic formalism can be extended to show how computations are to be performed and the state of a given computation.

I am interested in this example because it makes explicit in a visual way the constructs and relations that are involved in conventional computational languages: type comparisons, temporary data storage in variables, calculation, named processes, and recursion. The idea of a dataflow graph begins to make a distinction that fascinates me, too: The graph represents a structure stored in LTM, but the computational process occurs as flow of data through the structure. The procedure is not necessarily copied and applied step by step, but is executed in place, as it were.

Could actor-like operations occur in a neural system? Or should we view types, assertions, requests, and the process of computing referents as more akin to the reasoning over time of a conscious person? Might there be a simpler mechanism by which such thought becomes possible? In section 2.3, I consider several attempts to discover a "subsymbolic" neural level, the operations that make the computations of actors possible.

2.1.4 Hidden Markov Models

Conceptual graphs are useful for representing fixed, algorithmic processes. Markov models provide a way of representing a process with steps that vary probabilistically. Conventionally, a *Markov chain* is represented as a set of states and a transition matrix that indicates the probability of the next state, given the present state (Fig. 2.8).

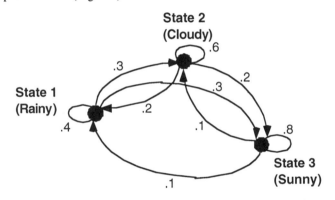

Fig. 2.8. Markov chain with three states; links indicate probability of state transitions.

Fig. 2.8 shows three states representing the three kinds of weather. Directional arcs indicate transitions from each state to each other state, with labels indicating the probability of the transitions. For example, if the weather is sunny, then the probability is .8 of remaining sunny (the next state will be sunny), .1 of rain, and .1 cloudy. Markov models can be contrasted with finite-state automata, in which the transitions are deterministic and indicate an observation (a condition that is true in the world; cf. Fig. 5.5).

As a method of representing a statistical process, a Markov model is interesting to consider as a model of procedural LTM. The multiple arcs from each state allow representing multiple possible associations (or next activations) from a given neural "state." Furthermore, Markov models are stochastic—only one next state is selected—a useful feature for modeling sequential memory.

Of special interest is a hidden Markov model (HMM), used most notably for speech recognition. In a simple Markov model, "each state corresponds to an observable (physical) event" (Rabiner, 1990, p. 269). In an HMM, each state is itself a Markov model; that is, what will be observed is itself the output of a stochastic process. For example, in a HMM of words in some language, each word could be represented by an HMM with states that are Markov models at the phonemic level.

The probability of transition between states might take into account more than the immediate predecessor state. In Lee's (1990) "triphone" models of speech, both the predecessor phoneme (state at $t - 1$) and next phoneme (state at $t + 1$) are referenced in computing the phoneme (state at Time t) that best fits the current input. This assumes that the states are ordered strictly chronologically—a "left–right model." The duration of each state is ignored (in other applications, the state might be viewed as held or repeated for some count).

As a model of human memory, Markov models are limited by assuming that memory consists of a fixed matrix of discrete states. That is, there is no learning: The states and the probability of transitions are always the same each time they occur and the number of states is strictly countable. The most interesting aspects of HMMs for the investigation here are the temporal, probabilistic sequencing of states and embedding of sequences. The context-sensitive nature of triphone models fits the idea of a categorized sequence: The next state is biased by a high-order organization in which "look ahead" activation occurs before the next state is activated (examples also occur in speaking slips and typing errors; see chapter 6). The success of HMMs for speech recognition suggests that this activation process, so different from a conventional computer memory, at least partially describes what is happening at the neural level.

2.1.5 SHRDLU's Procedural Knowledge

Conceptual graphs and Markov models treat procedures as being internally structured and organized like facts. Coming from the other direction, Winograd's (1972) program SHRDLU explored how facts might be stored as procedures. More precisely, the idea is to represent a program's experience, behaviors, and grammatical understanding of language in procedures, rather than separated into different knowledge bases. Winograd's intuition was that a strictly procedural memory would allow more specific association between problem-specific information and procedures for manipulating that information (to be contrasted with strictly separate "data" and "program" that must be combined at runtime). Winograd hypothesized that such a scheme would provide greater flexibility in learning and efficiency when understanding natural language (Anderson & Bower, 1980, p. 59).

In the technical terms of the day, Winograd attempted to show that "declarative" memory could be stored as "procedural" memory. Recalling the indexed array example (Fig. 2.1), the representation of "book" in an array is called declarative memory because the data structure representing the word is stored separately from the procedures that operate on it. In contrast, a strictly procedural memory of "book" might be a program with four steps: "Print b,

Print o, Print o, Print k." There is no separate data structure representing the letters, just a program for printing the word.

In Winograd's scheme, the emphasis was not so much on combining types of memory (e.g., words and programs) but of uniformly representing all types of memory as procedures:

> Knowledge in the system is represented in the form of procedures, rather than tables of rules or lists of patterns. By developing special procedural representations for syntax, semantics, and inference, we gain flexibility and power. Since each piece of knowledge can be a procedure, it can call directly on any other piece of knowledge in the system. (Winograd, 1972, p. 1)

In Piagetian terms, a procedural approach emphasizes that knowledge is active; meaning is formulated as procedural "calling" relations in the context of use. In contrast, pure deduction systems represent all statements in predicate calculus, and hence make it difficult to specify how to pursue certain kinds of problems efficiently (what knowledge to use must be inferred).[3]

To illustrate how a procedural representation works, Winograd (1972) gave the example that "Words like 'and' could be defined as 'demons' which interrupt the parsing whenever they are encountered, and start a special program for interpreting conjoining sentences" (p. 45). Thus, rather than representing a dictionary and grammar separately, the dictionary is viewed as a parsing procedure. This fits the activation trace view I am exploring: Words (e.g., "and") are activating in a bottom-up way, triggering procedural sequences (e.g., a phrase conjoining operation). Instead of having a separate master *control procedure* that interprets separate grammar and dictionary *networks*, Winograd suggests that the modeler "think in terms of programs and interrupts." Rather than different kinds of memory and separate librarian and executive programs, an attempt is made to integrate all the relations and operations in the way they work together when sentences are comprehended. This is a process memory—"what to do when."

The distinction between the declarative and procedural approach is especially evident when a parsing failure occurs. In the declarative approach, when matching predicate calculus descriptions, a blind backup occurs from a failed match to a previous choice point. In contrast, the SHRDLU model of language understanding is "an intelligent parser that can understand the reasons for its failure at a certain point, and can guide itself, rather than backing up blindly" (Winograd, 1972, p. 46). The basic idea again is that knowledge consists of processes, rather than statically stored nodes and links that another program must read and manipulate.

---

[3]Genesereth (1983) responded to these challenges with a system called MRS (Meta Representation System), in which metastatements can be made about kinds of problems, indicating for example how inference should be directed according to characteristics of the domain models being operated on.

Attempting to reconcile the approaches, Winograd (1972) suggested that the procedural approach might just be a viewpoint: "Grammars described as networks and grammars described as programs are just two different ways of doing exactly the same thing" (p. 44). Nevertheless, the functional equivalence of the two perspectives does not reduce to equivalent implementations. For example, rather than an "and" demon, in a declarative network one would require "a separate arc marked 'and' leading from every node in the network" (p. 45). This would work, but appears implausible as a model of human memory. The implementations are not doing "exactly the same thing."

A declarative modeler could rebut that Winograd's procedures are just logic statements in a programming language, For example, the modifier "which supports no pyramids" is represented as:

```
(THNOT (THPROG (X2)
       (THGOAL (#IS $?X2 #PYRAMID))
       (THGOAL (#SUPPORT $?X1 $?X2)))))
```

But it is the content of the statements that makes the representation procedural: (a) domain predicates and operations (e.g., "support") are associated within procedures, (b) knowledge is primarily state-specific and active (factual relations are expressed as operations for determining or ensuring validity), and (c) "pieces of knowledge" activate when necessary (as opposed to always being searched for, matched, and interpreted).

In many respects, the contemporaneous production rule approach of Newell and Simon, dating from the early 1970s, has these same properties, which I explore in detail in the next section.

2.2 PRODUCTION RULE MEMORY

The production rule architecture of Soar combines the advantages of the declarative and procedural approaches by representing procedures as separately activated situation–action associations, constituting steps that are combined into more complex procedural chunks through experience. In this section, I review the production rule memory architecture, critically examine how procedural memory is encoded in productions, and reformulate the examples according to a conceptual coordination perspective.

2.2.1 Production Rule Basics

Production rules are a very common way of modeling associative memory. In the simplest form, production rules are just conditional "if–then" statements—given some situation, a certain action is taken. For example, the linked list notation of Fig. 2.5 may be viewed as a trace of the production system:

>Rule X: If State is S1 and A is observed, then the next state is S2.
>Rule Y: If State is S2 and B is observed, then the next state is S3.

Notice how activation relations in a neural system are represented as explicit address locations in a Lisp implementation and explicit state names in a production rule implementation. The underlying issue is how do independently learned steps become associated in memory: As address locations? As state names? The reader should see by now that I am trying to get rid of the idea of addresses and names as a mechanism for modeling sequential memory. In examining Soar, we see that the use of state names becomes problematic for modeling sequential experience.

But let's back up a bit and consider why the production rule architecture—with inherent learning and a globally available "working memory"—represented such an important advance in modeling sequential memory. Anderson (1980) summarized some of the points at issue.

First, in stimulus–response (SR) theory, each learned step is independent and remains that way. For example, by the view of SR theory, rats that learn to run a maze are not learning a procedure, they are just learning to recognize and react moment by moment to each turn in the maze. For instance, there might be two SR associations:

>S1: <stimuli at first turn> → turn left
>S2: <stimuli at second turn> → turn right

The conditions for each association are stimuli for a particular place-location. In such a model, nothing general is being learned or pieced together. But experiments show that rats are learning more global orientations and orderings, not just independent SR associations (Tolman, 1948).

The evidence therefore suggests that learned steps become proceduralized, such that a sequence is "executed" as a unit (as in learning to play a musical piece by first practicing the phrases). There must be a memory mechanism by which individual steps are combined into sequences. Sequences may be internally organized and controlled (as in complex human problem solving). Steps are not just environmentally stimulated or reactive. And goal-directedness of behavior shows that internal states act as a context to activate (or prime) what happens or is experienced next.

By conjecture, what ties individual steps together are the internal categorizations that they independently operate on. Rather than viewing knowledge exclusively in terms of procedures being executed, as Winograd (1972) suggested (or as found in a common programming language), one shifts to viewing knowledge in terms of operations on a data structure called *working memory*. Insofar as which operations may activate is controlled by what is present in working memory, the ability to activate procedural steps independently is constrained—not every step may be activated at every moment.[4]

Production rules thereby combine the event schema notion that sequential memory is stored as units (e.g., if-then statements) and the procedural notion of Winograd that memory combines different kinds of knowledge opportunistically, according to experience (Fig. 2.9). In adopting such a mixed architecture, the declarative–procedural distinction breaks down. Indeed, the dichotomy was rarely mentioned after the debates of the 1970s.

CONDITIONS	*ACTIONS*
<list of expressions that must be matched in working memory>	*<transformations to make to change working memory>*
IF the goal is to generate a plural of a noun and the noun ends in a hard consonant	THEN generate the noun + s

Fig. 2.9. General form of a production rule and an example (Anderson, 1980, p. 239).

Production rules, although represented separately as independent operations, are context-sensitive by virtue of the conditions. The body of productions, which has even been called a "knowledge soup," constitutes a *content-addressable memory*. For efficiency, productions may be "compiled" into a single network to remove redundancy (e.g., the Rete algorithm; Forgy, 1979). Compiling may be viewed as a way of getting rid of the state and goal names that are otherwise required to make the productions flow together into coherent sequences. In evaluating the production model as a model of human memory, we must then be clear how the more verbose individual productions are to be interpreted: Are they literally units stored in memory? Or are they *specifications* of associations (i.e., a theoretician's descriptions of the subject's knowledge) realized in the brain in another way, such as a RETE network? Are goals literally names in individual production rule steps or are they categorized sequences (e.g., C in Fig. 1.6)? Furthermore, learning is not inherent in the RETE architecture itself; another program reads and manipulates the full productions, which name states and goals. Is there an intermediate kind of mechanism, with the directness of the RETE network for combining steps, but by which sequencing and composition could occur at "run time," not in a later learning stage, but while the person is

---

[4]In the late 1970s, the idea of directing execution of procedures according to the contents of working memory was elaborated into *blackboard architectures*. Knowledge sources (either production rules or arbitrary procedures) are activated by the contents of the blackboard, where they post transformations to an evolving situation-specific model, such as a diagnostic model of a patient's disease or a therapy plan.

behaving? These are the questions that arise when we attempt to reinterpret descriptive cognitive models in neurobiological terms.

On the positive side, we must acknowledge that the production rule architecture was a great leap forward in cognitive modeling. In a comprehensive model of cognition (Newell, 1990), specialized productions relate working memory to sensory signals on the one hand and motor operations on the other. The production view is thereby a rejection of the SR view that behavior is always in some sense immediate or "one-step." Internally, the mind is examining structures and matching, retrieving, and transforming these structures. Thus, the theoretical shift is from a purely reactive "empty organism" (Newell & Simon, 1972), to a creature with internal representations of the world and behavior: "The production system is responding to abstract propositions stored in memory rather than to external stimuli" (Anderson, 1980, p. 245). Production conditions are not restricted to single features (e.g., "hard consonant"), but may be *categorizations* (e.g., "noun"). Productions therefore may be abstracted behavior patterns, not only local reactions to local features.

Perhaps most important, the adoption of the production rule architecture for modeling human memory represents a theoretical shift in explaining behavior in terms of *goal-driven processes*, to be contrasted with SR bottom-up, feature-driven processes. In particular, internal representation of goals appears necessary to account for the organization of complex behavior, such as in playing chess or solving cryptograms.

Productions mention goals, not just stimuli, hence they model deliberately controlled, "top-down" behaviors. However, the emphasis on goal-driven problem solving in the 1970s and early 1980s led to a corresponding lack of consideration about how perception is coupled to procedural memory. The focus on working memory transformations also makes production firing appear to be independent of action, as if searching and matching are not deliberating (because they are subconscious) and deliberating is not acting (because it does not change the world).[5]

Moreover, models of learning highly formalized mathematical and scientific problem solving give the impression that proceduralization (the subconscious process of composing multiple productions into "single step" operations; Anderson, 1980, p. 268) is a *compilation* process. As in computer language compilation, a "higher-level language" is reduced to primitive operations, which are packaged into sequences that carry out procedures. For example, a common operation requiring application of several theorems in geometry may be composed into one single-step production. But is this a reflection of the properties of human memory or the properties of the geometry problem domain? Indeed, C. Lewis (1981) showed that composition alone is insufficient; experts also converted multiple-pass to single-pass procedures. That is, people are

---

[5]See Clancey (1997c), chapter 14, for a discussion of how the issues of perceptual coupling and timing have been handled in Soar.

reasoning about their experiences and *noticing* patterns. Can we factor out which aspects of proceduralization require conscious deliberation and which are more fundamental memory processes? In the next section I analyze the effort to model procedural memory in Soar as a way of teasing apart the relation of production rule models to automatic neural processes.

2.2.2 Procedural and Episodic Memory in Soar

In this section I review a paper by Rosenbloom, Newell, and Laird (1991) that explores how Soar can be used to represent procedural and episodic memory. I present an activation trace perspective and consider to what extent Soar might be viewed not literally, but as a specification for what a neural architecture must accomplish.

Soar is "an architecture for a system . . . capable of general intelligence" (p. 75). The definitions given by Rosenbloom et al. (1991) already assume what an architecture is, as they make explicit:

> A computer systems level consists of a *medium* that is processes, *components* that provide primitive processing, *laws of composition* that permit components to be assembled into systems, and *laws of behavior* that determine how system behavior depends on the component behavior and the structure of the system. Existing levels (and their media) include the device level (electrons), the circuit level (current), the logic level (bits), the register-transfer level (bit-vectors), and the program (or symbol) level (symbols, expressions). In terms of these levels, an architecture is a register-transfer level system that defines a symbol level. (p. 76)

To paraphrase these terms, the corresponding levels in the theory I am pursuing consist of: the device level (neurons), the circuit level (neural maps), the logic level (classification couples = categorizations), the register-transfer level (neural activation sequences and scenes of coupled categorizations), and the program (or symbol) level (referential conceptualizations contained within inferential conceptualizations).

Given this neural interpretation, we might still agree with the next sentence in the Soar definition: "In terms of these levels, an architecture is a register-transfer level system that defines a symbol level." That is, the neural activation architecture enables the capabilities of a reasoning system. However, I am moving toward an architecture level in which a symbol processing operator is the operating medium itself. That is, the symbols (names, images, "any pattern that denotes") are not *encoded* in the register-transfer level, but *process arrangements* (categorizations of categorizations) that constitute a "program." By this view, verbal problem-solving knowledge is not stored in the architecture, but a system of higher-order categorizations of lower-level categorizations in different modalities (image, sound, gesture).

Put another way, the medium is not *processed* in neural systems per se, but rather the medium is a process that operates on other processes (or as Marshall

McLuhan [1967] put it in another context, "the medium is the message"). The relation between levels is also not quite as protected as in digital computer systems, where for example, circuit behaviors are designed within tolerances that allow them to be predictably controlled by higher levels. Interactions between levels are visible in slips (chapter 6).

My first break with Soar is precisely over the distinction between procedures being stored recipes versus the activation relations I have described:

> The first form of knowledge to be examined is *procedural* knowledge. Procedural knowledge is knowledge about the agent's actions. It includes knowledge about which actions can be performed, which actions should be performed when (control knowledge), and how actions are performed. The second form of knowledge to be examined is *episodic* knowledge. Episodic knowledge is knowledge about what objects, actions, and action sequences have occurred in the agent's past. It allows answering questions such as "Did this object, action, or action sequence occur (in this context)?" and "What objects, actions, or action sequences occurred (in this context)?" The third and final form of knowledge to be examined is *declarative* knowledge. Declarative knowledge is knowledge about what is true in the world. (Rosenbloom et al., 1991, p. 77)

These definitions suggest that knowledge is like stuff in a database, consisting of *descriptions*—of objects, actions, and action sequences—about the agent's behavior and about the world. This is not an arbitrary intelligent creature, but a conscious being with a language for modeling behavior and the world. Procedures are viewed like recipes, experience is recorded in a diary, and the encountered world is captured by a logician's propositions.

With this view of knowledge, it is no surprise that the architecture of Soar looks like Leonardo's workbench. Procedural knowledge is supposed to be a kind of prescriptive knowledge, "what you should do when," and episodic knowledge a record of "what occurred." But the idea of occurrence in Soar, cited in the definition of episodic knowledge—"action sequences have occurred"—is the experience of a conscious observer, quite different from mere activation relations in a neural system.

Analyzing Soar's representation of episodic knowledge in particular is a good way of highlighting assumptions about present-day computer languages I am questioning as inappropriate for a memory architecture. We can focus on episodic knowledge, first, because it is most related to the kind of phenomena I want to study (such as typing slips), and second, because even within Soar it is viewed as more primitive than procedural knowledge:

> The procedural knowledge that Soar learns can be viewed as really being episodic knowledge about the past behavior of the system. To use this episodic knowledge as procedural knowledge, there is an implicit assumption that what is descriptive of the past is normative for the future. (Rosenbloom et al., 1991, p. 93)

The first distinction I introduce is that episodic knowledge need not be descriptive at all; it can simply be a sequence of activation relations, as in a habit. In part, in Soar terms I am addressing a different domain of knowledge, not problem solving, but simpler temporal relations in physical behavior (such as finding a path in a maze). Also, I am claiming that such processes are operating even in complex problem solving, and they account for important differences in what people can do relative to our best problem-solving programs (see chapter 12). So I focus here on Soar's treatment of episodic knowledge.

To begin, some of the constraints of Soar's architecture are important to review:

- "Soar cannot examine the conditions of productions" (Rosenbloom et al., 1991, p. 93). That is, matching productions occurs tacitly (is not cognitively penetrable) and when retrieved, Soar has no access to the condition itself, just to the changes it brings to working memory. (Soar may "use background knowledge . . . to reason" about what events are in a condition.)
- "Episodic knowledge is acquired by chunking problem-solving episodes . . . . [T]he system monitors its own performance, and creates declarative structures representing what has transpired" (Rosenbloom et al., 1991, p. 94).
- "The system . . . examines a representation of the perceptual event and the context, and generates as a subgoal result an occurred predicate covering them" (Rosenbloom et al., 1991, p. 95).

Aside from the important constraint on examining preconditions, the process of recording episodic knowledge in Soar resembles the manner in which a journalist writes a story—a process of reflection and description—"information storage is based on an understanding process" (Rosenbloom et al., 1991, p. 98). By this view, episodic knowledge cannot be found in creatures that lack the ability to describe events and understand their causal relations. Studies of rat navigation show this to be false (chapter 5).

Rosenbloom et al. (1991) associated Soar's remembering operations (using episodic knowledge) with the reconstructive process of Bartlett. However, Bartlett described both the neural processes by which schemas re-form and the story reconstruction aspect of conscious remembering. Which level is modeled in Soar? Apparently Soar is only concerned with the semantic operations of a conscious being. In Soar, "the storage process is semantically penetrable," (p. 98) in the sense that other knowledge can affect what is remembered and stored. Such interactions fit the well-known memory bias studied by Loftus (1979), for example. But such a mechanism does not address or explain interactions that are subconscious, except to posit that subconscious operations are the same as what the agent does consciously, only hidden, faster, and operating on a different medium. For example, the Soar model of learning implies that subconscious chunking is identical to consciously reading over and combining a description of steps used to solve a problem.

To understand better the assumptions and problems with how Soar models episodic knowledge, let's explore an example given by Rosenbloom et al.

(1991) in detail. Consider how one represents the events of pulling a knob and turning a knob when setting the time of a watch. Using Soar's mechanism for representing how operators can be applied, *events* (episodes that have occurred, i.e., the subject's *experience)* are represented as operators applied in a particular sequence:

> →
> (occurred e1 event s1 context c1)
> (sequence s1 operator1 a1 operator2 a1)
> (operator a1 name pull-knob)
> (operator a2 name turn-knob)
> (context c1 name setting-time-on-watch)

This production states that an event (e1) occurred in the context of setting time on the watch (c1). The event is a sequence (s1) of two operators, a1 and a2, pulling and turning a knob. This production has no conditions. Alternatively, the last (context) proposition could be converted to a condition, restricting retrieval to that context in the future.

An important constraint assumed by Soar researchers is that the structures posited as part of the episodic knowledge are the structures used in problem solving (i.e., setting the watch is viewed as a problem-solving episode). This is more parsimonious than positing additional predicates that the Soar model has not heretofore required. For this reason, "pull-knob" is referred to as an operator rather than an action. Following this principle, the newly introduced "sequence" predicate could be replaced by a "preference" predicate, which Soar already uses in problem solving, so "(sequence s1 operator1 a1 operator2 a1)" and the definitions of the operators would be reformulated as:

> (preference a1 value acceptable role operator goal g1 problem-space
>   p1 state s1)
> (operator a1 name pull-knob)
> (preference s2 value acceptable role operator goal g1 problem-space p1
>   state s1)
> (preference a2 value acceptable role operator goal g1 problem-space p1
>   state s2)
> (operator a2 name turn-knob)

The first preference says that pull-knob is the preferred operator for the first state, s1. The second preference statement says, "State s2 is preferred in problem space p1 when the current state s1 has the operator pull-knob selected." That is, S2 follows S1. The next preference says that the operator turn-knob is preferred in the state s2. Thus, contexts (more precisely, descriptions of contexts) and sequences are recorded in memory as state relations, called *preferences*.

Interestingly, Rosenbloom et al. (1991) emphasized that although the mechanism they sketch results from adhering to the assumptions presently built into Soar's architecture, the result is not at all parsimonious: "The overall picture of episodic knowledge...[is] relatively complicated and messy" (p. 99).

"If we were to sit down to design a capability for episodic knowledge from scratch, with no constraints, we would be unlikely to design it as currently embodied by Soar" (p. 98).

However, they ironically concluded that yet more complex reasoning should be incorporated to store experience so its use is more error free, as in scripts (Schank & Abelson, 1977) and E-MOPs (Kolodner, 1984). They appropriately suggested that the proper research question is "the extent to which the level of support models human capabilities, and the level of constraint models human limitations" (p. 99). My interest is to address precisely these questions by reexamining both the Soar model and human experience.

In particular, what episodic memory might result from simply having the capability to reactivate operators in the order they were serially active previously? Rather than working downward from what a conscious problem solver does, let's work upward from how an animal without problem solving capability might learn.

Using the activation trace notation introduced in chapter 1, we might represent the same watch-setting sequence as a categorized sequence of two operators coupled to two operands (Fig. 2.10).

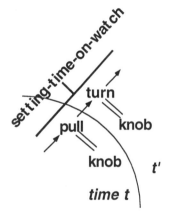

Fig. 2.10. Neural activations in categorized sequence of setting time on a watch.

Four categorizations are depicted: the categorization of a knob (a thing), the categorization of two actions (pull and turn), and the categorization of a sequence (setting-time-on-watch). These are the categorizations of an agent and not the psychologist–observer. The higher-order categorization "setting-time-on-watch" is a categorization of an *activity*, WIDN—a capability characteristic of a conscious being. Nevertheless, there is nothing in this representation that requires that the being be capable of naming and describing objects, events, states, or action sequences. The names in this diagram are our labels as scientists for describing categorizing processes that are occurring in the subject's brain.

The extent to which complex sequences can be chunked in this way without language is an open question. However, the evidence from ape learning, such as chimpanzees teaching their children how to open nuts with a stone (Boesch, 1991), suggests that such procedural knowledge can be learned without a modeling language (that names things, states, events, and their causal relations in action sequences).

The example just presented can be generalized (Fig. 2.11).

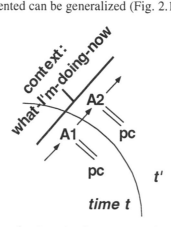

Fig. 2.11. General form of categorized sequence of operators, Ai coupled to a single perceptual categorization, pc.

Fig. 2.11 shows an event sequence as a series of categorized operator activations in time (A1 → A2); the operators are coupled to perceptual categorizations (of a single knob in the example); and the categorization of the sequence is a contextual, higher-order categorization. Alternatively, one could omit the capability to categorize sequences and move the context to a precursor, serving as a condition, as Soar conditionalizes "retrieval" by explicitly representing the context as a condition (Fig. 2.12).

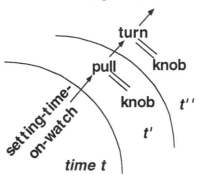

Fig. 2.12. Goal/context interpreted as a precondition.

In this diagram, the categorization of "setting-time-on-watch" is an initial state. This appears less parsimonious because the term setting-time-on-watch suggests an encompassing goal, a conceptualization of the overall activity, not an isolated state or condition. Later we see that attitudes such as hunger or emotions in general could constitute a contextual condition that organizes a sequence, so conceptualization of the sequence (the intention or purpose) would not be required (see chapter 8).

In contrast with activation relations of categorizations, Soar explicitly stores descriptions of preference relations that are about states. Although this idea of preference is not comparative, it nevertheless is a statement about an internal event (a state). If categorizations are sequenced directly, as I indicate in the activation trace diagrams, such statements are not required. Or put another way, Soar's theory of episodic memory should explicate when a *statement* is required (which involves a linguistic ability involving conscious coordination of behaviors and descriptions), rather than a simpler activation relation (which is subconscious).

As another example, the episodic knowledge that "the token 'gaf' occurred in list 1 of experiment 2" would be represented in Soar as:

(context c1 experiment 2 list 1) → (object o1 name gaf)

Fig. 2.13 represents this production as an activation trace.

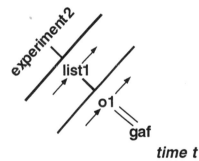

time t

Fig. 2.13. Object "gaf" conceived as an element in a list, conceived as a part of an experiment activity.

Here "gaf" is shown as a single perceptual categorization, categorized as being an object (o1), which is part of a categorized sequence (list1), which is part of a categorized sequence of a broader activity (experiment2). In contrast, Soar automatically associates perceptual information with "the state in the top problem-solving context" and must posit a special kind of chunking process called a *familiarity chunk* to explain how the "gaf" perceptual information becomes associated in memory with the specific sequence, list1. The activation perspective (Fig. 2.13) posits that the perceptual categorization is necessarily associated with the categorizations that subsume it and are active at that time, namely the higher-order categorization of a list and the higher-order categorization of the activity of participating in an experiment (WIDN). Again, these are all categorizations of a conscious being, but do not presuppose language for modeling experience.

The activation relation perspective more parsimoniously explains how a gorilla like Koko (Gordon, 1995), for example, can participate in recognition games (such as an experiment) without being able to articulate that objects have names, for example. More fundamentally, this analytical approach naturally leads to questions of what is required to categorize a list (list1) as being "the first" or an experiment as being "the second"—the agent requires a categorization of *series*, a higher-order categorization that a sequence is numerically ordered. Numeric ordering is therefore a categorization about *kinds of categorized sequences*. Yet, in Soar objects, states, and events are named and counted as if this is nonproblematic—it comes from the architecture for free. Therefore, Soar is not a good place to start if we want to understand how children learn to count or what mathematical limitations Koko, the gorilla, might have relative to people.

To reiterate the main point about memory, in Soar's episodic memory a sequence is a set of statements about the preference ordering of objects and perceived information, as they are referenced in operator sequences. In the theory I am pursuing, sequential memory is not necessarily a description of named objects and events, but of activation relations between categorizations. Four basic kinds of categorization are postulated: perceptual (e.g., a letter), coupling (simultaneously active features constituting an object or scene), sequential (e.g., an ordering of operators), and a categorized sequence (a chunked, conceptualized ordering). Because Soar's memory is about states and objects (versus a memory of temporal relations of categorizations), the constituent components must coexist and be physically associated in an LTM (the production memory). Because the components are concepts and their relations are consciously discerned, what is being stored may be affected by reasoning.

The architecture I am describing is far simpler and is highly limited in its capabilities. The agent does not "retrieve" memories, but experiences them. Despite such a simple set of assumptions, even the examples cited by Rosenbloom et al. (1991), of setting a watch or learning a list of nonsense syllables show that the activation perspective is relevant and insightful. Indeed, the conclusion by Rosenbloom et al. that "there has not been a great need for episodic knowledge in the tasks that have so far been implemented in Soar" (p. 92) reveals how many interesting and central aspects of memory are presumed or ignored by Soar's architecture and what remains to be investigated by adopting a more constrained memory architecture. Perhaps the apparent irrelevance of episodic memory follows from the researchers' focus on tasks involving verbal reasoning, rather than simpler aspects of conceptual coordination. As Rosenbloom et al. indicated, episodic knowledge is particularly relevant for simple "recognition and recall tasks," which I consider in the study of slips (chapter 6) and paired-associate learning (chapter 11.3).

Finally, the reader should note how the term *knowledge* is used in Soar to refer to constructs and processing in all aspects of remembering and problem solving. This follows from the attempt to adopt a uniform architecture, in which processes operating at lower levels are similar to those required for complex problem solving. The danger is that terminology developed to describe and explain complex goal-directed behavior has now been imported to the elementary levels of the architecture. So now even states have names. In response, the Soar researcher might suggest that these names are just arbitrary stand-ins for "neurally implemented" symbols, which are not necessarily part of a language. And so "name gaf" is just a way of representing what I am claiming is a perceptual categorization (gaf), coupled to an object-thing categorization (e.g., "nonsense syllable"), activated within a sequence (list1). I believe that this is a fruitful way to proceed (see especially chapter 12).

2.3 "SUBDELIBERATE" AND "SUBSYMBOLIC" MEMORY

By the mid-1980s, a number of cognitive scientists were growing increasingly uneasy with the way complex problem-solving notation and operations were part of theories of memory, perception, and learning. Reflecting on the state of cognitive science, J. R. Miller, Polson, and Kintsch (1984) wrote:

> As if it were the most natural thing in the world, purposive terminology has been imported into an information processing framework: subgoals are stored in short-term memory; unconscious expectations are processed in parallel; opinions are represented propositionally; the mind contains schemata. (p. 6)

If the meaningful names programmed into Soar's models, such as "name gaf" are just placeholders for a yet unspecified neural process, what is that "subsymbolic" mechanism? If learning can occur without reflective reasoning over the particulars of problem-solving episodes, what are the "subdeliberate" processes by which "implicit learning" occurs? Where do long-term productions come from? By assumption, productions in LTM are all compiled from explicit (declarative) components. What is the origin of the primitive tokens and perceptual-motor productions?

Viewed from slightly afar in the late 1990s, the range of research from early symbolic models through Soar and connectionism shows an awkward puzzlement about what memory does. Simpler models appear more felicitous, but accomplish less. For example, more than 20 years earlier, the EPAM model of memory showed how the history of stimuli might construct a discrimination tree for recognizing context-sensitive sequences. But EPAM can only recognize sequences, not generate them, so the problem-solving capabilities that drove Soar's design are not provided.

Nevertheless, many researchers were willing to give up the reasoning capabilities offered by a production rule architecture to reconsider perhaps more fundamental aspects of memory and learning. Several efforts emphasized how simultaneity in architectures of competing processes could produce output relationships such as binding, rules, tense, and so on, that were otherwise explicitly encoded in symbolic, stored description models:

- Rumelhart and McClelland (1986) demonstrated that an unordered collection of overlapping triples could generate sequences.
- Hofstadter and Mitchell et al., developed computational models of analogy formation at the perceptual level (see chapter 7), building on Selfridge's Pandemonium architecture (see article in Shapiro, 1992, p. 1081).
- Smolensky, Miyata, and Legendre (1993) described an "integrated connectionist-symbolic" architecture," which aimed to improve symbolic explanations by developing models with a deeper level of *systematicity* (simpler, underlying relations). These models provide better explanations of *productivity* (e.g., how syllabic vowel–consonant patterns are constrained by phonemic relations).
- Touretzky (1990) demonstrated several "revisionist symbolic processing" architectures, such as BoltzCONS, which had "the ability to construct and modify composite symbol structures *dynamically*, by representing them as activity patterns rather than weights" (p. 7).
- Hetherington and Shapiro (1993) used SRNs to model how hippocampal place fields "encode" remembered locations, such that feed-forward activation produces goal-directed behavior.
- Bickhard and Richie (1993) described "interactive control structures"—emergent functional organizations, arising from "certain patterns of material processes" (p. 57) and providing the basis for phenomenological representations (e.g., experienced categorizations, intentions) (pp. 17, 80 ff).
- Hanson and Burr (1990, Fig. 1, p. 472) described networks of competing processes that are nonlinear, recurrent, and error-correcting.
- In the *multiple drafts* idea of Dennett (1992) "all varieties of thought or mental activity . . . are accomplished in the brain by parallel, multitrack processes of interpretation and elaboration of sensory inputs" (p. 111).[6]
- Rosenfield (1992) described remembering in terms of "dynamic progression of coherent responses" (p. 85); conceptual relations are temporal coordinations (not labeled links).

Research on neural networks listed here falls on a spectrum (Fig. 2.14). On the one extreme, the "implementalist" approach to connectionism hypothesizes that

---

[6]The term *draft* does not imply a representation and nondialectic creation of something later incorporated or interpreted and revised.

symbolic models of cognition accurately describe a mechanism that neural networks in the brain implement. That is, neurobiology will not lead to revising theories of memory, reasoning, and learning, but only explain how such mechanisms are manifest in the human brain. Touretzky's (1988) BoltzCONS architecture and related work was an attempt to investigate this hypothesis by finding ways to represent variable binding, rules, trees, and so on, within the constraints of a connectionist architecture. By this view, Soar's architecture is literally accurate; consideration of the neural level changes nothing.

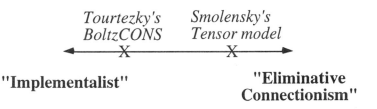

Fig. 2.14. Spectrum of approaches to Connectionism (based on discussion in Pinker and Prince, 1988).

At the other extreme, the "eliminative" approach to connectionism hypothesizes that symbolic models are at best good descriptions of what the brain is doing and should be taken seriously. But investigations should attempt to invent new, more flexible, and integrated mechanisms in a different computational framework. That is, neurobiology will lead to revising theories of memory, reasoning, and learning. Smolensky's (1988) research and his well-known treatise on this approach exemplifies this point of view.

I endorse both the implementalist and eliminative approaches as reasonable and important in bridging symbolic (descriptive) modeling and connectionism. However, my preference on the implementalist side is to seek new architectures that go beyond conventional data structures and processing, rather than merely mapping them into a neural implementation. Moreover, rather than taking a particular cognitive phenomenon and attempting to model it, as Smolensky did, this investigation seeks to specify more broadly and fundamentally the characteristics of serial learning by considering a variety of human experience. That is, holding the connectionist efforts in mind, I am working top down, looking for empirical evidence that can direct future modeling, moving from behavior and experience to architectural specifications.

At the same time, I attempt to extend two "eliminative connectionist" models: (a) Edelman's (1987) theory of neuronal group selection, which models categorization learning in terms of coupling between neural maps; and (b) Elman's (1989) simple recurrent networks, which model sequence learning by a "hidden layer" that represents the context of "current inputs" and the internal (recent) history of stimuli. I present these in detail in the next chapter.

In summary, the point of subsymbolic research is to reconsider how apparently complex organizations of behavior in problem solving might be learned and regenerated from a simple architecture based on activation relations of entities that are not representations in themselves (such as groups of neurons). This quest emphasizes:

- Bottom-up processes (from sensory stimuli).
- Self-organization (learning without a trainer or conscious inspection and reflection).
- Feedforward activation (one state activates the next, as opposed to top-down sorting and instantiation).
- Reconstruction of previously active relations (as opposed to a search and reassemble process overseen by a memory librarian and an executive, controlling process).

In general, the metaphor shifts from a memory of descriptions (what is true) to a memory of processes (what is related how and when).

2.3.1 Reformulating the "Executive"—Implicit Learning

An essential problem for subsymbolic models is to explain how controlled sequential behavior occurs. In problem-solving models, an executive controller handles the indexing, copying, assembling, and comparing of internal, textual components, such as the productions of Soar. Dennett (1992) summarized some of the features of the executive controller that the eliminative approach to understanding consciousness seeks to avoid: a *theater* (a stage where schema assemblages are presented), a *witness* (a subconscious, describing observer), a *central meaner* (an internal agent who represents what a person intends to say before he or she speaks), and a *figment* (what the brain creates to fill in perceptions to make them continuous, imagined sounds, colors, etc.) (p. 246).

In particular, Dennett (1992) emphasized that we must avoid the assumption that there is one construction where the brain assembles what it is really doing or what is really happening. A person's experience has an *apparent* seriality, but the psychophysical evidence suggests that attention, perception, and memory are coming together in many ways at once—such that different organizers developing simultaneously in different modalities are competing, supporting, organizing, and elaborating each other. My diagrams should be viewed as showing the neural system through a peephole; the point of view is very narrow.

As a first step, most of the early connectionist work focused on how categories and hierarchies might emerge as connectionist representations. How is complex, controlled behavior previously managed by executive processes to be explained by such bottom-up fragmentary models of memory and learning? Bickhard and Richie (1983) argued that there must be an emergent, developed *interactive system* that arises from lower-level neural processes. This systemic, intermediate-level organization forms the basis of learned patterns in human behavior, as well as phenomenological aspects of consciousness (e.g., holding ideas in mind, manipulating imagery [Kosslyn, 1980], having a goal). The intermediate level comprises both the *patterns* of experience and the *control processes* for creating new compositions and sequences:

> Organizations of potential such selections of activity, however, *are* control structures. Thus motivation too is an *aspect* of interactive competence, and representation and motivation turn out to be intimately related aspects of the same interactive control structures, not separate and disparate *components* as in the classical view . . . . There are no other possibilities. (Bickhard & Richie, 1983, p. 80–1)

The multifaceted aspect of categorization—as sequence and as unit, as recognized pattern and as memory creator, as functional indicator and as substitutable entity—is perhaps most evident in the study of grammars. For example, a subfield of learning research, focusing on *implicit learning*, considered how sequence patterns might be learned using a kind of activation memory.

In implicit learning experiments, subjects are presented with event sequences such as nonsense syllables to determine whether, by mere repetition, they detect and produce the patterns experimenters have used to create the event sequences. This is referred to as learning with "no intention to learn." Cleeremans and McClelland (1991) discovered that subjects' learning fit the capabilities of a simple recurrent network (SRN).

Such research supports the idea that "cognitive structures may emerge naturally out of associationist learning" (Patterson, 1991, p. 35). Mandler argued much earlier that associational memory not be viewed as isolated pairs, but as "temporal and probabilistic linkages of inputs and behavior which are available in functional units" (Mandler, 1962, p. 415, quoted by Patterson, 1991, p. 36). The functional view of associational structure embraces everything from habits to scripts, and fits the idea of categorization of a sequence (Fig. 1.6):

> Integration refers to the fact that previously discrete parts of a sequence come to behave functionally as a unit; the whole sequence . . . behaves as a single component response has in the past; any part of it elicits the whole sequence. (Mandler, 1962, p. 417)

With the emphasis on temporal relation, Mandler made association not a static lookup relation (index by inputting A and getting back B), but an internal, sequential activation (A activates B). Elman's simple recurrent networks, detailed in the next chapter, formalize how implicit learning might work.

2.3.2 Systematicity and Compositionality in the "Language of Thought"

To conclude this survey of activation theories of learning, I briefly consider Fodor and Pylyshyn's (1988) critical analysis of connectionism. One of the continuing ideas, developed earlier by Fodor, is the notion of a *language of thought (LOT)*, "representational states that have combinatorial syntactic and semantic structure" (p. 3). On first glance, LOT appears to fit the descriptive cognitive modeling approach, by which the language is a mechanism for describing the world and behavior (e.g., rules, scripts, procedures), and thought is a linguistic process. LOT appears to make the mistake of importing conscious, problem-solving mechanisms into the architecture of memory and learning. Nevertheless, a looser definition of "language" enables interpreting Fodor and Pylyshyn's analysis in a way consistent with the conceptual coordination perspective.

In particular, Fodor and Pylyshyn (1988) focused on the properties of systematicity and compositionality, which they rightly argued are characteristic of cognitive behavior and yet not supported by simple connectionist (neural network) models: "Cognitive capacities always exhibit certain symmetries, so that the ability to entertain a given thought implies the ability to entertain thoughts with semantically related contents" (p. 37). This implies that "the mind/brain architecture is not Connectionist at the cognitive level" (p. 37). For example, "the ability to produce/understand some sentences is *intrinsically* connected to the ability to produce/understand certain others" (p. 37). A native English speaker cannot understand "John loves the girl" without also being able to understand "The girl loves John." Put another way, sentences have constituents that are *compositionally* related. In the first sentence, the relation of John to the girl is the same as the relation of the girl to John in the second sentence.

The ideas of compositionality and systematicity suggest the existence of rule-like pattern comprehension and generation. I claim that such patterns result from categorization of sequences (e.g., Fig. 2.13), with later reactivation of sequences admitting substitution of subsequences and couplings. The processes of temporal sequencing, substitution, ongoing generalization, and compositional reconstruction provide an explanation of *productivity*, roughly, the ability to understand and produce relatively unbounded expressions from finite means (e.g., see Fodor and Pylyshyn, 1988, p. 33).

Most important, the architecture must be such that conceptual structures form without an executive assembly process that interprets a descriptive language of features, parts, types, orderings, semantic associations, and so on. The process of constructing categories, sequences, and compositions of them is the "language" of thought—although at this level, it can only be a poetic use of the word. Consideration of grammatical comprehension (chapter 10) suggests that some examples considered by Fodor and Pylyshyn (1988), such as the capacity to understand deductive arguments, may be *learned* forms of conceptual coordination. In general, higher-order semantic relations, as in logical deduction, may be dependent on simpler conceptualizations that are also learned, such as the conception that a sequence is an *inference* or even that a categorization is an *object reference*.

As Fodor and Pylyshyn (1988) required, the activation view of memory I am pursuing, by relating processes of sequence, coupling, and substitution, is neither strictly distributed nor strictly associationist. My investigation in this book may be viewed as exploring how far simple temporal and containment relations will go in explaining the patterns Fodor addressed in the LOT, without importing logic and language itself into the neural mechanism.

2.4 CHAPTER SUMMARY

In this chapter I have surveyed a variety of metaphors that have been applied to modeling neurobiological memory: replaying fixed sequences (executive model), moving pointers through fixed networks (interpretive model), reactivating sequences (data-driven model), and searching problem-solving paths (goal-driven model). In these efforts, cognitive scientists have struggled with the fundamental problem of explaining how behavior becomes patterned, or as many researchers would have put it, how patterns are learned. The shift since the 1980s has been to view the memory system as a *pattern creator* rather than a mere digester or recognizer. This active view of learning is combined with the view that performance itself is reconstructed, rather than rotely replayed (behavior is pattern reenacting and reexperiencing, not so much pattern following). Thus, the patterns are not to be viewed as either input and stored, nor as created internally and retrieved. Rather, behaving, learning, and remembering are all part of one more fundamental process of *internal structuring* that is experience. The case-based memory approach has pushed the idea that there is no understanding (problem solving) without learning. The extended shift, which looks more deeply at the neural processes of memory, is that aside from reflex actions, there is no behavior at all without learning.

"Conceptual coordination" refers to a developmental mechanism that replicates described patterns of behavior (e.g., grammars, semantic relations) without building the description into the mechanism, and thus presupposing what is to be explained. Connectionist theory has essentially the same goal, but often presupposes objective features, and separates mental representation from physical behavior. To make "schemata properties of entire networks," as Rumelhart et al. (1986, p. 8) aspired (see this chapter's opening quote), the behavior structuring properties of the network must be emphasized. Rather than distributed storage of static things, as simple connectionism views concepts, we have the coordinated construction of experience in time.

Building on ideas from Bartlett, Vygotsky, Piaget, and others, we can hypothesize that the internal structuring process has two basic aspects:

- Categorizing processes relate to each other in ways in which they worked together previously (actively related by time and physical subsumption).
- Every categorization is a generalization (i.e., not constructed from scratch, but a variation of some previous categorization).

Once we allow for categorizations to operate on themselves and substitutions to occur during the activation process, it is possible that we could discover an architectural mechanism with the full capability of procedures in programming languages, including variables with substitution and hierarchical composition. Such an architecture would have flexibility for improvisation (and error) that a conventional stored program does not have. The following chapter discusses neural network models that begin to deliver on this promise.

3

Neural Architectures for Categorization and Sequential Learning

The reader will remember that what we are aiming at here is the solution of a psychological problem. To get psychological theory out of a difficult impasse, one must find a way of reconciling three things without recourse to animism: perceptual generalization, the stability of memory, and the instabilities of attention. As neuropsychology, this and the preceding chapter go beyond the bounds of useful speculation. They make too many steps of inference without experimental check. As psychology, they are part of the preparation for experiment, a search for order in a body of phenomena about which our ideas are confused and contradictory; and the psychological evidence does provide some check on the inferences made here.

—Donald Hebb, *The Organization of Behavior: A neuropsychological theory,*
1949, p. 79

Although we cannot yet build a machine with the capabilities of the human brain, we can describe structures and processes of categorization and sequence learning that we believe are neurologically plausible. A combination of different scientific efforts is required: *analytical specifications* based on studying cognitive experience (e.g., activation interpretations of Kolers' color phi phenomenon; Fig. 1.15), *computational models* of neural processes, and basic *neurobiological science*. Put another way, researchers specify what processes they believe are occurring, model those processes in computer simulations, and search for neural structures and processes that fit the specifications and models (perhaps discovering bits and pieces whose functions are not known).

In most of this book, I am analyzing cognitive experiences to produce descriptions of neural processes (the activation trace diagrams). In this chapter, I present two computational models that are inspired by neurobiology. Thus, in effect my efforts are two steps removed from neurobiology: The computational models presented here are uncertain characterizations of how the brain works, and my explanations of cognitive experience are based on extensions of these uncertain computational models. My objectives in this chapter are to show that the specification I am producing has a plausible neurobiological interpretation and to show that the specification is useful for extending existing computational models of the brain.

In particular, I present Edelman's (1987) theory of categorization and Elman's (1989) theory of sequence learning. Edelman's theory explains categorization in terms of groups of neurons constituting "maps" that bidirectionally activate each other. That is, Edelman provided a computational model of what I have called the simultaneous, *coupling* relation. I extend Edelman's model by suggesting that global maps (maps of maps) might activate each other in time. That is, I build on Edelman's model to show how categorizations produced by coupling might become *sequences of categorizations.*

The computational model of sequence learning developed by Elman and others is couched in terms of neural networks, an extension of the parallel-distributed processing (PDP) connectionist architecture. The model postulates that sequences of categorizations are learned by way of an internal structure, called a *hidden unit.* Hidden units are a key aspect of connectionist models of learning. This model is particularly important to my investigation because the hidden units relate categorizations in time. As I show, the activation of sequences with hidden units provides a mechanism for sequence learning without storing descriptions of the sequences, and thus fits the specifications I have laid down in the last two chapters.

Putting these pieces together, my extension of Edelman's neurobiological model can be used to ground Elman's connectionist model by identifying the hidden units with global maps that activate each other in time.

3.1 TNGS: NEURAL MAP ACTIVATION OVER TIME

Edelman and his associates have developed a computational model of how categorization occurs in the brain. Specifically, they modeled the simplest possible categorizations, which they called *perceptual categorizations.* In a perceptual categorization two neural maps, each containing many groups of neurons, activate each other; this processes is called a *classification coupling.* Bidirectional activation is called *reentrant mapping.* The model is an implementation of the broader theory of neuronal group selection (TNGS; Edelman, 1992).

The square boxes in Fig. 3.1 illustrate a classification couple at two points in time. The classification couple is one of several such categorizations that may feed into a "map of maps" at that point in time, shown as a rectangle. I am extending Edelman's theory in this diagram. Edelman focused on multimodal coupling of neural maps in the basic form of *classification,* that is, integrating maps from several sensory systems. For example, the left square might be a sensory map activated by light stimuli and the right square might be a sensory map activated by tactile stimuli. In this figure, I suggest that we consider how map activation occurs over time in behavior sequences. In this figure, a given set of maps (the rectangle and two squares) are reactivated at a later time. With similar inputs, there is similar output. The groups and the reentrant links that are activated are always prone to change because of changes in the external environment and changes in the correlations activated throughout the neural system. TNGS claims that every activation is a *generalization* of past activation relations. Put another way, every activation is a *recategorization*, as opposed to a literal match or retrieval operation.

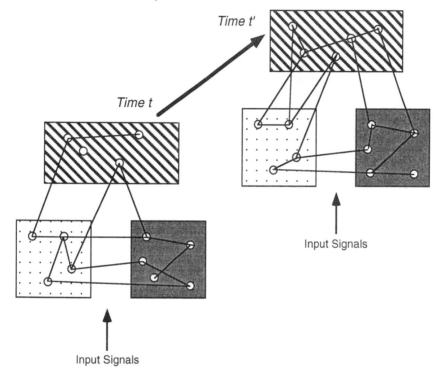

Fig. 3.1. Memory as recategorization. Inputs categorized similarly produce similar "output" relations. Circles are neuronal groups (perhaps thousands of neurons); lines indicate bidirectional activation; squares are "maps"; rectangles are maps of maps. (Adapted from Edelman, 1992, Figure 10-1, p. 103. Copyright ©1992 by BasicBooks, Inc. Reprinted by permission of BasicBooks, a division of Harper Collins Publishers, Inc.).

By explaining categorization in terms of more primitive sensory stimuli, TNGS is an attempt to avoid the usual approach in cognitive modeling by which meaningful categories are input to the program, usually as letters and words. The idea is that categories are internally constructed units, and stimuli are only organized, indeed only noticed, with respect to internal processes that are organizing and driving behavior.[1] To fit TNGS to what we already know about cognition, we must conclude that recategorization is always occurring simultaneously within a larger sensorimotor coordination. The higher-order construction of maps of *types of maps* is what we commonly call *conceptualization*. Conceptualization may involve different modalities, such as image, sound, touch, body position, rhythm, and so on. In particular, verbal concepts are not stored like dictionary entries, but involve a complex activation relation among many high-level neural maps.

In conventional psychological terms, a perceptual categorization corresponds to what is called *item memory* and accounts for recognition of an object or event as familiar.[2] A coupling relation corresponds to *associative memory*. A sequential activation corresponds to *serial memory*.

I have suggested that a basic form of conceptualization is simply the categorization of a sequence of maps activating over time. Neural evidence for these processes is tentative and incomplete; for voluntary movements at least, the cerebellum appears to play a role in sequencing. By one theory, the cerebellum constitutes a kind of content-addressable net that has some of the properties I describe (e.g., see Cowan & Sharp, 1988).

Braitenberg, Heck, and Sultan (1997) detailed the different functions of the cerebellum and their relations:

> The cerebellum is a large collection of individual lines (Eccles' "beams" . . .) that respond specifically to certain sequences of events in the input and in turn produce sequences of signals in the output. We believe that the sequence-in/sequence-out mode operation is as typical for the cerebellar cortex as the transformation of sets into sets of active neurons is typical for the cerebral cortex, and that both the histological differences between the two and their reciprocal functional interactions become understandable in light of this dichotomy. (p. 229)

The cerebellum has feed-forward activation, which in computational terms could be described as a one-dimensional beam:

> The cerebellar cortex is essentially "feed forward." Patterns of activity in the input are transformed into patterns of active output fibers through different sets of internal neurons which do not involve intracortical excitatory recurrent loops. The most numerous kind of interneurons, the granular cells, simply shift signals through their axonal branches (the parallel fibers) from their origin in the input in opposite directions along the laterolateral coordinate of the cortex at a low and fairly constant speed. Thus output neurons will be relaying input signals which arrived at different

---

[1] In Clancey (1997c) I described the philosophy and mechanisms of TNGS and related architectures in detail.

[2] The definitions here come from Murdock (1995, p. 111). Face recognition is most likely a higher-order, conceptual categorization, involving multiple simultaneous perceptual categorizations and a categorization of the relation of the other to the self; for example, see Barresi and Moore (1996).

times in the past in different places—the farther back in time, the farther away their origin. (p. 231)

In contrast, in the cerebral cortex a positive feedback occurs via recurrent loops (e.g., excitatory pyramidal cells connecting to each other). This fits the "explosive" buildup of activity that appears to occur in perceptual categorization (Freeman, 1991).

Broadly speaking, the (neo)cerebral cortex operations corresponds to the classification coupling that "form[s] internal representations of classes and subclasses of objects, using perceptron-like procedures" (Cowan & Sharp, 1988, p. 96), which correspond to the perceptual categorizations hanging off to the right in activation trace diagrams (e.g., Fig. 1.13). The cerebellum's operations correspond to the sequential activation of maps over time, as represented by activation trace diagrams (a one-dimensional beam).

In short, the ideas of classification coupling, sequencing, and their coordinated interaction in time are becoming identifiable as brain structures and processes. Hence, these are plausible architectural features on which to build a theory of conceptual coordination. For instance, I am assuming that mechanisms for fine motor control are similar to or replicated in the sequencing of higher-order maps.

My central hypothesis is that higher-order maps are sequenced in some way in the brain. As shown in Fig. 3.2, different maps of maps are linked to different high-order maps. The lower-level categorizations, often perceptual details, may involve locations, objects, words, and so on—what we commonly call "things in the world." The higher-order maps are physically linked by reentrant connections. However, the second higher-order map (labeled *time t'*) only becomes activated after the first map has become active (labeled *time t*). In this manner, I conjecture that maps of maps are sequenced over time via physical subsumption. The number of possible connections in the brain is so large that there are sufficient links to establish a link between any sets of maps, as required by activity. Furthermore, all learning is categorization over time. This means that all learning is activation "in place" of preexisting links, which are composed over time into, and always within, sequences of activation. As Edelman (1992) stated, there must be some way of holding such activations so they can be compared and further coordinated, allowing for continuity in our experience. The function of higher-order categorizations is to "activate or reconstruct portions of past activities of global mappings of different types—for example, those involving different sensory modalities. They must also be able to recombine or compare them" (Edelman, 1992, p. 109). This capability to hold active and categorize multiple maps in time is a key aspect of conceptual coordination.

Although the diagram depicts one global map as physically activating the next, nothing in this book depends on that particular mechanism. Neuronal groups may activate the next map by direct feed-forward activation, as I show, or there may be other (or additional) means by which sequencing and timing are brought about. The key hypothesis is that learning of behavior sequences (or procedures, habits, and routines) involves physical activation of maps in sequence as part of sensorimotor coordination. I will often refer to this as *next–next–next ordering*.

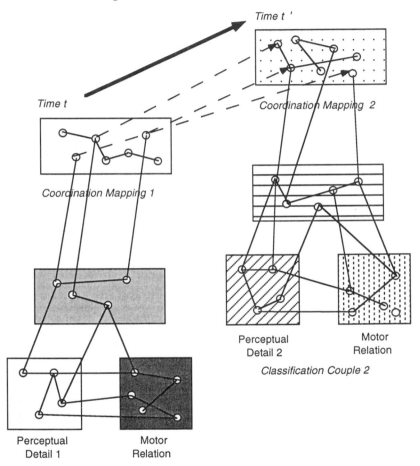

Fig. 3.2. An extension of TNGS. Higher-order maps, including categorizations of global (cross-modal) maps, physically activate in sequence over time, serving as the memory of how perceptual details are coordinated within an activity. Solid lines indicate co-activation in a circuit; dotted lines indicate activation over time.

The memory of next–next–next ordering is not described, stored someplace else, and later retrieved and applied. Rather the memory of sequence is embodied in the physical activation of categorizations (neural structures) in time (hence the subtitle of this book, "How the Mind Orders Experience in Time"). The simplest hypothesis, as depicted by Fig. 3.2, is that each global map activates the next map in sequence, as a kind of triggering. As already summarized, the cerebellum is a leading candidate for this mechanism—"A main function of the cerebellum is to link sequentially the sensorimotor components of a synergy [constructed in a global mapping] in a feed-forward fashion" (Edelman, 1987, p. 229).

The second essential hypothesis is that sequences themselves may be categorized and composed. Feed-forward activation of a categorized sequence activates maps in the sequence concurrently, so the activation of the sequence may be a construction, rather than strictly built up over time (as in Kolers' color phi phenomenon, section 1.2.2). Sequential ordering is central in my examples and discussion, primarily because my main goal is to reformulate stored procedural models of memory.

Formation of categorized sequences may occur through what Damasio (1994) called *convergence zones*: "Dispositional representations exist as potential patterns of neuron activity in small ensembles of neurons I call 'convergence zones'" (p. 102). Dispositional representations are acquired patterns that "make neural activity happen elsewhere" (p. 102). A paradigmatic example is the convergence zones related to imagery:

> Convergence zones whose dispositional representations can result in images when they fire back to early sensory cortices (which) are located throughout the higher-order association cortices (in occipital, temporal, parietal, and frontal regions), and in basal ganglia and limbic structures. (p. 102)

The higher-order categorizations I am postulating may also be termed dispositional representations: "imageable knowledge that we can recall and which is used for movement, reason, planning, creativity; and some contain records of rules and strategies with which we operate on those images" (p. 105). However, I emphasize that such "representations" are not records as in descriptive cognitive models, but dispositional in Damasio's sense—activity patterns of which we are not necessarily conscious. Also, by "imageable" Damasio did not mean only visual representations, but any topographically organized representation, such as an auditory sequence. And topographical does not mean necessarily a spatial relation to objects in the world, but any neural map in early sensory cortices, in Edelman's sense of a neural map. Thus, the neural patterns are topographical with respect to sensory surfaces.[3]

---

[3]Hull (1935) explained the capability of rats to efficiently assemble previously learned paths by a mechanism of moving the effect of stimuli forward in a series: "similar components of all reactions in any given series tend to come forward and become associated with the external stimulus component in the same manner" (p. 229). The effect

In summary, a dispositional sequence may include the whole range of sensorimotor categorization: visual imagery, sounds, taste, and even broad body feelings like being contained, smothered, fear, and so forth. By this view, categorized sequences would be dispositional representations that activate other dispositional representations, indirectly resulting in activation of sensory and motor cortices (cf. Damasio, 1994, p. 105). Damasio described how such higher-order activity in convergence zones may develop through feed-forward relations to sensory and somatosensory (including emotional) brain activity, similar to Edelman's theory of reentrant categorization based on "value." Consistent with the coordination sequencing property I am emphasizing, Damasio said that a convergence zone "preserves the order of the onset of brain activity and in addition maintains activity and attentional focus by means of feedback connections to the two sites (sensory and somatosensory) to the two sites of brain activity" (p. 162). Although it is far from clear that such a mechanism is sufficient for producing all behavioral sequences and their hierarchical organization, the idea of a convergence zone is plainly the beginning of a neural theory for categorization of categorizations and their temporal ordering. As such, a convergence zone idea may be viewed as a global mapping, in Edelman's sense, in which attentional focus and connections to multiple, simultaneous forms of brain activity are synchronized to form a higher-order ensemble.

With this background, in the next section I present a connectionist model of sequence learning, which I will reinterpret and extend in terms of neural map activation.

3.2 SEQUENTIAL CONNECTIONIST LEARNING

It is well known that practiced behavior, such as speech, is inherently sequential, more commonly called *serial* in cognitive psychology. Descriptive cognitive models are especially good at representing sequential relations of association and procedures, by using production rules, frames, scripts, and so on, to represent behavior patterns. Connectionism was devised as a means of modeling memory in a finer grain of detail, such that certain patterns would develop in the model by a learning mechanism, rather than being built in by a researcher developing a model. On the other hand, an ordinary connectionist network is designed to store associations between input–output pairs, and thus cannot directly capture temporal relations, which are so easily encoded in conventional procedural languages. Elman (1989) devised an extension of connectionism, which he called a *simple recurrent network* (SRN). In SRNs, preceding events in a sequence of input provide a context for associating new inputs (Fig. 3.3).

---

is that stimulus-response associations do not always act in isolation, but may be combined as if anticipating a goal—yet this occurs without reasoning.

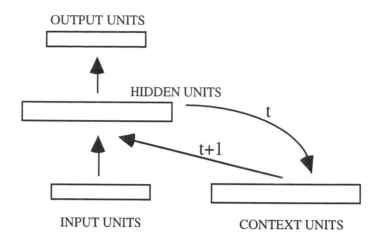

Fig. 3.3. Simple recurrent network. The arrow pointing "backward" from the hidden layer to the context layer indicates that the weights associated with the hidden units at time *t* are copied; they become part of the input at Time *t* + 1. This design avoids having to present a "moving window" of input by which sequences associated with different times are presented in parallel. (From Elman, 1989, p. 18. Copyright ©1989. Reprinted by permission of Lawrence Erlbaum Associates, Inc.).

This architecture was inspired by the recursive networks of Jordan (1986) that used a direct feedback approach, using *output units* from Time *t* as part of the inputs of Time *t* + 1. But "such a network learns how to use the representation of successive states [denoted by the output units], it does not discover a representation of the sequence [encoded in the hidden units]" (Servan-Schreiber et al., 1988, p. 4). For this reason, Elman's model feeds back the *hidden units*, rather than the output. In this way, hidden units now...

> encode not only the prior event, but also relevant aspects of the representation that was constructed in predicting the prior event from its predecessor. When fed back as input, these representations could provide information that allows the network to maintain prediction-relevant features of an entire sequence. (p. 411)

Experiments indicate that such networks "learn to approximate the frequency of occurrence of successor words" (Elman, p. 18) in two- and three-word natural language sentences, using a lexicon of 29 nouns and verbs. Such a network was trained on six passes through a corpus of 10,000 sentences, with no breaks between sentences:

> The network is not able to predict the precise order of words, but it recognizes that (in this corpus) there is a class of inputs (viz., verbs) which typically follow other inputs (viz., nouns). This knowledge of class behavior is quite detailed; from the

fact that there is a class of items which always precedes **chase, break, smash**, it infers a category we might call *aggressors*. (p. 19)

This information is of course in the input; the encoding merely re-represents sequential orderings appearing in the original sentence.[4]

To understand how the network operates, a record of hidden unit activations is retained for each word in the lexicon; these data are then analyzed by hierarchical cluster analysis. The categories in the resulting tree correspond to what we call nouns, verbs, animates (broken into small and large animals and humans), inanimates (broken into breakables, edibles, and miscellaneous). Elman (1989, p. 19) summarized several essential properties of the encoding by the hidden units:

- "The category structure is hierarchical." Considering all possible values of the hidden units as constituting a "space" of representation, then "higher-level categories correspond to larger and more general regions of the space."
- "The categories are not discrete . . . category membership may be marginal or ambiguous."
- "The content of the categories is not known to the network." Unlike language learners, the network has no way to "ground" its emergent categorizations in the real world.

Instances of words appear as the terminal nodes of the tree (because of course the data were collected on this basis as the network operated). But we find that words are separated by the lexical type distinctions and no others. Even occurrences of the same word (such as a noun appearing as object and subject of different sentences) are clustered to distinguish between the tokens of different types. "For instance, tokens of **boy** which occur in subject position tend to cluster together, and apart from tokens of **boy** in object position" (Elman, 1989, p. 20). Further experimentation with more (but still restricted) complex sentences (averaging more than five words), incorporating relative clauses and punctuated, demonstrate that the network can predict how classes of words follow in sequence (e.g., distinctions between verbs requiring, optionally permitting, or never allowing a direct object).

Elman (1989) concluded from his work that connectionist representations need not consist of atomic (isolated) associations, but may encode "systematic patterns which are immanent in the primary data" (p. 21), such as syntax. Further, these representations are highly context-sensitive. Indeed, the SRN "binds the semantics of reference with the syntax of representation" (p. 21). Elman's experiments suggest that the "distinction between syntax and semantics may be quantitative in nature and do not stem from any deep distinctions." Finally, the activation of hidden units over time "make use of state space and state dynamics" (p. 21). Of course, the grammatical categories are implicit in the

---

[4]See the critical discussion in Chapter 3 of Clancey (1997c).

data, but the point is that the SRN architecture is able to represent these categories, and does so in an open-ended way. Elman concluded by reminding us that "language presents many problems of a highly complex nature, and the simple successes obtained here should not cause us to forget just how difficult those problems can be" (p. 22).

In detailed experiments, Servan-Schreiber et al. (1988), showed that an SRN, when presented with structured sequences of inputs generated from a finite state grammar, can adapt to become a finite state machine that recognizes the sequences. Analysis showed that the SRN initially learns to distinguish between different inputs, "independently of the temporal context" (p. 35). Subsequent modifications indicate that

> different occurrences of the same event (e.g., two occurrences of the same letter) are distinguished on the basis of immediately preceding events—the simplest form of a time tag. This stage corresponds to the recognition of the different "arcs" in the particular finite state grammar used in the experiments. (p. 35)

Finally, subsequences are discriminated, corresponding, for example, to where a noun phrase may appear in a relative clause. These experiments show why the SRN requires multiple presentations of the entire data set to learn the sequence patterns. This of course is not unreasonable when the patterns are occurring over and over again as in natural language. The experiments do not suggest that "SRN can learn to recognize *any* finite state language" (p. 36). The data must be context sensitive so, for example, the variations in embedded sequences depend on information preceding the embedding.

Servan-Schreiber et al. (1988), pointed that we do not typically use finite-state automata (FSA) to encode nonlocal information such as the length of sequences. But this is because of the awkwardness of designing such FSA machines: The SRN develops its own state transition diagram, may encode billions of different patterns through the use of the hidden unit layer, and continues to operate even when it "encounters an undefined state transition" (p. 21).

In comparing SRN as a kind of mental representation to conventional descriptive cognitive models, Elman (1989) said:

> As words are processed there is no separate state of lexical retrieval. There are no representations of words in isolation. The representations of words (the internal states following input of a word) always reflect the input taken together with the prior state. In this scenario, words are not building blocks as much as they are cues which guide the networks through different grammatical states. Words are distinct from each other by virtue of having different causal properties. (p. 21)

Elman (1991) compared the SRN architecture to a combination lock:

> In this metaphor, the role of words is analogous to the role played by the numbers in a combination. The numbers have causal properties; they advance the lock into different states. The effect of a number is dependent on its context. Entered in the correct sequence, the numbers move the block into an open state. The open state may be said to be functionally compositional (van Gelder, [1990]) in the sense that

it reflects a particular sequence of events. The numbers are "present" insofar as they are responsible for the final state, but not because they are still physically present.

The limitation of this combination lock is of course that there is only one correct combination. The networks studied here are more complex. The causal properties of words are highly structure-dependent and the networks allow many "open" (i.e., grammatical) states. (p. 221)

3.2.1 Experiments with Nesting and Timing

To understand better how sequences are encoded in SRNs, Cottrell compared Jordan's state networks architecture to Elman's context networks for simple arithmetic problems, such as adding two multi-digit numbers (Cottrell & Tsung, 1989). The input consisted of the two digits of the current column; the output consists of an action (e.g., "WRITE the sum of the two digits," "note that there is a CARRY," "shift the input window to the NEXT column of digits" [p. 60]) and a result (e.g., the digit of a WRITE action). To enforce the need for context, Cottrell supplied input that required the network to learn the program: WRITE result, NEXT, CARRY. Shifting to the next column before checking for a carry requires memory of the previous column.

Cottrell and Tsung (1989) discovered what now seems obvious—"networks with only output histories cannot remember things about their input that are not reflected in their output" (p. 64). Because the Jordan networks did not record the information needed for *carrying* in the output, they were unable to learn the algorithm. On the other hand, SRNs can

> learn simple programming constructs that are not nested. In particular, these nets can do simple sequencing, looping, and branching. Also, values necessary for future processing [as in carrying] can be stored over short periods by the context network. (p. 65)

It should also be noted that Cottrell's network had to be trained 10,000 times on the data set of 3,000 problems before it reached a state of generalization that allowed good performance on the remainder of the training set of 4,096 problems.[5] Children learn, even those who have difficulty, on far fewer examples and certainly without doing the same problems 10,000 times! It is obvious that the pattern extraction capabilities of SRNs are capable of learning the task, but the learning mechanism is far less capable than what children employ.

Nesting or subproceduralization, which SRNs cannot do, corresponds to categorizing sequences (cf. Fig. 1.6). SRNs merely repeat associations in sequence; they do not compose and substitute sequences. To handle this problem Miyata (1989) devised an architecture that attempts to replicate the practice law,

---

[5]This corresponds to the possible combinations in base-4 arithmetic with addends up to three digits.

in which performance increases as a power function of the number of trials. He chose the problem of learning to type. His architecture uses two Jordan networks, such that the action corresponds to finger movements and the input corresponds to "a conceptual representation of the action sequence to be performed" (p. 11). This approach allows for subsequences to be recognized and to prime the behavior, so with practice typing shifts from serial to parallel processing.

However, the training of the network was quite contrived, requiring pretraining, very restricted input–output pairs (four "actions" A, B, C, and D and only three inputs), and controlling the "planning" level so it only operates once for every three steps of "execution." In effect, Miyata had encountered another inherent limitation of this architecture: The mechanism operates in a timeless way, behavior is sequential but not temporal.

Cummins (1993) explored the temporal capabilities of SRNs further, investigating how they can be understood as encoding patterns via movement in a phase space. A network is trained to recognize sequences in which elements in a given order (such as O, A, B, C) are presented for different lengths of time or "rates." For example, the network will recognize OAAABC, OAABBBBCC, but not BAOC or some other permutation. The rate of presentation is defined as the number of times an element is presented. In this sense, Cummins' model can be said to recognize repeated "beats," or input in a common sequence presented at a different rate.

But again, in Cummins' (1993) model the input is actually provided in a rate-independent way, with an arbitrary time between inputs, unlike a rhythm, which exists in time. OAAABC might be presented so there is a gap of 1 sec between O and A, but only 1/3 sec between the As. Cummins' network would not notice the difference in *timing*. The "temporal" nature of this network is only sequential and involves *counting* discrete, uniform units. Recurrence of an element is not the same as timing. The so-called rhythm being recognized is actually rate invariant because the network does not detect temporal differences.

Related arguments are made by Bickhard and Richie (1983) in analyzing the inability of a Turing machine to model temporal aspects of processes:

> A Turing machine is not, and cannot be, truly interactive in any interesting or important way. It cannot be because its environment, the tape, is static and provides nothing (interactively) interesting to be interacted with.

> There is a deeper point behind this one, however, and that is that interactive competence in an environment requires *skill*, and skill requires not just formal "information processing" or "symbol manipulating" capabilities, but also timing and temporal coordination capabilities, and Turing machine theory has no natural way of introducing such considerations. There is no natural timing unit in Turing machine theory, nor even any sense in which the processing steps take the same or determinate multiple amounts of time as each other: the steps are simply serially ordered with no metric time considerations at all. There is, for example, nothing equivalent to an oscillator in Turing machine theory, and no way to construct one

without adding to the fundamental assumptions of the formalism. A related point is that interactive functions such as multi-system environment monitoring or coordination intrinsically require simultaneous processing across the various systems involved, while Turing machine theory is intrinsically logically serial and temporally sequential. (p. 90)

The point is clear: Memorizing a sequence of supplied inputs is not the same as learning to coordinate behavior in an environment over time. Interactivity involves relating sensory fields to movement and coupling movements with the timing of other agents and artifacts—prominent in the rhythm and intonation of speech, but ignored by simple connectionist models.

Related work on modeling aphasia shows that interactivity is occurring inside the brain, too. Aphasia is the "partial or total loss of the ability to articulate ideas or comprehend spoken or written language, resulting from damage to the brain caused by injury or disease" (*American Heritage Electronic Dictionary*, 1992). Research (French, 1997) indicates that language learning disabilities can be tracked to internal breakdown in how parts of the brain interact with each other. Specifically, recurrence relations normally enable hippocampal "training" of the neocortex.

The entire experimental paradigm of training networks by supplying inputs may be wrong-headed: The organism must be organizing its own learning through its own activities, and internally a codependency between organizers speeds up the construction of useful generalizations. My position on this nature versus nurture dichotomy is that once the idea of learning by training is replaced by learning by active organizing, the influences of both environmental and internal processes will become more salient. The examples in Part II and III shed some light on this matter.

In conclusion, the SRN architecture is a useful extension of connectionist networks, but falls prey to the limitations of descriptive cognitive modeling. An SRN model provides no explanation of why human language has grammatical forms, but only stores the product of grammatical speaking. Although the use of a context layer provides an enticing glimpse of how sequential behavior might be learned, there is no mechanism for composing sequences into chunks or any kind of hierarchical organization so prominent in the cognitive models of knowledge. In effect, the storage-encoding paradigm is continued, with little insight into the nature of how behavior is *functionally ordered* and *composed* in time.

3.2.2 Reinterpreting SRN in Terms of Neural Activation

Because the input and output units of the SRN mechanism are given data items and no perceptual categorizations or complex motor actions are involved, we need a more complex representation to describe what and how people learn. In this section, I consider how we can extend the SRN model by reinterpreting it in terms of neural map activation.

Recall that in the SRN architecture the hidden units of Time $t - 1$ become the context units at Time t, combining with the input units of Time t to produce output units via hidden units (t). The hidden units of Time t then become the context units of Time $t + 1$, and so on. In this re-representation of an SRN architecture (Fig. 3.4), I use a different node to represent each state of the hidden units over time (this turns out to be pivotal in the neural interpretation of slips, chapter 6). The output units may be a conceptualization of WIDN (which would be represented as another network) or a categorization of a coordinated sensorimotor sequence (such as pulling a knob). By the neural activation perspective, input units are not necessarily "raw sensory data," but may be output units from perceptual categorization. Following the key idea of connectionist modeling, the hidden units are generalized on each cycle; in my interpretation a cycle is some combination of perceptual categorization and movement (or reconceptualization). That is, the hidden units of the next cycle are a generalization of the context on the previous cycle, and in general this context involves perception and movement.

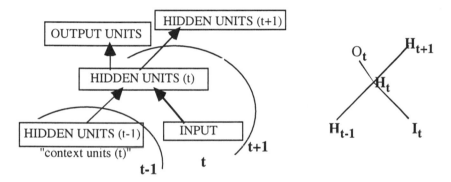

Fig. 3.4. Simple recurrent network (SRN) shown using an activation trace notation (compare to Fig. 1.5). Hidden units form the "maps of maps" backbone of a sequence. Right diagram shows participating processes of each coordination at Time t. In a sequence activated by the previous hidden unit H(t - 1), the Input(t), Output(t), and H(t) categorizations are biased to form a coupling if they have previously co-occurred.

A node in the activation trace diagram may be identified with a categorization of a global neural map, in contrast with a simple vector in the hidden unit model of SRNs. In contrast with SRN modeling, I do not refer to the $h(t)$ sequence as an internal encoding, but rather a process that coordinates perception and motion in time. Obviously, SRNs in themselves do not realize what is required for replicating the coordination processes of the brain. Elman's (1989) examples and those provided in related research suggest that human behavior fits the properties of an SRN, but the mechanism of neural coordination involves much more. To summarize some of the differences:

- The "input units" of conceptual coordinations are perceptual categorizations (as in TNGS), not supplied tokens. Neural learning starts by organizing a dynamic sensory field, not by receiving whole letters, words, or descriptions in an input buffer.

- Perceptual categorizations have different modalities and temporal relations, such as pitches and rhythms.

- The "hidden units" of the brain may be higher-order categorizations of WIDN.

- The "output units" of human behavior may include speech processes of saying what was experienced, not the categorizations themselves.

- In the brain, the formation of the hidden units *(t)* and input units*(t)* are codetermined in the manner of a classification couple. That is, categorizing WIDN and perceptual categorizing constrain each other—the coordinating process participates in the construction of the "input" (e.g., see the interaction of seeing and interpretation in the paintbrush inventors in chapter 7; see also the discussion of EPAM's learning strategy in chapter 11).

Rather than viewing the recurrent networks as a means of storing things, the activation perspective suggests that the basic characteristic of a sequence is that the agent is recategorizing "what is happening." What is especially missing from SRNs is a mechanism for *compositionality* (Fodor & Pylyshyn, 1988), by which sequences may be categorized simultaneously on multiple levels. In the next section, I briefly reconsider how compositionality of procedural programming languages might be reinterpreted in neural terms.

3.3 REINTERPRETING STORED-TEXT PROCEDURAL MODELS AS NEURAL PROCESSES

At a high level of abstraction, it is at least plausible that a neural map construction process of classification, sequencing, substitution, and composition could be dynamically reconstructing the relations of ordered steps, variable bindings, conditional statements, and subgoaling described in procedural models of human memory and reasoning (Fig. 3.5).

Specifically, each variable binding (a variable receives a particular value) would be an occurrence of a particular categorizing process reactivating. For example, if C is a variable representing a class of objects, such as cards in a playing deck, then C could be a (higher-order) categorization constituting the conceptualization that an object is a playing card. C receiving a different value in a program would be like this same neural process (one physical structure) being reactivated and coupled to a different combination of perceptual categorizations (in the manner that both the king of spades and the queen of hearts are categorized as being playing cards). Of course, a key distinction is that C is not merely being "assigned" a different value, but is being recategorized (generalized); what C means is changing each time it activates by virtue of the other categorizations it is coupled with. In this manner, each time the "neural procedure" (a sequence of global maps) is "reapplied," a kind of substitution is possible. Part II provides many examples of such generalization and substitution during sequence reconstruction.

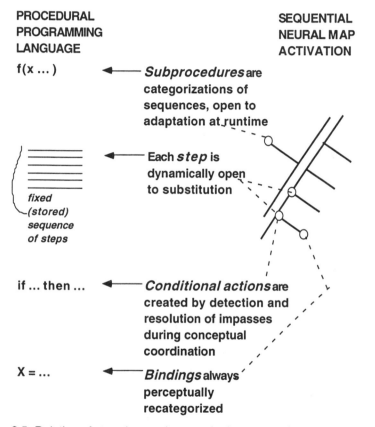

PROCEDURAL
PROGRAMMING
LANGUAGE

SEQUENTIAL
NEURAL MAP
ACTIVATION

f(x ...)   ◄——— *Subprocedures* are
                 categorizations of
                 sequences, open to
                 adaptation at runtime

                 ◄——— Each *step* is
                 dynamically open
                 to substitution

fixed
(stored)
sequence
of steps

if ... then ... ◄——— *Conditional actions* are
                 created by detection and
                 resolution of impasses
                 during conceptual
                 coordination

X = ...   ◄——— *Bindings* always
                 perceptually
                 recategorized

Fig. 3.5. Relation of stored procedures and rules to neural map activation.

Similarly, the idea of a conditional statement (if–then statement) in a programming language could be reinterpreted in terms of a sequence in which the "if part" is a categorization that must be "observed" and the "then part" is the next global map in sequence. That is, without the simultaneous occurrence of another (often perceptual) categorization, the next global map in the habitual sequence is not activated.

Procedures themselves are categorized sequences, which can become "subprocedures" or "steps" in other sequences. That is, compositionality or proceduralization is enabled by categorizing sequences, making them units in their own right. Constraints on reusing a categorization in an active sequence are visible in natural language comprehension (chapter 10). Indeed, in comprehension we can see strong evidence that categorizations are indeed physical structures that are reused, and not arbitrarily copied or "reinstantiated" as is permissible in conventional programming languages.

Coming from the other direction, we find that human coordination capability exceeds what most programming languages allow. For example, speaking grammatically is a complex manifestation of conceptual coordination, involving multidimensional reconstruction from previously constructed sequences (grammar) and categorization couplings (images, references, goal concepts, etc.). In programmatic terms, reconstructing sequences in this way would be like remembering and reenacting *stacks* (a sequence of procedural calls and variable bindings). Indeed, the Soar architecture already shows how an ordering of steps and binding constraints could be reestablished without running the procedures themselves; this is what chunking provides.

The usual procedural interpretation of Fig. 3.5 is that a procedure on one level invokes a subprocedure and transfers control to that subprocedure. The higher procedure is held in quiescence on a stack. Control returns to the higher procedure when the invoked subprocedure is complete. But a composition of categorized sequences operates quite differently: Each of the sequences remains active and continues to affect the construction of lower-level (subsumed) units. Brooks (1991) called such a simultaneous activation of organizers on multiple levels the *subsumption architecture*. In my neural interpretation, the higher-order categorizations constitute ongoing "interests" and orders, which provide a contextual bias on what is noticed and incorporated in ongoing serial behavior. In most general terms, this simultaneous, hierarchical organization accounts for how a person sustains a coherent identity throughout the day, as a family member, citizen, employee, customer, and so on.[6] In the construction of specific gestures and expressions, such integrative, multiple-layered effects are exemplified by the sustained timing in typing, even as incorrect letters are substituted (see Fig. 6.4).

To restate my underlying purposes, my exploration of a neurally plausible "process memory" aims to reveal aspects of sequencing, categories (variables), "binding," and so forth, that are taken for granted in most computational models of memory and learning. At the same time, I hope to discover capabilities, especially flexibilities, that a process memory allows, but a stored program

---

[6]See Clancey, 1997b; see the elaborated example of Cohen's identity in chapter 1 of Clancey (1997c).

memory does not have.[7] Table 3.1 summarizes the terminological correspondences between the conventional programming view of stored procedures and a neurobiological view of processes.

Table 3.1

Relation of Procedural Constructs to Neurobiological Processes

Procedural Construct	*Neurobiological Process*
Variable	Conceptual categorization
Binding	Classification coupling (recurrent mapping)
Sequence	Global neural map activation
Condition	Current (perceptual) categorization and global map
Production	Sequential activation, plus motor actions
Procedure	Categorized sequence (higher-order map)

In short, the neural activation perspective is a tool for visualizing where stored descriptive models do not fit neural processes: Neural categorizations are not merely instantiated templates, but *regeneralizations*; conditional actions are not merely fixed stored steps, but *recomposed sequences* (again regeneralizations). Substitution of details (perceptions and conceptions of objects) and entire sequences (conceptions of activities) might occur through similarities categorized at "run time" (during activity). Indeed, such a comparison leads us to question why hierarchies of problem-solving steps (called *problem spaces;* chapter 12) are formed at all in human knowledge and where the lowest levels in such constructions come from (the *primitive terms* in descriptive models). In short, by the neural activation view, learning is inherent in behavior itself. The typical machine-learning approach is that some activity generates a trace, which is then inspected in a secondary, "reflective" process, and "lessons" are stored. New behaviors are only generated from previous descriptions, rather than allowing both perceptual and conceptual change at "run-time."

---

[7]Drescher (1991) used a related notation to represent perception–action–result schemas. His work more systematically explored learning visual-motor controllers; I am more interested in describing *experience* (phenomenology); but the work is complementary.

3.4 REINTERPRETING ACTIVATION TRACE DIAGRAMS
AS A NEURAL THEORY

Throughout this chapter we have been relating preliminary neurobiological theory, such as Damasio's (1994) convergence zones, to simple connectionist models of categorization and sequence learning. In this section I reiterate the neural interpretation of activation trace diagrams and emphasize the details that remain to be worked out.

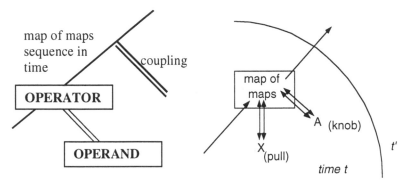

Fig. 3.6. Relation of operator–operand and map activation views. Operators, coupled to operands, are sequenced. Alternatively, right side shows that both operators and operand may be coupled to a global map (compare to Fig. 2.10).

In summary, the activation trace diagram illustrates two basic temporal relations of different levels of neural organization: Categorizations are simultaneously related (coupled) to higher-order categorizations (maps of maps), which are themselves sequentially related (left side of Fig. 3.6). In diagramming a behavior sequence, we conventionally show an operator as a node and operands as hanging off the side (as in the depiction of Pull-Knob in Fig. 2.10). This makes sense because in most models of cognition, and as will be evident in the examples of Part II, operators are sequenced and operands are substitutable. But in moving to consideration of neural maps, as in Edelman's model (Fig. 3.2), it appears more reasonable to interpret the motor relation (operator) and perceptual categorization (operand) as both coupled to a map of maps (right side of Fig. 3.6).

More careful comparison of the figures reveals that to account for how multiple modalities are related at a point in time (speech, visual image, smell, and so on), the nodes of the activation trace are not simply maps of maps, but maps that contain maps of maps (see Fig. 3.2). Thus, a categorized sequence would be a map of maps of maps. As I have indicated, TNGS does not show sequencing of maps of maps, let alone categorization of such sequencing. In the absence of a good neurological model of such sequencing and categorization, I have adopted SRNs as the best computational envisionment of what is occurring.

Details about how neurons are organized—groups, maps, convergence zone, hypercolumns,[8] and so on—although exceedingly interesting and potentially relevant for understanding cognition, are beyond what I can consider in this book. For example, the hierarchical form of cortical regions, areas, modules, and columns is suggestive evidence that the brain is capable of forming the categorizations of categorizations that my analysis assumes. Rather than working with neurobiological specifics, which is not my area of expertise, my analysis instead works from more abstract architectural assumptions about categorization:

- Categorization is a basic memory process that operates on its own products.
- Inclusion of categorizations in a behavior sequence is an activation process, not a copying process.
- "Instantiation" of a categorization is a process of both generalization (changing the categorization) and coupling to other categorizations (e.g., perceptual details). That is, categorizations are not things that are merely reused, but always adapted relations and always part of functional circuits within activity.
- Concepts are higher-order categorizations.
- Categorization of sequences is an essential part of a mechanism by which behavior becomes hierarchically organized (corresponding to problem spaces in descriptive cognitive models).

Adopting such a framework, we can attempt to interpret empirical data to the best extent possible, and only delve into questions about neural details when there is evidence for more detailed structuring. For example, traditional psychological experiments suggest a difference in ability to recall elements in a list depending on their position: "The beginning of the list is best recalled," with a recency effect, "the end of the list is next best" (Murdock, 1995, p. 110). This suggests that activation of the categorization of the sequence activates the first element (cf. Fig. 2.5), and if there are activation links to every element, they are comparatively weak. (However, "overlearning" experiments investigating implicit learning suggest that by repeated practice it may be possible to pick up a

---

[8]A hypercolumn is a hierarchical processing module having a specialized function, "composed of columns of cells which process a related function (e.g., processing lines of a given orientation for a given portion of the visual field). Each column contains large numbers of cells (e.g., 40,000 in a column) and are further organized into modules that share input and output functions" (Schneider, 1999, p. 342). These modules are further interconnected to form 500–100 cortical areas that are further organized into cortical areas, which apparently relate to different aspects of coordination (e.g., vision, motor output).

sequence at multiple points.) How are categorizations of sequences formed? Possibly all maps in the sequence have a transient, retained threshold that degrades over time. Either by raising activation of the elements so they are simultaneously active (categorization held in "working memory") or by lowering the threshold required for formation of a coupling, the sequence is grabbed and thus "held as a unit" with a special activation to the head.

Alternatively, the conceptual categorization might be the first node in the sequence (as suggested by Fig. 2.12). This categorization is generalized to include the subsequent global maps, including them both temporally and by reentrant links. In this way, the sequence is subsumed within a global map, but is the global map itself. The global map operates by activating included maps as a process over time. The unit is a coordinated sequence over time. Is the end marked, does it loop back to itself, or does the sequence simply stop, like the last line in a computer program? Some sequencing and timing mechanism is required to prevent looping or stuttering, yet allow controlled repetition. Such issues are relevant to understanding typing errors and other slips, and they are considered further in Part II.

Indeed, the examples in Part II illustrate a variety of reconstruction variations: figure–ground shifts, slips, repetition with addition on the end, and "seeing as" analogy. My arguments in the next chapter are intended to show that such activation patterning and reconstruction has a neurobiological explanation. The basic structuring processes include:

- Perceptual categorization (including figure–ground shifts and simultaneous relations).
- Categorization as generalization of previous activation relations.
- Coupling of categorizations (modular, but codetermined).
- Sequencing of categorizations (habits).
- Subsumption of categorizations in time (generalization of WIDN)
- Categorization of sequences (a kind of conceptualization).
- Hierarchical composition of categorized sequences (conceptualization of problem spaces), and sequential learning of lines of reasoning across conceptual levels (chunking).

In conclusion, I suggested in this chapter that we attempt to straddle three domains of investigation: empirical descriptions of behavior and experience, computational (connectionist and symbolic) models, and neurobiological theories of brain structures and processes. The temptation for the cognitive modeler is to anchor everything with computational models, for they are the most precise of the three elements of our investigation. However, as I have indicated in this chapter, such models typically take too much for granted. Adopting the current modeling paradigm leads too often to building in what needs to be generated by cognition. Chief among the biases that must be questioned, in connectionist and symbolic modeling alike, is the view that memory is primarily a place where things are stored, rather than a primary capability to relate and reconstruct experience in time, that is, a coordination mechanism.

My investigative approach is more like juggling, with apparently three balls in the air: Do not hold on to any one piece for too long, and keep moving. I have adopted an intermediate specification description in terms of categorization, sequencing, substitution, and so on, which is applied to a range of apparently different forms of human behavior and experience in Part II. The questions at issue are to what extent this simple model frames and stimulates a new analysis of familiar phenomena, and how the framework guides further consideration of neurobiological details. After showing that the implications are substantial, I then reconsider symbolic models of verbal memory in Part III to show what they take for granted and how they might be improved by taking the extant models as only simplified, abstract descriptions of what is actually occurring in the brain.

PART II

SERIAL LEARNING AS PHYSICAL COORDINATION

4

Coupled Perceptual-Motor Conception

...it was a long time before I fully realized the importance, for many psychological experiments, of putting the situations which are used to produce response into sequential form.

—Sir Frederic C. Bartlett, *Thinking*, 1958, p. 141

Consider how we use a computer interface for sending electronic mail (e-mail). Typically, the sequence of reading, buttoning options, and filling in forms flows smoothly. Attention shifts from one message to the next, and familiar operations are enacted: select, read, delete; reply, address, send; forward, address, comment, file, and so on. The person's interactions with the computer screen can be understood in terms of coordinating multiple, simultaneously active neural processes for focusing attention, comprehending, composing, and operating on the message material.

As we see in this example, perceiving forms visible on the screen organizes and sustains other neural processes: If we change what is on the screen, we disrupt the active neural processes. The organizing process we are observing is not a program running in the brain, to which the screen is merely input, but an interaction of processes on the screen and processes in the brain. When we describe patterns arising in this interaction in terms of reading, buttons and writing, we are describing dynamically constructed and coordinated *behaviors.*

Put another way, a simple example using an e-mail interface explicated in this chapter reveals how multiple neural processes are organizing physical materials. The analysis suggests that perception is tied to conceptualized activities in such a manner that recall is easy (seeing a form reminds you of what you were doing), but *reassignment is difficult* (viewing a form as meaning something else disrupts the previous activity. Most of the elements of a theory of process memory are brought together here in a deceptively simple, momentary experience, which nevertheless illustrates how a repetition is coordinated without copying or naming neural processes.

4.1 THE EXAMPLE: MULTIPLE MESSAGE WINDOWS

In this example, I examine how I typically used the Xerox–Lafite e-mail system in the early 1980s (for simplicity, I use present tense). The process is as follows: I decide to send a message to a particular person, and select "Send Mail" in the Lafite control window (Fig. 4.1, top center). Then, perhaps before typing anything in the message window (W1), I remember that I want to send a message to someone else, so I button "Send Mail" in the control window a second time to produce a second message window template (W2).

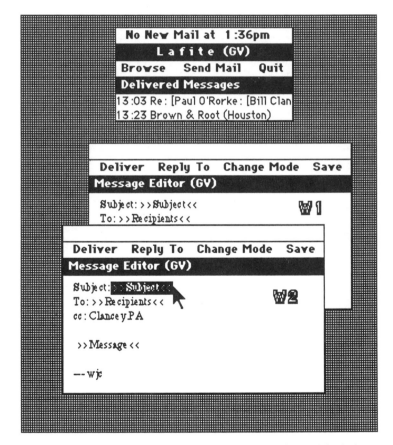

Fig. 4.1. Example of two active "Send Message" windows, labeled W1 and W2.

Why do I create a second window rather than using the first one? Why do I find it so easy to later return to the first window and send the message I first intended, when it may be unlabeled and I have no notes about what I intended to do with it? Why does it feel difficult to hold the first message in mind and reassign the first window to the second message?

The impression I have is that the first window, W1, is assigned; it embodies my intent; it has meaning already. I see W1 as "a message to Person 1." Using W1 to send a message to the second person means seeing it in a new way. My feeling is that this disrupts my thoughts. It is much easier and obvious to create a second window.

Using the terminology of Bamberger and Schön (1991), the physical structures visible on the screen, W1 and W2, are *reference entities.*

> A reference entity serves to single out, externalize, hold for current attention some emergent object or relation. A reference entity serves the function of on-the-spot naming within, and as part of, the making process.

Related to these reference entities are conceptualized activities, which I describe as "the process of sending a message to person 1" and "the process of sending a message to Person 2." Crucially, I see W1 and W2 as being related to these activities, what I am currently doing and planning to do. Somehow, through neural processes inaccessible to me, W1 and W2 are bound or viewed as part of different activities.

To reassign W1 is to see it another way and to reconceive its meaning. However, because W1 embodies the process of sending a message to Person 1, to see W1 in a different way is to disrupt that process. This is a crucial observation: Seeing materials in a different way may require disrupting an ongoing neural process, an active coordination between what we are seeing and what we are doing, that otherwise has no observable manifestation.

Significantly, "doing" has the larger sense of what I am doing during this current e-mail session. In some sense, I am still sending that message to Person 1, even although I have shifted my focus to Person 2; the neural aspect of seeing and sending that message is still active. Conventionally, we would say that I am still "intending" to send the first message.

Instead of disrupting the first process, I *hold it aside* and start up a second process, embodied by W2. I send the second message and then return to W1. The windows on the screen serve as my external representation of messages I want to send. I do not even need to type in something in the TO: or SUBJECT: fields in W1. I can remember how to see W1. I know what it means.

The following aspects of this coordination are striking:

- Visible spatial reminders on the screen allow me to coordinate multiple activities. I can interrupt what I am doing, both physically and mentally setting it aside, and pick up the activity later where I left off. I do not disrupt the interaction; I hold it active, keeping it current but making it peripheral.

- The capability to create multiple processes in the e-mail program facilitates my mental coordination. Activating the second "Send Mail" process in the mail program parallels and facilitates my allowing a second activity (sending a message to Person 2) to take form. Indeed, the idea of setting aside Message 1 and beginning Message 2 is afforded by the concreteness of W1 now in place and the "Send Mail" button, allowing a repeated operation to occur. Selecting back and forth between W1 and W2, by buttoning the mouse in each window in turn, is shifting my attention back and forth between the activities of sending the two messages. The effortless flow and context shift as windows shift forward and backward parallels my experience in thinking about the messages. The window I am seeing is the activity I am doing.

- Completing the second message first is a bit odd. The impression is of a stack: I need to get rid of the second message before I can return to the first. The feeling is that the second message is more pressing. If I do not do it now, I will forget it. The idea of sending the second message arose effortlessly from the process of sending the first; but somehow the second message, as an interruption that only came to mind as a second thought, needs to be handled immediately.

4.2 DISCUSSION: FIGURE–GROUND PRIORITIES

To develop these points further, consider the many alternative ways of using the Lafite system for sending two messages. Table 4.1 summarizes how one might *reassign* the windows or *reorder* the sending of messages. Reassign means to use an already open window for a different message than first intended; reorder means to send the messages in a different order.

Table 4.1

Alternative Ways of Sending Two Messages

	Keep Interpretations	*Reassign Windows*
Keep order	A) W1 ← msg1	C) W2 ← msg1
	W2 ← msg2	W1 ← msg2
Reorder messages	B) W2 ← msg2	D) W1 ← msg2
	W1 ← msg1	W2 ← msg1

For example, in the combination labeled C, one keeps the order (sending the first message first), but reassigns the windows, so the first message is typed into W2 (i.e., W2 ← msg1). One returns to W1 to send the second message (W1 ← msg2). In Combination D one reassigns W1 to the second message, and then creates a second process for the first message (W2 ← msg1) after sending off the second message. There are other possibilities:

1. Type in reminders about the contents of the first message in W1 before creating W2.
2. Type in reminders about the contents of the first message after creating W2.
3. Immediately type in reminders for the second message in W1, then create W2 and use it for sending the first message.

The coordination I developed (Combination B) was to reorder messages, but not to reassign windows. And I did not use reminders. Assuming that this selection bears some relation to neural processes, what conjectures can we make about how neural processes are activated, held active, coordinated, and reactivated?

First, in my experience, it is difficult to reassign W1. The impression is that I would lose the process of sending the first message. There is no way to remember it, aside from reaching for a pad and making a note. It is difficult to switch contexts, to see W1 as being about (or for) the process of sending a message to Person 2. The meaning persists; perceived forms are coordinated with activities. To destroy or reassign perceived objects is to lose the coordination; to lose a way of seeing is to lose an activity.

Second, it is difficult to do Message 1 before Message 2. Message 2 is active now, after "Send Mail" was selected a second time. I am doing *that* now; I do not want to disrupt Message 2 now. There would then be two disruptions. I need to keep going forward. (In chapter 10, I relate this observation to the inability to "move noun phrase references," a key pattern in Chomsky's Universal Grammar.)

Oddly, it seems easier to remember what I intend to do with W1 than to make the effort of typing in some TO: or SUBJECT: information as a reminder. Typing anything in W1 after already pulling down W2 feels like actually doing the first message—going back to it. Crucially, I immediately pull down a second window by buttoning "Send Mail" at the same moment that I realize I want to send a message to a second person.

Thus, we have a curious and fortunate balance: It is difficult to reinterpret forms (reference entities) that are part of a sequence of activity (a chain of thought). But it is relatively easy to recall how materials were previously perceived and engage in that process again. These possibilities work together here because interrupting the first process is perceived as holding aside, not a disruption, by the representation on the screen. The first message activity is held active, not reorganized or ignored; it is visible peripherally on the screen. The activity is set aside like an object in the physical world, and can be picked up again at the click of the mouse.

The effect is like illusions that reorganize the visual field, such as the Necker Cube, the duck–rabbit, old–young woman, and so on (Fig. 4.2). Buttoning one of the windows makes that activity the *figure* and the other activity part of the *ground*. Fixing a figure–ground relationship on the screen by bringing W1 or W2 to the fore corresponds to making that activity WIDN and every other process in which I am engaged is *peripheral*.[1]

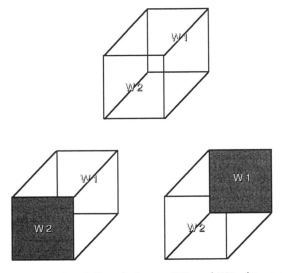

Fig. 4.2. Figure–ground relations between W1 and W2 shown as a Necker Cube.

Shifting from one message activity to another, the previous focus becomes part of the background; the associated neural maps are still active, but I am not conceiving "sending W1" as WIDN. Looking at the screen in different ways is analogous to looking at the cube in Fig. 4.2: "I am looking at the cube and seeing it as W1" or "I am looking at the cube and seeing it as W2." An activity, a way of coordinating perception and action, is reenacted, but activating and hence incorporating different perceptual categorizations. Grounded in the activity, the details (person–topics) are mutually exclusive—I am only literally sending one message at a time. I argue that the higher-order categorization, "I am sending multiple messages," is a conjunction of two sequences, but only one categorization (idea) of sending a message is active at a time.

---

[1]See the discussion of Arbib's model of the schema assemblage (section 1.2.1) and the paintbrush example of figure–contrast relations (chapter 7).

4.3 WHY DID THE REMINDER OCCUR?

To better understand how the neural processes are created and held relative to each other, I use the activation trace notation (introduced in chapter 1) to show how the W2 process develops in the context of W1.

Why did I experience the idea of sending a message to the second person just when I was about to write to the first person? When such an interruption occurs, I experience an image or name relating to the second person. Bartlett (1932/1977) identified this phenomenon of working with a focus detail with the process of remembering. The ongoing activity of sending a message apparently enables effortlessly beginning the process of sending a different message. This is apparently similar to the effect of seeing two ducks or two rabbits in sequence (Fig. 1.11), as if conceptual coordinations are biased to repeat. Building on this clue, and Bartlett's model of remembering (which I present in chapter 8 to summarize Part II), I illustrate the relation of the two processes (Fig. 4.3).

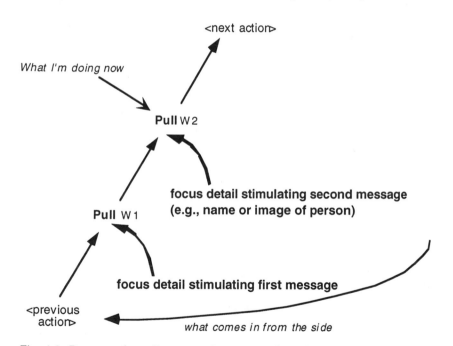

Fig. 4.3. Process of sending second message viewed as a generalization of the active process of sending a message.

Fig. 4.3 shows the coordination just after I have opened W2. Just after opening W1 a detail came to the foreground (e.g., the idea of another person or message).

The diagram shows this second focus detail coming in from the side. Because of the materials available to me, I did not experience a sense of disruption (an impasse). For example, without the multiple-process capability of Lafite, I might have been forced to turn aside and write something down about Message 2 on a sheet of paper. Instead, I immediately repeated the current activity of writing a message, pulling down W2. By this coordination, I incorporated the detail; I made it WIDN. The relation is nonsymmetric: I can button back and forth to *see the windows as different activities*, but I resist actually doing the first message activity after I have pulled down W2.

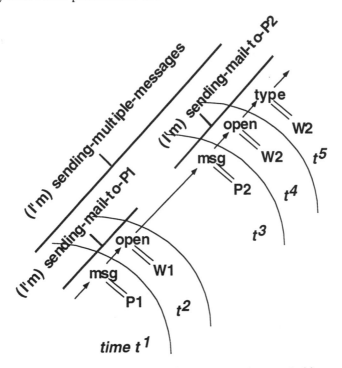

Fig. 4.4. The process of sending mail to someone is repeated by reactivating the categorization with a different focus (person–topic P2 instead of P1) by a coordination that categorizes the reactivation as a conjunctive sequence.

The two activities are parallel and coordinated, as if they indeed integrated in my understanding. Fig. 4.4 represents this sequence; WIDN is sending multiple messages. Narrowly, my focus is on sending the second message, but broadly, my coordinated activity still includes the idea of the first message. This conceptual coordination parallels our analysis of seeing multiple duck–rabbits (Fig. 1.13). Following the idea that a categorization is reactivated and *not copied* in a second "instantiation" (as in conventional cognitive models based on class-instance programming languages), one can hypothesize that there are two active processes of "I am sending mail" only by virtue of the higher-order categorization of (the idea of) a conjunctive sequence. The reference entities (W1 and W2) locate these processes in space and constitute the only "explicit" physical manifestations of the messages as being two things. That is, unlike a conventional programming language that would represent multiple (recursive) invocations of a given procedure on a stack as multiple objects representing multiple invocations of processes, a person may use perceptual categorization to coordinate repeated processes.

Let us go over these ideas more carefully, for this example is deceptively simple and yet illustrates a great deal of taken-for-granted complexity in how the brain coordinates ideas. First, the very idea of a *repetition* poses a major question if we follow the assumption that the brain does not have a data structure like a program stack for naming and storing an indefinite number of references to work in progress. Instead, I argue that the mechanisms available are *to hold a categorization active by anchoring it* (and only one internal anchor or "pointer" is available) or *to embed a categorization in a higher-order categorization* (which may occur as a conjunction, as in this example, or center-embedding). I illustrate and support these claims in subsequent analyses of path learning, slips by substitution, analogical reasoning, and constraints on natural language comprehension. That is, I am applying ideas about mechanisms in this send message example that only become clear in the context of other examples—in the manner of the math teacher showing you the nice formulation without all the mess of how the proof path was found. The analysis presented here is backed up with a variety of data in other chapters.

Fig. 4.2 breaks the experience of sending two messages into five time slices corresponding to two sequences with three distinguished aspects:

- Having the concept of a message to send to someone (categorizations of persons, labeled P1 and P2).
- Opening a new message window (labeled W1 and W2).
- Typing a message into a window.

The times indicate that the idea of sending a second message occurs after opening W1 and before typing in it (i.e., the coupling of categorizations type = W1 has not occurred). The meaning of the open message window, W1, is retained by holding categorization P1 active while a second message sending activity is completed. Then attention returns to the first window and the first message sending activity completes.

Subsequent analysis of natural language grammars (chapter 10) suggests that the problematic repetition is not just the conception, "I am sending mail," but individual categorizations of two message windows having two different meanings. In grammatical terms, it is as if "open-window-for-message" is a grammatical category like "noun phrase" and P1 and P2 are two nouns in a sentence. Studies of comprehension of natural language reveal certain constraints in how two or more noun phrases can appear in the same sentence. In this case, we have an apparent conjunction, "I am sending mail to P1 and to P2." But of course, the relations being kept active are more complex: Distinct topics are remembered for each person and the assignment of windows to the two person–topics is remembered. In this respect, my analysis in Fig. 4.4 is simplified because it leaves out the topics.

The essential claim I am considering, again based on the natural language comprehension data, is that, in an open, ongoing conceptualization of WIDN, a categorization, such as "open-window-for-message" cannot be simply reused in the manner of a copy or two instances of a class. Instead, if there are multiple open-window-for-message processes being coordinated at one time, references to them must be held in some way other than some kind of copying operation.

Of course, it is equally true that a conventional von Neumann computer cannot apply a given procedure in two different contexts at the same moment. A conventional computer architecture uses a stack that holds the name of a procedure and its arguments (or pointers to them). In this respect, a stack works by copying the name of the procedure (as well as arguments in "call by value"). My claim that the brain works differently is based on several sources:

- Holding W1 aside rather than reusing it suggests that the binding process is a physical interaction—not all in the head; the meaning of the visible display is being held fixed to coordinate the activity in time.
- The ability to flip back and forth, reminding oneself of the meaning of each window ("now I am doing this") suggests a mutually exclusive assignment—just as only one window can be forward at a time, only one sending-mail-to-person categorization is active at one time (copying is not required, any more than a conventional program must be copied for each invocation).
- An analogy with the Necker Cube suggests that the previous figure (P1) becomes ground with respect to the repeated categorization (sending a message).
- Evidence from slips and related errors suggests mechanisms of generalization, substitution, and repetition by higher-order categorization.
- Evidence from natural language comprehension limitations supports the use of a single anchor, embedding in high-order categorizations, and limitations on role assignment (a categorization can fill or be bound to only one role in a sequence).

In this example, the previous focus (the topic of the first message) is not stored in a buffer or register constituting what we call short-term memory. Instead, the neural links create physical structure "in place," such that different perceptual categorizations are activated at different times and incorporated in the higher-order maps. A sequence of maps is constructed that includes the different ways of viewing the screen and my current activity, such that the containing structure *conceptually* relates the activity and present focus.

At the same time, notice that I am not claiming that the brain cannot have multiple processes active at the same time—for clearly the categorizations of topic of a message and a perceived window on a screen are being coordinated. Indeed, the very idea of *reference*—this window refers to this message for this person—involves a higher-order categorization of multiple, simultaneously active categorizations. But we are getting slightly ahead of the story.

Let us back up and summarize the main points. The primary conjecture is that "Open W2" literally reuses the neural maps involved in "Open W1," but coordinates them with different perceptual categorizations (which we might call details or figures). Remembering what W1 means requires that the reference (conventionally called a binding) be able to be reactivated in some way after the second message is sent. The secondary conjecture is that this reactivate–repeat process is not accomplished by internal *descriptions* of what is happening (in the manner of names in a conventional computer stack), but by a higher-order process that incorporates the first "use" as a detail within a sequence.

Significantly, the new focus detail, P2 (the person–topic of the second message), bears the same relation to "Opening W1" as the first focus detail, P1. The second focus detail is *an instance of* "what I am already doing" (opening a window to send a message to someone). Put the other way around, the send message process has been *generalized* to subsume P2 in the same manner it subsumes P1. The process of sending the first message (involving opening and typing processes) is reactivated, but I do it with respect to a different figure (the name or image related to the second person–topic that came to my attention).

Crucially, the mechanism we are attempting to specify must include the use of reference entities—physical objects in the world interpreted as standing for different concepts. The mental coordination and remembering process is not limited by how neural maps might be related internally, but leverages how physical objects are externally related. To repeat Bamberger and Schön's (1991) definition, "A reference entity serves the function of on-the-spot naming within, and as part of, the making process." "Naming within" is categorizing, not necessarily describing. Arranging windows while writing and reading mail is a kind of larger activity that Bamberger and Schön called a "making process"—it is a kind of design or layout activity.

The essential point is that the activity we are studying is not merely a kind of mental gymnastics, but an interactive—mind–world—coordination of physical stuff and categorizing (neural stuff). The experience—what the person is doing—is not merely trying to remember two messages but laying out objects on the screen and thus, remembering what two windows mean. By virtue of having the reference entities, the activity need not be strictly sequential, always moving forward, as suggested by Fig. 4.3 and Fig. 4.4. Instead, an overarching higher-order categorization may form, indeed analogous to "I am seeing two duck–rabbits"—"I am moving back and forth between two message windows" (a categorization of a sequence). That is, when I start buttoning back and forth between W1 and W2 I am recoordinating my activity; it becomes something new. A given coordination is repeated (the process of sending a message), but physically composed ("instantiated") with different perceptual and conceptual maps (respectively, the window being used and the person–topic of the message). This might be the most simple kind of sequencing: Doing something again, but acting on different objects in the world.[2]

4.4 DISTINGUISHING BETWEEN AWARENESS AND REPRESENTATIONS

The tree form of the diagrams presented here should not suggest that there is a data structure that is being traversed, inspected, or otherwise manipulated by some other process in the brain. The neural mechanism is not a process of moving pointers up and down a tree or restoring a previous organization by writing it into a buffer for execution. Representing occurs for sure in the message sender's mind, but not necessarily by propositions that describe the world and what the person is doing. Put another way, statements such as "how the subject is representing the windows to himself," must be distinguished from "how the subject is *describing* the windows to himself." We must not equate "representations in the mind" with "descriptions," either in our analyses (such as Fig. 4.3) or the subject's own reflections ("Oh, I need to send a message to

---

[2]*An aside about interface design:* The message example reveals our capacity to associate visibly identical screen objects with different activities, and how easily interactive contexts can be restored without requiring special reminders to describe them. The example reveals the potential difficulty of being forced to take every operation to completion once it begins. These observations help explain the ease of use of popular computer features such as multiple windows, multiple instantiations of a process, and ability to save and restore contexts.

In this respect, it is significant that many word processors do not operate in the same manner as the e-mail program I have described. Usually, when you start a word processor, an "untitled" blank window is opened. If you immediately open a previously created file, the untitled window is automatically closed. Suppose, however, that you started the word processor with the intention of starting something new, but this reminded you of the intention of revising, examining, or copying another file. By closing the blank window, the program is aborting the first activity. This disruption illustrates how the kind of analysis I have presented here is relevant to the design of computer interfaces and has perhaps been ignored in the design of word processors.

Related analysis might help guide design of features such as "publish and subscribe" links between documents. For example, when figures and spreadsheets are modified, one can arrange to have the documents in which they are incorporated be automatically updated. But we might find that people prefer to cut and paste than to have what is perceived as a copy be automatically inserted elsewhere. As sending two messages indicates, structures that appear identical on the screen might be perceived as being about different things. This is possible and perhaps encouraged by the structures being spatially distinct and created at different times, in the context of different activities.

Wendy"). The fundamental form of representation is categorization, and categorization is not necessarily verbal. Perceptual categorizations (e.g., of windows) coupled to conceptualized activities (e.g., sending a message to someone) may be formed tacitly, without conscious commentary.

Compare my experience in sending two messages with my asking an assistant to finish my work: He is given two identical, blank windows, already open on the screen. He is told to send two messages to different people. Further suppose that I require him to assign the windows in the same way I viewed them when they were created. Now I must describe these windows for him: "This is the window for Mike's message; here is the one for Wendy." Without such instructions, my friend cannot replicate the activity I was engaged in: He needs to be told what the two open windows represent.

Commonly, we would say that in sending the two messages I know what the windows represent (or similarly, "what they mean"). However, this means that if asked, I could tell you what I am doing, not that I necessarily view the windows as being representations. However, when buttoning back and forth, as I conceive that "I am in the activity of jumping back and forth," the two windows become representations of messages. I shift from perceiving spaces in which I type to categorizing the forms as windows.

Engaged in the initial flow of sending two messages, the windows *are* the messages I am in the process of sending, not representations of them. Given that the windows are identical except for spatial location, they are *indexical* representations (like the word *now*). The conceptual coordination process of *seeing as* "registers" each of the windows with respect to different person–topic conceptions. This registration is a higher-order, conceptual categorization of a window–location categorization and a person–topic categorization.

Zhang (1997) argued similarly that descriptive cognitive models have postulated more mechanism than is required for organizing attention over time:

> The key assumption of the framework is that external representations need not be re-represented as an internal model to be involved in problem-solving activities: they can directly activate perceptual operations and directly provide perceptual information that, in conjunction with the memorial information and cognitive operations provided by internal representations, determine problem solving behavior. (p. 5)

The perceived representational forms directly constrain mental processes without going through an intermediate state of being described. The conceptual relation of my understanding WIDN is not between descriptions, that is, a verbal, internal model of the world and behavior and how they relate. Instead, seeing places on the screen is inseparable from interacting with them, what I am doing with them. As (1949) said, demonstrating know-how (doing) is not two things: knowing-that (articulating facts) plus doing. What I am perceiving, my way of categorizing my experience, is literally part of the construction of what I am doing. I do not describe what I am doing when I return to W1; I simply reconstitute that process from the ground, making that place and the topic the new figure of my conception.

4.5 THE ROLE OF SOCIAL CONTEXT
IN COORDINATED ACTION

In this chapter, I am primarily concerned with neural process explanations of behavior. However, I want to emphasize again an issue that cannot be ignored when we study human behavior, namely the nature of self-reference and its relation to consciousness. Throughout, my approach to describing human experience is always to posit a high-level categorization by which the person is conceiving WIDN. This is more than keeping track of what the person is doing (goals) or what is happening in the world (information). Experience is not merely *something* experienced, but the coordinated activity of a conscious agent.

By self-reference, I mean that a person is always constructing experience with respect to an ongoing understanding of *personal role*. Human activity is inherently personal, it is monitored, interpreted, and oriented subjectively. To paraphrase Shakespeare, all the world is a stage and people are always sustaining a sense of the role, norms, and dynamics of the ongoing interaction—a sense of who he or she is, what is happening, and what kinds of interactions make sense socially (social norms). Indeed, we cannot understand human *experience* or what it means to be an agent without taking social constraints into account (e.g., see Goffman, 1959). Descriptions of experience in terms of "sense making" that only refer to information processing, for example, are missing the complexity of interactions and conflicts that people are conceptually managing.

The idea that the construction of a persona frames and shapes cognitive experience is more often cited in the social sciences than in cognitive psychology, although these ideas were fundamental to William James' theories:

> The key to the experience of consciousness, as James . . . notes, is self reference, as experiencer or agent: "The universal conscious fact is not 'feelings exist' or 'thoughts exist' but 'I think' and 'I feel.' (Kihlstrom, 1984, p. 152)

Inquiring how "mental activities can proceed apparently involuntarily, and outside of phenomenal awareness," (p. 192) Kihlstrom (1984) emphasized the role of ongoing construction of a self-image, coordinated with the possibilities of perceptions, memories, and actions:

> To paraphrase James: Conscious awareness does not consist in the recognition that "This is happening"; but, rather, "I am doing this, or experiencing this, here and now." Central to the experience of consciousness, then, is linking activated concepts representing percepts, memories, thoughts, and actions with others representing the self as agent and experiencer on the one hand, and the spatiotemporal context of the event on the other. (pp. 192–193)

The nature of this self-reference will become more clear in subsequent examples. The essential idea is that what constitutes *context* for a person always includes the understanding of being a social actor (Bannon, 1991). In conventional terms, context is not merely bottom-up facts about the external world, but top-down, internal points of view. Human activities in the large are framed by an ongoing understanding of social relations, which constrain what is perceived, thought about, and done.

Thus, for example, my sending a second message must be understood not only as "another task I need to do," or a second activation of a neural process, but as occurring within my sense of WIDN—both narrowly in terms of sending messages and broadly in terms of my ongoing interactions with my correspondents. Understanding why the reminder occurred requires considering the higher-order *conceptualization of context* that sustains my activity. In people, the content of this context is an understanding of the self as a social being. In some important sense, my "top-level" activity is always *the activity of being a person.* Thus, even when I am alone, my behavior is shaped by my often tacit view of myself as an actor in a community of practice, a choreography of interactions.[3]

In this book, I do not focus on questions about the nature of intentionality and consciousness. However, my point in this section is that such issues cannot easily be ignored. We can, to a certain extent, focus on neural processes, but we must at least mention social context in passing. Any content analysis (descriptions of what the person is thinking about) must make some mention of a personal point of view, WIDN. So although I may appear to present an apparently reductionistic account of behavior in terms of neural processes, the transactions being studied are social behaviors and the higher-order categorizations are tacitly constructions of identity. Whenever we ask, "Why did the repetition occur?" we need to distinguish between the content (social) explanation of why the behavior was *relevant* and the mechanism (neural) explanation of why the behavior was *possible.* Even on the apparently safe ground of understanding typing slips, where attention is most narrow and automatic, we will find, as Freud emphasized, that social concerns bias what substitutions or reorderings occur. In effect, the evidence suggests that there is no such thing as an exclusively neural event in human experience; in this respect, a person is not remotely like a symbolic calculator or expert system.

---

[3]For a more detailed discussion of these ideas, see Clancey (1997c) chapter 1. Perhaps the most accessible introduction for cognitive scientists is Greenbaum and Kyng's (1991) *Design at Work.* More elaborate discussion appears in Wenger (1998).

5

Extending a Felt Path

We humans certainly have a passion for stringing things together: words into sentences, notes into melodies, steps into dances, narratives into games with rules of procedures. Might stringing things together be a core facility of the brain, one commonly useful to language, storytelling, planning, games, and ethics?

—William H. Calvin, The emergence of intelligence, *Scientific American*, 1994, p. 104

In this chapter I consider a few simple examples of serial behavior in children and animals. Again viewing memory in terms of categories activating each other in time, I reconsider some of the basic processes of repeating a sequence, adding to a sequence, and restructuring a sequence. The examples illustrate the extent of our ignorance about how procedural learning is possible, at the same time hinting at the neural building blocks at work in repetitive behavior and play.

The learning pattern of conceptualizing a sequence and extending it on repetition, called *progressive deepening*, is well known in cognitive science. Behavior is explained in terms of a mental search of a *problem space* that represents the goal the subject is trying to achieve, the present situation ("state"), and differences from the goal and present state. In a typical cognitive analysis, "search in a problem space" suggests that the subject is always manipulating abstract state *descriptions* of goals, situations, and operations to perform. By such an analysis, the subject necessarily formalizes the world into named things and places in a coordinate system (such as standard musical notation). Knowledge and memory are viewed almost exclusively with respect to *reasoning*, or making deductions, which occurs in a disembodied, timeless way.

However, in any human behavior, reasoning or otherwise, perception, emotion, and physical constraints are involved, too. Indeed, reasoning behaviors often involve interactive, physical processes, as when we write and speak. Insofar as our interest is to understand how behavior sequences are shaped and remembered, we need to complement the problem space analysis with an interactive analysis. That is, we consider how behavior develops in a *transactional space* that is mental, physical, and social.

Put another way, our understanding of the neural mechanism of conceptualization is improved when we view the behavior as developing within a dynamically constructed problem space of interacting constraints: *mental constraints* (internal categorizations and their temporal activation relations), *physical constraints* (objects located in the person's world), and *social constraints* (goals and activities conceived with respect to other people).

Aside from mere repetition, exemplified in sending two consecutive messages (chapter 4), the simplest form of a conceptualized behavior sequence is a *felt path*, exemplified in this chapter by the representation of a melody and a child playing in a pool. These are compared to studies of animal learning to show how behavior is constrained by rote sequential reconstruction and to what extent conceptualization makes felt paths into units that can be related and more flexibly recoordinated. In particular, this analysis shows how properties of the subject's world are *projections*, relative to and coupled with serial behavior. Understanding this, we are then in a position to consider how conceptual coordination enables categories to become known independently of action, such that they are "defused from the situation" and known more abstractly as the objects and named attributes—a mental coordination process that a traditional descriptive ("symbolic") cognitive analysis usually takes for granted.

5.1 THE FELT PATH OF A MELODY REPRESENTATION

Over more than a decade, Bamberger (1991) studied children's representations of simple melodies. In these experiments, students are given unlabeled bells that look alike, but play various pitches. The students are asked to "build a tune with the bells," such as "Twinkle, Twinkle, Little Star."

One of the most striking patterns in one child's early development (whom Bamberger named Jeff) is the procedure he uses for arranging the bells into a tune path (Fig. 5.1): After putting a new bell into position at the end of the path (F), he would always return to the first bell and play the entire tune from the beginning before searching for the next bell in the unsorted array of bells on the table top. That is, Jeff's performance procedure for playing the tune appears as part of his search procedure for finding the next bell: His strategy for *representing* a tune is inseparable from his strategy for *playing* a tune. This is why Bamberger emphasized that when Jeff first learned the scale-tune, it was still a *figural* way of knowing—he always needed to begin at the beginning of the scale.

In Bamberger's terms, Jeff's action path in the figural stage is "simply to 'go straight ahead' along the bell path":

> We call this strategy of construction a *felt path strategy* by analogy with the familiar experience of marking the chronological occurrence of chosen landmarks as one walks, through time, along a path from here to there—next–next–next. The temporally experienced landmarks then become a description of the path—the way one remembers it. (p. 25)

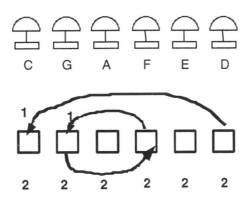

Fig. 5.1. Arrangement of Montessori Bells on a table and child's "instructions" indicating the order and number of hits for playing a tune (the "action path"). (Adapted from THE MIND BEHIND THE MUSICAL EAR by J. Bamberger, 1991, p. 218. Copyright ©1991 by the President and Fellows of Harvard College. Reprinted by permission of Harvard University Press.).

In a felt path, remembering and doing are inseparable; what is remembered is the coordination over time and space of what you saw and how you turned. The strategy of felt path construction is of course one aspect of Cicero's well-known memorization technique (S. Rose, 1994), in which one visually places things to be remembered in a familiar setting and orders the sequence by visualizing a walk through the space.

The "qualities of a felt path construction—bell path, action path and sequence of events go always straight ahead, never turning back, never skipping" (Bamberger, 1991, p. 53) are arguably the most fundamental aspect of perception–action learning. If "learning in doing" consists most basically of learning a felt path (literally "feeling your way along"), then explaining this neuropsychological process in more detail will provide a start for understanding more formal representational strategies, such as musical scales and notation. Studying examples of felt paths in different contexts may help us better understand this process of "knowing as representing."

5.2 A FELT PATH IN A SWIMMING POOL

One summer day, I was in a swimming pool with my 4-year-old niece, Caitlin. She entered the pool at the steps on one side, and holding to the edge, shuffled her hands and worked her way along to the left, into deeper water. But after proceeding forward a bit, she returned all the way back to the entry steps. At this point, she repeated the process, each time exceeding her previous motion to the left by a foot or so, each time returning to the start, near the steps, before adding another foray into deeper water (Fig. 5.2). There were five or six cycles before she stopped (on the shallow side).

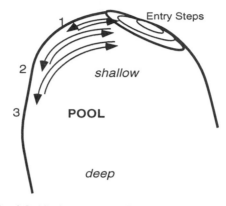

Fig. 5.2. Felt path of Caitlin in the pool—Developing a sequence by returning to the start before extending a segment.

Caitlin moved by shuffling along, shifting the left hand left, followed by the right. The shuffle itself is a coordination that is repetitively reactivated to create a sequence over a distance. The movement to the left is coupled to the perception of the curve of the pool and the depth of the water; there is no need for her to count how many hand motions she makes in a cycle. This shuffling should also be contrasted with random movement back and forth, which would cause her to lose sense of WIDN—even the right side would be a new frontier; there would be no anchoring place.

Moving to the left, every step is a coordinated motion of left–right hand shuffling, coupled to awareness of being in familiar terrain. But I can see on Caitlin's face and hear in her breathing her excitement in moving out over the deeper water. Eventually, the territory appears unfamiliar and she perceives she has extended her range too far. At this point she returns to the start. The experience of unfamiliar terrain, with a sense of breakdown in the familiar coordination, apparently ends the path. Each traversal from the steps to the deep water is an *action path*. Each traversal is analogous to Jeff's playing as much of a tune as the bell path under construction allows. Extending the path by returning to the start would therefore appear to be a basic aspect of the felt path strategy of adding a new element to a coordination sequence. But why is this so?

Caitlin starts at the beginning because each traversal from steps to deep water is a unit, even although it is composed of many movements. Going back to the start completes the sequence—with an assumption that tension is also lowered—and thus anchors the activity of constructing a sequence of sequences. This is visible graphically in Fig. 5.2. Each motion from the steps to new territory is a *segment*, a new action chunk. Caitlin knows the beginning, the feeling of being coordinated throughout, and the tension of the end. We can see in Caitlin's smile, as she reaches the beginning and then starts out again, that there is pleasure in taking on something new; each sequence is extended by a move or two left. (Indeed, her grandparents and uncle are watching; this audience provides a safety net for exploration, as well as a setting for demonstrating competence in the water.) But the tension Caitlin experiences toward the left requires returning "home" to establish that she can get back and is in control. The pattern suggests that each repetition is an accomplishment, reinforced by the satisfaction of landing back home at the safety of the steps, away from the deep water.

One way of viewing felt path construction is that the coordination is only experienced and performable as a whole. Caitlin can move out to the deep water, but only in one, unbroken sequence of movement from right to left. Like Jeff playing a tune, each performance has the same beginning. Commenting on the story of Caitlin, Bamberger (private communication, 1995) said,

> Next–next–next involves no turning back, no comparing of events or things distanced in time and/or space. You are where you are and where you were is gone. See Lorenz's story of the shrew in "King Solomon's Ring." This is the "felt path" idea: a kind of experience where making and following are going on simultaneously. This is profoundly sequential: where you are leads you to where you go next (like jazz improvisation). If you are interrupted by yourself or by something outside, you have to start over again to build up the context for the next move. A lot of our "knowledge" is of this sort.

Caitlin's return to the beginning involves literally retracing her steps; she does not demonstrate flexibility to simply *be* anywhere in the path. She is either moving out to extend her path or she is returning home. She has no other reference point for conceiving WIDN without experiencing fear and trouble.

Konrad Lorenz's (1952) description of the water-shrews is relevant and illuminating:

> In their accustomed surroundings, my shrews proved to be very strict creatures of habit . . . . In the water-shrew, the path-habits, in particular, are of a really amazing immutability . . . . Unless the little animal is severely frightened, it moves, in strange surroundings, only step by step, whiskering right and left all the time and following a path that is anything but straight. Its course is determined by a hundred fortuitous factors when it walks that way for the first time. But, after a few repetitions, it is evident that the shrew recognizes the locality in which it finds itself and that it repeats, with the utmost exactitude, the movements which it performed the previous time . . . . When placed on a path which it has already traversed a few times, the shrew starts on its way slowly, carefully whiskering. Suddenly, it finds its known bearings, and now rushes forward a short distance, repeating exactly every step and turn which it executed on the last occasion. Then, when it comes to a spot where it ceases to know the way by heart, it is reduced to whiskering again and to feeling its way step by step. (p. 123)

Like Caitlin, the shrews turn around and start again when they arrive in unfamiliar territory:

Any major alteration in the habitual path threw the shrews into complete confusion .
. . . If I moved the stones out of the runway, placing both together in the middle of
the table, the shrews would jump right up into the air in the place where the stone
should have been; they came down with a jarring bump, were obviously
disconcerted and starting whiskering cautiously right and left, just as they behaved
in an unknown environment. And then they did a most interesting thing: they went
back the way they had come, carefully feeling their way until they had again got
their bearings. Then, facing round again, they tried a second time with a rush and
jumped and crashed down exactly as they had done a few seconds before . . . . This
method of going back to the start, and trying again always reminded me of a small
boy, who, in reciting a poem, gets stuck and begins again at an earlier verse. (pp.
123–124)

Lorenz went on to contrast the shrews' adherence to "motor habit over
present perception" to a rat learning a maze, which "would not dream of trying
to jump over a stone which was not there":

A rat or mouse would be quick to discover that it was making an unnecessary
detour, but the water-shrew is no more able to do so than is a toy train to turn off at
right angles at a level crossing. To change its route, the water-shrew must change its
entire path-habit, and this cannot be done at a moment's notice, but gradually, over a
long period of time. (p. 125)

Lorenz (1952) contrasted the "true observation" of a human to the water
shrew's "learning by heart every possible spatial contingency" (p. 125). Coupled
with its very fast racing along known pathways, the shrew's method for
navigating is more effective than the whiskering and nosing required to
reperceive the surroundings each time. The quickest path is not a newly
optimized straight line, but the accustomed path taken at breakneck speed.
    White and Siegel (1984) made the same observation about exploration:

Generally, spatially mobile and territorial creatures occupy new territory in a
stepwise fashion. They find a secure place, use it as an anchor point, explore out
from it, and retreat back toward it depending on their needs. This pattern is
embodied in the toddler's ranging out from mother as an emotional basis . . . . Rats
explore in a new environment by using a known part as an anchor point or base of
operations. They then appear to construe the rest of the environment as a network of
topological relationships extending outward from that anchor point. (p. 245)

In contrasting the examples, a distinction can be made between the rote
learning and reproduction of paths by the water shrew, the apparently attentive
reconsideration of the rat, and the child's deliberate, playful repetition and
exploration. The rat or mouse, according to Lorenz, adapts paths to new
surroundings and is known to explore a new maze. Caitlin's behavior has these
properties, but adds another dimension of systematic extension within a social
interaction (with adults watching and tacitly encouraging). The behavior of
wolves and other animals with social interactions may be organized in similar
ways (Gould & Gould, 1994).

In conventional terms, a water shrew demonstrates a relatively inflexible procedural memory (a rote replaying of a path sequence), to be contrasted with an ability to more flexibly use past experience to orient behavior. For example, Tolman's (1948) famous appraisal of cognitive maps in rats showed that rat exploration is not strictly rote. Indeed, Tolman's more fundamental argument is that rat learning was not merely a set of localized stimulus–response reactions, but was indeed episodic in nature. The rat differs from the shrew in that individually experienced paths are *integrated*, "indicating routes and paths and environmental relationships" (p. 192). This integration is visible in the rat's active learning: "He often has to look actively for the significant stimuli to form his map and does not merely passively receive and react to all the stimuli which are physically present" (p. 201). This active learning is characterized as running "through a succession of systematic choices" that indicate *repetition of a coordination* with different physical "bindings":

> The individual animal might perhaps begin by choosing practically all right-hand doors, then he might give this up for choosing practically all left-hand doors, and then, for choosing all dark doors, and so on. These relatively persistent, and well-above-chance systematic types of choice Krech called "hypotheses." In using this term, he obviously did not mean to imply verbal processes in the rat but merely referred to what I have been calling cognitive maps. (Tolman, 1948, p. 202)

Most important, when paths are blocked, the rat's investigation and deliberate movements suggest knowledge of the orientation, the general direction in which to go:

> After going out a few inches only on one path, each rat finally chose to run all the way out one . . . . The rats had, it would seem, acquired not merely a strip-map to the effect that the original specifically trained-on path led to food, but, rather, a wider comprehensive map to the effect that food was located in such and such a direction in the room. (Tolman, 1948, p. 204)

Thus, the idea of the food has become related to location in a spatial area, and the coordination of going to the food becomes dynamically coordinated with respect to the relative location of the food. In this respect, the rat is oriented and the map appears to be comprehensive. In what sense is the map comprehensive and what is its neural form?

Integrating several theories of neurobiology and ethology, Wan, Touretzky, and Redish (1994) developed a computational neural model of rat navigation. This model combines a *path integration system* that tracks the current position, relative to reference points, with a *sequence memory*. Reference points are not landmarks themselves (with necessarily distinct sensory cues), but internally created distinctions (associated with "place cells") that track the angle between landmarks, which is invariant with respect to orientation and head direction. "The path integrator maintains position with respect to several reference points simultaneously" (p. 16) in a context-sensitive way. The number of points being tracked depends on the sense of familiarity; when disoriented, bias shifts toward perceptual inputs, rather than recognition-driven sequencing. Wan et al.'s (1994) model generally fits the pattern of categorization in sequence I have described, providing more details about what perceptual categorizations are constructed for navigation. My own analysis emphasizes the next–next–next ordering of "place cells," an aspect of the rat navigation model that is implicit in Wan et al.'s block diagrams.

Glenberg (1997) recently proposed a model of memory based on "how separate patterns of actions can be combined given the constraints of our bodies" (p. 1). He called this combination *mesh*, evoking the lattice-like arrangement of the cerebellar cortex (section 3.4). His primary example involves path finding and strikingly fits the example and analysis of rat navigation and Caitlin's "search" of the pool space:

> Thus projectable properties of the environment (arrangement of rocks, twigs, and soil) are encoded in terms of how you (with your particular body) can interact with that environment (e.g., whether the distances between rocks in the creek can be broached). Other patterns of interaction come from memory, for example, patterns representing goals such as "get home without getting wet." In conceptualizing the environment as a path, the spatial-functional patterns based on projectable properties from the environment are combined and meshed with patterns from memory. (p. 6)

The term *encoded* is inappropriate here because the properties are perceptually categorized or conceived as objects and locations, not mapped onto a coordinate system. Also, as I discuss further later, the goal of getting home is not necessarily represented, but may be either the categorization of the sequence itself as an activity (just as "finding the food" is a higher-order categorization of a sequence) or a result of exploration leading to unfamiliarity and a strategy of returning to the beginning. Nevertheless, Glenberg's (1997) ideas of "clamping" and a continuously reconceptualized path-making activity appear appropriate and insightful:

> Projectable properties are clamped and then embodied memories mesh to produce a particular conceptualization (e.g., the path home). At this point, either an action is taken (e.g., a step along the path) or projectable properties of the environment change (e.g., a barrier appears). In either case, the system is forced to settle into a new conceptualization . . . .
>
> Updating is not encoding a memory trace. Instead the shift from one pattern of possible actions (one conceptualization) to the next is reinforced. That is, what is updated is how one situation flows into another. I will refer to this flow as a "trajectory" . . . . Actions humanly possible under the current conceptualization are biased by what was possible in the previous conceptualization, just as pronunciation of a vowel is biased by the pronunciation of a preceding consonant. (p. 7)

I disagree with Glenberg (1997) that the environment must be "seen for what it is" and hence projectable properties (perceptual categorizations) are somehow independently held (clamped) so they are not distorted by how the path is conceived ("projectable properties of the environment are primary"). This is more often true when *deliberating* about what the facts are and what they mean (illustrated in chapter 7), but less relevant or possible in quick movement through space. If properties are categorized with respect to motor activity, as Glenberg rightly said, then motion on the felt path must influence how the environment is perceived. Perception of steps and barriers occurred originally during action, and thus they are rightly called projectable properties. The categorization is not an encoding, but a relation to action—like the landmark angle invariants in Wan et al.'s model—and this is what makes them *situated*, the "embodied memory" Glenberg (1997) otherwise argued for.

5.3 RESTRUCTURING AND PROGRESSIVE DEEPENING

The most important aspect of Glenberg's (1997) theory is viewing a "pattern of possible actions" as a conceptualization. But the conscious aspects of monitoring and controlling exploration need to be articulated more carefully. How can we characterize Caitlin's sequential behavior in terms of recurrent processes, breakdown, and recovery, all within the exploratory mode of playing in the pool?

To begin, we might reconsider how felt paths are related to descriptive schemes like musical scales and computer programs. The example of Jeff's playing is useful, because he has not yet learned the formal coordinate system of standard musical notation. Thus, his understanding of ordering and "musical instructions" is strongly grounded in his experiences. The notation he developed (bottom of Fig. 5.1) illustrates a semiformal approach. Jeff is learning to describe tunes by articulating his experience, such as using squares to represent bells he has arranged on the table and numbers to indicate repetition. These instructions are overlaid on the occurrence of the bells in the tune itself, not the abstracted ordering of pitches in a scale. As for conventional notation, the meaning of the "instructions" and music making are mutually constraining: Jeff is learning how to coordinate what he hears and plays with what the description means.

Bamberger and Schön (1979), building on the work of Piaget, emphasize that the process of inventing representations, illustrated by Jeff's notation, involves restructuring experience:

> We believe the work of restructuring can be understood in terms of the following kinds of processes: the differentiation and conservation of properties, the construction and conservation of new structures, and the development of schemas for co-ordination. (p. 40)

One way of understanding the work of restructuring would be to explain why certain patterns develop so easily in learning, and then to account for what work is involved to change those patterns. In our examples here, we observe that adding an element on the end is easily accomplished by just extending a felt path. However, when out in the deep water or encountering an unexpected obstacle, a process of reorientation is required, which in these examples involves returning the way you came and starting again at the beginning. That is, one way of reconstructing a habit is to follow the previous pattern until it breaks down, and then incrementally add new pieces on the end.[1]

This exploration strategy, called *progressive deepening* (which the pool example illustrates very well), is well-known in cognitive psychology. The term was coined by de Groot in the mid 1960s in his analysis of chess playing; most generally it signifies "selectively extending the main continuation of interest" (Shapiro, 1992, p. 231; see also de Groot, 1965). More formally, Newell (1990) described the process as follows:

> The search can be seen to have a definite pattern, it does not just wander at random or jump around. The pattern is called *progressive deepening*: search down in a depth-first fashion; then return all the way back to the initial situation; then search back down again, following an old path for a while, before either going deeper or branching out to the side. (p. 10)

Depth first means the path is extended before all alternative moves are considered at each step. More generally, this kind of behavior is characterized as search in a problem space and is depicted using a graph notation I discuss subsequently.

In the case of Caitlin—and perhaps the water shrews and rats—emotional experience is inseparable from the perceptual and physical coordination process. Bamberger and Schön (1979) described the learning process as shifting from the immediacy of first encounters to the establishment of landmarks and multiple coordinating schemes:

> The work of restructuring involves processes such as the defusing of situational and formal properties of phenomena, the creation of new fixed references, and the building of schemas for co-ordinating these representations with one another. (p. 63)

For Caitlin, part of the "defusing" of situational properties is the emotional shift from mild trepidation and excitement to familiarity and self-confidence. (which is partially established by demonstrating competence in her family's presence). This shift could be facilitated by establishing new, fixed landmarks,

---

[1]Compton and Jansen (1990) used the idea of "adding new pieces on the end" to develop a novel production rule architecture called *ripple down rules* (RDR). In RDR, a chain of rules constitutes a kind of decision tree, with conclusions or actions at the ends. If an existing rule set needs to be modified, a new condition is added to the end of a chain, constituting a kind of contextual switch that refines the outcome appropriately. In effect, the new condition and outcome constitute, in combination with the preexisting chain, a new path. As a representational system, RDRs have proven to be a good way of developing a complex decision network. In effect, they avoid the memory overhead otherwise required in naming branches as new subprocedures or adding arguments to existing procedures. All changes are local; no insertion or reordering is involved. This efficiency of this engineering design may be more than a coincidence, for Compton's invention was inspired by the contextual aspects of human memory.

so she could say where she is (perhaps by reaching the ladder). Naming points on a felt path is certainly a basic part of being able to deliberately move back and forth, and skip about. In effect, in naming landmarks, a secondary scheme is imposed onto the physical arrangement, so places are perceived as being things in themselves. Simpler navigation is more limited by sequential memory, as in Wan et al.'s (1994) navigation model; categorizations of reference points are relative angles, not particular objects or places in the world.

The shift from relative references also occurs in Jeff's experience as bells are perceived to be pitches on a scale; a difficult step when one realizes that even identical bells can sound differently depending on their sequential relations in the path. Jeff generalizes and relates bell sounds: A sound becomes the concept of a sound by virtue of its relation to other sounds, independent of musical context, which we call a *pitch*. Thus another aspect of "defusing situational properties" is the generalization of perceptual details in a sequence to become a kind of vocabulary by which sequences can be described. [2]

5.4 ALTERNATE REPRESENTATIONS OF A FELT PATH

So far we have seen that describing how paths develop in experience is a fruitful way of understanding the learning process. Rather than beginning with a coordinate system that we want someone to learn, such as giving Jeff standard musical notation, we observe the work that is required in moving from paths to sequences that can be described. We reexamine learning in terms of hand–eye–ear coordination, rather than assuming that language is the central controller of behavior. Such coordination is demonstrated by Jeff, as he adds a new bell to the end of a developing sequence. Similarly, on a larger scale using her whole body, Caitlin in the pool illustrates the same process of learning by adding a motion to the end of a sequence.

This perspective can be contrasted with a view of skill learning that posits sequence learning is always assembling already practiced pieces—"discrete parts of a sequence come to behave functionally as a unit" (Patterson, 1991, p.

---

[2] Bamberger and Schön's (1977) analysis goes further in articulating how Jeff learns a coordinate system, such as the conventional musical scale, for naming and arranging pitches and playing tunes. Multiple representations of pitch, phrases in a melody, and action paths must be coordinated. Learning a formal strategy, then, involves perceiving features that become fixed references, and coordinating them with a new action strategy:

What Moore and Newell describe as multiple seeing becomes understandable as the selection of different combinations of features and relations discovered in figural representations of information-rich experience. What they describe as accommodation may be usefully re-described, we think, in terms of the work of restructuring involved in the figure<->formal transaction. (p. 63)

36). In felt path learning we have an extension process—adding a sensorimotor coordination at the end of a learned sequence—suggesting reactivation of a global neural map (Fig. 3.2). Repetition is a simpler process than constructive assembly of discrete, independently known parts. But as I have said, the usual view of learning, starting with the experimenter's descriptions in some coordinate system, posits that the parts exist and have a meaning independently of how they function together. This is the view of the schoolteacher, not the child creating order by moving and arranging things in the world.

Similarly, I wish to emphasize that the conceptualization of an activity is not necessarily verbal or talked about. The conventional definition appears to emphasize the articulated aspect of concepts: "A concept is a family of constraints, affordances, and abilities that practitioners in a domain refer to in their communication in and about their activities" (Greeno, 1995, p. 71). It is surely the case that practitioners refer to their conceptualizations. But, first, as Greeno indicated, the articulation (the descriptive map) is not to be confused with the "constraints, affordances, and abilities" (the conceptual territory). Second, verbal conceptualizations constitute a subset of conceptual knowledge. More generally, concepts are organizers for coordinating perceptual-motor systems, manifest in movement, attention and ordering of behavior in time. To rephrase Greeno's definition, in a way that I believe is consistent with his intent: Conceptualizing within activities constructs abilities that *incorporate* constraints and affordances. Thus, Caitlin's exploratory activity is constructing an ability to go out into the deep end, which incorporates the constraints of her endurance and how the pool side affords a hand-shuffling action. Articulating concepts is part of *reflective learning*, which most learning research prior to connectionism at least implied was the central mechanism of all cognitive development. Such articulation is surely necessary for theorizing and design (section 7.6); its role in other aspects of development, such as Caitlin's swimming, is unclear.

How might we represent behavior so we can understand the learning mechanism, without positing that descriptions of paths and motions are driving the process from the start? Jeff's notation illustrates very well how the figural, next–next–next capability develops prior to being able to articulate in words and formal notation the musical tune. Indeed, this notation is not equivalent to his original experience, but restructures it and changes its personal character. (As after learning to speak French, it no longer has the musical sound we first appreciated.)

Perhaps the most well-known notation for representing exploration is the *problem behavior graph* (PBG), introduced by Newell and Simon in their studies of human problem solving in the 1960s. This notation was developed to capture the sequence of alternative operations over time, as a person explored the states in problems such as chess playing, cryptarithmetic, and (later) computer programming (Kant & Newell, 1984). The notation has the advantage of depicting recurrent "states" and repeated sequences of operators (paths). Fig. 5.3 schematically shows the form of a PBG. Each node in this graph is a "state of knowledge"; operators (or actions) are labeled links, which transform the state from one situation to the next. Time proceeds from left to right and from top to bottom.

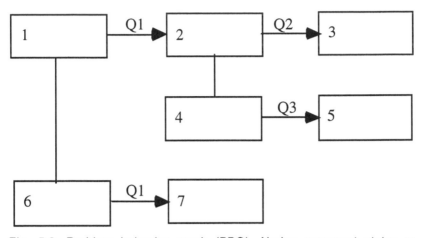

Fig. 5.3. Problem behavior graph (PBG). Nodes represent states or situations in an exploration, encountered or created in the numbered sequence shown. Q numbers indicate operators or actions. Vertical links indicate return to a previous state; thus after State 3, the person returned to the same state indicated by Node 2 and after State 5 returned to the initial situation. (From HUMAN PROBLEM SOLVING, Newell & Simon, 1972, p. 173. Copyright ©1972. Reprinted by permission of Prentice-Hall, Inc., Upper Saddle River, NJ.).

We can represent Caitlin's actions in a PBG (Fig. 5.4). The graph notation shows the return to previous states, return to the beginning, and repetition of paths—all characteristic of progressive deepening. For example, the sequence 1, 2, 3, 4, 5 shows two movements left (ML) to the end point (3), then a return to the beginning (Place 1 is the same as Place 5). However, the "move right" operation in physically returning is not shown because returning to a state of knowledge is not an action in the PBG notation. But for Caitlin, returning to an earlier state (place in the pool) involves an action, moving right. Thus the ideas of a state of knowledge and exploration situation are not equivalent. The PBG notation was of course devised to represent abstract descriptions of object configurations (such as the placement of pieces on a chess board), not the person's oriented location in physical space. A notation for behavior sequences in time and space must show the operation of return to a prior state more explicitly.

Alternatively, we could use a finite-state automata (FSA) representation for felt paths (Fig. 5.5). There are additional pitfalls in using and interpreting such diagrams, so we must proceed carefully. A reasonable assumption in making such diagrams, including the PBG, is that each transition should relate to Caitlin's awareness—what she is perceiving and feeling—as she attentively coordinates her movement. Therefore, I call this particular application of FSA notation a *situated-action FSA*. The diagram indicates that Caitlin generally continues what she is doing while she is in a familiar place, shifting direction only when encountering a dangerous place and reaching the safety of home.

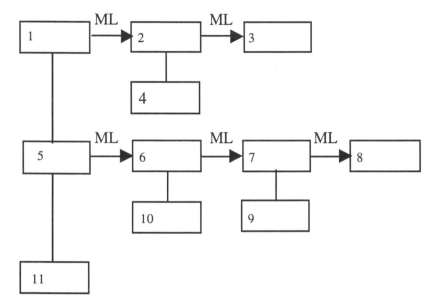

Fig. 5.4. Caitlin's explorations in a pool, a progressive deepening strategy, shown as a problem behavior graph. ML indicates a "move left" operation. Nodes 1, 5, and 11 represent the pool steps. For simplicity, each exploration path is shown as adding a single step.

Notice that the role of nodes and links is reversed from PBGs—here a node is an action and a link is a condition or situation. The notation makes it clear that certain ongoing conditions enable an action to repeat. In this respect, acting in some way is itself a state (which emphasizes that states are abstractions indicating lack of change from some observers' analytic perspective, not states that are fixed internal configurations).

The FSA notation brings out some important properties of a simple learned path not evident in the PBG notation. First, notice that being outside the pool and reentering the water are shown as part of the path—overall one sequence is repeated, with entering the pool as a necessary beginning. Second, notice that the loops in "going left" and "going right" naturally enable extension. As long as the place is familiar, this action will be repeated. Third, notice that Caitlin's range of movement changes on each cycle (Fig. 5.2) because places that were perceived as dangerous on one cycle are more familiar the next time around. In effect, the PBG records actual behavior (actions taken), whereas the FSA notation represents a general procedure. Fig. 5.5 describes a single process with results that change on repetition because the world is recategorized during each cycle of the interaction, producing the progressive deepening pattern (Fig. 5.3).

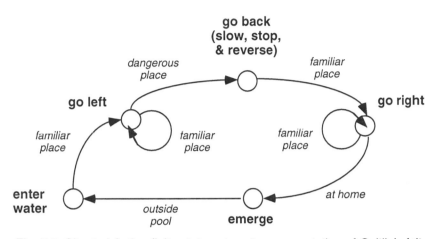

Fig. 5.5. Situated Action finite-state automata representation of Caitlin's felt path.

The nodes in this description are *coordinated operations*, sensorimotor processes. Typically states in computer models are viewed as static properties of a system that persist for some measurable time, such as Newell and Simon's (1972) reference to "knowledge states" in chess playing. However, the nodes in this diagram are more like fixed points in a dynamic framework; they are recurrent *relations* between what Caitlin perceives and how movement occurs. Hence, "going left" is a state in the sense of a stable relation between categorizing "I am in a familiar place" and "I am moving left—out into the deeper water." Such recurrence of temporal relations between categories, which also appears in Wan et al.'s (1994) model of rat navigation, is characteristic of a conceptual coordination process.

Unlike the problem space formulation of the PBG notation, the FSA notation indicates directed coordinated action in a physical space, with actions coupled to perceptual processes. Oriented movement is not like a mathematically formal operation. A physical movement does not have fixed characteristics, such as moving a specific distance left or right. Nor does returning to earlier situations involve returning to a specific place. In conventional cognitive science jargon, the familiarity match is "fuzzy." Caitlin's idea of being in a situation is not an abstract description of a state, but a complex combination of a recognized location, an emotion, and an ongoing movement orientation. Simply put, the very idea of states imposes an analytic order on human behavior that abstracts and to some extent obscures the work involved in coordinating perceptual processes with actions in physical space.

In particular, the FSA representation is deficient for representing dynamic aspects of coordination. For example, it does not represent slowing or the competitive tension between a categorization of familiarity and danger. An activation model of competing processes would account better for differences in speed during the cycle. But especially, the FSA representation does not explain why Caitlin is moving all the time, or that the "go back home" action is a kind of strategy for reestablishing orientation, and why this is important. To this end, we move to the neural level.

In terms of a theory of neural activation, outlined in chapter 3, each node in Fig. 5.5 represents a global mapping, repeatedly reactivated, tentatively represented by Fig. 5.6. This sequence represents one motion from the start of the steps out into the deep water, extending the path, and returning back to the steps. Reversal (going back to the beginning) occurs when the place appears unfamiliar, relative to the sequence developed so far. The landmarks (or correlations among them) perceived along the edge of the pool are represented as perceptual categorizations hanging off the right side of the diagonal; they become part of the constructed coordination.

On repeating the motion into the space around the pool—a kind of exploring activity—a point will be reached where the place is not familiar. We can conjecture that this new place is categorized as dangerous because there is deep water all around, leading Caitlin to "go back home" by reversing her motion. At this point, she turns her head and looks to the right instead. Now once again the place is familiar, but it is perceived within the activity of moving back. That is, a path is still being followed, but now with motion to the right coupled with a view to the right, in the direction of the increasingly familiar and safe. Finally, Caitlin arrives back at the steps and leaves the pool, completing the path development activity.

This notation raises many interesting questions. Should we say that there are two activities: *exploring/extending* a path and *reorienting* by going home? Are time durations equal? Fig. 5.6 arbitrarily extends the diagonal where Fig. 5.5 shows a recurrent loop, a transition pointing back to the original state. But a description of repeated states alone, as in Fig. 5.5, gives no understanding of why the development occurs or how it is possible. In this respect, the activation trace notation represents more than the chronology of experience, of perceptual categorizations within movements. It leads us to consider how sequences become concepts.

Recurrent or stable coordination in people often involves conceptualization: Caitlin is not dumbly moving, as if caught in a repetition, or racing along like the water shrews playing out a program. She is deliberately repeating an *activity*, just as Jeff knows that he is adding a bell to extend the melody representation. In playing a melody, Jeff must remember every bell location–sound to play back the sequence. Remembering the sequence requires reconstructing a temporal ordering of perceptual categorizations. Therefore, each bell–sound–hit would be a global map in the neural activation sequence. But in the case of Caitlin's motion, it appears unnecessary to say that, for example, every shuffle of the hands left is reified in the same way as every bell–sound–hit. We can collapse the representation to indicate a larger-grained activity, representing Caitlin's conceptualization (Fig. 5.7). The conceptualized activity—in general an answer to the question, "What I am doing now?"—is "Continuing to move out, recognizing this place."

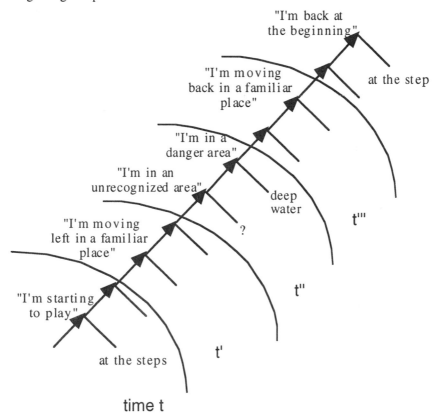

Fig. 5.6. Provisional activation trace representation for Caitlin in the pool (compare to Fig. 5.5).

In contrast with playing a melody, it is not necessary to remember the sequence of the landmarks, just the relative relationships of the scene (reference points). The curve, visible depth changes of the water, filter outlets, furniture on the deck, variations in the deck, and so on, provide a varied enough terrain that we need not conjecture that Caitlin is deliberately remembering her turning point or counting hand motions. Further, because she is aware that she is engaged in an activity of extending her path (going further each time), all she needs to attend to is the *familiarity of the scene*. Finally, in moving back to the steps, she is naturally lead to walk up the steps because she cannot continue her hand shifting. The entire sequence can therefore be represented more simply (Fig. 5.8).[3] This aggregated description highlights that, as Newell (1990) described search in problem solving, "attention is focused on locally experienced difficulties" (p. 10). Caitlin's overall conceptualization is a matter of conjecture. Yet given her age and expressions, it is reasonable to assume that she was deliberately demonstrating competence to be allowed in the deep end.

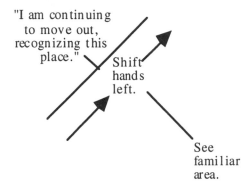

Fig. 5.7. Simplified representation of Caitlin's following a felt path.

After a repetition, this sequence becomes a kind of procedure that is repeated. But on the first occurrence, we might conjecture that a more general process of reorienting has come into play. Thus, the cycle of going out and returning we observe (Fig. 5.2) is a combination of exploring and reorienting that has become a practiced sequence—indeed, Caitlin's idea of a new game she is playing. In discussing Bartlett's model of remembering (chapter 8), I consider the idea that reorientation is part of the neural architecture, which develops into consciously controlled restructuring strategies.

Jeff's activity in adding a bell to the sequence by first playing every bell can be represented similarly: Continuing to hit the bells in order, followed by searching for the next bell in the working space, followed by adding the bell to the end of the row. Bamberger's routine of humming or clapping the tune with

---

[3]Newell and Simon (1972) commented at length about the problem of representing behavior sequence in a way that is too disaggregated or too superficial. They concluded that even if the representations are more like observer summarizations than steps corresponding to mental states, hypothesized mechanisms can be tested (pp. 186–190). I must be a bit more careful because I am making claims about neural processes. However, my descriptions are inevitably gross summaries of complex neural interactions.

Jeff before he attempted to order the bells is a kind of training phase that establishes the idea of coordinating physical actions with sounds.

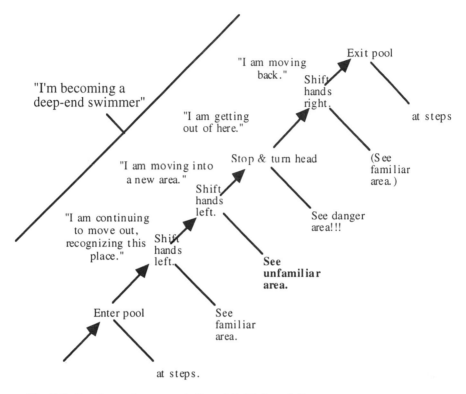

Fig. 5.8. Condensed representation of Caitlin's activity.

Table 5.1 summarizes the different analyses I have presented in this section. Each of the notations is useful. In simple terms, a *PBG* shows the history of state transitions with respect to problem situations; a *situated-action FSA* shows how transitions are coupled to perceptual and emotional categorizations (constituting situations); a *neural activation trace diagram* shows how categorizations are reactivating and physically related to each other. This comparison brings out that a situation is problem-centered in PBG analysis (e.g., a characterization of a puzzle or technical problem). However, in general a situation from the subject's perspective need not be a described (verbally modeled) construction: Categorizations can be perceptual or sequences of behaviors. Further, relations are not necessarily all inferential ("this factual condition implies this other set of facts or heuristically suggests this action"), but may be coupled "reactive" coordinations ("see danger area—flee").

Table 5.1

Comparison of Analytic Notations of Procedural Learning

	Problem Behavior Graph	*Situated Action Finite State Automata*	*Neural Activation Trace Diagram*
Meaning of node	States or situations in an exploration	Physical action	Neural map constituting a categorization
Meaning of link	Operators or actions; including return to a previous state	Subject's observation of conditions (familiar, at home), causing transition to next state (or repetition)	Subsequent activation of categorization (neural map), simultaneous (coupling) activation, or categorization of a sequence
What does the diagram describe?	Subject's search behavior; a space of problem states internally describing the situation	How subject's categorizations cause state changes (i.e., actions)	How categorizations are ordered and temporally related.
Appropriate or common task domain	Usually a puzzle or game (closed, mathematically defined world)	Any, preferably one involving interactive behavior	Any interactive behavior, preferably not a predefined problem to be solved
Mechanism assumptions	Sequences are stored in a secondary memory (LTM), from where they are indexed by content, retrieved (copied), and executed (instantiated and loaded into an instruction processor)	Actions can repeat indefinitely (e.g., no fatigue).	Categorizations reactivate, but are not copied; activations occur "in line"; all activation involves generalization; sequences are higher-order categorizations; no separate memory, processor, or learning step except as conscious behavior
Representation of world	World objects and relations fully modeled internally	Links indicate categorized internal conditions or aspects of world	Perceptual categorizations and higher-order categorizations involved in perceptual-motor coordination

The activation trace notation emphasizes that a higher-order conceptualization of WIDN is always orienting a person's activity. This conceptualization is not a goal, per se, but an understanding of role–position–status. Such conceptualizations are often tacit and may organize behavior without being articulated at all (Hall, 1966/1982). PBGs leave out the person's conceptualization of being stuck, of doing well, of recognizing a loop, and so forth. Human actions are not merely state changes on a game board, but transactions that sustain or transform a conceptual coordination of what is happening to him or her, which includes the person's conception of what kind of game or experiment is being played. That is, each action bears some relation to understanding of what constitutes a good move, danger, what is familiar, how others view the behavior, and other norms. In descriptive cognitive modeling, such aspects of knowledgeable behavior are often called *expectations.* Again, they are not necessarily descriptions but may be perceptual categorizations (unnamed properties) or categorized sequences (unnamed coordinated "steps" in time).

Furthermore, in the PBG each action is a local state change operation; the activation trace perspective shows that each categorization changes the nature of the sequence being constructed—it can be sustained further in the future or it bears a more general relation to the environment. The PBG notation assumes that knowledge is static, retrieved, and applied; the activation trace perspective claims that learning is always, inevitably occurring.

Further comparisons are considered in the next section, relative to the length of sequences and how sequence construction can be coordinated by higher-order categorizations.

5.5 SHORT-TERM MEMORY OF BEHAVIOR SEQUENCES

Progressive deepening—adding a step to the end of a sequence of movements—is quite striking in Jeff's and Caitlin's behavior. In each example, a procedure is repeated, which we represent in the activation trace notation as a label of WIDN associated with some sensorimotor activity. The procedure is a style or strategy for coordinating behavior. A sequence of categorizations (sounds, bells, scenes) is chronologically sequenced. The same action (from the observer's perspective) is applied repeatedly, but in a different place (hitting a different bell, moving further along the pool). In computational terms, the varying details of particular bells and locations along the pool constitute a variable input to a fixed procedure in which actions are "operators." However, the activation trace analysis emphasizes that what is remembered is a hand–eye–ear coordination; a sequence of coordinations is reenacted "from memory." As Bamberger (private communication, 1995) stated, "you are where you are" and this "leads you to where you go next." When interrupted, you "start over again to build up the context for the next move." Rather than viewing the tune or a map of the pool as input, the sequence of sounds and places are specific experiences embedded in inherently sequential activity. Through repetition such details become defused and hence conceptualized to being the landmarks of pitches or known places.

If each landmark must be physically integrated into a sequence, how long a sequence can a person construct? The traditional answer in psychology, given by the work of Miller (1956), is that 7 plus or minus 2 units can be perceived and recalled. In terms of neural activation, this implies that we can construct and reenact from memory a new coordinated sequence of behavior of 7 ± 2 steps, in which each step is a sensorimotor coordination, coupled to a detail categorization (e.g., a letter or number). Thus, we can easily learn a sequence of seven digits in a phone number, and PBGs for chess playing are usually 10 steps or shorter. However, it is also known that if subsequences can be chunked by familiar organizers (such as area codes), the hierarchical order that results can be much longer. For example, Chase, Ericsson, and Faloon (1980) studied a long-distance runner who learned to memorize sequences of more than 100 digits by reconceiving subsequences as being known running times for different distance races.

Similarly, by the generalization that repetition in a particular place allows, Caitlin's memory of the sequence needn't be restricted by enumerating locations or counting hand motions. She need only recognize whether a place is familiar. Jeff can remember a tune requiring more than seven bells because music is segmented into phrases that repeat and are hierarchically organized by design. In Jeff's playing, the sequence is strictly ordered and nonreversible (perhaps because the elements are perceptual categorizations that cannot be held active and reordered in the manner of higher-order, conceptual categorizations). Caitlin returning home does not have to find her way, because she can literally feel her way along the edge of the pool. But the water shrews must actively sniff their way about to rebuild their path. Lorenz's description suggests that the shrews do not literally retrace their steps, but either go back and turn around once a place is familiar again, or establish a new path back to the nest. This is a crucial point: The chronological next–next–next sequence, represented by an activation trace diagram is not reversible; only movement in space is reversible.[4]

Newell and Simon's (1972) studies showed that progressive deepening is characteristic of a broad range of human behavior: motor control, skill learning, and problem solving. Crucially, this is a description of what people do, not a requirement imposed by nature of the work to be done. For example, most chess playing programs, which are not intended to model human behavior, use a more

---

[4]Wilden (1987) explained nonreversibility in terms of the development of a coordination, a system of interacting parts:

  The reason for the nonreversibility of emergent quality in living and social systems is that such systems create system-dependent behavior between system-dependent parts—parts that cannot normally develop or exist outside the context they are in. (pp. 170–171)

general depth-first search (Newell, 1990, p. 12). Of course, in general, computer programs needn't be limited to exploration paths of 7 or 10 steps. According to the problem space formulation, the difference between human "information processors" and these computer programs is simply the limitation of short-term memory in people. The (human) strategy of progressive deepening is advantageous because it may be performed by "holding a single temporary state."

> In particular, the general depth-first strategy, which exhausts the explorations of each state and then backs up to the immediately prior state, is not possible because the stack of prior states along the search path cannot be kept in mind. Progressive deepening, however, is a search strategy precisely adapted to this demand. (Newell, 1990, p. 11)

The earlier work of Bruner, Goodnow, and Austin characterized such approaches as lowering "cognitive strain," which Newell and Simon (1972) summarized as follows:

> No complicated internal housekeeping is needed to keep track of where the search is. Only a single position need be stored internally, and it can be *stored in terms of the way it differs from the base position*, which is under continual surveillance (thus providing a continuing memory of all the things that have not changed). (p. 720; citing Bruner et al., 1956; italics added)

It is striking how well Newell and Simon's choice of language fits Caitlin's and Jeff's explorations as well as rat navigation, despite Newell and Simon's focus on formal problems and not action in physical space. By my analysis, the "single position" held in short-term memory is not a single named state or symbol, but a complex conceptualization relating *the activity* of WIDN, the *perceptual categorization of the current situation* (perhaps just a sound or scene), and an *attitude*. Thus, short-term memory contains not the value of a variable, but consists of a partly abstracted physical coordination, a dynamic perceptual-motor relation within an exploration. As internal constructs, these relations are reference points; when categorized as *objects* they become reference entities; when abstracted further they become instances of a coordinate system. The attitude within the conceptualized coordination is the person's orientation of doing something familiar, getting into trouble, recovering, and so on. Newell and Simon (1972) made such distinctions between "rework" and "explore," but did not mention the emotional aspect of such behavior.

5.6 USE OF AN ANCHOR IN DELIBERATE SEQUENTIAL COORDINATION

To explicate better how the single position in memory mentioned by Newell and Simon (1972) is not just a pointer to a problem state, but part of a complex conceptualization that is coordinating the activity, I conclude this chapter with another simple example from language learning. Here two ideas are highlighted: The role of an anchor for holding one's place (a *base position*) and the nature of a sequence as a relation between the current action and the anchor.

It is no surprise that in reconstructing a tune from memory, one proceeds from the first note and not the last. But adding to the front of a sequence is possible, and may be preferred in some forms of learning. For example, one method for learning to pronounce a long word or a phrase is to build it up from the *middle*. For example, to learn to pronounce *C'est un inconvénient*, one might build the phrase by saying the following sequence:

> *con-vén*
> *convén-ient*
> *in-convénient*
> *un inconvénient*
> *C'est un inconvénient.*

The method begins with an already familiar word, syllable, or root in a sequence to be learned (*con-vén*). If there are following familiar pieces, they are added at the end (*convén-ient*). Now, with this anchored sequence, new syllables are added on the front: *in-convénient, un inconvénient,* and so on. Like Jeff playing the bells, the phrase learned so far is repeated each time, but the new piece is placed at the front![5] In this example, starting with a stressed ending may provide useful information for "getting into the rhythm" that the accented syllables and segmentation into words requires. The example reveals that for language learning at least, with context-sensitive, embedded compositions, human sequence construction capability is much more flexible than the felt path examples suggest.

As another example of deliberate sequencing, consider what happens when you are read outloud a sequence of letters, such as "d-r-o-w," and asked to say what the word is, were the letters to be reversed. According to Schneider (1999), four visual modules (each a *hypercolumn,* a map, of tens of thousands of neurons) are activated and held (short-term memory). You then alter your attention to scan the modules sequentially in reverse order. Relating this to my analysis, each module corresponds to a node in the activation trace diagrams; the sequence construction process involves conscious direction of attention and construction of a new sequence, "w-o-r-d." Note that the four modules corresponding to "d-r-o-w" need not be simultaneously active, as in a buffer. Instead, the experienced sequence need only be *reactivated,* one letter at a time. Two sequences are therefore being coordinated. An anchor holds the temporal position in the heard sequence as each letter is added on the end to the newly constructed sequence. (Of course, when the word becomes recognized as familiar, a higher-order conceptualization corresponding to the word then helps to hold and complete the result.)

---

[5]In the discussion of grammar (chapter 9), we find that adding to the front is a recurrent pattern in relating noun phrases to verbs.

The "d-r-o-w" example highlights several points. First, the analysis exemplifies what conventional computational modeling too often takes for granted, namely how multiple categorizations can be active and related in the brain. Ignoring this conceptual coordination process in turn diminishes our appreciation of what consciousness accomplishes. In particular, the example exemplifies the ability of higher-order consciousness to move deliberately through a previously experienced sequence and to create a new sequence. More complex coordinations involve logically comparing categorizations or reordering categorizations in a causal story. Such capability goes well beyond felt path behavior, but builds on the same inherent nature of neural activation: sequential relations (e.g., the heard letter sequence and the created reversed sequence) and simultaneous relations (e.g., an anchor constituting focal attention shifts from one active module to the next, called *binding* in conventional programming).

The generalization of the examples I have presented—constructing felt paths, learning pronunciation, and reversing letters—is that we "repeat what we have done so far" and "add a piece"—precisely de Groot's (1965) idea of progressive deepening (Fig. 5.3). By conjecture, a conceptualization is required to coordinate attention during learning to where a new piece is added. Indeed, in the pronunciation example, conceptual coordination is required merely to segment the sequence of phonemes into ordered syllables and words. The process of adding an element is not a mere repetition (as appears to be the case for the rats), but a coordinated learning strategy, a conceptualization of how to learn a new sequence (even in something so apparently simple as reversing heard letters). In particular, the relation between the new piece and the existing sequence is conceptual, not merely an episodic, highly "situated" addition onto a next–next–next sequence. In the examples presented, this conceptual organization involves relating multiple sequences by use of an anchor (the steps in the pool, the middle syllable in a word, a letter in the heard sequence). In summary, progressive deepening may fit the behavior of water shrews, mice, and people, but *conceptual organizers* allow for more flexibility in how new actions relate to the existing sequence. (The learning strategy may become arbitrarily complex, as illustrated in my analysis of how EPAM learns in section 11.3.)

In summary, my concern in this book is with development and learning over a time period of just a few minutes to understand the overarching processes that produce organized behavior in the first place. Consideration of neural processes suggests that a sequence recurs by next–next–next activation when it is reconstructed, but it may be developed through orthogonal conceptual relations (such as "word," "root," "suffix") that are tacitly evoked and composed. (By *orthogonal*, I mean that a single sequence is ordered by different higher-order categorizations, which themselves may be repeated and ordered.) Examples in the next chapter illustrate how substitutions, reversals, and so on, are possible and hence reveal how this orthogonal composing process works.

To understand the nature of conceptual coordination, I am attempting to juggle a broader view of human activity with a narrow view of neural map activation. The comparisons of simpler animal behavior and children's explorations to studies of complex problem solving show striking commonalities, but also differences that are taken for granted. There is a difference between the episodic, next–next–next learning of the water shrew and the conceptualization of sequences evident in the language learning. On the other hand, emotional attitude may be an important way of sustaining orientation in animals (implied by Bartlett's analysis; chapter 8), but is ignored in information processing models. Too often emotion has been viewed as a reaction to a situation or a kind of flavoring that distorts thinking, rather than an organizer for initially prompting that "a situation has occurred" and framing the categorization of "what is happening to me now" (see the discussion of Damasio's theory in section 8.4).

Most important, I am claiming that conscious human behavior is never a mere application of a procedure or rote reenactment from memory, but is part of an overarching construction of the persona. We say that Caitlin is conceptualizing; she has a sense of WIDN, not just "where I am." Put another way, Caitlin is engaged in an *activity*, just as Newell and Simon's (1972) subjects were engaged in a laboratory activity that is taken for granted in the interpretation of PBGs. An activity is a higher-order, conceptual organizer of motion over time in space. Caitlin is not merely solving a problem, but with her family watching, she is engaged in demonstratively overcoming fear and gaining the right to go into the deep end of the pool. When the broader aspect of human activity is ignored, as in much of the study of human problem solving, the nature and role of emotional organizers may also be obscured or distorted.

Cognitive modelers have been well aware that human capabilities are different from the full generality of modern computer languages. However, both the broader conceptual organizers and the more basic attention and sequencing processes need to be reconsidered. In this chapter, we have moved beyond the taken-for-granted aspects of the information processing architecture of knowledge states and short-term memory to consider an animal's felt path behaviors. We find that we must consider exploring and learning itself to be a coordinated activity, modulated by a complex of repetition, rhythm, feedback, and emotion.[6]

In this chapter, I highlighted the idea that a sequence can become conceptualized and hence repeated as a unit, which may be extended on repetition. Thus progressive deepening and PBGs may be reformulated in terms of learning behavior sequences. This analysis is to be contrasted with the more

---

[6]Various aspects of "temporally extended patterns of motor activity (e.g., fixed-action patterns)" are illustrated by Beer's (1995) models in the realm of "computational ethology." Relevant mechanisms at the neural level include network oscillators that generate rhythmic patterns, positive feedback loops, and chemical modulation of activity (pp. 7–8).

abstract model of behavior as search in a problem space consisting of abstract state descriptions that formalize situations into named places in a coordinate system. The situated action FSA approach moves the analysis from searching trees to *constructing paths in an interactive behavior space*. The activation trace moves us further toward understanding a "single dynamic state," not as a stored description, but more generally as a sustained conceptual relation, a kind of physical coordination. By considering behaviors as physical movements in space, we saw how the encountered location of objects (perhaps deliberately arranged as in the case of Jeff's bells) can serve as part of the "memory" of a procedure. The environment is not merely input to a procedure, but leaned on and reordered. To elucidate this transactional aspect of cognitive behavior, subsequent examples examine in more detail how constraints and flexibilities of internal activations themselves interact and blend, especially conceptual organizers.

6

Slips and Composed Parallel Binding

Wild chimpanzees use about three dozen different vocalizations to convey about three dozen different meanings. They may repeat a sound to intensify its meaning, but they do not string together three sounds to add a new word to their vocabulary. We humans also use about three dozen vocalizations, called phonemes. Yet only their combinations have content: We string together meaningless sounds to make meaningful words. No one has yet explained how our ancestors got over the hump of replacing "one sound, one meaning" with a sequential combinatorial system of meaningless phonemes, but it is probably one of the most important advances that took place during ape-to-human evolution.

—William H. Calvin, The emergence of intelligence, *Scientific American*, 1994, p. 102[1]

In this chapter I consider simple discoordinations of timing and repetition, primarily involving language, such as misreading words, "slips" in typing and writing, and mishearing speech. Such examples are commonplace and deceptively simple on the surface. Analysis reveals patterns of *rearrangement* and *substitution*, which indicate an ordering and grouping mechanism that is operating in parallel on hierarchical levels to reproduce sequential relations in behavior. The conscious process and result is, as Bartlett (1932/1977) put it, "an imaginative reconstruction" (p. 213) of past experience. We find especially that perception is not a kind of input stage to understanding and action; rather, processes of scanning, forming units, and stringing sequences work together. More specifically, the examples reveal:

- Experienced behavior in writing/typing and reading/hearing is serial; one thing follows another.
- A learning process makes new units from input fields (discretizing images and sounds) and reconstructs previously formed units in time.

---

[1]Of course, some phonemes are words, too: "Oh, are you a bee? I see!"

> That is, parallel processing is constrained by learned, sequence-specific timings, rather than being fully "distributed."

- Parallel processing involves activation of multiple alphabetic, phonological, and syllabic units ("inputs") in time, as well as multiple links between lower and higher levels.
- Higher-order organizers compete for and "lock up" lower-order units in recognition "binding."

Taken together, the evidence suggests that language understanding and generation involves learned sequences of categorizations, organized on different levels, as multimodal coordinations in time.

6.1 SEEING WHAT YOU ARE SAYING

Here is an example of a misreading discoordination: I was looking at a newspaper airline advertisement that listed cities with special airfares. The name "Spartanville" came to my attention (as if I had said the name to myself). "Where in the list is it?" I wondered. I scanned the list and found "Greenville/Spartanburg."

The example illustrates bottom-up production of a description (the articulation, Spartanville); I was not coordinating the words I was saying to what I was seeing. Put another way, when we interact with newspaper material we normally coordinate our conceptualization of WIDN to what we are seeing. But as in this example, you may read a paragraph and find that you do not know what you are looking at, despite having a fully formed idea in mind. My search for Spartanville in the list was evidently an attempt to reestablish a coordination between what I was seeing and what I was saying.

The example also demonstrates the phenomenon of reconstruction (here, saying the word *Spartanville*). Obviously, I did not literally see "Spartanville"—it was not on the page at all. But a process of visual categorizing constructed this process of speaking (perhaps by combining *Spartan* and the adjacent *ville*).

The reader might want to try representing how this process developed (in any favorite notation) before examining my representation. Fig. 6.1 shows how I first represented what was happening in the Spartanville story. This awkward, hierarchical depiction shows that how one experience leads to another is not obvious.

This representation is hierarchical, according to the conventional idea that WIDN is controlling what I see and do. By this view, I have a procedure for reading newspapers, by which goal-directed comprehension processes are interacting with bottom-up recognition processes. In browsing the page (undirected reading) I saw something and said "Spartanville." Because this did not fit into my current understanding of what I was reading (a description "posted" in an internal short-term structure), an impasse occurred and a repair procedure was invoked. I now began to search for "Spartanville"—"Where is it in the list?" I am now engaged in directed reading, scanning the list sequentially (perhaps sampling different areas). Matching the item "Greenville/Spartanburg" against the target I am holding active, "Spartanville," I decide that *Spartanburg* is the word I must have seen earlier.

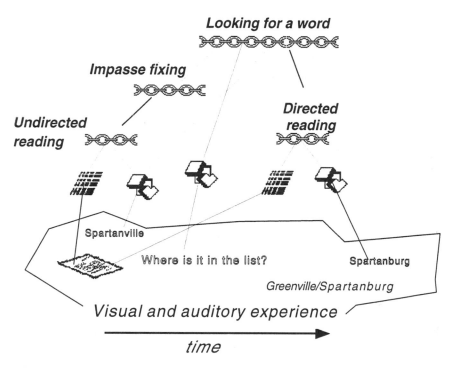

Fig. 6.1. Initial representation of the discoordination in reading "Spartanville" instead of "Spartanburg" (Key. chain = interactive controlling process; black diagonal boxes = reading; angular boxes = silent speech [saying a word to oneself]).

But now consider the activation trace representation (Fig. 6.2) of the Spartanville incident. This representation better reveals the sequential aspects of learning and attentive experience in time. As discussed in previous chapters, each bold node on the left represents a process, part of WIDN. I am reading and imagine the name "Spartanville," a focus detail that "comes in from the side" (undirected reading). I am stymied because I am reading, but not seeing the word I am hearing (an attitude of unease, a sense of discoordination). I am saying, "Where is it in the list?" (WIDN: Trying to find a word, *Spartanville*). I attend for a moment and next I am seeing and saying to myself

"Greenville/Spartanburg," believing at once that it is what I had been reading (Spartanburg).

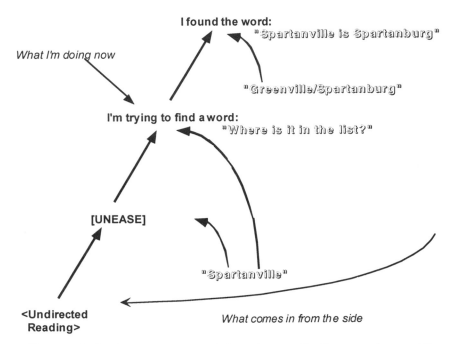

Fig. 6.2. Activation trace representation of recoordinating experience while reading. Ideas being coordinated (in outline font on the right) arise spontaneously in consciousness ("come in from the side"); overarching conceptualization of WIDN appears on the left.

The relation between the two focus details, "Greenville/Spartanburg" and "Spartanville" is obviously pivotal for the conclusion of the episode. When a correlation is accomplished, the search stops. Superficially, we can compare this sequence to the example of sending two messages (chapter 4):

- A focus detail comes from the side to change what I am doing (saying "I need to send a message to Mike"; saying "Spartanville").
- A new activity is started, which is the previous activity (sending a message, reading) qualified by this focus detail.

The key difference between the two examples is that the idea of sending a message to Mike arose as an automatic transition, whereas the idea of "Spartanville" arose as a problem, a *discoordination*. In reading I must *find* a correlation for the first focus detail (looking for a correlate of Spartanville). The arrival of "Spartanville" is thus like the arrival of the focus on Mike, a direct correlation with the previously held focus. In each case, the focus detail coming in from the side (Mike, Spartanville, Spartanburg) is not arbitrary, but is already correlated with what I am currently doing.

When Spartanville comes to my attention while I am deliberately reading, I reconceive what I have been doing. Because I do not actually find Spartanville, the construction requires a *descriptive rationalization*, a kind of knitting operation, which is simply stated, "Spartanville is Spartanburg." I realize that when I became stuck I must have been reading Spartanburg ("that's the word I was reading"). Colloquially, we might say that my demeanor is now composed. My sense of closure is a combination of my conceptualization of the episode as being a misreading and my verbal description of what happened.

In conclusion, the relation between the statements "trying to find a word" and "I found the word" is not an immediate *reenactment*, like sending a second message, but a *paraphrase* of the past sequence of actions. Schön (1987) called this "Reflection-in-Action"—I talk about what I have been doing while I am engaged in the activity. The (reflective) conception of WIDN is all-embracing: The conception broadens to include the overall episode, over time, here marked by an incident that constituted an impasse and anchored by the focus detail, Spartanville. In my directed reading, I held onto the saying–hearing of Spartanville, hoping to compose it into some new conceptualization that would include it, and hence explain its occurrence.

Again, my sense of WIDN is a handle on a coordinated sequence of perceptions and actions, not just a momentary behavior. As a conceptualization, WIDN concerns an engagement, an activity in time, as opposed to an object, simple event, or even a "goal." As a generalization of past WIDN experiences, the conceptualization has both general and specific aspects. For example, when I am trying to tell a story, WIDN will be both a very general, complex "choreography" of linguistic roles and orderings in trying to tell a story and the specific details I am intending to incorporate.

In the descriptive language I have been using here, *intending* involves holding active one or more categorizations (focus details) within a categorized coordination (conception of WIDN). A focus detail is something I am working with. The overarching conception is, in Bartlett's terms, the "main stream of interest." For example, to resolve the impasse in my reading, I require a conceptualization of WIDN that brings the incommensurable detail of Spartanville into the main stream of interest. That is, saying Spartanville earlier can be *viewed as* part of the normal activity of reading the paper. Thus closure is attained because I can conceive WIDN as one thing, a coherent sequence.

6.2 UNDERSTANDING "SLIPS"—ROLES IN A SEQUENCE

The Spartanville example illustrates the perceptual aspect of analogies, which has been investigated by Hofstadter (1993, 1995a), Mitchell (1993), Mitchell and Hofstadter (1990), and others in their research group. For example, in solving a jumble puzzle in a newspaper, one might be given the token, *telkin* and asked to rearrange the letters into an English word. Hofstadter and associates have devised a set of programs that make transformations like those used by people, producing guesses like *knitle* and *keltin*. The program attempts to replicate our sense of style of real words: "intuitions about letter affinities, plausible clusters and their stabilities, syllable qualities, etc." (Hofstadter, 1985, p. 641). These intuitions are explained by how associations between letters are represented in memory and how clusters form during the search process, summarized by Hofstadter (1995a, pp. 84-5) as theoretical themes:

- The *inseparability of perception and high-level cognition,* leading to the idea of a perceptual architecture being at the heart of cognition.
- The fruits of high-level perception being *easily reconfigurable multi-level cognitive representations* held loosely together by bonds of different types and different strengths.
- The idea of *subcognitive pressures*—namely, that the more "important" a concept or a representation is, the greater an influence it should be allowed to exert, in a probabilistic sense, on the direction of the processing.
- The *commingling of many pressures*, both context-dependent and context-independent, leading to a nondeterministic parallel architecture in which bottom-up and top-down processing coexist gracefully.
- The *simultaneous feeling-out of many potential pathways* at differential rates governed by quickly made estimates of degree of promise.
- The centrality of the making of analogies and variations on a theme in high-level cognition.
- The possession, by cognitive representations, of *deeper and shallower aspects,* with the former remaining relatively immune to contextual pressures, and the latter being more likely to yield under pressure (to "slip").
- The crucial role played by *the inner structure of concepts and conceptual neighborhoods* in all these goals, particularly context-dependent conceptual overlap and proximity, and context-independent conceptual depth.

These themes are generally consistent with the theoretical thrust of my own study.[2] The differences are matters of emphasis. Hofstadter (1995a) rightly emphasized that analogies and variations are central to cognition (as opposed to being merely errors). On the other hand, I emphasize the temporal aspect of conceptual organizing (preferring not to use spatial metaphors such as inner structure and neighborhood).

---

[2]Lakoff (1995) provided a similar list of findings from cognitive linguistics, related to Damasio's convergence zones, which I discuss in section 8.4.

Transforming Spartanburg to Spartanville follows the kind of logic Hofstadter was exploring. For example, this transformation obviously combined the *ville* suffix of the previous word with the *Spartan* prefix. Significantly, the pieces—*ville, spartan,* and *burg*—are familiar units, appearing alone or in combination with other units (so indeed, Spartanville is a plausible name for a city). The construction of Spartanville involves *superimposition* of different sequences. Similar transformations occur as mistakes in typing or writing, often called *slips.* These are not deliberate reorderings, but transformations in coordination that produce the wrong word or nonsensical words. Like other researchers, I have collected and studied my own slip experiences. About a third of the examples in my typing and writing are "early capture" elisions, such as "be key" → "bey" and "EPRI Net experience" → "Epri Nex." Another third are substitutions of similar-sounding words: "bring" → "brain," "egos" → "eagers," and "locomotion" → "location." As in the example of reading Spartanville, a word appears without my intention to produce it; I am typing along and realize that the wrong word has appeared on the page.

Hofstadter and Mitchell's models of analogy formations postulate that these transformations are evidence for multiple, parallel activations occurring in anticipation of incorporation in sequential behavior. Typing studies clearly show how an expert typist's fingers begin moving and arrive over a letter key before it needs to be pressed (Gentner, 1981b). Broadly speaking, Dennett (1992) called this the "multiple drafts" model of consciousness: The temporally ordered, coordinated sequence of behavior and experience is produced from multiple, simultaneous "tracks" of interpretation (bottom-up) and elaboration (top-down).

However, we must be clear that slips are evidence of *physical discoordination*, not just syntactic reorderings of *products.* That is, perceptual-motor action is being organized, not letters. The rules of transformation we use to describe reorderings or slips must be further related to neural sensorimotor processes of activation, composition, and sequencing. The concepts of slippage and temperature in Mitchell's (1993) Copycat program (and related connectionist systems) are a good start. However, Hofstadter and Mitchell's interest is to model creative analogy formation, in solving problems like "abc is to abd as xyz is to what?" Their architecture is designed to flexibly apply a variety of structure comparing and structure-building rules to nonsense sequences; they do not model errors derived from a preexisting vocabulary (Chalmers, French, & Hofstadter, 1992)[3] A neural theory must be both a model of learning and a model of recoordination, that is, based on recomposition as well as reactivation.

---

[3]Chalmers et al. (1992) realized that perception cannot be separated from analogy formation, but in saying that "Copycat is not intended as a model of learning" (p. 209), they suggested that coordination is not learning. They meant that Copycat does not model perceptual categorization; the program operates on a fixed set of letter combinations.

6.2.1 Slip Patterns: A Coordination Mechanism or Stored Templates?

Related work by Dell, Juliano, and Govindejee (1993) and other researchers uses SRNs[4], a form of connectionist architecture involving activation links between letters; in this way, using a given vocabulary, they model different slip phenomena that actually occur in human speech. Their models of slips support the psycholinguistics hypothesis that linguistic structure processing (syntax) is to some degree independent of linguistic content processing (semantics). That is, they show how slip patterns are general, not specific to particular words, but relating to patterns of letters and segments. Moreover, in using SRNs to model the patterns observed in such slips, they demonstrate that structural patterns (such as transpositions) are not described and stored separately as abstract rules. Instead, the law-like patterns we observe "emerge from the storage of many individual linguistic strings" (p. 155). That is, patterns in slips are the product of how sequences are learned (and hence the nature of particular learned sequences) and the process of reactivation and serializing of previously active sequences.

In considering Dell et al.'s (1993) work, I contrast it to other frame-based models that describe slips as if they were produced by separate transformation operators (abstract rules or laws) operating on the vocabulary. I ultimately find, after considering Chomsky's theories in some detail (section 9.2), that learned sequences embody the results of general coordination (composition, sequencing, generalizing) processes. Hence, in the attempt to locate the cause of behavior patterns, the debate about syntax versus content and "in the mechanism" versus "in the learned behavior" is a false dichotomy. Very general operations are at work, and these to some important degree are the basis of the logical relations in our behavior and meanings (cf. opening quote by Vygotsky, chapter 1). However, these operations are *inherent in the mechanism* of neural recoordination (temporally relating categorizations to each other), not a separate set of verbally modeled rules (e.g., grammars found in descriptive cognitive models). Thus, slip behavior can be law-like without a body of laws being part of the mechanism that creates observed patterns. The transformation operations are inherent in how categorization building blocks may combine with each other.

In Dell et al.'s (1993) model,[5] the laws of slip transformation include:

---

[4]The motivation and accomplishments of the SRN architecture are detailed in section 3.2.

[5]To model letter sequences, Dell et al. (1993) used a recursive network that combines a copy of the previous output (as in Pollack's [1990] recursive networks) and a copy of internal relations between the previous inputs and outputs (called *hidden units*). The algorithm that combines activation weights (called *back-propagation* in such connectionist models) is viewed as a kind of feedback, error-correcting procedure, which

- Slips produce sound sequences that almost always occur in the language being spoken.
- "When one segment replaces another, the replacing and replaced segments are in the same basic category" (p. 150): Vowels are replaced by vowels, consonants are replaced by consonants. This is supported by patterns of phonological speech errors (e.g., *a reading list* → *a leading list* illustrates phonological movement, anticipation of /l/).
- "When an adjacent vowel and consonant are both replaced in a slip, the [changed] sequence is more likely a VC than a CV. So, for example, *dog* → *tig* would be less likely than *dog* → *dit*." One explanation is that "a VC is more likely to be a single subsyllabic unit," that is, a rhyme constituent.
- "Initial or onset consonants are more likely to slip than noninitial ones."

As in the NETtalk model of speech (Sejnowski & Rosenberg, 1990; see also Clancey, 1997c, chapter 3), the program of Dell et al. (1993) internally manipulates and outputs *encoded descriptions of sounds*, not word spellings or sound signals. Dell et al. referred to this as "patterns of sound." But is not the role of the model to explain why sound patterns occur? Dell et al. agreed that their model simply replicates the patterns found in the input vocabulary: "Thus [the model] begs the question of why the vocabulary has the structure it does. A theory of phonological competence should explain *why* certain sound patterns are present and why others are not" (p. 180). For example, constraints on articulation—how the mouth can create sounds—affect phonological segmentation. The model's input vocabulary therefore embodies certain (unexamined) constraints that affected the evolution of human speech and the cultural development of particular phonetic-syllabic systems. Also, in not considering "higher" organizers, the model omits how metrical and prosodic structure of sentences influences pronunciation of single words.

Nevertheless, the Dell et al. (1993) model compares favorably to other work that separated slip pattern generators from the vocabulary. Previous models processed the input stream of letters simultaneously (multiple words at a time) and mapped the input onto theoretical constructs such as onset (initial letters), vowels, and codas and other frame slots (e.g., letter relationships in words). Such constructs were motivated only by the observed slip (or more general pronunciation) regularities. That is, the modeler designed the processing architecture to incorporate observed phonological patterns. The patterns the model is expected to produce are explicitly built into the model via stored properties of words (frame slots) and processing rules—what I call a stored

---

is inherent in human learning. Dell et al. trained the network on three-letter words. Experiments showed that a limited vocabulary of 50 words produced slips similar to those observed in adults. Other experiments involved randomly degrading weights and introducing a much larger vocabulary; both were less successful in replicating the slip patterns.

grammar model. In contrast, the Dell et al. SRN model relies on sequential ordering alone to replace a deliberate encoding of serial ordering, phonological features, and constraints between features.[6] By basing slips on the vocabulary itself, the model produces violations of known patterns, and such violations are observed in human speech. This flexibility and discovery is not possible in models that generate slips from fixed rules for generating slips.

On the other hand, the Dell et al. (1993) model, being restricted to sequential orderings in the vocabulary, does not produce *speech movement* errors across words. Of special interest are exchanges, such as saying "lork yibrary" instead of "York library," which involve "similar sounds occupying structurally similar positions" (p. 184). Analysis of such errors shows that more than 70% of exchanges between words involved initial consonants. Are the frame-slot models more correct here? Are there "slots" that label the position of consonants in words (such as "first consonant in a word") and a structure exchange rule (such as "swap first-consonant in adjacent words")? (And why would there be a "slip rule"?) Or is there something special about the first categorization in a sequence of neural activations? Some kind of hybrid model is required that incorporates the structure of the vocabulary in the slip mechanism.

6.2.2 Exchanges and Bindings

To produce effects such as exchanges between words, processing must involve more than a sequence of letters of single words. The slip evidence indicates that a "contamination" occurs between a sequence of *words*. The word-initial effect may be explained by the presence of a boundary, such that when beginning to say a word, the effect of the context (subsequent letters of the word) is lessened, increasing the chance of a replacement. Nevertheless, the Dell et al. (1993) model would not tend to produce an exchange. For example, in the phrase *York library*, if /l/ replaces the /y/ in York, there would not be an increased chance that /y/ replaces the /l/ in library. A frame-based (explicit rules) approach can produce such exchanges because the mechanism involves mapping and binding tokens—once the /l/ is used to produce /lork/ it is no longer available, leaving /y/ in the pool of letters for assembly into *yibrary* (p. 185). Indeed, the data suggest that sounds are manipulated as units that have a kind of independent existence from words themselves, such that they can be swapped over word boundaries. Frame-slot models, such as the Mitchell–Hofstadter program, accomplish this exchange by incorporating competition between units and inhibition of assignment. A binding process thus relates units and the higher units that

---

[6]"Encoding" means that features of words, also called *frame slots* (e.g., "initial letter") are described in a language devised by the modeler; the vocabulary is represented by the modeler in terms of this language; and processing rules use the same language to manipulate the input.

subsume them. It is this higher-level coordination organization that the Dell et al. model, which is based on sequential ordering alone, lacks.

In my own experience of learning to recognize and pronounce French phrases, I have found striking examples of this binding effect. For example, while listening carefully to a tape on repeated trials, I continuously heard *je ne les ai pas vu* as *je nez e' pas vu*. From the context, I knew that an *l* sound should be present, but I could not hear it because I kept mapping the second unit I perceived onto the expected *ne* (depicted in Fig. 6.3). Put another way, although I knew that the first two words could be combined into *J'ne* as they were in the actual recording, I heard the second two units as combined: *ne + les -> nez*. In my hearing, the *n* sound was not bound to the first *j* (as in the English *June*), but was heard as the start of the second word (which is permissible, but not the pronunciation on the tape). That is, the expected binding of the consonant *n* as a word onset was stronger in the final construction than the actual phonemic unit on the tape (*j'ne*). This top-down effect was so dominant, it persisted even when I tried on multiple attempts to hear the consonant *l,* knowing fully well that it must be present.

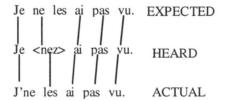

Fig. 6.3. Five phonetic units perceived in input were mapped onto six expected word units, resulting in creation of incorrect elided sound *nez* and subsequent "blind spot" to hearing *l*.

A similar binding effect occurs at the phonemic level alone, when one is trying to learn a new phoneme. For example, I listened to the phrase *est-ce que vous les avez vu* eight times before I could hear and say *vu* as something other than *veux*. I have found that in learning a sound in French that does not occur in English, my perceptual categorization sometimes oscillates between known phonemes. For example, I realized that I was in the process of learning the correct pronunciation when I repeatedly replayed the tape and heard *v u* oscillating in a kind of sound-illusion between *veux* and *vous* on different trials.

In explaining the *lork* slip, I mentioned a boundary effect. I have found other examples in which the initial words and final words are caught, but everything in between is lost. This relatively well-known pattern suggests that:

- Activation of the first and last units is higher (or they are more easily reactivated and held active).

- The number of intermediate units that may be kept active is limited while a larger composition is occurring.

For example, in listening to the sentence, *je connais un bon café place de la cathedral*, I was listening carefully, wanting to hear whether the adjective was *bon* or *beau*. On listening to the tape repeatedly, I knew that an adjective was being said—I heard one of the two choices—but by the end of the sentence all I could remember was *je connais* and *place de la cathedral*. That is, I had no experience of what occurred. In conventional terms, we would say that my short-term memory was full (with nine syllables); but in terms of attention and compositional structuring, much more is happening. The effect is as if I "get for free" the beginning and end in memory, and am busy hearing each of those syllables and what the words mean. (Indeed, my wife, a native French speaker, complained early in my learning that I pronounced each syllable with equal emphasis, and this sounded unnatural to her.) Thus, an activation model, based on sequences, units at different levels (as in the Chase model), competitive bindings, and special relations based on position explains more than a model of memory in terms of a linear data structure of 7 ± 2 units. The example also nicely illustrates that although we often loosely talk about hierarchies of sequences and composition, "which units subserve which is context dependent" (Gallistel, 1981, p. 617). Because of binding and mappings between levels, serial behavior and experience have an implicit hierarchical order, but the soup of potentially activatable strings at any one time is a *heterarchy*.

Returning to our comparison of binding in different models of slips, Dell et al. (1993) mentioned another movement error that suggests consonants move to form clusters similar to those in the original text. For example, *big glass* → *blig glass* is more likely than "*big lass* → *blig lass* suggesting that the moving /l/ 'knows' that it is part of a cluster" (p. 186) (namely *bl*). Again, a frame-slot model, based on categorizations and assembly rules, would suggest that a categorization such as "the word begins with a cluster" would exist independently from the segmentation of individual words. Indeed, the data suggest a kind of fixation may occur at a certain categorical abstraction (such as "the word begins with a cluster"). The flow of recognition is not just in a sequence of sounds and bottom-up, but involves neighboring words (other levels of segmentation) and recognized patterns in these segments.

The examples of sound substitution I have found in my own collection of slips, such as *egos* → *eagers*, suggests further that auditory-motor categorizations—not just words and letter clusters—may select letter sequences. Recall that I stated at the onset of this discussion that Dell et al.'s (1993) model is limited because it does not examine how sound patterns are generated. Put another way, Dell et al.'s emphasis on storage of a vocabulary misses the constructive aspect of sequencing occurring on several dimensions of categorization, which allows substitution and swapping across word boundaries. In general, the data suggest that a persistent influence from different sequential and sensorimotor organizers constrains local processing.

One of the most elegant demonstrations of the relation between learned patterns and the coordination process is Grudin's (1982) explanation of transpositions in typing. Grudin found that where letters were exchanged, the timing is nevertheless preserved until after the error occurs (Fig. 6.4). For example, in typing *and* as *adn*, the *d* is typed when *n* would normally occur and the *n* is typed when *d* would occur. A very nice particular example occurs in typing *Teh* instead of *The*—a transposition that occurs only when the *T* is capitalized. Here the right hand is effectively busy hitting the shift key: "This 'spatial dislocation' of the hand might result in the right index finger taking longer than usual to arrive in place to strike the h̲. The e̲, however, typed by the unaffected left hand, would be ready to go on schedule" (Grudin, 1982, p. 12). The timing is preserved: The letters are not only swapped, they are typed precisely when letters would be typed in a correct sequence.

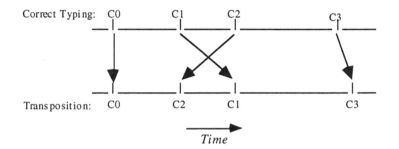

Fig. 6.4. "Timing Pattern in Transpositions" (from Grudin, 1982, p. 13; reprinted with permission). Transposed characters are designated as C1 and C2. Adjacent characters (perhaps spaces) are C0 and C3.

Such comparisons are possible because experienced typists develop characteristic timing patterns for typing familiar words, with different intervals between letters. Statistical analysis of 74 instances in one typist showed that the wrong letters are typed at the same time they appear in correct typing sequences, with a delay after the error. Grudin (1982) concluded that serial production is not fully distributed, such that output ordering is reconstructed on each trial from the competing activations of independent letters. Instead, a learned timing particular to sequences is preserved and in some sense controls the sensorimotor coordination: "There is some general timing pattern, and signals to strike keys are issued according to that pattern" (p. 20). The delay after an error may indicate the effect of coordinating a new (incorrect) sequence. Grudin used the term *central* to contrast with the fully distributed model, but he means "specific to the sequence being typed," not something like a metronome or global controller.

The claim that timing is learned and replicated is also apparent in the data reported by Gentner (1982) that professional typists produce familiar sequences faster than they produce double letters, which are the fastest sequences for beginners. However, with practice, parallel effects do appear to dominate. So although timing of two- and three-letter combinations recurs, the pattern is more dependent on surrounding context than specific to particular words (Gentner, 1981b). This does not mean that sequences are not being reconstructed. Rather, by maximizing preparatory overlap (fingers hover in anticipation), practice has sped up each learned word sequence, so that physical limits of the keyboard layout now dominate. For example, typing *bit* takes significantly longer than *wit* because of the movement required by the left index finger. Timings can thus be attributed to run-time constraints rather than idiosyncratic, learned patterns.

6.2.3 Evidence for Parallel-Hierarchical Activation

Rumelhart and Norman (1981) produced yet another detailed study and computer model. Typing timing and errors were for the most part successfully modeled by the activation of letter schemata, ordered by strings created by a perceptual (reading) process. That is, all timings and errors are generated at run time, not from replaying sequences. A pivotal consideration in the development of this model is the presence of doubling errors, which I have not yet discussed, for example typing *mpaaing* instead of *mapping*.[7] This suggests that repetition is a kind of motor schema, and the letters are types not tokens. A neural map corresponding to the letter *a* is reactivated, rather than there being two such maps (or a copy) in a sequence. That is, a type (such as the categorization of a letter) is reactivated instead of there being two physical copies (such as two maps representing a letter, or tokens). Furthermore, doubling errors suggest that the binding between the repetition schema and the letter schema to which it applies is weak and changeable.

Both transpositions and doubling errors suggest that practiced sequences are not activated and need not be performed in order. Instead, in Rumelhart and Norman's (1981) model, letters in a word are activated in parallel, with the initial letter having the strongest activation, and each letter inhibiting the activation of its successor until it is deactivated (Rumelhart & Norman, p. 12). This fits the idea that a sequence becomes a chunk by virtue of being categorized by a higher-order map, allowing all elements to be activated at once and providing a handle to the start (Fig. 6.5, cf. Fig. 1.6 and linked list representation, Fig. 2.5).

Fig. 6.5 shows four global mappings, with one subsuming three others that activate each other in sequence. The activation trace representation suggests that, rather than there being an inhibiting link from, say, A1 to A2, the relationships are inherently sequential (A1's incorporation in a sensorimotor

---

[7]This is my own slip. For some reason, I like Norman take particular pride in indicating which errors I produced by myself, perhaps because they embody the creativity and uniqueness emphasized by Hofstadter. Yet they are still mistakes!

coordination at run time activates A2). Nevertheless, both A1 and A2 are in a partial state of activation (allowing for ordering errors to occur) by virtue of the activation of the higher-order categorization of a word that subsumes them. The head (A1) and tail (A3) are perhaps more strongly activated or more often remembered (as in my *place de cathedral* example) for different reasons: The conceptual categorization directly activates, and thus sustains, the head and the tail is more recently activated.[8]

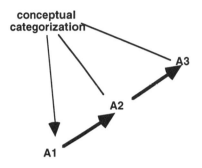

Fig. 6.5. A conceptualization categorizing an activation sequence, involving a possible "feed-forward" activation to the head of the sequence (A1), with couplings between the global map of the conceptual categorization and subsequent global map categorizations (A2, A3).

If a letter is doubled, does that same map appear twice in the sequence? If so, the map activates itself. This is perhaps acceptable if the higher-order categorization of the word strongly controls the sequential invocation of the

---

[8]Noting that an "internal representation of a goal occurs first" and then placing it at the end of a chain of action–events, Grossberg (1982) asked, "How can the goal representation occur both last and first?" (p. 502). He then presented an alternative hierarchical notation, with a plan node tied to action-events and asked, "What mechanism tells the plan which of the events came first, so that it will be able to perform them in a proper order?" (p. 504). Grossberg adopted a hybrid notation (p. 509), which resembles my Fig. 6.5. For Grossberg's "plan" node, I substitute a categorization of the sequence (which remains a chain), with direct activation to the head. That is, a categorized sequence is not a hierarchy itself, but a special kind of chain that can be partially activated as a whole and has a special "pointer" to the head. In this way, a conceptualized sequence can correspond to what we call a *goal*, be activated first, and activate the sequence. Indeed, Grossberg posed this hypothesis as the question, "Are adaptive coding (or chunking) and the learning of order information dual processes in a feedback system?" (p. 523). I do not know any more than Grossberg how this occurs neurally, but data indicate that the mechanism is something like this. In particular, experimental evidence (e.g., see Murdock, 1995) of the primacy effect ("the beginning of a list is best recalled" [p. 110]) and the recency effect ("the end of the list is next best") indicates that serial learning involves a special activation from the sequence categorization to the head.

individual letters, but by assumption each categorization in the sequence activates the next one in line. Indeed, this is a defining example for a theory of sequential activation (cf. Fig. 3.2). How is an infinite loop avoided? There are two obvious, interacting possibilities: First, a word with repeating letters could be typed by a direct "see and hit" higher-order coordination. Confronted by *maaaaaping*, you mark your way along, typing each letter as you see it. Alternatively, repetitions are consciously detected and the action is generalized—as suggested by Rumelhart and Norman, a *conceptualization of doubling* (Fig. 6.6) controls the sequence's production (corresponding to their repetition schema).[9] Because doubling is itself a categorization, delays in finger movement and activation noise (an important part of Rumelhart and Norman's model) may then cause the categorization to apply to an adjacent letter.

In practice, nearly all repetitions are doubles, and we come to recognize them; even triples can be recognized as a unit (e.g., in *maaaping* the repetition is by inspection conceived as a triple). Thus, to retain my claim that each categorization in a sequence activates the next, repeated letters in a word (itself conceptualized) must be chunked. Indeed, by introspection it appears impossible to learn a sequence such as *maaaaaping* without counting or composing the sequence in a cadence—*m-aa-aa-a-ping*. A necessary interpretation of my theory is that repetitions in a sequence cannot be learned without being coordinated with respect to a counting or rhythm-creating process.[10] This is difficult to check experimentally without turning off the chunking processes we routinely apply. Even a sequence of fewer than seven repetitions, which perhaps might be recalled by remaining activated (short-term memory), is prone to be counted or heard in rhythm (Kotovsky & Simon, 1973). Even if we can quickly repeat back a repeated sequence, we could not recoordinate such a sequence from memory (if my claim about sequential activation is correct) without categorizing repetitions in some way.[11] The idea that cadence (rhythmic stress)

---

[9]Just as most doubled letters appear normally within a word (not at the start), most doubling errors reported occur within the word.

[10]In effect, I adopt the mechanism in SRNs and Jordan Networks (vs. buffer models) of using "the same structures to represent identical events occurring at different time steps" (Cleeremans, 1993, p. 143). Consequently, generalization occurs to recognize longer embeddings than occurred in the training set. I am claiming that in people such repetition is not indefinite, but is itself categorized *as a repetition,* as in groupings in a cadence. That is, unlike SRNs, human sequence learning involves ongoing categorization of sequence patterns (chunking).

[11]In a related analysis, it can be shown that representing sequences as overlapping subsequences will fail to represent duplicating the same length as a sequence: "So a system, for example, which represented the spellings of words as sets of letter-*pairs* would not be able to represent the word *yoyo*, and even if the breadth were increased to three, the system would still not be able to represent words with duplicate triples such as *banana*" (Pollack, 1990, p. 80). These examples illustrate that the categorization of duplication may be essential and obviate the length restriction.

is a basic organizer is appealing because it is so obviously a physically felt and experienced process. Thus, a sensorimotor coordination serves to group categorizations so they may be conceptualized as units—precisely the kind of hierarchical architecture we might expect, both from evolutionary and developmental viewpoints.

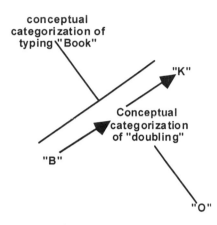

Fig. 6.6. Conceptualization of typing *book* represented as a sequence that includes a categorization of doubling, which is a sequence containing one perceptual detail, the letter *o*.

As shown in Fig. 6.6, categorizations of the three letters (*B, O, K*) and doubling are all activated, as in the Rumelhart–Norman model, but I claim that their relationships are reactivated in the conceptualization of this word (*book*), not just created from scratch by processing the perceptual output ("see and hit"). Correspondingly, the Rumelhart-Norman model does not account for capture errors (Greenville + Spartanburg → Spartanville), which requires incorporating a preexisting vocabulary (ville + Spartan) and letter cluster relationships. Also, Grudin's (1982) transposition data (where *e* is typed when *h* should occur in *The*) suggests that some memory is retained of previously typed sequences and their timings. Similarly, Mozer (1983) showed that letter migration errors require some kind of hierarchical structuring of memory, with parallel-activation and run-time resolution of constraints (as in Rumelhart & Norman's [1981] model).[12] Of course, Rumelhart and Norman (1981) were not opposed to a

---

[12]Mozer analyzed letter migration, which appears to be an effect of copying dominated by higher-order organizers and "spoonerisms," which are exchanges, as I have described here. Mozer emphasized that letters "move" as clusters (such as "Sparta" and "cus" in the Spartacus example). He rejected a bottom-up, staged model of feature registration and integration, demonstrating the importance of positional effects and parallel processing at the word level (Mozer, 1983). His subsequent connectionist model, BLIRNET (Mozer,

theory incorporating a memory; they merely sought to show how much could be accomplished without it (and how much performance was dominated by circumstantial, highly situation-specific constraints, such as key position).

In conclusion, the analysis of reading and typing errors supports the idea that memory is a hierarchy of categorizations, in which some categorizations are sequences, as depicted by the activation trace diagrams. Sequences are not merely replayed as orderings, but are physically reconstructed as a sensorimotor coordination in time (cf. Fig. 3.2). The resulting ordering and timing is the product of multiple constraints:

- Learned temporal sensorimotor patterns and "run time" orderings that compete as different levels are reconstructed in parallel.
- Sensory similarities (such as how words sound) cause new units to participate.
- Physical constraints (such as keyboard layout) produce circumstantial delays and inadvertent actions.

Similarly, Dell et al. (1993) concluded that there is a combined effect in how (speech) slips occur:

> The PDP [parallel distributed processing] model can be taken as a demonstration that sequential biases, similarity, and the structure of the vocabulary are powerful principles in explaining error patterns . . . . Phonological speech errors result from the simultaneous influence of all words stored in the system, in addition to the set of words in the intended utterance. (p. 188)

They stressed that the creativity produced at the syntactic level is so different from what is required for pronouncing single words that the SRN mechanism appears to be too simple to do the job. "There may be other effects best explained by structural knowledge that has been separated out from linguistic content" (p. 189).

In terms of neural activation, this "structural knowledge" would consist of sequences of recurrent letter combinations and sounds, plus conceptualization of segmentation and grouping (such as doubling and elision as in *j'ne*). Units are chunked on different levels to form words, which are activated on the basis of their inclusions (letter combinations and sounds) and what includes them (categorizations of meaning[13]). The assembly mechanism by which an utterance (whether heard, spoken, or written) is coordinated is constrained to preserve the *positional timing* and *number* of syllables, word boundaries, and sounds. But the multiple dimensions of organizers activate multiple sequences (multiple drafts) that occur in the vocabulary, allowing for movement and substitution that, under

---

1986) indicates that reading words may be modeled by 6,000 letter cluster units. Put another way, sequences of letters appear to be bound into clusters, which act as units that may be transposed, copied, substituted, and so on, in the recognition of words.

[13]Thus, one may type "Barbara, thanks" instead of the intended "Barbara, things are going well."

certain conditions of relaxation or fatigue, operate relatively independent of the conceptual organizers.

In this respect, the theory of coordination that I am proposing, which is based on sequential patterns of activation, incorporates the *discrete* characteristics of a frame model like Mitchell's (1993) Copycat, as well as the *vocabulary-based* patterns of Dell et al. and Mozer's (1986) connectionist models. That is, the patterns that occur are learned sequences, but *sequence entities* are competing and organizing substitutions and exchanges. Sequences are activated as units, suggesting that sequences are categorized and incorporated within other sequences. In this way, the *gos* and *gers* sequences are categorized similarly in coordination dominated by sound perception (just as the words Spartanburg and Spartanville are related). Furthermore, there is no need for assuming categories such as word-initial consonant—this is not the person's *knowledge*, but a binding and boundary effect inherent in how sequences are constructed at the neural level and reassembled. (For related discussion of the knowledge-mechanism distinction, see Table 7.1 and Table 12.2.)

A categorized sequence, such as sensorimotor coordination for typing a word, corresponds to the idea of a token in descriptive cognitive models, but it is a coordinated sensorimotor process, not a static thing (i.e., not like the symbols in conventional symbolic models) or a description that needs to be interpreted like a computer program. I call a particular categorized sequence the *conceptualization* of typing a particular word. Such neural organizations exist only temporally and within ongoing activity. By virtue of being categorizations, they function as discrete units that can be incorporated with some degree of flexibility in behavior sequences. The separability of timing (in Grudin's [1982] data) and doubling indicates that motoric patterns may become "abstracted" and operate relatively independently from conceptualized content—just as one may learn and apply a song's melody to different words. This separability, which must routinely be coordinated in practice, illustrates the general case in which serial experience is the product of multimodal conceptualization (e.g., visual, auditory, syntactic-linguistic, rhythmic).

Returning to our discussion at the start of this section, we have seen that although content and structure are relatively independent, this does not mean that processing is separate in the sense of serial or parallel-independent modules. We must be careful in using terms like *controlling, monitoring,* or *editorial process* to avoid suggesting a process of examining pieces created elsewhere and applying rules of transformation to produce an output stream, whether it is grammatical text, jazz improvisation, or a game. Dennett (1992) emphasized that there is no central place where things are coming together:

> Most important, the Multiple Drafts model avoids the tempting mistake of supposing that there must be a single narrative (the "final" or "published" draft, you might say) that is canonical—that is the actual stream of consciousness of the subject, whether or not the experimenter (or even the subject) has access to it. (p. 113)

For example, the *un bon café* example emphasizes that knowing "what happened" is itself ongoing and reconstructive. Elements may fade away or only be describable in abstract terms. The answer to "What did you experience?" may be a description that combines what we can now reconstruct and something else that failed to occur. In some sense, in my example a "draft" was constructed that incorporated *bon* as an adjective modifying *café*, but like words fading on the paper, all I now conceive is that "I know . . . the location of the Cathedral."

In particular, we realize again that an activation trace diagram is a descriptive representation, a story about experience. We must be aware that first, observed and experienced behavior is not all that is going on (other details and conceptualizations are vying for development), and there is no hard and fast logic for why a particular interactive flow forms. Indeed, the PDP model emphasizes distributed knowledge and processing, but what is really most distributed are constraints and physical influences. What we, as observers, view as conscious, deliberate experience is an emergent construction. The constructive process is an ongoing accomplishment, not a preordained or predetermined order, such as by templates or fixed rules in a program. There is no storyteller or master carpenter inside. A person's deliberate, intentional experience is always a balance between trying to get somewhere (a goal) and working with the materials that rise up, sometimes unbidden, in awareness.

6.3 NORMAN'S THEORY OF ACTION

The study of linguistic transformations we have considered is only part of a broader, well-known study of unintended actions, ranging from Freud's interpretations of subconscious wishes to analyses of tragic errors in operating complex machinery. A broader consideration of slips is highly instructive for comparing different neural architectures and reveals the advantages of a sequential activation and composition perspective. Here I will reformulate Norman's (1979) study, which is based on his own corpus of slips and Reason's (1979) data and model. Norman's and Reason's studies build on Miller, Galanter, and Pribram's (1960) feedback model of testing and correcting performance relative to planned behavior. The notion of levels and intention in Norman's model—as well as the catalog of errors—can be simplified and perhaps better explained by a mechanism of sequencing, substituting, and composing categories in time.

The most salient aspect of Norman's (1979) model, from the perspective of the present study of coordination, is the idea that action is organized by a process of decomposition from abstract specifications. Reflecting on the example of driving a car out of a parking lot, he said:

> Each level of specification of the intention must be decomposed into more basic
> levels in order for an action to take place, each new decomposition more finely
> dividing the actions required, more precisely specifying what must be done. And
> each new level of specification is, in turn, decomposed into its basic components

until some primitive level of act specification is reached. The scheme is *not* a hierarchy: it is a spawning of independent action systems, each complete with the possibility of feedback monitoring of its own performance. Each system is a schema, with the decomposition process being the activation of schemas, the feedback mechanism being the attempt to satisfy some of the internal conditions required for triggering (or the cessation of triggering) of the schema. (p. 23)

Although allowing for independent development and nonhierarchical organization, this architecture emphasizes top-down decomposition, relying on *conditions* for triggering schemas. The nature of these conditions is pivotal in the theory, producing explanations of "failure to trigger" and "loss of activation." Norman (1979) viewed a condition as being a *description* of features. For example, a *description error* is a slip that occurs when a "description of the desired act is insufficient" (p. 12). In this case, the conditions are ambiguous, leading to slips such as "replacing of a lid to the sugar container on the coffee cup...or throwing a soiled shirt into the toilet rather than the laundry basket" (p. 12). But such ambiguity is a problem for a reader or listener who is interpreting descriptions, not a mechanism that could be operating subconsciously. Can we drive the analysis to a neural level, rather than suggesting that slips are the constructive products of a deliberating, conscious person?

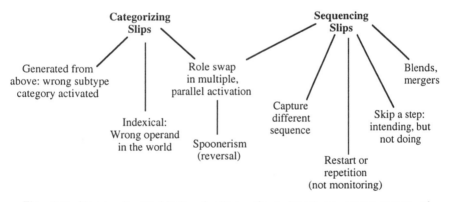

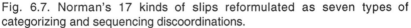

Fig. 6.7. Norman's 17 kinds of slips reformulated as seven types of categorizing and sequencing discoordinations.

Norman (1979) appropriately pointed out that the descriptive errors he illustrated involve "similarly shaped containers." Perceptual similarity is involved, not the interpretative ambiguity of meaning that the term *description* suggests. The mechanism is not a matter of deduction over descriptions, but a matter of *discoordination*. Viewed this way, we wonder how such errors of *incomplete description* are different from another category called *data driven*, such as putting a coin into the wrong (adjacent) vending machine. A better analysis can be given once we move from the idea of manipulating and inspecting subconscious descriptions of behavior to the problem of coordinating competing activations. Indeed, a strong claim can be made that all of the 17 errors cataloged by Norman can be reformulated as discoordination of categorizing and sequencing (Fig. 6.7). This analysis also attempts to unify what Norman called *slips* and *motor errors* rather than making a distinction between intellectual and physical skills.

The following examples illustrate this classification:

- *Generated from above:* "They have Chinee—Japa—Mexican food to go" (called "associative" by Norman; p. 12). Illustrates higher-order conceptualization activating categories that it subsumes.

- *Indexical:* Pouring orange juice into the coffee cup (description error). Illustrates perceptual coupling of "right categorization, wrong thing in the world." No mediating description occurs; if it did, the error would be less likely to occur.

- *Role swap:* "'I got my degree at Harvard and was a post-doc and faculty member at Penn.' (Exactly the reverse of the facts.)" (loss of activation; p. 16). Illustrates reordering of components activated in parallel when composing a sequence (exchanges). Typing transpositions occur at the letter level; Spoonerisms occur at the syllabic level.

- *Capture different sequence:* Counting pages at a copying machine: "'1, 2, 3, 4, 5, 6, 7, 8, 9, 10, Jack, Queen, King.' (I have been playing cards recently.)" (capture slips; p. 14). Illustrate elements of a sequence activating another sequence that includes them (Mozer's letter migration).

- *Restart or repetition:* "Engaging the starter of an automobile after it had already been started" (loss of activation or mode error; p. 17). Illustrates lack of closure of a sequence (inadequate strengthening of the subsuming conceptualization?).

- *Skip a step:* "Think of typing the special character that deletes the line...the '@' sign was only thought, not actually typed" (faulty triggering; p. 18). Illustrates conceptualization without motor activation of a subsumed component.

- *Blends and mergers:* Saying "financed by the Rockebrothers, un, the Rockefeller Brother's Foundation" (p. 18) and (my own example) "you two [people] could just swip" instead of *switch* or *swap*.

From the perspective of neural activation, all the slips in Norman's catalog now appear to be variations of "right category, wrong instance" and coordination of sequence activation. They are problems of activation within a compositional process. Some slips are categorical, in which a fitting thing in the world or other categorization is incorporated within an otherwise correctly accomplished sequence. We "capture" the wrong thing in the world (orange juice into coffee cup), the wrong subcategorization (kind of ethnic restaurant), or the wrong element in a series (swapping names of universities). Other slips appear to derive from "disattentive" sequencing, again within an otherwise correctly accomplished sequence. We "capture" another sequence with a similar head ("9, 10, J, Q . . ."), a completed subsequence (restarting the engine), a skipped subsequence (i.e., as if it had occurred), or a subsequent sequence too soon (such as the elisions in typing). In short, viewed from the perspective of categorization and sequencing, the many kinds of errors classified by the terms *association, triggering, mode, capture, intention,* and so on, appear to be just a few kinds of neural constructions based on *activation* and *inclusion.*

At the same time, my analysis highlights the unknown character of the coordinating mechanism that Norman (1979) also emphasized, namely the process of monitoring or feedback that keeps a sequence coordinated. How do we know that an error has occurred? Within the parallel, nonhierarchical process of activation, there is a constraining aspect that produces coherent sequences, such that higher-order conceptualization (intention) and similar categorizations are "appropriately" related. Although a form may be functionally a container and conveniently at hand, it must be the right container. Although a word (e.g., *Japanese*) may be functionally an ethnic-place-for-eating, it must be the place I was thinking of going to a moment ago. This conceptual coordination operates over time, to sustain a relation between our ongoing activity and things in the world. In conventional terms, this is the problem of *reference* or grounding between names and objects. By my reformulation, intentionality involves a coordination process that sustains conscious activity: An intention is an active conceptual relation between what we are manipulating, what we perceive, and how we are ordering behavior in time.

The data suggest that processes (neural map sequences) categorized as similar may substitute for one another. Part of paying attention to what we are doing is sustaining an activation and continuing to work with it. The data suggest that this is an effortful process, and over time we become tired by doing it. Here the physical character of cognition is salient.

To explain how we sustain coherence, most theories of action suppose some kind of feedback and monitoring mechanism. The coordination perspective suggests that we seek some constraining process at the neural level that is inherent in the compositional, constructive ordering in time, and reserve the secondary "watching" role for the person. That is, we want to distinguish between how a discrepancy arises at the neural level and a person's conscious perception and description of an error. For example, in typing errors we distinguish between the production of the typed sequence and what the person does in examining what was actually typed and in fixing the error. Specifically, I question the idea that "a different system must compare the intended word selection with that actually being uttered (or triggered for utterance)" (Norman, 1979, p. 23). The idea of "different levels for different purposes" (p. 23) claims that the architecture constructing coherent sequences has (at least) two distinct processors, one assembling and the other *comparing* and detecting errors. But as Edelman and others have emphasized (see Clancey, 1997c, chapter 3), there is nothing for the neural system to compare to; the constructions are all made "inline" out of components that worked together in the past.

Norman (1979) recognized that errors must be "detected within the action selection mechanism" (p. 22) or otherwise a complex process would be required to get back to the more abstract "intention" level. Nevertheless, he still envisioned a separate "feedback comparison process" that "looks at" the operation of the system in different ways. This still presupposes the separation of intention and action, mediated by a description of a plan, which specifies in propositional form what action is to occur. We need instead a notion of comparison that does not operate on descriptions, but is occurring inline, as part of the composing process itself, such that intending and acting are one process (excluding, of course, when the person does formulate a descriptive plan[14]).

The simplest assumption, again deriving from a physical coordination perspective, is that the newly composed sequence strengthens or reinforces the conceptualization that is organizing the sequence. Rather than comparing static things, the neural system need only detect novel constructions. The resulting composed sequence is not "wrong" per se; it is a new categorization or contains a new categorical component, where nothing new was sought. Rather than a feedback signal per se or a comparison against something held fixed (as in retrieval models of memory), a breakdown occurs in actively sustained sequencing—a new categorization develops that does not fit within the ongoing conceptualization. For this to occur there must be a certain resistance to accepting substitutions. A coffee cup must not be too readily taken to be an orange juice container. Another restaurant must not be too readily substituted for one recently conceived. This "fit" is not a personal or social judgment (such as understanding the norms of conversations about where to eat), but something structural and mechanical in the sense that a square peg does not fit into a round hole.

Furthermore, slips come to conscious attention—they are conceived as slips—because we have the capabilities to detect an inconsistency within the range of an organizer, stop what we are doing, hold active the ongoing construction, and categorically "reconstruct" what has happened (as in going back to try to find "Spartanville" in the paper). Consciousness is very much concerned with this ability to reconceive the process that guides behavior—indeed, to make an object of the conceptualization process itself. Furthermore, reconsideration cannot be arbitrary without leading to a discoordination in terms of our sustained identity in time. We will find that consciousness so understood is intricately related to the idea of "identity"—of having a sustained sense of WIDN (as mentioned in the discussion of Caitlin's playing, chapter 5). Thus, understanding the evolution and function of consciousness is related to understanding the nature of people as *personas*, that is, agents whose on-going, constructed categorization of WIDN has historical integrity. In terms of coordination, this means that categorizations are being

---

[14]Studies of dreaming (Clancey, in press) indicate that verbal conceptualizations may organize experience without being formulated as models of the world or plans.

activated consistently as recategorizations of sequences (conceptualizations) and not freely substituted or reordered in all ways that parallel neural activation allows.

For purposes of our present discussion, the presence, detection, and resolution of errors relies on several conceptual coordination capabilities:

- The ability to hold a conceptualization active.
- To form new categorizations as behavior proceeds (such as inappropriate similarities).
- To then formulate a new conceptualization that may be "held against" the intended one.

We may visualize this as two processes, one that is forming or guiding (e.g., a conceptualization of saying something) and the other that subsumes what actually occurred (e.g., what you actually said), both of which are now in some sense held active, such that a contradiction may be conceived. Viewed as cycles of behaving and reconceiving WIDN, the monitoring process is occurring in time, as a behavior, with previously active conceptualizations still active or able to be deliberately reactivated so they may be described and worked with. This is Bartlett's (1932/1977) notion of conscious reflection as "turning round upon its own 'schemata' and making them the objects of its reactions" (p. 202). The jarring experience of discoordination is "remembering" that "this is not the way it is supposed to happen."

In summary, we realize a failure has occurred because the (often perceptual) categorization of the present situation does not fit our ongoing conceptualization of WIDN. Given that each construction is a recoordination of many levels operating in parallel, the "feedback" that drives subsequent reflection and correction is just the detection that higher and lower categorizations (e.g., a word conceptualization and subsumed letter categorizations) or categorizations in different modalities (e.g. hearing and seeing) are out of joint. No reflective level or monitoring process is required. Rather, the persistence of activation in time of the different dimensions of a coordination allows the agent to *experience an incompatibility* between organizers that normally work together. This is an emotional experience, an attitude of surprise or being confused—the direct result of a physical incompatibility, not the result of a homunculus, meta-knowledge process that is waiting around for errors.

By virtue of being able to deliberately reactivate and hold components active as focus details, the person may then deliberately work with the original, earlier conceptualization (e.g., "reading the newspaper") and its components (e.g., words silently said and seen). The often-supposed reflective level in computer architectures, which does control perceptual-motor constructions in computer programs, corresponds to a person's later conceptualization of a discoordination and its aspects.[15] As Norman points out, slips are detectable as a matter of course, but mistakes, as in faulty reasoning, require a propositional *argument* to be developed. By my reformulation, slip detection comes for free because it is part of the automatic process of conceptual coordination.

Rather than an architecture operating through stages of intend, select, and act, which decompose an intention specification by selecting actions in a descriptively comparative way, categorizing and sequencing processes operate as co-constructors. Higher-order categorizations of sequences are held active over time and constrain lower constituents, but flexibly allow for bottom-up recategorizations of what is occurring. Consequently, what you expect does not rigidly prevent you from perceiving what you have actually done. The intention conceptualization is "constructed up" in activity as much as being "broken down" in preparation for action. Components are not triggered by descriptive conditions, but activated in-line, as part of next–next–next ordering and timing of behavioral units (compare Fig. 6.1 and Fig. 6.2). Categorizations subsume or are subsumed by other categorizations in a sequence, such that similar sound, appearance, function, and so on, allow substitution or inclusion. Sometimes this recategorization gives us a great new idea, sometimes it is just an incidental use of an available material, and sometimes it does not fit what we are doing.

The term *slip* is appropriate because the inclusion is always categorically right within the sequence; the error is that the inclusion may be early, redundant, tangential (as in Norman's playing cards example), or substitute an inappropriate instance (thing, place, event) in the world. Multiple higher-order conceptualizations may be operating, such that a substitution fits, that is, is appropriate with respect to our conception of our interactive behavior. However, the fit may be with respect to another relation we did not intend at the moment—allowing for a "Freudian" interpretation of the behavior. Blends and mergers reveal how the cause of action may be nonlinear and indeterminate, contrary to the intend–select–act model. Intention may be incoherent, yet still organize behavior in time.

In short, the conceptual coordination reformulation of monitoring only superficially fits the test-operate-test-exit (TOTE) cycle of Miller et al. (19??). Incongruity detection is the awareness of a discoordinated construction. Comparison and revision processes occur as reflective behavior in time, which is itself conceptually organized. Holding processes active so they can be described constitutes a kind of store, but labeled boxes such as "intention store" and "action store" in TOTE feedback models must not be taken literally (cf. Reason, 1977, p. 33). In short, an expectation or plan at the neural level is not a mediating description, but a previous categorization of a sequence (perhaps just recently constructed when conceiving a plan), which is coordinating behavior in time.

---

[15]Though, with practice, as in typing, reflection occurs in parallel with action and errors may be detected and fixed without mediating descriptions.

Although I have been generally critical of the control model on which Norman (1979) relied, his work on slips is distinguished for its concern with naturalistic data (behavior in the context of everyday life) and its attempt to relate cybernetic theory to schema models. He recognized that "the analysis of slips requires study of the intersection between the cognitive control system and the motor control system" (p. 19). My focus on physical coordination suggests that we strengthen this claim by viewing conceptualization as a sophisticated kind of motor control.

We have micro- and macro-coordinations that are both relatively fixed and emergent, depending on the circumstances. Through processes of learning inherent in coordination itself, we can reconstruct these sequences; they are multi-layered and the layers interact in a sometimes synchronous and sometimes asynchronous way. The emergence of the coordination depends largely on the relationship the agent has at the time with the environment. Sequences are "knitted" together to suit present demands. This perspective provides an insight that what we perceive to be behavioral "grammars" are really microsequences that emerge during the course of interplay between the agent and the environment. When attention lags or the physical relations of the body and the perceived environment allow, slips can occur.[16] From a cognitive psychologist's perspective, the take-home message is that speaking, reading, and typing are physical activities that are conceptually coordinated in time like pouring orange juice and driving a car. From the neurobiologist's perspective, these odd flups and slibs reveal how categories are forming, sequencing, and composing as neural map activations in time.

---

[16]This summary is based on a private communication from Joe Toth.

7

The Paintbrush Inventors: Analogy and Theorizing

The depths, the mysteries, of nature are nonrational. The business of reason is not to extinguish the fires which keep the vitality seething, nor yet to supply the ingredients which are in vital stir. Its task is to see that they boil to some purpose.

—John Dewey, *Character and Events*, 1929, p. 587

Qualities and characteristics may stimulate functional activities long before their precise nature is known.

—Sir Frederic C. Bartlett, *Remembering*, 1932/1977, p. 306

I have illustrated how behavior may be coordinated automatically—by neural processes of activation repetition, generalization, substitution, exchanges in a sequence, figure–ground mapping, and so on. Such processes help explain human experience of assigning meanings to a computer interface, progressive deepening in playful exploration and navigation, and slips in language production. In this chapter, I focus on the character and role of verbalization as a means of relating perceptual and conceptual categorizations. In this example, a group of inventors articulate and refine a causal theory of how a synthetic paintbrush works. This example extends the conceptual coordination perspective to include deliberate, model-based human inquiry. My analysis shows that rationalization is a means of knitting experiences together and directing subsequent perceptual-motor experience.

The discussion in this chapter relates different models of metaphorical reasoning and reconsiders the nature of storytelling in the context of making something. My thesis is that the capability of consciousness to hold multiple details active provides a *mechanism of coordination* that is extended in time. In effect, cognitive studies of problem solving have only described the flow and products of this mechanism, wrongly attributing aspects of conceptual thinking to subconscious perceptual processes and misconstruing the coupling of perception to conception as another form of interleaved inference.

7.1 INVENTING A SYNTHETIC PAINTBRUSH

In his critique of descriptive cognitive models of analogical reasoning, Schön (1979) analyzed an example of a group of people inventing a synthetic paintbrush.[1] At first, the synthetic brushes created by the design team do not spread paint properly. Perceiving gloppiness in the painted surface produced by the synthetic brush, the inventors use a natural hair brush again and again, looking for new ways of seeing how it works. Suddenly, a new contrast comes to their attention: They see that paint is flowing between the bristles. Perceiving the spaces as *channels*, someone proclaims, "A paintbrush is a kind of pump!" With this new orientation, they look again at painting: In what ways is this way of viewing the brush appropriate? They look again at their well-practiced use of a brush and observe that they vibrate a brush when they paint, causing the paint to flow. Finally, they develop a theory of "pumpoids" (is a cloth rag a kind of pump, too?) and relate their observations in a causal model of how flexible bristles allow vibrating, even flow, and hence smooth painting.

Schön argued that the invention of the synthetic paintbrush proceeded through several representational stages:

- *A similarity is conceived* in terms of the flowing of a liquid substance: "A paintbrush is a kind of pump." The old idea of a pump is used metaphorically to represent what a paintbrush is. Painting is put in the context of pumping.
- *New details are now perceived and described:* "Notions familiarly associated with pumping . . . project onto the painting situation, transforming their perception of pumping." Spaces are seen between the bristles ("channels"); bending the brush forces paint to flow between the channels (paint is not merely scraped off the bristles).
- *An explicit account of the similarity is articulated* as a "general theory of pumpoids," by which examples of pumps known previously are understood in a different way.

This development process occurs during "the concrete, sensory experience of using the brushes and feeling how the brushes worked with paint":

> At first they had only an unarticulated perception of similarity which they could express by doing the painting and inviting others to see it as they did, or by using terms like "squeezing" or "forcing" to convey the pumplike quality of the action.

---

[1]Unless otherwise indicated, all quotes in this section are from Schön (1979, pp. 258–260). Most of the text in this section and the next (with the exception of Fig. 7.1) has been reprinted and revised from Clancey (1997c), chapter 9, with the permission of Cambridge University Press.

Only later, and in an effort to account for their earlier perception of similarity, did they develop an explicit account of the similarity, an account which later still became part of a general theory of "pumpoid," according to which they could regard paintbrushes and pumps, along with washcloths and mops, as instances of a single technological category.

The contrast of the painters' experience with description-driven models of invention is stark:

- *New features are created, not supplied as data to be reasoned about or retrieved from previously constructed descriptions.* For example, spaces between the bristles were not even seen as things to be described until the pump metaphor developed.

- *Perceptual categorizing is not comparing,* although it may be constrained by a (deliberate) reasoning sequence. Perceptual similarity is not "detected" by searching and matching descriptions, as in inductive models of discovery, but by perceptually recategorizing the sensory field.

- *A metaphor is not "applied" or "mapped" as a fixed set of previously known features, but itself constructed to fit the circumstances.* New properties (e.g., channels, flowing) were attributed to pumps after the metaphor was conceived. What a pump is, is reconceived with respect to this example; it is not a general category that is just instantiated or matched against the situation.

- *A metaphor develops as a coupled perceptual–conceptual process, not sequential "interleaving" of modules.* Seeing the paintbrush as a pump is a parallel-dependent process, which is poorly modeled by co-processors (computer programs that mutually supply and consume data). Knowing what the situation is and categorizing it (as objects and events in a generalized causal story) develop together. "The situation" and "the metaphor" are not source and target (or givens and goals) that need to be only deductively related in a descriptive network. Previous ways of seeing and previous ways of talking are both changed by a coupling (simultaneous categorization) process.

Each of these ideas is examined in more detail when I compare different models of analogical reasoning. First, I would like to elucidate nonobvious aspects of the paintbrush invention process.

The first thing to notice is that new terminology is being invented as the theory of "pumpoids" is developed. Rather than being merely retrieved, matched, or assembled in some subconscious way, descriptions of the paintbrush and pump develop incrementally within the painters' inquiry: "The making of generative metaphor involves a developmental process. . . . To read the later model back into the beginning of the process would be to engage in a kind of historical revisionism" (p. 260). Unlike many psychological experiments, the conditions of the painting situation are not given, but represented–categorically

as perceptions and conceptions and as descriptions–by the participants
themselves as part of the inquiry process.

Crucially, the idea of what a pump is develops during the invention process:
"Both their perception of the phenomenon and the previous description of
pumping were transformed." This is an essential property of metaphorical
descriptions: In perceiving and saying that one thing, the paintbrush, is an
example of something else, a pump, we change both how we view paintbrushes
and how we view pumps. Thus, the metaphorical conception is *generative* of
both perceptual features and descriptions. Indeed, the painters' experience
indicates that the previously articulated features of these objects are
incommensurate at first; all they have is a sense of similarity (in the seeing) and
a sense of discord (in the saying). The new way of seeing and the tentative way
of talking arose together, but the painters do not yet have a descriptive model to
explain this relation.

A common view of scientific understanding is that creating a mental model
involves parsing perceptions in terms of theories. This is the idea that discovery
is driven top-down by a descriptive hypothesis, which allows recognizing and
relating data. This may fit certain aspects of scientific reasoning, but it does not
capture all aspects of discovery. To paraphrase Schön's analysis, experience of
similarity is not description based. Conceiving that a similarity *exists* (a
paintbrush is like a pump) precedes and forms the basis for describing what the
similarity is (the spaces between bristles are channels). Seeing-as (perceptual
categorization) and conceiving that you are seeing X as Y (a conceptual
categorization) precede the sequential, incremental process of descriptive
theorizing. You conceive relationships before you can articulate a model. You
do not speak by translating internal descriptions of what you are going to say.
But the effect does go the other way over time: Describing relationships in an
inquiry process (e.g., trying to create a causal story) constitutes a systematic way
of creating new conceptions.

The conditions that will give rise to articulations are tacit in past experience
because knowledge of pumping and painting includes perceptual-motor
coordinations. How these coordinations are related neurally is hardly understood
at all, yet it is the basis for our ability to synthesize experience. For example,
viewing painting as pumping generalizes previous processes that were active in
the experiences of talking about, seeing, and using pumps. I hypothesize that
different activities and ways of perceiving are correlated by the neural
mechanism of composing a sequence into a new conception of WIDN (as
constructions of sending two messages, Fig. 4.4, and hearing Spartanville when
seeing Spartanburg, Fig. 6.2).

The sense-making process maintains an ongoing conception of WIDN; it is
not just a process of manipulating descriptions of activities and objects, or
strictly driven by such verbal comparisons. The physical, sensorimotor
processes involved in describing, perceiving, and using pumps and paintbrushes
are reactivated and recoordinated. As the painters talk, where do the descriptions
of vibrating, pumps, and channels come from? Categories are generalized

(*channel* is applied to the almost invisible, flexible space between bristles), and new properties are tentatively claimed (the bristles are vibrating). This process bears some discussion to understand how it is different from the strict retrieval-indexing and matching model of most explanations of analogical reasoning.

7.2 COMPOSITIONS OF ACTIVITIES AND PERCEPTIONS

The painters' sense of similarity is an example of what is often called *tacit knowledge* (Polanyi, 1966), but this term can be misleading. On the one hand we have descriptions of knowledge (e.g., statements of belief, theories about pumps). On the other hand, we have active neural processes coordinating what we are doing and how we are perceiving the situation (what Schön called "knowing in action"). In this respect, knowledge as a capability to coordinate perception and action is always tacit or implicit. Descriptions are always explicit because they are consciously created and perceived. How interpreting (explicit) descriptions reorganizes (implicit) ways of seeing and talking is precisely what we now need to understand.

The paintbrush example is useful for understanding how coordination develops over time as part of a deliberate activity, which Dewey (1938) called *inquiry*, of developing a new conceptualization. How are ways of seeing and talking related? How does what we are doing influence what we see? Concepts are not merely applied, but transformed by the coordinations in which they are composed. The painters *change* the old concept of a pump, they do not merely apply it. Transferring a concept from one situation to another or using a metaphor is a matter of recategorizing and recoordinating relations, not merely mapping labels in a template. The terms *transfer, use*, and *apply* suggest a process of direct copying or instantiation that occurs in conventional programming (cf. Fig. 1.1), but is not what the brain is doing. As I indicated in the Spartanville example, representing the paintbrush example without building the outcome (the invention) into the beginning of the story requires moving from a top-down procedural control view to a bottom-up, perceptual activity view. Fig. 7.1 was my first attempt to visualize the paintbrush story in this way.

The interpretation of Fig. 7.1 is as follows: The designers are engaged in the process of painting. They are moving the brush, dipping it into the paint, paying attention to the result, and so forth. In the activity of using the synthetic brush, the painters see that the resulting surface is not how it normally appears: They perceive details of discontinuity and gloppiness. They go back to the natural hair brush and use it, now paying more attention to what the desirable effects are, when they are produced, and what corresponding events are experienced. They perceive the detail of vibrating the brush. Thus, routine activity comes to be described in a way that is relevant to the invention process, but has little or no role in everyday, practiced painting.

In Dewey's (1896/1981b) terms, the designers are not merely sensing patterns of light; they are engaged in the coordinated activity of looking to determine how painting happens. They are recoordinating how they usually look when they are painting. Such purposeful, exploratory transforming and reperceiving of materials exemplifies the transactional aspect of inquiry.

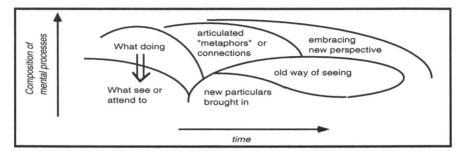

Fig. 7.1. Representation of changes in painters' perceptions and conceptions over time. New compositions coordinate ongoing activities, details of what is observed, old activities and ways of seeing, plus new and old ways of talking.

The painters are not (only) looking for previously named features; they are not merely searching the world to recognize a fit to previously created categories. They are also seeking a new way of seeing, which involves *recoordinating* what they are seeing (new categories) and how they talk about paintbrushes (new vocabulary). They do not know in descriptive terms what they are looking for; the properties they need to create an explanatory story have not yet been articulated and (in this case) will be new to the objects being investigated (cf. Dewey's distinction cited in the preface between objects/events and propositions). In this deliberate process of reperception, the familiar becomes strange as new particulars are brought in. For example, *vibrating* was not a description that was part of the professional procedure of how to paint, just as *channels* was plausibly never part of their description of properties of brushes. *Vibrating* and *channels* are in the general vocabulary of the painters, but are reconceived in the context of inquiring why undesired effects occur. Looking is directed by the conception of inquiry itself, "How, other than the conventional ways, might I see what the brush is doing?"—a complex *contextual constraint* for organizing perception (cf. Jackendoff, 1987).

Perceptual details that are noticed over time are given meaning by describing what is happening (e.g., "vibrating the brush is pumping" subsumes the detail that bristles are curved).[2] Thus the meaning of the perceptual experience is a

---

[2]Note that I might have said: "given meaning by statements that represent what is happening." This phrasing is more common, but shifts from viewing describing as coupled perceiving–conceiving–description creating to locating meaning in statements.

relation between details, metaphoric conceptions, and verbal explanations. The verbalizing process creates a conceptualization that holds active disparate experiences. These experiences were originally associated by only a superficial perceiving-as coupling (of image, sound, gesture, odor, and so on). With the disparate details now subsumed (in a still unarticulated categorization), a more abstract conceptualization can be constructed that relates to still other pumping experiences, a *theory* of pumpoids.

Dewey (1938) described how perceptions and theoretical concepts are intricately linked in time:

> Perceptual and conceptual materials are instituted in functional correlativity with each other, in such a manner that the former locates and describes the problem while the latter represents a possible method of solution. Both are determinations in and by inquiry of the original problematic situation whose pervasive quality controls their institution and their contents. . . . As distinctions they represent logical divisions of labor. . . . The idea or meaning when developed in discourse directs the activities which, when executed, provide needed evidential material. (pp. 111–112)

The "original problematic situation" is the sense of discord (and despondency) on seeing gloppy paint on the wall. The breakdown in prior coordinations of seeing and doing (how paint should flow as the brush moves along the wall) drives the painters' looking, conceptualizing, and subsequent theorizing. New ways of seeing and describing, "developed in discourse," direct subsequent physical experiments and talk. Now, in feedback (or what Schön called *back talk),* the new stuff on the wall stimulates further ways of seeing and talking about experience, provoking commentary about the meaning of what is seen and heard ("needed evidential material"). Fig. 7.2 illustrates this feedback relation. This diagram represents the effortful experience of acting, hearing-seeing-smelling, and doing that occurs when making bread, drawing something, playing music, writing, and so on.

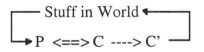

Fig. 7.2. Coupling, inference, and feedback in transactional processes. Changing stuff in the world during inquiry to see its properties and looking in new ways changes what we perceive; perceived similarity shifts to a different domain (P ⇔ C, where ⇔ demotes a subconscious, neural coupling relation); general ways of coordinating the inquiry may lead to hypotheses about causal relations or decisions about things to try next (C → C', where → denotes a conscious inference).

The more common working makes description manipulation appear to be the only mechanism and conflates different kinds of internal categorization with statements.

Working with the new particulars (the spaces, the flow, the vibration), the painters develop the metaphor of a pump. The painters recoordinate their seeing, doing, and talking so that the process of painting is conceptually like the process of pumping. Certainly, saying things like "flow" and "forcing the liquid" is part of this correlation of activities. Again, however, the description-matching model of analogy comprehension is incomplete. Remembering is itself a transformation of previous experience. The currently active details transform and generalize what pumping means.

Schön summarized why the reconstruction and generalization of past experience are inadequately modeled by a mechanism based on manipulation of descriptions alone:

> [T]he two descriptions resisted mapping. It was only after elements and relations of the brush and the painting had been regrouped and renamed (spaces between bristles made into foreground elements and called "channels," for example) that the paintbrush could be seen as a pump.

This regrouping involves a perceptual recategorization (a figure–ground shift in seeing channels) and a conceptual recoordination that subsumes and hence transforms painting, as well as the old way of seeing pumps. The old way of seeing pumps influenced what the painters were seeing and how they were talking before anyone thought to talk about pumps ("the researchers were able to see painting as similar to pumping before they were able to say 'similar to what'"). This is the essential shortcoming of descriptive cognitive models: "Knowledge in action may often be that which an individual knows how to do but cannot yet say" (Bamberger & Schön, 1991).

Put another way, the painters experience similarity, but do not at first notice similarities. This experience of similarity might be explained in descriptive models in terms of a subconscious discovery of a match, which is later translated into speech. My claim is that this match is sometimes a perceptual reconfiguration and may involve relating new, generalized conceptual categorizations not previously attributed to the objects in question. The coupling categorization is experienced as similarity.

The statement, "a paintbrush is a kind of pump" makes concrete the sense that there is something familiar here, and thus makes an explicit, overarching connection between painting (what the painters are doing) and previous ways of seeing and talking about pumps (middle of diagram). Salient details about painting and pumps (articulated as *channels*) are the basis of the new composition. Again, this composition is not a description, but a conceptualized activity that incorporates a way of seeing.

Finally, with talking about pumps now incorporated in the painters' activity, they look again at the natural and synthetic brushes, the painting process, and the resultant surfaces. Now they notice how the flexibility of the bristles (the angles of bending) affect how the channels are compressed, and hence how the liquid is forced out. This leads to the goal of smoothing the bending angle by changing the construction of the synthetic brush. The embracing new perspective of what a pump is, which includes washcloths and mops, helps guide their further activity as they go back and consider freshly how pumping works.

In summary, the conventional characterization of the invention process as relating descriptions of data and explanatory hypotheses that are independently preexisting and need only to be linked via a mapping process fails to capture or explain a wide variety of phenomena in human experience:

- How and why new perceptual features are constructed and new properties attributed to materials.
- How physical coordinations are coupled to ways of perceiving and talking.
- How subsequent theorizing requires realizing (conceiving) that you are seeing something *as* something else; that is, categorizing categorizations as "events I experience" objectifies experience by constructing an I–world–subject–object higher-order relation (the idea that a categorization is subjective, that an understanding can be objectively wrong).
- How theorizing requires categorizing talk as being about something; that is, categorizing a conceptualization as *referring to* other categorizations, as "being about" them, makes the talk a description of experience: "My talk is about *that!*"
- How the brain holds disparate conceptualizations active so that noncoupled aspects can be related; that is, the categorizations I am holding active (*"that"* stuff in the world that I have experienced and am referring to) function as symbols in inferential associations (*"vibrating* forces the *liquid* to . . . ").
- How inferential, verbal categorization in descriptive modeling (such as causal talk about pumpoids) constructs a unifying conception that itself remains tacit.

Of course, the invention process can be informally described (as I have talked about it here) or modeled in computer programs (what Hofstadter, 1995b, calls the frozen caricatures of structure-mapping engines). But naturally occurring human invention involves feedback and coupling on different levels of neural, physical, and social interaction. In particular, we have only the vaguest understanding of the ongoing, multitracked, multimodal neural process that is reactivating and recomposing the painters' previous perceptions and actions as they paint, look, listen, and speak.

7.3 ACTIVATION TRACE REPRESENTATION OF THE PAINTERS' EXPERIENCE

Applying the activation trace perspective to this example, Fig. 7.3 represents the painter story as a conceptually coordinated sequence of perceptions and actions.

In Bartlett's (1932/1977) terminology, the main diagonal represents the "main stream of interest." Perceptions in the form of details come in from the side. Each composition recharacterizes WIDN, recoordinating what I am doing and perceiving.

This notation has the advantage of showing the sequence in which details are perceived and described. As we have seen in other examples, details arise through either deliberately looking to see if there is anything interesting (and this is not strictly matching or filtering) or by an automatic process of noticing something (e.g., being surprised). As in the example of sending two messages (chapter 4), we find that perceptual reorganizations may involve transforming or incorporating the ground into a figure. The conventional figure (bristles) becomes ground for another figure (bristles become walls for channels). The sequential perspective emphasizes that perceptual details (such as seeing liquid flowing between the bristles) play a crucial role in the development of a generative metaphor (the paintbrush is like a pump). The sense of similarity arises because of a perceptual correlation between the bristle space and channels previously seen. Perceiving bristles in this way is coupled to generalizing what a channel is. That is, the reperception and the reconceptualization arise together (P ⇔C in Fig. 7.2).

Further, as Fig. 7.1 aims to show, the conception of the activity changes over time, broadening to incorporate new details and their interpretations. This broadening is a kind of generalization process by which sequential conceptualizations are coupled (C⇔C'). For example, conceiving that the "vibrating brush is pumping" elaborates and hence generalizes the realization that "a paintbrush is a kind of pump" by virtue of incorporating what becomes a causal detail, "bristles are curved." That is, besides the idea expressed by Vygotsky (the opening quote of chapter 1) that every thought is a generalization, I am suggesting that sequential analysis shows that a thought tends to broaden and elaborate the immediately previous thought. This perspective on conceptual development emphasizes the (temporal) activation relation of categories and not just the structural aspects of the final product. For example, a purely structural analysis would suggest that the painters are looking for evidence of a causal hypothesis that a paintbrush is a kind of pump. A temporal analysis leads us to focus on the order in which ideas are formed, and how thus new ways of perceiving and thinking can develop at all. In this case, a figure–ground shift in the perceptual field is evidently pivotal in the development of a new way of conceiving painting.

Fig. 7.3 represents the coordinations of one person.[3] For present purposes, I assume there is a member of the design team whose experience strongly

---

[3]Nodes in activation trace diagrams have now been used to represent opening an e-mail window, placing hands on the rim of a swimming pool, letters in words, and now causal explanations. It may appear that I am using a single notation, which after all is supposed to have some relation to neural processes, for wildly different levels of categorization and action. First, using a single notation for many levels of analysis is not

paralleled the description given by Schön. This is not necessarily true. Indeed, because of the distributed, collaborative process of the invention, individuals must be capable of such a coordination process for incorporating the claims uttered by others in the group within ongoing individual experience. Thus, even if there were several individual contributions, each person following along must look at similar details (perhaps after they are pointed out) and conceive the same shift in how paintbrushes are viewed (although it is easy to suppose that some members of the team could find the analogy obscure and jump directly to reconsideration of the bristle material).

In particular, I want to distinguish between the experience of the person who first conceived the metaphor and the experience of the team on hearing his description. Schön said that the metaphor led the researchers to project notions of the pump onto the painting situation, and only then did they view the spaces as channels. This is evidently true for most members of the team, but, according to the theory of metaphor I am developing here, the creator of the metaphor might have perceived a detail first and stated the metaphor before being able to articulate what he was seeing. It is quite true that the metaphor once articulated generates new perceptions. But there must be some correlation process—not feature matching—that underlies the first experience of similarity.

The idea of "seeing as," pivotal to this example, is essentially what Gestalt theorists called the *Höffding step*. According to Wertheimer (1985), the Höffding step is the phenomenon in human behavior of recognizing a new situation as similar to one you have encountered before, so a particular kind of solution applies. Without this step, one must assume that a blind search occurs, requiring description and matching against problem schemas, as in a descriptive cognitive model of analogical reasoning. People experience instead a more immediate recognition, in which relations are grasped as a whole, from which parts can be articulated. This is the basis of analogical reasoning in people:

> Transfer of a solution for a familiar problem (A) to a new problem (A') can occur only if the problem solver is capable of seeing the similarity between the two. Recognition of this similarity is the crucial step, the Höffding step, that makes transfer possible. It is a step that requires insight into the applicability of the old

---

unusual in cognitive science; for example, hierarchies have been used to represent relations between neurons (Grossberg, 1982, p. 503, 522), arbitrary concepts (e.g., Minsky's [1977] frame theory), tasks, procedures, and domains of knowledge. Second, I am specifically claiming that certain kinds of behavior that conventionally are shown as hierarchically controlled in a copying or instantiation process may develop and be sequentially constructed through perceptual-conceptual coupling. In some cases these sequences are subconsciously related (as in typing); in other cases they are paths of deliberate conceptual development, marked by ongoing reframing of WIDN (as in the present example of the paintbrush inventors). The nodes in activation trace diagrams represent different kinds of categorizations. Within a given diagram the level of analysis must be the same (as is also true in hierarchical analyses); see the discussion of problem space formation in section 12.3.

solution approach to the new problem, that is, insight into the structural but not superficial similarity of the new problem and the old problem whose solution is already understood. The crucial step in insight or understanding is knowing what solution strategy to try; thereafter, application of the particular strategy is relatively trivial. (p. 24)

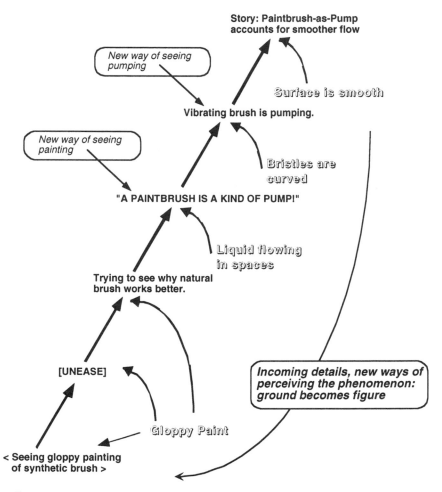

Fig. 7.3. Interactive activation relations for paintbrush invention. Perceptual constructions, influenced by the currently active way of coordinating perception and action, are incorporated with respect to conceptual generalizations of "what I am doing now." Time proceeds from left to right.

This analysis "recognizes the primacy of the whole and its decisive role in articulating the parts." That is, a relation is grasped that defines the new situation and the old way of seeing with respect to each other. The meaning of the new situation is seen through the old understanding, and this occurs as one, integral coupling process, as one experience, which we call *insight* (which I denote by ⇔ in contrast with inference,→).

7.4 ALTERNATIVE MODELS OF ANALOGICAL THOUGHT

Schön's paper, which first appeared in a seminal volume about metaphor in 1979, was a direct response to prevalent descriptive cognitive models. Most computer models had omitted the perceptual aspect of forming analogies, or modeled perception as a process of manipulating descriptions. At about the same time, Hofstadter (1995a) and his students began developing new computer models, based on the idea that "analogy-making is closely related to perception and should be modeled with techniques inspired by models of perception" (p. 286). Their central example is the Copycat program, which I described in the last chapter. Here I consider how the paintbrush inventors' example bears on the debate about analogy programs. I conclude that most computer models to date omit key elements of human experience:

- Materials are reperceived as they are reorganized in the world (Fig. 7.2).
- Perception is coupled to conceptualization within a coordination process; "mapping" the analogy in stages occurs only over *cycles* of conscious action and reperception.
- Forming and comprehending analogies are interleaved in scientific and engineering practice; in contrast, examples presented as puzzles or classroom exercises tend to separate these processes into something created whole and something given whole, viewing comprehension as a kind of digestive process and disguising its creative aspect.

To begin the analysis, consider Hofstadter's (1995a) summary of the "fluid concepts" approach:

Very few (if any) other computer models focus, as Copycat does, on the construction of representation for source and target situations, and on how this construction interacts with the mapping process. Few (if any) other models attempt to deal with the question of how new, previously unincluded concepts can be brought in and can come to be seen as relevant, in response to pressures that emerge as processing proceeds. In short, no other computer model of analogy-making of which we are aware attempts, as Copycat does, to integrate high-level perception, concepts, and conceptual slippage (p. 275)

The first criticism Hofstadter raised is that other computer models presuppose that descriptions already exist of a source and target, and these need only to be mapped onto each other. This is essentially Schön's claim that theories of analogy work with the *product* and engage in historical revisionism, rather than beginning with inarticulate, perceptual experience of similarity. By supposing that the world comes pre-described, such models fail to explain how cognition

cuts up the world in the first place, as Hofstadter (1995b) explained in his
critique of work by Holyoak and Thagard (1994):

> They do not seem to realize the hugeness of the gulf between a full situation as a
> human perceives it—having no sharp boundaries, woven intricately into the fabric
> of one's knowledge and life experiences—and a handful of predicate calculus
> formulas . . . .
>
> They constantly refer to "the objects," "the attributes," "the relations," and "the
> higher-level predicates" in situations, as if distilling Hamlet or World War II into
> two dozen lines of predicate calculus were a mechanical task not meriting
> discussion in a book on analogy. (p. 76)

In Holyoak and Thagard's (1994) work, analogies are found between stories.
Even here, where text is necessarily the starting point, Hofstadter (1995b)
objected that the conceptual process of grasping a story's gist has been ignored:
"Getting from the story to the story's gist, something that occurs swiftly yet
almost invisibly in a human mind, is as central a mystery of cognitive science as
any that exists" (p. 76). Similarly, he said that SME ("structure mapping
engine"; Falkenhainer, Forbus, & Gentner, 1990), a well-known program based
on Gentner's theory of analogy, deals "only with the end result of a mapping
while leaving aside the problem of how situations become understood and how
this process interacts with the mapping process" and hence "leaves out some of
the most important aspects of how analogies are made" (Hofstadter, 1995b, p.
285). In summary, the criticism is that conventional models do not explain how
descriptions are ever generated (except from other descriptions) or how new
perceptual features are created. Descriptive cognitive models suppose that
experience of similarity is only and inherently a verbal phenomenon.

Morrison and Dietrich (1995) have formulated an appealing response to this
criticism: "SME explains what is happening *in the comprehension of* an analogy
. . . it is not being proposed as a model of discovery through analogy" (p. 680).
They argued that "analogy comprehension might be separated from analogy
production" (p. 680). This is partially true, for in Schön's example there is a
difference between the process of conceiving the paintbrush-as-pump analogy
and understanding what "A paintbrush is a kind of pump" might mean.

But Morrison and Dietrich's analysis (like most of the work on analogy)
leaves out what happens *in practice* as analogies are formed in the service of
some larger activity. For example, given the pump analogy, other painters were
able to reperceive the painting situation and reconceive the mechanism of bristle
movement as pumping. Understanding the pumping metaphor within the inquiry
of inventing a new paintbrush required perceptual figure–ground
recategorization, not just mapping between descriptions. Secondarily, the
painters had to develop a new causal theory of painting, not just map two old
theories (of painting and pumping) onto each other. This is the generative aspect
emphasized by Schön. Indeed, Schön talked about metaphor and not just
similitude, because as a metaphor the paintbrush-as-pump conception is a way
of recoordinating seeing, acting, and theorizing. It is not just a static mapping in

a kind of isolated analogy puzzle: "Paint is to bristles as liquid is to what?" As nearly as I can tell, the entire cognitive science approach to date, including Copycat and the research Schön criticized, leaves out the function of comprehending analogies in the practice of sensing and *making something*—it's not just a puzzle to solve in a newspaper or a question to answer in a test.

Forming analogies is not staged into producing and comprehending, and may be distributed in a group of people over time. Morrison and Dietrich's (1995) analysis supposes that one person first produces an analogy whole, and then that person or others apply it. What if the analogy develops in inquiry (Dewey's term), as aspects of a situation (gloppy paint, vibrating, stiff bristles) are reperceived over time, while people are articulating aspects of an analogy and indeed formulating causal explanations (channels, flow, forcing liquid, pumping)? Then some people are comprehending what others are saying, and some people are off by themselves trying different brushes and getting new insights for developing the analogy. In short, producing, comprehending, and applying analogies in practice may be interleaved, as well as distributed in time in the group. The examples of analogy comprehension as well as the playful games of Copycat and its ilk are idealized models of both production and understanding—like a school test—not plausible models of how analogies develop and are conveyed in human activity.

Evaluating computer models is notoriously difficult. We must be especially careful about what is a placeholder descriptive abstraction or simplification and what is put forth as the mechanism. In the literature, we find researchers who work on letter puzzles criticizing research on story comprehension as being shallow, wooden, rigid, and so forth. Is not a puzzle more shallow and trivial a task? Here I consider some of the important dimensions for sorting out the debate and respective contributions.

Copycat operates in a "toy domain" and it operates on presupplied elements (letters and predicates), but its scientific purpose is to formulate a general mechanism of neural processes. Hofstadter's scientific claim is that the perceptual-conceptual slippage process Copycat models also operates in more complex situations involving comprehension and invention (as the paintbrush story illustrates). Thus the argument that the "domain" of letter play is too small and simple is irrelevant, if indeed the same mechanism is involved in broader activities.

A recurrent criticism bantered back and forth is that one program or the other only operates on handcrafted representations. This argument becomes confused when researchers view all representations in the brain as being descriptions. Thus, if a program generates new descriptions from old descriptions, it is claimed to be automatically generating representations. But as Schön and Hofstadter emphasized, these models are ignoring how descriptions are created in the first place from previously unarticulated perceptual and conceptual relations. We are back to the fundamental criticism I have made throughout, that descriptive cognitive models ignore the multimodal, physical coordination aspect of conceptualization and instead reduce all experience, knowledge, and thought to words. This is most obvious in programs that automatically generate descriptions from input graphics (Larkin & Simon, 1987). Rather than demonstrating that a program can operate on nonverbal input, they model perception as mapping from descriptions *onto* images—a historical revisionism that equates internal, subconscious processes with interactive behavior in time.

Although Copycat begins to address the perceptual-conceptual dimension, the model is unrealistic by separating learning from analogy formation. The set of predicates in Copycat are hard-wired and cannot be changed by the program (Forbus, personal communication, 1995). Therefore, such a model cannot in itself explain how the conceptions of painting and pumping were both changed by virtue of forming an analogy between them. As I described, the process of seeing one concept as another is a process of generalization. The concepts become coupled, so they are mutually defined. Structure mapping theory certainly begins to address how the two domains become interleaved, especially by focusing on how relations are related (such as the flow relation between liquid and channels in the painting and pumping domains). What is missing from the structure-mapping model is how a perceptual correlation can be the basis of a new conceptualization (which in the paintbrush example subsumes the previous ways of conceiving painting and pumping; Fig. 7.1). By leaving out perception, as Hofstadter (1995b) noted, a fundamental mechanism of analogy formation has been only described and not replicated.

The best-developed mechanistic aspect of Hofstadter's theory (which I summarized in chapter 6) is the temporal aspect of activation and competition in dynamic perceptual processes. The figure–ground shift in viewing bristles is a good example of such dynamic regrouping. Copycat and related models model the psychological process by which competing, incommensurate possibilities "pop to mind" with different activation strengths (not all at once), and some are generated only after others do not fit (cf. Fig. 1.7). Again, in the paintbrush story, it is important that the idea of pumping was part of the set of ideas that the painters started with. But the idea of pumping only became salient within the physical behavior of moving the brush and seeing liquid flowing.

Table 7.1

Comparison of Theories of Analogy

Researcher	Schön Bamberger	Hofstadter Mitchell	Holyoak Thagard	Falken- hainer Forbus Gentner
Domain	Invention of physical tool (paintbrush)	Word puzzles	Complex historical and literary analogies	Understanding scientific (causal) models
Input given to subjects	Sensation	Perceptual categories (letters) and word (letter-string) concepts	Descriptive models of objects and events	Perceptual, conceptual, verbal
Behavior studied	Relation between perception, conception, and theory of painting	How new words come to mind; temporal aspect of activation and competition in "dynamic perceptual processes"	Causal explanation of event histories	Compre-hension of analogy
Mechanism attributed	Coupling process mutually constrains visual figures, conceptual generalization and talk	Integrated high-level perception, concepts, and conceptual slippage	Use of abstract causal schemas to relate incidents in different domains	Different conceptual domains are interleaved by structure mapping
What theory handles especially well	$P \Leftrightarrow C$ Coupling between perception and conception	$C \Leftrightarrow C$ Coupling between conceptions	$C \rightarrow C'$ Inference using descriptive models	$C \rightarrow C'$ Inference using descriptive models
Explanatory limitations	No neural theory; why is story construction pivotal?	Omits learning inherent in analogy formation; no evaluative context	No perceptual aspect, all verbal reasoning	No difference between perceptual and conceptual mechanisms, No coupling

7.5 IMPORTANCE OF LEARNING AND ACTIVITY CONTEXT

Without addressing learning, none of these programs (Table 7.1) can address the pragmatics of analogy formation in practice. Although Hofstadter emphasized that Copycat models what concepts mean (e.g., Copycat can generate as well as recognize examples of "successor"), the program does not model the situations and activity in which analogy formation occurs. Thus, the researchers have ignored the practical context for forming and using appropriate analogies. Without an evaluative component, the process of forming analogies is arbitrary. Even if analogy formation is treated as a kind of entertainment, the social aspects of play need to be considered. I explain these aspects of learning and context in more detail.

First, Hofstadter (1995b) noted that Holyoak and Thagard (1994) "point out that Copycat lacks a pragmatic unit, as if this were a glaring defect. But our philosophy was not to tell our program what mattered in a situation; it was, rather, to let the program itself figure that out" (pp. 283–284). The issue is not merely that of predescribing situations (a weakness of SME at all levels and Copycat at the perceptual level), but the functional aspect of conceptualization (which none of the models acknowledges at all). Hofstadter was right that Holyoak and Thagard's model predescribes pragmatic interests of certain situations, but he ignored that his own model, Copycat, has no understanding at all of what situations are in a human cognitive sense. Copycat has no activity as a social actor and no identity or relation to other actors. Copycat's analogies have no purpose.

Contrast Copycat with Hofstadter's (1995a) and Mitchell's (1993) own understanding of analogies. For them, analogy puzzles are a form of intellectual play and amusement. Analogy-making constitutes part of Hofstadter's sense of himself as (previously) a *Scientific American* columnist, trade book author, and AI researcher promoting such microworlds for enjoyment as well as scientific value.

Thus, the Copycat model of "what matters in a situation" is significantly impoverished relative to human experience. Copycat does not figure out what matters, in the sense of what analogies are *valuable within an activity,* for it has no conception of its own activity. Answers to puzzles like "aabc => aabd; ijkk => ?" cannot be evaluated in the same way we usually resolve scientific or engineering problems. The puzzle's answer has no impact on the program's interaction in the world. Indeed, for Hofstadter and others, the personal psychological experience of working with a puzzle informs the developing theory of slippage. Theory formation as an AI researcher is part of the "situation" for doing such puzzles and Copycat has no understanding of that. Hence Copycat's lack of self-awareness is not just in the basics of how to avoid getting stuck, but as a participant in science.[4] So when Hofstadter said "hjkk" is the best answer according to many people, but I come up with "ikkk," all we can fall back on for evaluation is the aesthetic-emotional experience of our surprise at such a "weird" response. Then we move on to what really matters in this situation—our theorizing and understanding of the nature of representing, problem solving, analogy, and so on—an activity in which Copycat does not participate.

In summary, in replying to Holyoak and Thagard (1994), Hofstadter (1995b) focused on the difference between static (presupplied) and dynamic (emergent) models of what is important to the program. However, because letter play is a toy world, there is no importance in the usual social and pragmatic context of science and engineering. One might say that Holyoak and Thagard helped us understand the social-pragmatic *content* (which they descriptively build in), whereas Hofstadter helped us understand the *neural mechanism* of how ideas come to attention and are dynamically related.

To address the issue of learning in somewhat more detail, consider Hofstadter's (1995a) claim that "mechanisms for deciding which things to concentrate on and which mappings to make involve semantics" (p. 281). That is, his research program addresses the nature of concepts from the perspective of what understanding is and how it is inseparable from issues like what to concentrate on and what mappings to make. In contrast, the model elements in other analogy programs, which other researchers describe as real-world in comparison with his "toy examples," appear to be inadequate representations of concepts:

> These programs are purported to make very high-level analogies involving the concepts heat and water, and yet ironically, the programs have absolutely no sense of the meaning of heat and water; that is, the much more fundamental ability to recognize instances of these categories is completely absent from the programs. (p. 289)

As Hofstadter noted, his argument has been raised often, and resolving this problem is central to his alternative approach.[5]

Forbus, Gentner, Markman, and Ferguson (1998) responded to Hofstadter's criticism in another paper, "Analogy looks just like high level perception: why a domain-general approach to analogical mapping is right." Here are key points where I believe they misunderstand the other point of view:

- "The structure-mapping algorithm embodied in SME approach can capture significant aspects of the psychological processing of analogy" (p. 232-233). As a descriptive model, the algorithm may fit, but this is not

---

[4]Compare with Hofstadter's (1995a) discussion on p. 309; see also my related analysis of Cohen as an artist versus the Aaron program in chapter 1 of Clancey (1997c).

[5]I describe these issues in Part 1 of Clancey (1997c).

the mechanism by which perceptual and conceptual categories are formed and related.

- "The processes that build representations are interleaved with the processes that use them" (p. 234). Coupling between perception and conception is not the same as interleaving of computer processes; coupling is a mechanism of *simultaneous codetermination*, not sequential co-processing.

- Referring to the visual analogy posed by Fig. 1.8, "When compared with the four-pronged creature, the hypothesis that the creature [with three prongs and a bump] has four prongs might lead to the dismissal of the size difference as irrelevant" (p. 243). But this analysis treats the features (prongs, bumps) as given, as aspects to be *compared*, ignoring that the spaces might be perceived instead. Notice the term, *four-pronged creature*—as if this is a fixed and absolute aspect of the problem. Consider how a slight modification to "C" must be ignored (not categorized as a prong) if "C" and "D" are to be conceived as similar. The perception of a feature depends on the context for which it serves as a discriminating influence (just as an explicit definition of a conception depends on the context; Wittgenstein, 1953/1958). Perceptual categorizing is not comparing; comparing is a higher-order, inferential process that occurs sequentially in time.

D

Fig. 7.4. Related to Fig. 1.8, does this figure have four or five prongs? What constitutes a "prong" is not given, but a perceptual categorization (e.g., of protuberances as opposed to channels) that is coupled to higher-order contextual conceptualizations (e.g., these are "creatures with prongs").

- "The map analyze cycle allows representation and mapping to interact while maintaining some separation" (p. 243). This reveals how Forbus and Gentner's psychological concern is with cycles of perceiving and acting, rather than the relation between perception of features and conception of objects ("pronged creatures") to be related.

- "This example suggests that perceptual processing can, in principle, be decomposed into modular sub-tasks" (p. 243). It is decomposed in our analysis, but not decomposed in fact, as illustrated by how the constructed conception of prongs and creatures arises as part of the perceptual process of scanning the field of examples in Fig. 1.8.

- "Both the weights on predicate pairs (the Slipnet) and the conceptual depths of individual predicates are hand-coded and pre-set . . . . [T]hese representations do not have any other independent motivation for their existence" (p. 245). The weights represent neural activation relations, a level of concern that SME ignores.

- "It [Copycat] cannot capture what is perhaps the most important, creative aspect of analogy: the ability to align and map systems of knowledge from different domains" (p. 245). This is a different level of concern, presupposing that theoretical descriptions ("knowledge" in SME) have been generated by some other means, which is precisely the creative aspect that Copycat is starting to address.

- "SME, despite its seeming rigidity, is in important ways more flexible than Copycat" (p. 245). This is irrelevant, for obviously reasoning over descriptive models is more "flexible" than perception.

- "A consequence of Chalmers *et al.*'s [1992] argument that perception cannot be split from comparison is that one should not be able to make domain-independent theories of analogical processing" (p. 247). This does not follow. Copycat is a "domain-independent" theory of how perception cannot be split from comparison. The point is that perceptual categorization and conceptual categorization occur together, not that we cannot describe the mechanism in a domain-general way.

- "The ban on having more than a single mapping bond between any two objects is a simple form of the one-to-one matching criterion found in SME . . . . Human beings . . . have no problem matching along multiple dimensions" (p. 248). This again illustrates a level confusion, a failure to understand that perceptual categorization is different from conceptualization and inference. Copycat is modeling a perceptual aspect of simultaneity that occurs in coupling of *features*; in contrast, the *conceptual categories* that SME models may be sequenced and composed "along multiple dimensions."

- "Compare the letter string domain of Copycat with the qualitative physics domain of PHINEAS" (p 249). This is a good illustration of the level confusion of viewing all "knowledge" as stored and manipulated descriptions—letter strings are about perceptual-conceptual coupling; qualitative physics is a matter of inference over descriptive models. Copycat and PHINEAS are not concerned with different domains of knowledge (like sports and cooking); they are models of different levels of processing.

- "Copycat ignores the possibility of memory influencing current processing" (p. 251). No, that is what the weights represent and how they function.

- "Mitchell's (1993) analysis of Copycat demonstrates that it can be analyzed into modules" (p. 253). This again fundamentally confuses a descriptive, analytic model with the mechanism itself, the neurobiological phenomenon being modeled. We must distinguish between the modules found in Copycat and the neural mechanism those modules imperfectly replicate.

▪ "Hofstadter's failure to take seriously the distinction between a model of analogical mapping and a model of the full discovery process" (p. 242). Indeed, this argument can be leveled against SME and all the other models of analogy, as indicated by Schön's analysis of the paintbrush inventors.

At the same time, Forbus et al. (1998) made many valid points about weaknesses of Copycat, relative to their interest in inferential analogy, such as that Copycat ignores how people learn scientific theories via analogy. To understand Hofstadter's contribution, notice first of all that he is dealing with conceptions that are coupled to perceptual experience, not inferred from descriptions. This is clear when he uses the phrase, "perception of instances of those concepts in the letter-strings" (Hofstadter, 1995a, p. 281). An example of a concept that is coupled to perception is "sameness group," such as the *a*s in *aabd*. Activating such a concept happens "directly" from the perceptual categorizations, just as we can conceive that something is an apple by feeling its shape. In contrast, distinguishing between a Delicious apple and a pippin for most people involves describing features and then deductively combining several *descriptions* of shape, color, presence of bumps on the bottom, and so on. The concepts in examples by Holyoak and Thagard (e.g., "events leading up to WWII" [p. 76]) and Falkenhainer (1988) (e.g., heat flow between bodies at different temperatures) are not usually activated in one step from perceptual categories. But a Copycat concept such as "group length" is defined in terms of perceptual categories. The concepts in the painter story arise by a combination of perceptual coupling (e.g., channel) and multiple-step deductive inferences (e.g., how vibrating affects flow).

I conclude that there is a difference between real-world examples and letter analogies in the role played by description and deduction. The real world examples deal with causal explanations of event-stories. The concepts being related in these analogies are more than descriptions of static perceptual relations (e.g., adjacency, "alphabetic first"), but are conceptions of objects and events changing in time. Such conceptions often must be described in several alternative ways before they can be related and understood. This does not detract from Hofstadter's main claim about the importance of perceptual processes. Rather the work of Holyoak and Thagard (1994) reminds us that the process of getting to a *useful* description involves more than perception, and one cannot simply apply Hofstadter's approach to satisfy the constraints of the story understanding and scientific discovery domain.[6]

---

[6]The distinction between perceptual coupling and deductive inference is further elaborated in Clancey (1997c, chapters 12, 13).

Finally, the relative complexity of causal-story concepts in real-world examples relates to the role of learning in forming causal analogies. As I have indicated, the concepts of painting, paintbrush, and pumping all changed in the painters' experience. Hofstadter (1995a) said that "Copycat is not meant to be a model of learning" (p. 294), and I believe he has gotten away with that simplification because the concepts he was dealing with are perceptually defined, mathematical notions like "sameness group." Similarly, his use of microworlds also explains why he believed that analogies (and metaphors) are discovered, not invented. Although focused on creativity, and emphasizing the "fluid" nature of concepts, Copycat ignores how conceptual change relates to modeling the world for a purpose, and thus can only be an impoverished model of creativity in the large. I agree with Hofstadter that the mechanisms apply up and down the line, from perception through conception. But, as Schön (1979) emphasized, analogy formation in the large—in practice—cannot be treated independently of theory reformulation in the service of science and engineering design. In practice, new features are discovered and others become more or less relevant. Language changes. Again, this is part of the pragmatic content Holyoak and Thagard (1994) were trying to include (but which they treated descriptively, rather than by a generative mechanism). In short, Holyoak and Thagard have a better model of conceptual content; Hofstadter and his colleagues have a better model of generative mechanism.

Just as Hofstadter and others take a hard line that perception is essential, I will say similarly that learning is essential. The issue is not just conceptual similarity, but generalizing to form an embracing theory. Here is precisely where structure mapping will be helpful. As I have said, although Hofstadter was right that very often we first have perceptual similitude—as when the bristles look like channels—some talk is often then necessary to develop the analogy. Learning involves a combination of the conceptual slippage Hofstadter models and structure mapping between descriptions. Some of this mapping may indeed be subconscious and proceed by the kinds of "pressures" and "activation proximities" in Copycat. Some of the mapping will take the form of *argumentation*, with evidence being pointed out, objections raised, and new connections sought—all as materials are being rearranged in space and previously coordinated interactions are being reexamined and described for the first time.

The metaphor of "a paintbrush is a kind of pump" may have been discovered, but the theory of pumping that resulted and the new brush must be invented through descriptive modeling and discussion. In subsequent sections, I consider further how such talk and conceptual coordination are related.

7.6 STORYTELLING AS COORDINATING

In their conversation, people organize their experiences into stories
(Bruner,1990; Linde,1993). This sense-making process develops as a kind of
compositional process. Over time, through a *sequence of conceptualizations* of
WIDN, we subsume details and activities into a coherent way of seeing and
talking (Fig. 7.1 and Fig. 7.3). In effect, storytelling is a process by which
participants deliberately represent (and hence distinguish into components) the
processes that they intuitively sense have come together in their thinking. Schön
(1979) reviewed the process in the paintbrush example:

> It is significant that the participants are involved in a particular concrete situation; at
> the same time that they are reflecting on the problem, they are experiencing the
> phenomena of the problem. In the pump-paintbrush case, the researchers
> experimented with what it felt like actually to use the brush . . . . The cognitive work
> of restructuring draws upon the richness of features and relations which are to be
> found in the concrete situation. There one can notice the gentle curve of the natural
> brush and the sharp angle of the synthetic one. (p. 277–278)

The imposition of narrative structure on experience becomes generative of
future experience itself, as conceptual ordering strategies:

> In the context of a particular situation, the participants work at the restructuring of
> their initial descriptions—regrouping, reordering, and renaming elements and
> relations; selecting new features and relations from their observations of the
> situation. As this work proceeds, they represent their experience of the situation
> through strategies which capture the "next-next-next" of temporal experience of
> events; and from such representations, of which storytelling is a prime example,
> they draw the restructured groupings and relations of elements which they are able
> to embed in a new, coordinated description . . . .
>
> The old descriptions are not mapped onto one another by matching corresponding
> elements in each, for the old descriptions resist such a mapping.   Rather the
> *restructured* descriptions are coordinated with one another. (p. 278-279)

The storytelling strategy of representation, perhaps accompanied by a
diagram, "enables inquirers to hang onto and convey the richness of their
experience of the events themselves . . . without being constrained by the initial
category-schemes with which [they] begin" (Schön, 1979, p. 278). In effect, an
implicit conceptualization, which subsumes some set of details at a particular
time, is given a name, enabling a similar correlation and sequencing to be
constructed at a later time. Ways of talking are themselves conceptions, so that
phrases, particularly names for stories and key events, are categorizations that
can be reactivated and potentially reexperienced as details, within a fitting
ongoing activity. In this way "pump talk" arose within the paintbrush inquiry. In
contrast, description-based models, like those Schön and Hofstadter critiqued,
assume that definitions and features of concepts are physically linked in a
database-like memory. According to the conceptual coordination perspective,

previous ideas arise because we are coordinating processes of perceiving and speaking in ways that are reproducing or similar to those active in the past.

Schön (1979) made the important point that details that may have played no part in or had a different significance in your original experience will be reconstructible at a later time. This is another way of saying that your experience is not stored in memory as descriptions, but are structures within a physically-embodied, conceptual coordination of sensing, doing, and talking. In remembering you are reactivating processes and thus able to re-present what happened and give it different interpretations. For example, listening to someone else's re-creation of the paintbrush experience hours or days later, one of the researchers may reexperience a detail (perhaps an image) that he or she noticed originally, but allowed to pass without conceiving or articulating its significance. Our sense of the "richness" of our experience is manifested by the incorporation of such multimodal details.

Seeing something in a new way stimulates articulating an explanatory theory. This is because perceiving involves generalizing. Seeing the brush as a pump creates a kind of impasse; there is a pull to identify, to make an identity relation, but also a felt resistance (the brush is not a pump). Describing the experience is a method for creating a new coordination, of composing your activity now with how you have segmented experience and spoken in the past (Fig. 7.1). Articulating the metaphor—verbally developing its perceived parts and relations—resolves the tension of the over-generalization: The designers create a model of pumping that adjusts their way of viewing brushes as well as pumps, articulating a theory that *rationalizes* why they saw brushes and pumps as similar. The subsequent composition—a *description* of pumping—incorporates both the generalized way of seeing, plus the perceptual details of painting that caught their attention. Resolving impasses by rationalizing details is central to Bartlett's (1932/1977) constructive model of memory.

How does a story explanation influence inquiry? Chi, de Leeus, Chiu, and LaVancher (1994) studied how explaining ideas to oneself aids understanding and memory of scientific concepts. Crucially, self-explanation is not simply retrieving from memory and *translating theories* about how a problem was solved, but part of the process of solving a problem itself. Storytelling is how new theories are developed, as the paintbrush example illustrates.

We can summarize the development of a theoretical description by building on Schön's idea of reflective conversation in action (Table 7.2). The right column of the table indicates the levels of descriptive activity, in which one names things, frames situations, tells stories, and develops causal theories and plans.[7] Cognitive processes we associate with each kind of description are listed parenthetically. These are nested such that we move from *names* to *event descriptions* to *stories* about incidents and recurrent patterns (scripts) to

---

[7]For further discussion, see Schön (1987) and chapter 9 of Clancey (1997c).

theoretical causal models to *designs* based on such understanding. For example, in history telling one might describe how the paint is flowing in particular cases; in design one moves to more abstract theories of pumps and why brushes bend in different ways.

Table 7.2

Descriptive Development Viewed as Composing Different Kinds of Relations in Sequence, Over Time

Relational Recoordination	*Descriptive Activity*
TYPE Things in the world *Concepts*: outlines, form, extent *Examples*: gloppy paint, channels	**Naming, Framing** (describing metaphorically, seeing as, visualizing, bounding, identifying, classifying)
ORDER Temporal sequence; changes to properties in the thing over time; contrast; dynamics *Concepts*: spatial interaction; size, reach, location; adjacency; alignment; containment *Examples*: Liquid flowing, vibrating brush	**History telling** (sequencing, reexperiencing, ordering, recounting, juxtaposing events, ideas, and emotions; conceiving scripts and cases, seeing a sequence as a thing; projecting, imagining, anticipating events)
CAUSE Behavioral effects, internal relations of structures and processes *Concepts*: genesis, development, evolution; ecological codetermination; settings and purposes. *Examples*: pumping action, curving brush forcing flow of paint	**Design** (theorizing, explaining, modeling processes causally; planning; describing origins and correlations)

The left column lists three kinds of conceptual relations or ways of reifying experience: type, order, and cause. These build on one another:

- Describing a type is conceiving an experience in itself.
- Describing an order is conceiving a relation of types.

- Describing a cause is conceiving a sequence (order) of events.

(We might also say that "order" and "cause" are higher-order or meta-level types.) Causal *reasoning* thus involves higher-order conceptualization of conceptualizations. This is not especially a novel idea. But as Hofstadter (1995b) pointed out, many descriptive cognitive models use terms like *heat* and *flow* as if they are primitives. Hence internal categorical relations—especially perceptual relations—are ignored in the model of the analogy mechanism.

In Table 7.2, examples are given for conceptual relations in the development of the invention of the synthetic paintbrush. For instance, the idea of alignment of bristles (an order) relates the perception of channels (a type) to the conceptualization of pumping (a cause). In effect, the analysis summarized in the table describes how feature categorization and theory formation are related. The table is not meant to imply that there are definite stages in particular experiences, although over time a given metaphor may develop from perceptual experience to new designs, as in the paintbrush story. In practice, a paintbrush inventor could begin with a competitor's successful brush, and work "down" from the design to understanding why it works (reverse engineering).

Such an account of conceptual relations is to be contrasted with the view that we proceed from descriptive theories to selecting and comparing features. For example, Schank's (1986) account of explanation patterns broadly fits the painter story—failure, questioning, case-recalling and storytelling, explanation, and generalization. However, his account of "expectation failure" is based on stored descriptions of the world and a set of "questions already present in our minds" (p. 186) not a *physical discoordination* between perceiving and acting.[8]

7.7 CONCEPTUAL COORDINATING AS CONVERSING WITH MATERIALS

The process of commenting on what we are seeing or experiencing as we move things about, what Bamberger and Schön (1991) called "conversing with materials," is an essential part of creating new models of the world. By painting, shifting the brush around on the wall, examining and probing at the painted surface, and commenting on all of this activity, the form of the paintbrushes and (liquid) paint come to have different meanings for the painters. Similarly, Jeff (section 5.1) moves bells around and compares different sounds to represent the melody he hears in his head. This illustrates why Bamberger and Schön viewed "cognitive processes as a kind of 'making.'" In these examples representations being reflected upon (e.g., an arrangement of bells on the table) are created in interactive commentary, they are not inaccessible or subconsciously

---

[8]Compare with the experience of the paintbrush inventors; see section 11.2 for further discussion of Schank's model of memory.

manipulated mental constructs. The process is dialectic: "Knowing in action" reshapes materials (the bristles and paint); then reperceiving the changed forms, the painters articulate a new description (Fig. 7.2). Forms, categories, and descriptions are mutually constraining, although progressively developing in time within an overarching, purposeful activity conception (e.g., trying to invent a synthetic paintbrush, being a member of a large company's research and development team).

Schön (1987) described architectural drawing similarly: Descriptions of what the drawings for a new design stand for (what they represent) are substantially produced *after* the drawings are made, as perceptual and conceptual recategorizations of serendipitous effects. A person reshapes materials and then is changed by interpreting the new forms. This process occurs in writing, speaking, drawing, music, and design of all kinds. In effect, Bamberger and Schön (1991) lead us to view all cognition as a kind of design: "Making something through reflective 'conversation' between makers and their materials in the course of shaping meaning and coherence . . . . Meaning, itself, is a process of making" (pp. 69–70). Changed material is not only the "output," but part of the *conceptual* shaping and organizing; for the painters, the stuff on the wall is not a defined set of objective, prearranged things and relations, but subject to interpretation, held in place (a reference entity; see section 4.1), and reperceived. For example, by figure–ground reconfiguration, *spaces* (where nothing exists) suddenly become perceived features. The stuff on the wall is not just "input" to problem solving either, but a developing form the person is working with. The transaction of invention is an interplay of physical, perceptual, and conceptual reshaping (Fig. 7.2).

In their study of representational development, Bamberger and Schön (1979, 1991) were particularly interested in *transitional objects*, temporary arrangements that are "embodied and enacted representations of what agents know." In the paintbrush story, transitional objects include the painted surfaces, the experimental brushes, and sketches the painters used to describe their theories. In the example of Jeff and the bells, transitional objects are the bells Jeff arranges to "hold still meanings." They constitute a "materialized log of the making process." Deliberately placed objects hold still the relation of the not yet articulated, but conceived meaning. We saw this in the example of sending two messages (chapter 4), in which windows on the computer screen participate in and hold still the activities of sending messages. Coming the other way, to understand the influence of conventional symbolic notations on experience, other investigations consider how the language of mathematics constrains "just what are taken to be possible entities and relations in the stuff." A formal language (line, angle, and equations) provides additional materials that children arrange physically, perceptually, and in their descriptions (Roschelle & Clancey, 1992).

In many studies of learning, a student is confronted with a packaged interplay of materials and representations in a curriculum, by which learning experiences are designed. This is fine for certain purposes, but what is problematic for a learner is then no longer visible to the teacher, as all the focus is on channeling and controlling what is learned. From the inventor's view, all inquiry is a process of making something new. From the student's view, all learning is the process of digesting something old. Too often studies of learning look to the classroom rather than the workplace, and theories of intelligence are based too much on the teacher's perspective. Again, creating and comprehending have been separated, as they are not in the practice of science, business, or engineering.

If we wish to understand how invention is possible or how human capability is more flexible than a handcrafted vocabulary of a descriptive cognitive model, a transactional perspective is helpful. We view the compositional and sequencing processes of neural mechanisms as transforming (internal) categories, behaviors, and materials out in the world, as in the experience of the message sender, Jeff, Caitlin, and the paintbrush inventors. In fact, the possibility of perceptual, conceptual, and physical recoordination is the very source of originality in human behavior; but the product (what is understood and created) is a coupled (hence, transactional) relation between mental and physical constructs (Fig. 7.2).

In summary, structure mapping theories capture some of the high-level regularities found in human reasoning, but appear to imply that descriptions exist in the brain before we know what to say. In turn, they imply that reasoning is just a process of manipulating descriptions that were created in a previous perceptual stage. Such models generally assume that perception of features in the world is based on preexisting descriptions of what we can see. Schön's (1979) analysis turns this upside down: The experience of similarity involves nonverbal processes; describing what we are seeing helps orient how we reshape materials and how we reperceive what we are doing. Perceiving, describing, and acting may be coupled—developing together through the coordination process—without intermediate descriptions and inferences that control what we see, say, or do (Fig. 7.2).

In the paintbrush example, metaphors play a central role in the process of developing an appropriate feature language for describing paintbrushes, painting, and the painted surface. The painters must make sense of an unorganized visual field and usefully describe what they see. Because they want to build a synthetic brush, they must also explain why good and bad features are present. Thus, they are engaged in a conception of an inquiry that conceptually frames their metaphor generation and descriptive theorizing.

By carefully examining what designers are looking at, doing, and saying to each other, we can essentially study the lifecycle of a representation. The conceptual coordination perspective helps us understand the development and interaction of perception, metaphorical talk, and causal explanations (Table 7.2). The stages of invention can be modeled in terms of reconciling old and new ways of seeing and talking in a compositional process: Each coordination is built out of currently active and prior coordinations (Fig. 7.3). In this example the conceptualization of WIDN goes beyond simple actions and looking (as in the

Spartanville example, section 6.1, and the Copycat model), to encompass comparing different experiences and developing theories about them. Here we must also pay more attention to the social interaction influencing individual attention. The environment is constantly changing as other participants supply visible forms to be interpreted, as well as new descriptions and directions for what to do next.

With such analysis in mind, I turn in Part III to related theories of verbal learning to show how the conceptual coordination perspective fits experimental data and how it helps disentangle the various perspectives of biological development, memory mechanism, and descriptive patterns of behavior.

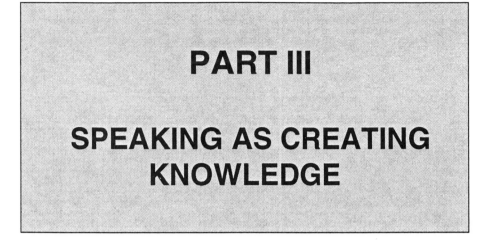

PART III

SPEAKING AS CREATING KNOWLEDGE

8

Bartlett's Reconstructive Memory

The "image" of memory and thought is derived by analogy to the image of art. The "trace" of a percept is analogous to the graphic act. The "storehouse" of memory is analogous to the museums and libraries of civilization . . . . These inventions do make possible the preservation of human knowledge for subsequent generations. But to assume that experiences leave images or traces in the brain, that experience writes a record, that the storage of memories explains learning, that, in short, the child accumulates knowledge as the race accumulated it, is stultifying.

—James J. Gibson, *The Senses Considered as Perceptual Systems,* 1966, p. 277

In the examples in Part II, I deliberately attempted to move away from top-down hierarchical descriptive cognitive models of memory, to understanding a mechanism that replicates and generalizes itself as behavior occurs. My exploration might be couched as follows: What if we apply Gibson's (1966) phrase, "senses considered as perceptual systems" to the next level, perceptual-motor coordination considered as conceptual systems? How far can this analogy apply? Where does similarity of mechanism between the categorization of perceptual features and conceptualization break down?

To pursue these issues, I delve more deeply in Part III into related theories of learning: Bartlett's model of memory (this chapter), transformational theories (chapters 9 and 10, focusing on natural language grammars), and descriptive stored-schema models of memory (chapter 11). I also reformulate problem-solving models in terms of conceptual coordination (chapter 12), and begin to explain a nagging limitation of the stored-descriptions approach, namely "where the lower problem spaces come from" (Lehman, Lewis, & Newell, 1991, p. 39). My aim throughout is to understand what is right about descriptive (or "symbolic") cognitive modeling, while revealing how remembering and acting are *physical* processes that are conceptually coordinated. Theoretical analyses and comparisons in this part show in more detail how perception-action sequences are *extended*, *categorized*, and *composed* to form paths, routines, and grammars, and (perhaps) descriptive theories themselves.

The title of Part III highlights that speaking, learning, and conceptual coordination are aspects of a complex coordination process, both as neurorobiological circuits and as conscious behavior over time. Knowledge is not retrieved and displayed in spoken form, in the way computer programs restructure diagrams and text on a computer screen. Rather, conceptualization occurs *as we speak*, and meanings are reflexively constructed as we interpret what we say (in the transactional relation shown by Fig. 7.2). I develop these ideas in this part of the book through detailed examination of models of memory, verbal behavior, and problem solving. What we normally consider knowledge is routinely created in the very act of articulating what we know.

My ideas about speaking, reconceptualization, and coordination, as well as the activation trace notation, were inspired by my interpretation of Bartlett's theory of remembering. In this chapter I show how the activity of recollecting described by Bartlett (1932/1977) resembles the pattern we find in reading "Spartanville" or inventing the paintbrush: an impasse, reperception, and experience of a focus detail experience, accompanied by a feeling of resolution and a descriptive rationalization. Trying to remember something is a kind of coordination problem. I begin by introducing Bartlett's model and relate it to the examples in Part II, reworking them to produce a more general theory of sequential coordination.

In this exposition, the reader should be aware that by *remembering*, Bartlett (like Gibson) means in particular the sequential, conscious process of telling a story about the past. Nevertheless, he (like Gibson) aimed to show that the neural processes are reconstructive, and not merely replaying stored procedures or instantiating stored descriptions (or "traces"). Thus, the reader should be aware that "reconstruction" refers to two levels operating together in remembering—subconscious, selective-compositional process of *neural recoordination* and the imaginative, *reflective investigation* of the conscious person.

8.1 REMEMBERING AS COORDINATING

Bartlett's (1932/1977) experiments in the study of memory involved having subjects recall a folk tale that was foreign to their culture. Bartlett was interested in the structure of the recollected story (inclusion and transformation of details), the process and experience of telling a story from memory, and the conditions that influence the person's performance (especially social conventions). Bartlett attended carefully to the running commentary during the reconstruction of the story:

> The story as he constructed it is full of rationalizations and explanations, and most of the running comments of the subject concerned the interconnexion of the various

events and were directed to making the whole narration appear as coherent as possible. (p. 78)

That is, Bartlett viewed remembering the story as a sense-making activity in which the explanations and rationalizations are playing an essential part. The experience of getting stuck (being unable to remember) and finding a way to continue is of special interest.

Bartlett's (1932/1977) main conclusion, stated in the preface to his book, is that "some widely held views have to be completely discarded, and none more completely than that which treats recall as the reexcitement in some way of fixed and changeless 'traces'" (p. vi). Writing today, Bartlett would be arguing against the idea that memory is a place where descriptions are stored. However, the argument against fixed traces is more general, emphasizing that memories are inherently *relational*: attitudes, images, and actions operating together, not independently existing ("lifeless") structures:[1]

> Remembering is not the re-excitation of innumerable fixed, lifeless and fragmentary traces. It is an imaginative reconstruction, or construction, built out of the relation of our attitude toward a whole active mass of organised past reactions or experience, and to a little outstanding detail which commonly appears in image or in language form. (p. 213)

> Whenever there is any order or regularity of behaviour, a particular response is possible only because it is related to other similar responses which have been serially organised, yet which *operate, not simply as individual members coming one after another, but as a unitary mass.* (p. 201)

That is, an ongoing conceptualization is generalized and elaborated by inclusion of additional categories in time (cf. Fig. 1.6). This whole ensemble is what is constructed and remembered:

> There is not the slightest reason, however, to suppose that each set of incoming impulses, each new group of experiences persists as an isolated member of some passive patchwork. They have to be regarded as constituents of living, momentary settings belonging to the organism . . . not as a number of individual events somehow strung together and stored within the organism. (p. 201)

Similarly, Rosenfield (1988) argued that what we view as static memory can be viewed as a process of coordinating past perceptions and actions with what we are currently doing. Thus, even when we view neural maps as corresponding to perceptual and conceptual categorizations, we should consider that categorizing is always embedded in conceptualized *activities*. Recollecting requires in some sense a reactivation of a way of coordinating activity, not just

---

[1]Referring to these passages, Anderson and Bower (1980) wrote, "We find such crucial passages a little hard to follow" (p. 58). My objective in this chapter is to help descriptive modelers understand Bartlett's theory by showing it makes fundamentally different assumptions about the brain.

reactivation of isolated categorizations, and at the neural level, certainly not indexing, retrieval, and matching descriptions (contrast with Fig. 2.7). Here activity can be viewed both narrowly, in terms of speaking grammatically, and broadly, in terms of retelling a folk story.

Bartlett (1932/1977) emphasized that a person's recollections operate "as a unitary mass." Although there is a sequential aspect to memory, concepts should not be viewed as individual members that are chained together, but as operating whole (cf. Figure 3.5). The "confederation" has "an organic and personal and historical unity"; that is, the living parts, the maps and procedures exist because they once *worked together* (Sacks, 1990, p. 50). No unit exists on its own. It came into existence because it fit sometime in past behavior. In this sense, neural maps, concepts, and ideas have a history, like two people who have done things together.[2]

Bartlett conjectured that the process of relating recollected details to an ongoing story employs the same mechanism involved in any physical activity. That is, routines are themselves constructed coordinations. Bartlett (1932/1977) gave the example of "making a stroke in a quick game" (p. 201), a postural recoordination that is reconstructed and hence generalized. Memory is *procedural*, a capability to recoordinate ways of perceiving and moving in ways similar to how they have worked together before. The idea is exemplified by Payne's (1993) reformulation of visuospatial mental models as reconstructed, not merely retrieved: "Subjects remember the mental operations they must perform to construct the model" (p. 596). Neisser (1976), a contemporary supporter of Bartlett's position, described the same idea:

> All ordinary perceiving has just these characteristics. Not only reading but also listening, feeling, and looking are skillful activities that occur over time. All of them depend upon preexisting structures, here called schemata, which direct perceptual activity and *are modified as it occurs*. (p. 9, italics added)

Physical structures are "manufactured" as living processes that were previously structured, called *schemata*. This manufacturing is a process of selection and recombination, not at all like reexecuting a stored computer program: "Every time we make it, it has its own characteristics." Neural maps that organized behavior before are reengaged, but are always adapted and integrated within the neural context of ongoing interaction.

The example of postures is also central to the analysis of Head, a teacher who inspired Bartlett.[3] The adaptation of postures within movement is to be viewed as a general categorizing and coordinating mechanism. Perceptual and

---

[2]The same process can be argued about a group of people. An individual makes sense to himself and other people as a person because of how he fits historically in a community. At the neural level, Minsky's (1985) society of mind should be viewed as interacting and overlapping communities (in which the "agents" are processes not conscious beings like people).

[3]See Rosenfield (1992) and the discussion in Clancey (1997c, chapter 3).

conceptual categorization within a cognitive activity incorporates and extends this kind of coordinating mechanism. Just as Hofstadter and others argue for extension of the perceptual mechanism into the process of conceptual analogy formation (section 7.4), Bartlett and Head extended physical recoordination of postures into the perceptual-conceptual arena.

Bartlett   (1932/1977) found that his subject's process of remembering involved a complex interplay of visual imagery and verbal descriptions. Asking his subjects to recollect the same story at later times, he observed processes of "invention, condensation, elaboration, [and] simplification" (p. 212). He described four facets to the story-construction process (Fig. 8.1):

- A *direct chain of reactions;* this behavior is unreflective in the sense that no representations of these actions are involved.
- A *subsequent encompassing (emotional) attitude* ("characterised by doubt, hesitation, surprise, astonishment, confidence, dislike, etc." p. 207) that breaks away from the preceding reaction.
- A *subsequent detail* (usually an image) is reexperienced, termed a "recollection" because it was heard or seen before.
- A *satisfying or fortifying rationalization* is constructed ("on the basis of the relation of this specific bit of material to the general mass of past experience or reactions, the latter functioning, after the manner of the 'schema,' as an active organised setting," p. 209).

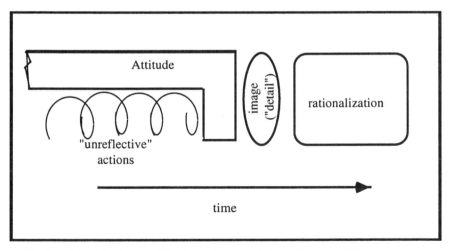

Fig. 8.1. Initial depiction of Bartlett's theory of story-reconstruction.

As in the preceding chapters, I show here my initial representation of these facets of remembering, for later comparison to the activation trace analysis. The idea of an encompassing emotional attitude is especially interesting: Although the person does not know what to say or do, he does have "a sense of himself." The compositional process is still ongoing; the detail has been incorporated, but for the moment only emotionally related. The emotion provides a way of holding the detail, of making it part of the current *meaningful context*, while a new categorization is attempted that makes it part of the *conceptual* story of WIDN.

The activation trace representation (Fig. 8.2) has the advantage of showing that the rationalization is *about* the detail, supplying a context that includes it, making the detail a held-in-place, referential representation of the constructed understanding (cf. Bamberger's analysis of Jeff's bell playing, section 5.1). The detail comes to attention ("from the side") and is held, as new descriptions are created that incorporate the detail and relate it to the main stream of interest. The detail *anchors* the new composition. Talking about the detail is an intricate part of creating a coherent composition that bridges the original impasse. In this respect, trying to remember a story is like trying to tell a new story, that is, to have a descriptive "theory" that relates the parts. Both involve narrative construction. One recalls details, the other looks for them or makes sense of them.

A coherent story provides a context, a way of coordinating ideas, that makes the detail meaningful. That is, the detail becomes a *referential categorization* (or "symbolic") by a compositional process that creates a generalization (rationalization) that includes it. I call this the *commentary theory of meaning*. With the detail included in the main stream of activity, behavior can become automatic again (i.e., without the need for deliberate search and storytelling). By this analysis, descriptive representing—articulating a generalization about what is true—plays a critical part in relating details in our experience to resolve conflicts in past ways of coordinating or to reconcile new details.

Winograd and Flores (1986) provided a related discussion of the breakdown and representation, but their analysis is a special case. For them, breakdown occurs when representations in the world are incompatible with our experience. For example, the vocabulary of a medical expert system might lead me to experience a breakdown when I cannot understand the program's questions. In this case, the incommensurable focus details are the words used in the expert system's inquiries. I am categorizing what I am seeing in a familiar way (I recognize the words), but I cannot incorporate them in my activity of using the program to treat a particular patient.

Bartlett (1932/1977) suggested more generally that breakdown occurs when any detail comes to our attention that does not fit what we are doing. Hence, breakdown is not a specific, inherent weakness of computer representations or other external notations. Breakdown arises from any incompatible categorization, relative to ongoing activity. For example, we experience breakdown when using an unfamiliar device, such as a shower faucet in a hotel (Norman, 1988). An impasse is any disruption in the otherwise smooth and unremarkable character of our coordination (what Schön called "knowing-in-action").

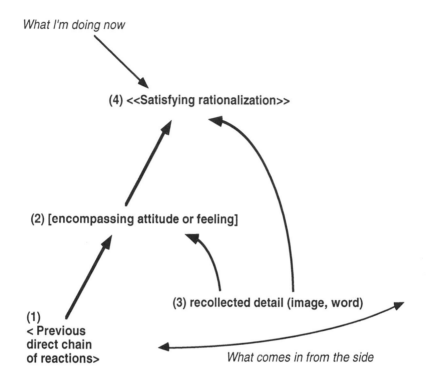

What I'm doing now

(4) <<Satisfying rationalization>>

(2) [encompassing attitude or feeling]

(3) recollected detail (image, word)

**(1)
< Previous
direct chain
of reactions>**   *What comes in from the side*

Fig. 8.2. Bartlett's theory of remembering. (1) Breakdown in ongoing experience is followed by (2) an emotional response to discoordination, (3) formation of a recategorized detail, and (4) reconceptualization of WIDN. All of this occurs within broader conceptualizations of activity (WIDN), that further organize the recoordination and rationalization.

Furthermore, disruptions are occurring all the time as we speak and are reminded of things we want to say or need to incorporate. Because we have learned to coordinate multiple ideas in a conversation, we can automatically recoordinate our sense-making process (what Schön, 1987, called "reflection-in-action"). Bartlett's (1932/1977) subjects experienced an image detail just as they recognized that an alternative conceptualization was possible:

> Images are particularly likely to arise when any slight check occurs, and that in the absence of this the whole process is likely to run on to completion simply in terms of language or of manipulative activity of some kind . . . .. A difference in present circumstances, as compared with those suitable to an automatic response, sets up in the agent a conflict of attitude or of interest. The appropriate response is then temporarily held up, and the image, an item from some scheme, comes in to help solve the difficulty. (p. 220)

Echoing Dewey's (1896) claim that a stimulus has no definite character until it becomes part of an activity (as opposed to being "given" or independently "input"), Bartlett (1932/1977) explained how the detail coming into our attention becomes part of the ongoing activity: "The main absorbing stream is crossed by another . . . . Nothing decisive can be said or done till the incoming detail has acquired a more or less definite relationship to the main stream of interest" (p. 217). That is, what the detail is, what it means, cannot be said without constructing a relation to ongoing activity. Images provide a special mode for relating ideas. Bartlett claimed that images, through their affective character can "combine interests of very different nature and origin" (p. 223). Consequently, images serve as a means for focusing on and articulating cross attitudes that are functioning simultaneously (Koestler, 1964).

Bartlett's (1932/1977) data and analysis provide the beginning for a computational model of the coordination process. Significantly, he revealed the intricate temporal relation in creating new coordinations: Images are perceived (often in imagination), automatic composition is interrupted, words are reconceived, and the details are commented on (making them meaningful). The coherent whole arising through verbal elaboration coordinates multiple, crossing attitudes, behaviors, and purposes.

A simple conjecture is that one focus detail is incorporated at a time (Fig. 8.3), and this constitutes a "step" in a conscious experience. A detail is something perceived in the environment (e.g., "Spartanville" in section 6.1; gloppy paint in chapter 7) or imagined (e.g., a recollection of someone or how something appeared or sounded). An incoming focus detail is correlated to the previous focus detail by the generalized activity or way of seeing (e.g., sending a second message in chapter 4); saying that "Spartanville is Spartanburg"; "the vibrating brush is pumping"). The detail serves to *qualify* the generalization. The effect is that the main stream of interest is *seen as* the incoming detail. (I see what I am doing as sending a message to Mark; reading the word "Spartanville" in "Greenville/Spartanburg"; "pumping paint.") The detail allows me to make the new claim; the claim allows me to incorporate the detail in what I am doing.

The relation of the meaning of the detail to the generalization of what I am doing is dialectic: By incorporating the incoming detail in the ongoing composition I am categorizing the detail, but I am also recategorizing what I have been doing (generalizing it), so that what I am doing includes the detail. Here the detail may be something that correlates with what I have been looking for (e.g., "Spartanville"; why the natural brush paints smoothly).

A detail may develop spontaneously and be incorporated smoothly as a *figure* because it correlates with what I am doing (a generalization is possible). This occurred when sending the second message, as well as when the first inventor conceived of a paintbrush as a kind of pump. However, the new figure may have significance because of an alternative way of coordinating, producing an emotion of surprise or disruption and requiring a recoordination. The resolution is marked by rationalization of the detail with respect to a new conception of WIDN. This happened on saying "Spartanville" and shifting to "trying to find a word."

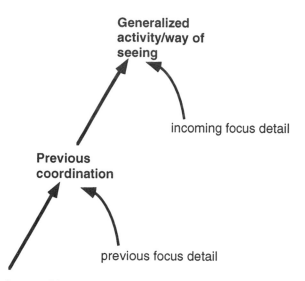

Generalized activity/way of seeing

incoming focus detail

Previous coordination

previous focus detail

Fig. 8.3. Compositional structure of serial activation of neurological categorizations.

Our examples suggest that the generalization may bear different relations to the previous coordination:

- *Immediate reenactment* of the previous activity by figure–ground recategorization of a sensory field (sending a second message)
- Perceptual recategorization and comparison (correlating details) through *interactive search* (finding "Spartanville" in the newspaper)
- *Rationalizing* a complex activity through interactive search and theoretical description (examining and explaining why the paint is gloppy).

In the first case, no description of the activity is necessary for recoordination; it simply happens because of how neural sequences form. In the second, a glitch requires some extended, cyclic activity, but the description is of the goal "Where is 'Spartanville'?"; the immediate process of searching for the word is reflection-in-action. (Schön [1987] illustrated this by how we respond in a game to a surprise move by an opponent, such as when a basketball player responds to someone taking the ball while he is dribbling.) In the third case, the panoply of descriptive modeling is employed: framing the situation, telling stories, articulating theories. The design process occurs within the activity of painting and dialogue about painting, but is guided throughout by alternative descriptions of what is being seen, what to do next, and how the paintbrush works.

In the case of sending two messages, the generalized activity is simply the repeated process of sending a message, coordinating ideas and actions as before. In reading "Spartanville," the generalization requires a conscious recognition that two details, appearing in experience as different words, are the same thing. In inventing a paintbrush, there are many new generalizations, involving new ways of seeing, talking, and coordinating painting (e.g., deliberately vibrating the synthetic brush).

Although there is a certain arbitrariness in how we segment behavior in an activation trace analysis, and the time scale varies greatly in the examples, the salient events are perceptions (details) coordinated within an ongoing sequence of behavior. The activation diagram establishes a relation between surprises, inquiry, and path changing (cf. Fig. 5.8). These relations are not primarily descriptive or theoretical structures, but determined by the agent's prior physical coordinations and immediate flow of experience. They are activation relations, not descriptive models of the world and behavior (what Ryle [1949, p. 40] called "prescriptions"). Thus, the agent's history, which as in other theories of memory plays a central role, is not a storehouse of descriptions of behavior, but the actual prior ways in which categorizations were temporally and compositionally related as they functioned together in a reflectively constructed perceptual-motor coordination.

8.2 "SCHEMA" AS AN ACTIVE, COORDINATING PROCESS

Perhaps now we can better understand Bartlett's (1932/1977) notion of a schema as a coordinating process, rather than a stored description of how behavior appears to an observer:

> "Schema" refers to an active organization of past reactions, or of past experiences, which must always be supposed to be operating in any well-adapted organic response . . . . All incoming impulses of a certain kind, or mode, go together to build up an active, organised setting: visual auditory . . . at a relatively low level; all the experiences connected by a common interest: in sport, in literature, history . . . at a higher level. (p. 201)

An activation trace diagram represents a schema in this sense: a composition or coordination of processes, which by its very coming into being (selection as an active map composition), is biased to reform itself again (through strengthening of neural connections). Here is the crucial idea of memory: Every neural organization that is physically part of the current sequence is liable to be activated again, precisely because of, and in composition with, the neural processes with which it is currently activated.

To make this shift from schema as stored and reassembled stored parts to schema as active processes generalized in use, Bartlett (1932/1977) found it necessary to explicitly reject Head's use of the term *storehouse*. In this example, he alluded to earlier experiments involving brain lesions, in which researchers attributed remembering (or the lack of it) to the changed sites (in the following example, the teeth are where poetry knowledge is stored):

Head gives away far too much to earlier investigators when he speaks of the cortex as "a storehouse of past impressions." All that his experiments show is that certain processes cannot be carried out unless the brain is playing its normal part. But equally those very reactions could be cut out by injuries to peripheral nerves or to muscular functions. One might almost as well say that because nobody who is suffering from a raging toothache could calmly recite "Oh, my love's like a red, red rose", the teeth are the repository of lyric poetry. In any case, the storehouse is a place where things are put in the hope that they may be found again when they are wanted exactly as they were when first stored away. The schemata are, we are told, living, constantly developing, affected by every bit of incoming sensational experience of a given kind. The storehouse notion is as far removed from this as it well could be. (p. 200)

Bartlett goes further in rejecting the term *schema*, as Head and other used it, as a kind of template (or in modern terms a *frame*) that is directly applied:

I strongly dislike the term "schema." It is at once too definite and too sketchy. The word is already widely used in controversial psychological writing to refer generally to any rather vaguely outlined theory. It suggests some persistent, but fragmentary, "form of arrangement," and it does not indicate what is very essential to the whole notion, that the organised mass results of past changes of position and posture are actively doing something all the time; are, so to speak, carried along with us, complete, although developing, from moment to moment. Yet it is certainly very difficult to think of any better single descriptive word to cover the facts involved. It would probably be best to speak of "active, developing patterns"; but the word "pattern," too, being now very widely and variously employed, has its own difficulties; and it, like "schema," suggests *a greater articulation of detail* than is normally found. I think probably the term "organised setting," approximates more closely and clearly to the notion required. I shall, however, continue to use the term "schema" when it seems best to do so, but I will attempt to define its application more narrowly. (pp. 200–201, italics added)

These remarks inspired my analysis in chapter 2 of conventional memory architectures, which were developed 30 to 50 years after Bartlett's critique! Again, the notion is that a conceptualization (which I identify with an "organized setting") is not articulated into parts and named relations, as one finds in conventional descriptive models of conceptual knowledge.

Building on Head's studies of sensation memory, Bartlett (1932/1977) described a schema as a chronological ordering of experience:

If Head is right, "schemata" are built up chronologically. Every incoming change contributes its part to the total "schema" of the moment in the order in which it occurs. That is to say, when we have movements *a, b, c, d,* in this order, our "plastic postural model" [in Head's terminology] of ourselves at the moment *d* is made depends, not merely upon the direction, extent, and intensity of *a, b, c, d,* but also upon the chronological order in which they have occurred. (p. 203)

A neural activation analysis represents this forward-moving, sequential aspect of activity. The chronological, next–next–next development of activity is represented by the main diagonal (Fig. 8.2 and Fig. 8.3). Bartlett's (1932/1977) schemas are *interacting processes*, not static representations like the descriptions encoded in semantic networks or production rules:

> Since its nature is not of that of a passive framework, or patchwork, but of an activity, it can be maintained only if something is being done all the time. So to maintain the "schema" as it is—although this is rather inaccurate language—a, b, c, d must continue to be done, and must continue to be done in the same order. (p. 208)

This model strongly parallels Dewey's (1902) principles of *continuity* (developing sense of WIDN) and *interaction* (coordinated perceptions and actions in the world):

> The two principles of continuity and interaction are not separate from one another. They intercept and unite. They are, so to speak, the longitudinal and lateral aspects of experience. Different situations succeed one another. But because of the principle of continuity, something is carried over from the earlier to the later ones. As an individual passes from one situation to another, his world, his environment, expands or contracts. (p. 519)

Continuity corresponds to the ongoing conceptualization of WIDN, as well as the idea that a sequence is reactivated and generalized in later experience. Interaction corresponds to the details hanging to the right, representing the ongoing relation of perception and motion (the "situatedness" of activity). As Dewey repeatedly emphasized, incoming details described by Bartlett are not independently existing entities, but experienced (categorized) within recoordinations.

For example, when the painters (chapter 7) experience an incoming detail such as "flowing in channels," this perception is not an objective thing in the world they suddenly take notice of, but a constructive *relation* codetermined by how they are coordinating their sense-making activity at that time. The descriptive modeling view would suggest that the painters are looking for *features* they have previously conceived (indeed, previously described). A dialectic perspective claims that a new visual organization developed because certain kinds of *contrasts* were part of their conception of what they were doing, and hence organizing where and how they looked during their painting activity. That is, their *interest* was not an internal description, but an active, coordinating process, a schema. Most cognitive models have not captured the nature and role of this ongoing conceptual, nondescriptive context in perceptual categorization: Perception is not peripheral or antecedent to movement, but rather arises *within* a comprehending, composing process (cf. the critique of analogy models for omitting pragmatic context, section 7.5).

Vygotsky's claim cited at the beginning of chapter 1, that "every thought is a generalization," views development as inherently a process of generalization. Of course, we do not mean descriptive generalization, in the sense that a named class generalizes a set of described examples, but coordination generalization, in the sense that WIDN *includes* processes already and previously occurring. This generalization occurs at different levels and relations between perceptual categorization, sequencing, and categorization of sequences. Descriptive rationalization is the most powerful way of reconceptualizing and hence generalizing behavior. In practice, talk and mechanical recoordination are integrated, so that a person is always like a dancer balancing his or her next steps against the inertia of past movements and a view of where he or she is going.

The resulting picture is a unification of physical and intellectual skills. Rather than viewing cognition as controlling or opposed to action, we place talk and conceptualization within movement:

- Descriptive phrases are not concepts themselves, but *representations* of conceptualizations; that is, grammatical language enables modeling the situation and activity.
- Conceptualization is a form of physical recoordination.
- The "main stream of interest" is developed through an ongoing process of conceiving WIDN (and this conception can be nonverbal).
- New conceptualizations subsume details and previous conceptions in a "dialectic" process of codetermination that recoordinates activity.

In subsequent sections, I relate other models of memory and learning to Bartlett's theory.

8.3 NOVELTY IN MANIPULATION OF MATERIALS

How are new schemas constructed? As Maturana and Varela (1987) emphasized, in their biological theory of knowledge, the neural system is structurally closed; changes are not imposed from outside by instruction or programming, but only induced during internal and external interactions. In Bateson's (1972) terms, the relations of neural processes are tautological with respect to themselves. That is, categorizations can only operate on the constructions of prior mental processes. To understand novelty, we must view the total *system* of neural processes, behavior, and how the environment is changed (cf. Fig. 7.2).

A fundamental insight of situated cognition is that introducing new materials in the environment—including especially speech and written notations—promotes new ways of categorizing. What I say can be news to me. Novelty and invention occurs in *cycles* of changing the environment and recategorizing (reperceiving and reconceiving meaning). The possibility for novelty lies in perturbations that the neural and external material organizations impose on each other. On the one hand, physical selections and recombinations occur neurologically; on the other hand, such operations occur in the conventionalized meaning-expressing forms of crafts, gestures, spoken language, writing, and roles of social organizations.

Bartlett (1932/1977) emphasized that consciousness, especially in speaking that models the world, provides a means to break out of the immediate coordination of behavior to deal with breakdowns deliberately:

> An organism has somehow to acquire the capacity to turn round upon its own "schemata" and to construct them afresh . . . . It is where and why consciousness comes in. (p. 206)

> A new incoming impulse must become *not merely* a cue setting up *a series of reactions all carried out in a fixed temporal order,* but a stimulus which enables us to go direct to that portion of the organised setting of past responses which is most relevant to the needs of the moment. (p. 206, italics added)

The detail arising to our awareness provides a handle for deliberately reconceiving a past experience, holding it against the needs of the moment. In this way, the automatic processes of the impasses, emotional experience, and recollected detail become material for description, and incorporation into a story of what is happening:

> To break away from this the "schema" must become, not merely something that works the organism, but something with which the organism can work . . . . What then emerges is an *attitude* toward the massed effects of a series of past reactions. Remembering is a constructive justification of this attitude . . . . The fact that it is operating with a diverse organised mass and not with single undiversified events or units, gives to remembering its inevitable associative character. (p. 208)

An attitude is the first aspect of a developing "novel" neural organization. As rationalization begins, the attitude and detail are already part of an ongoing activity, providing an orientation in the chronology of experience (cf. Fig. 7.1, Fig. 8.1, and Fig. 8.2). By virtue of the compositional process that includes them in the new global map, we view the attitude and detail as associated with the conceptualization of what we are doing. Reflection is the process of reifying these nonverbal experiences, making the "diverse organized mass" of attitude, concept, and image *discrete objects* to be named and related:

> If only the organism could hit upon a way of turning round upon its own 'schemata' and making them the objects of its reactions . . . . It would be the case that the organism would say, if it were able to express itself: "This and this and this must have occurred, in order that my present state should be what it is." And, in fact, I believe this is precisely and accurately just what does happen in by far the greatest number of instances of remembering. (p. 202)

Rationalization thus weaves a story, an ordering of diverse concerns in a *causal view* of experience and behavior: "I must have been thinking . . . ." "I guess I wanted . . . ." "I assumed . . . ." Where there was perhaps no talk before, we populate the mechanism of behavior with a chain of names, facts, assumptions, features, rules, and theories. Where even there was descriptive consideration (such as in reading instructions or discussing a situation with a colleague), we populate our subsequent behavior with interpretations and further inferential steps: "I must have concluded that . . . ." "I interpreted this to mean . . . ." "I guess I thought that wasn't important . . . ." So looking back between the original plan and the subsequent action, we posit more descriptions. This is the conventional, everyday process of sense making. As a psychological theory of human action, Schön (1979) cautioned us that such interposing of descriptive inference may be historical revisionism. Yet this is precisely how conventional descriptive cognitive models operate—by manipulating the already articulated products of the programmer's thought, rather than reifying a nonverbal experience (e.g., an attitude or an image).

Now, the great benefit of the conjectural talk of the conscious person is extending the self into the world. Descriptions are like clay or sketches, available for reshaping, reperception, and reinterpretation. The word, as well as the image, moves the determinants of behavior into experience itself, so a loop can form with action mediated by acts of representing:

> In fact, this is one of the great functions of images in mental life: to pick items out of "schemata", and to rid the organism of over-determination by the last preceding member of a given series . . . . This, too, could not occur except through the medium of consciousness. (Bartlett, 1932/1977, p. 209)

Representational artifacts—our speech, drawings, books, and so on—become part of the causality of human behavior, so what we do next is not merely a process of selecting and recombining neural maps (although it always depends on that).

> The possibility of being determined by really remote stimuli seems to be coincident with the development of specialised and widely ranging interests. And this, again, appears to demand a reshuffling and reorganisation of material. (Bartlett, 1932/1977, p. 211)

Bartlett (1932/1977) summarized the advantages of representational activity, particularly imagery and rationalization:

> Images are a device for picking bits out of schemes, for increasing the chance of variability in the reconstruction of past stimuli and situations, *for surmounting the chronology of presentations.* [An image] facilitates the operation of the past in relation to the somewhat changed conditions of the present. (p. 219, italics added)

Imagined statements and visualization become part of the environment of the coordination process, so instead of a linear stimulus–response or reactive system, the cognitive process is inherently based on feedback. This view directly counteracts the all too prevalent view that consciousness is "epiphenomenal" or "incidental," as suggested by Gibson (1966) and many others: "Perhaps conscious remembering is an occasional and incidental symptom of learning in the same way that sensations are occasional and incidental symptoms of perceiving" (p. 277).

Bartlett's characterization of consciousness is quite general. "Turning around on one's own schema" may occur without descriptions, in the conceptual rearrangement of objects and events of animals with primary consciousness (such as ravens; Heinrich, 1993). Indeed, such "event perception" underlies human linguistic ability. People and some primates have a secondary feedback loop internally allowing categorization of the conceptualizing process itself (and hence self-awareness; Edelman, 1992). Such reflective categorizing, externalized into linguistic artifacts, provides a *tool* for remembering and recoordination.

8.4 THE ROLE OF EMOTION IN CONCEPTUAL COORDINATION

Given the prominence of attitude in Bartlett's theory, and its corresponding omission in the vast majority of descriptive cognitive models of memory, further discussion of the nature and role of emotion in conceptual coordination is warranted. Here I briefly describe recent studies that have changed how cognitive scientists relate emotion to the information processing framework.

Damasio (1994) synthesized ideas about the brain and cognition in a way that is entirely consistent with the view of memory and knowledge I am exploring. He produced a comprehensive, balanced theory relating neural facts, a broad view of animal cognition, and the role of symbol processing in human society. Damasio's discussion of emotion is of specific interest with respect to our present consideration of Bartlett. His lucid prose provides its own summary:

- Certain aspects of the process of emotion and feeling are indispensable for rationality.[4]

- Feelings point us in the proper direction, take us to the appropriate place in a decision-making space, where we may put the instruments of logic to good use.

- Both "high-level" and "low-level" brain centers, from the prefrontal cortices to the hypothalamus and brain stem, cooperate in the making of reason.

- The dependence of high reason on low brain does not turn high reason into low reason.

- The essence of a feeling may not be an elusive mental quality attached to an object, but rather the direct perception of a specific landscape: that of a body . . . . A "feeling" is a momentary "view" of that body landscape. It has a specific content—the state of the body.

- Because the sense of that body landscape is juxtaposed in time to the perception or recollection of something else that is not part of the body—a face, melody, an aroma—feelings end up being "qualifiers" to that something else.

- The qualifying body state, positive and negative, is accompanied and rounded up by a corresponding thinking mode: fast moving and idea rich,

---

[4]These statements are all quotes from Damasio (1994, pp. xiii–xvi).

when the body-state is in the positive and pleasant band of the spectrum, slow moving and repetitive, when the body-state veers toward the painful band.

- Feelings are the sensors for the match or lack thereof between nature and circumstance . . . . Feelings are just as cognitive as other percepts. Our most refined thoughts and best actions, our greatest joys and deepest sorrows, use the body as a yardstick.
- The organism interacts with the environment as an ensemble: the interaction is neither of the body alone nor of the brain alone.

Thus, Damasio added certain details and qualifications to Bartlett's theory of remembering. Bartlett's "attitudes" are described more specifically by Damasio as a "feeling about the body," which he calls a *somatic marker*. Somatic markers are "a special instance of feelings generated from secondary emotions" (p. 174). Feelings are conscious experiences; secondary emotions are learned, as opposed to innate responses: "Those emotions and feelings have been connected, by learning, to predicted future outcomes of certain scenarios" (p. 174). The mechanism is essentially a process of conditioned response: "When the bad outcome connected with a given response option comes to mind, however fleetingly, you experience an unpleasant gut feeling" (p. 173). The association modifies attention, as well as the cognitive style, affecting the kind and number of action alternatives that will be considered: "Somatic markers probably increase the accuracy and efficiency of the decision process. Their absence reduces them" (p. 173).

Damasio's theory is actually much more complex, including consideration of the varieties of feelings and the possibility for somatic markers to operate subconsciously and to "utilize an 'as if' loop" (p. 288). However, at root, it is basically a conditioned-response theory: Secondary emotions are learned associations; feelings about emotions anticipate punishment or reward outcomes that occurred in the past; future action is modified by the present experienced feeling.

Damasio (1994) elevated this theory from being a simple, behaviorist model to a complex cognitive theory by:

- Relating decision-making behavior to emotional response.
- Emphasizing the role of dispositional representation in deliberately controlling emotional experience (as in projective, exploratory consideration of options during decision making).
- Relating emotional experience to the construction of a social self.

Thus, the organism is not merely reactive, but constructing a persona and evoking emotional experience within purposeful activity. His evidence comes from neurological dysfunctions, in which discoordinations occur in the preceding functions of consciousness.

Grounding his theory in what is known about neural systems, Damasio (1994) distinguished between sensory and dispositional representations, effectively corresponding to what I have called perceptual and conceptual categorization. Again, Damasio gave emotion a central role: "Dispositional representations . . . embody knowledge pertaining to how certain types of situations usually have been paired with certain emotional responses, in your individual experience" (p. 136).

Other aspects of Damasio's theory provide neurological supporting details for my notion of conceptual coordination. In particular, he related Lashley's (1951) idea of "sentential ordering" of behavioral "phrases" to criteria provided by somatic markers for selecting among sequences activating in parallel, which Damasio called "concurrent and interactive sequences" (p. 199). This is effectively a mechanism by which pragmatic context can affect the recombination and substitution of behaviors (cf. discussion in chapter 7 of what controls analogical constructions). Damasio also mentioned briefly how the ensemble of attention, feeling, and activity in sensory cortices may be synchronously coordinated by *convergence zones* utilizing feedforward and feedback connection (see also Pribram, 1971, and Minsky, 1985).

Acting as "third-party brokers" convergence zones "preserve the order of the onset of brain activity" and "maintain activity and attentional focus" (p. 162). This may explain why, in reflecting on an experience and recalling similar experiences, we tend to articulate how we felt at the beginning (as noted by Bartlett). Perhaps the early orienting attitude is what later subsumed, conceptualized experiences have in common. Or put another way, experience is conceptually categorized by associating perceptions that evoke similar attitudes. This attitude then "moves forward" in an automatic process of generalization, so it occurs earlier in the reconstructive, remembering process. Fears and pleasures come to mind first, appropriately inhibiting or enabling the enactment of the conceptualized coordination. Hence, you may have an oriented response (as in catching the quick sight of another person), prior to even trying to say what is happening to you.

Similar mechanisms are described by Barresi and Moore (1996), with respect to emotional attitudes (also called *psychological orientations*) of anger, fear, surprise/puzzlement, happiness, and so on. Insofar as emotion plays a pivotal role in relation to activity, it becomes associated with included objects and their properties. As observers, we may view an emotion as "directed toward an act or possible state of affairs" (p. 108) (a goal) and focus on the object and properties. Conventional analyses would suggest that the emotion is a reaction to the object. But, as Bartlett and Damasio emphasized, the agent's experience may be different: Perceptual categorizations are developing in an activity (kinesthetic and proprioceptive), with a feeling occurring as an overarching impression. That is, emotion is not just a *response to* objects, but an organizer playing a causal role in categorization of objects as *being present*. Feelings and perceptual categorizations thus arise together.

In summary, the significance of Bartlett's theory and recent reconsiderations of cognitive theory is in giving emotion a causal role, rather than making it always a passive response. On the other hand, a feeling is not just a trigger—for example, I became angry and therefore I shouted—as if a state of mind causes certain (usually viewed as irrational) actions. Rather, the relation may be synchronous: A state of mind (feelings), categorizations of what the situation is, and actions develop together.

8.5 SUMMARY OF FUNCTIONAL ARCHITECTURE OF REMEMBERING

The discussion to this point has only been a sketch of what must eventually be an elaborate theory, which integrates many previous observations and theories. The work discussed so far goes a long way toward bringing together the information processing, emotional, and physical coordination aspects of cognition. Nevertheless, the remembering process described here is already more complex than we know how to physically build. What we are doing here is developing an abstract specification of the remembering mechanism, which needs to be better related to cognitive experience and neurobiological processes, if we are to replicate conceptual coordination as it occurs in the human brain. Some key aspects of conceptual coordination, which I continue to elaborate in subsequent chapters, include:

- Reactivating ("replaying") a previously enacted sequence (e.g., habits).
- Conceiving phrases ("conceptual chunking," in contrast with just rote repetition, which become details within other sequences, forming hierarchies of substitutable coordinations (e.g., goal hierarchies).
- Ongoing selection and recombination into a stream of conscious activity by coordinating multiple perspectives (e.g., syntax and semantics).
- A reflective process by which a detail (a visual image or word) becomes the starting point for a new conceptualization that constitutes a new compositional coordination (e.g., inventive design).

In more detail, my conjectures about the functioning and production of neural processes represented by the neural activation diagrams are as follows (for simplicity a sequence of neural activations is referred to as a "sequence"):

1. Composition, correlation, and details
  a.   The sequence is constructed in real time,
  b.   by a composition process
  c.   that coordinates categorization of sensation and action (active processes)
  d.   by including a detail, usually an image or word, that "comes in from the side,"

e.   such that the new composition is a generalization of the one immediately preceding,

f.   often correlating the new image detail with the one just before.

2. Neural maps

a.   The composition process constructs processes by selecting neural maps, which formed ontogenically (i.e., as the brain physically developed early in life; Edelman, 1992).

b.   The huge number of possible maps of maps (compositions) gives the effect of constructing arbitrary links in real time.

c.   Global ("conceptual") maps may be organized with respect to (incorporate) an emotion or attitude,

d.   which is experienced at the same time perceptual details come to attention.

3. Coordinated sequences

a.   Usually sequence construction proceeds automatically, as a "direct chain of reactions,"

b.   so that previous constructions are reconfigured and incorporated immediately,

c.   producing what we recognize as practiced sequences of behavior.

d.   The chain is oriented temporally forward, so the person finds it easy to project or anticipate, but more difficult to return to an earlier step, and impossible to erase what is internally constructed.

4. Figure–ground

a.   Even a recurring, habitual sequence is adapted

b.   and never repeats a previous state (although the agent or outside observer may perceive the behaviors to be identical by his own categorizing).

c.   The current organization constitutes a figure relative to the potentially active categorizations, which constitute the ground.

d.   Figure and ground may be swapped under deliberate control,

e.   in a process that resembles self-organization between alternative attractors of chaotic systems (Freeman, 1991).

5. Focus of attention and analogy

a.   Current sequences direct attention

b.   by coordinating looking and listening

c.   with details deliberately held active by conscious awareness,

d.   such that new generalizations are created *(ways* of seeing, hearing, and so on),

e.   that incorporate details from previous experience

f.   in a process of "seeing as," which correlates old and new details (analogical reasoning).

6. Interactivity of coordination

a.   Coordination is fundamentally interactive: A coordinating process now becoming active must compose currently active processes of perceiving and acting.

  b. That is, in conscious behavior, the person is interacting with compositions of one's own construction, which constitute the context of ongoing behavior.
  c. Furthermore, a practiced sequence constrains and bounds perceptions and movements now being constructed (yielding biases and illusions).

7. Rationalization (descriptive representations of experience)

  a. Rationalizations are ways of conceiving and hence coordinating experience.
  b. Rationalizations are generalizations that include the immediately previous compositions on the main stream of interest and the current focus details (figures).
  c. Rationalizations state the validity of a categorization (the experience of similarity), giving meaning to an incoming detail.
  d. Rationalizing can occur automatically, as reflection-in-action, or after deliberate processes of search in physical materials and by construction of details from the ground.
  e. Strategies for rationalizing (i.e., making sense) may incorporate practiced sequences, which become the main stream of interest (as in the painters observing their painting and later talking about pumps).
  f. Descriptions of experiences of categorizing and doing (e.g., names for things and actions) reinforce stability by providing details (words) that become part of a sequence.
  g. Describing facilitates multimodal organizing (sound + image + movement) and hence facilitates deliberate reactivation of coordinated processes.
  h. Conventional narrative forms of discourse develop from the neural compositional process of coordinating current and past compositions (ways of making sense) against details of sensory experience (images and words).

8. Impasses

  a. Impasses occur when current categorizing—including higher level organizers of the ongoing story, previous incorporations, and contextually required inclusions—cannot be immediately composed with the main stream of interest (WIDN).
  b. An overarching composition is created by talking about (i.e., rationalizing) a detail that is only held for the moment by an emotional categorization.

By this theory, there is one overarching organizer for all learning in a conscious person—the generalization of WIDN. But there are two distinct contexts for learning depending on the scope of attention, corresponding to Dewey's longitudinal and latitudinal aspects of experience. When attention is focused narrowly on some detail, there is a one-step generalization that incorporates the detail (latitudinal). However, when attention is focused on the main stream of interest itself, there is the effect of reflecting on or reconceptualizing WIDN (longitudinal). Together, the compositional process has the essential characteristic indicated by Schön (1979, 1987) of history telling and re-*collecting* details in the path: "I noticed this; I tried to do this; then I realized such-and-such; and I concluded . . . ." The longitudinal includes the latitudinal: In my speaking I recategorize the details of my experiences (what I said, heard, or saw), then I describe the generalization (e.g., what it all—the sequence of experience—means).

Finally, building on Bartlett's notion of an organized mass, the very idea of a behavior "step" should be called into question. There may be an ongoing conceptualization (WIDN) that absorbs, shifts, and emphasizes experience. This conceptualization is only marked and broken apart in our discrete verbal commentary about events, lapses, and realizations. Even here a broader conceptualization of the person's activity ("I am writing the bills" or "I am planning for a trip") may remain relatively unarticulated, constituting a higher-level organizer that bridges impasses at the task level. An aspect of consciousness is that we always, necessarily, have some ongoing way of ordering thoughts. The breakdown of this broad view of WIDN is evident in obsessive-compulsive tendencies, when people become caught in repetitive behavior (brooding, cleaning, hearing voices), which they, as persons striving for a coherent self-story, cannot control.

To further elucidate the nature and operation of conceptual coordination, I examine in subsequent chapters a variety of related theories of learning and memory. My analysis shows that the picture I have just sketched fits a diverse range of psychological data, and it explains the flexibility and profoundly sequential aspect of cognition in a new way.

9

Transformational Processes, Grammars, and Self-Organizing Strings

Darwin's answer to the sources of the order we see all around us is overwhelmingly an appeal to a single force: natural selection. It is this single-force view which I believe to be inadequate, for it fails to notice, fails to stress, fails to incorporate the possibility that simple and complex systems exhibit order spontaneously.

—Stuart A. Kauffman, *The Origins of Order*, 1993, p. xiii.

In this chapter I relate conceptual coordination to Piaget's and Chomsky's theories of learning. I conclude that a coordination perspective bridges theories of *mechanism* (e.g., grounded in biological processes of neural map formation) and theories of *knowledge construction* (grounded in transformation of existing conceptual relations). On the one hand, we view development as mechanical or physically constrained, on the other, as functional or semantically constrained. Kauffman's (1993) theory of self-organizing processes, which spans phenomena from molecular genetics to language and economics, is a new way of bringing together the view of mechanism and cognitive product (knowledge). In particular, I consider how neural activation can be viewed in terms of autocatalytic sets of "grammar strings"—generalized coordination sequences that order and operate on each other. Viewing conceptual coordination processes as both the carrier and constructor of memory—content and assembly process—I suggest a way to disentangle the dichotomy between mechanism and meaning, variously described as syntax versus semantics, form versus content, and structure versus process.

9.1 PIAGET'S TRANSFORMATIONAL PROCESSES

Piaget (1970) described two processes relevant to conceptual coordination—*reflective abstraction* and *self-regulation*. In Piaget's terms, conceptual coordination processes are the "mechanism of construction of novelties." I briefly consider his theories here.

First, *reflective action* is the root of logical thought, by which Piaget meant conceptualization, not linguistic argument. The basis of reflective action is coordinated action, which is of four types that may be related to the neural activation relations we have considered (Table 9.1).

Table 9.1

Relation of Piaget's Reflective Action to Neural Processes of Conceptual Coordination

Piaget's Types of Reflective Action	*Neural Activation Relations*
Additive (joining)	Adding a category onto the end of a sequence
Sequential (ordering)	Categorized sequences
Corresponding	Generalization of a focus detail (cf. Fig. 4.3)
Intersecting	Incorporation of details in a mainstream of interest

Abstraction, the second aspect of reflective abstraction, fits the claim that every categorization is a generalization. However, Piaget had in mind a more important, organizing level, of coordinated activity, namely the transformations we learn, the ways of seeing and ordering, which Bamberger (1991) called *strategies of representation.* This was Piaget's main point: the ability to comprehend, focus, and make sense in logical ways (e.g., the notions of simultaneity and conservation) develops in experience. Piaget emphasizes that knowledge is *operative*—it is interactively (functionally) constructed and reengaged. Knowledge consists of capabilities, operations, transformational processes, ways of interacting, and coordinating. Crucially, Piaget's studies indicate that these ways of organizing experience develop in a human child before language develops.

Neural processes represented by activation trace diagrams partially account for the logical relations of *inclusion, order,* and *correspondence* by which people order objects and events in the world. That is, the logic of thought depends on relations between categories that automatically arise in our experience—perceptual categorizing, sensorimotor coordinating, conceptualizing, impasses, recoordination, generalization, sequencing, conceptualizing a sequence, holding a detail, categorizing conceptualizations, imagining a sequence, and so on. Piaget (1970) called such a hypothesis (although he did not explicitly present this list) the "fundamental hypothesis of genetic epistemology": "There is a parallelism between the progress made in logical and rational organization of knowledge and the corresponding formative psychological processes" (p. 13).[1]

For example, I may automatically conceive what I am doing as similar to what I did before (e.g., as in sending two messages in rapid succession; chapter 4). Reflecting on this relation (categorically grasping the relation of two details in the sequence of my shifting attention), I experience the meaning of *correspondence*. Subsumption and composition are conceived as *inclusion*: "I noticed this detail and included it in my design." Next–next–next chronology is conceived as *order*: "I did this and then I did that." These relations are immediately available in awareness. More complicated relations are constructed as perceivable units by the use of descriptive representations including diagrams, organizing materials in space, and language. By self-regulative processes, most evident in noticing and resolving impasses, we develop systems of transformation that have their own developed-in-use logic (e.g., what inventors or planners learn to do when they get stuck). (The breakdown in such systems results in the dysfunctions mentioned at the end of the last chapter.)

There is no control structure in the sense of a separate processor that interprets and assembles stored structures, as is prevalent in descriptive cognitive models. Rather, the controlling structure is the ongoing compositional process itself (recall the discussion of slips and Norman's theory; section 6.3). Holding a focus of attention, dealing with impasses, and executing a motor sequence are not separate operations handled by a scheduling program that manipulates models of behavior, but accomplished by the self-organizing process of physical coordination. In this sense, the generalizations of WIDN are not the controlling processes either, but just transitory organizations that influence the next compositional state. In these respects, Piagetian terms like *reflective abstraction* are misunderstood or incomprehensible from the descriptive modeling perspective, which views reflection as describing and abstraction as a description. So conventional cognitive models would equate reflective abstraction with conscious, meta-level reasoning—as opposed to the underlying subconscious neural mechanism.

---

[1]Reber (1993) called this "process-specific nativism" (p. 149) and contrasted it with a "content-specific nativism" that claims that apparent structure, as in grammars, is not the learned result of modality-general processing systems (such as the list I give here), but of physical modules that are genetically specified. As I indicate later, I believe Chomsky's (1980, 1981) view lies somewhere in between, not at the genetic-content extreme.

9.2 CHOMSKY'S MENTAL PHYSIOLOGY

Chomsky provided another—often viewed as opposing—account of learning. The nature of linguistic patterns (grammars) is of special interest as we tease apart theorists' descriptions, a person's behavior patterns, and neural processes. How do rules of grammar relate to conceptualization of sequences and their subsequent reactivation and generalization in coordinating speaking?

In essence, Chomsky (1980, 1981) argues for internal processes operating on representations of linguistic expressions:

> Chomsky has maintained that all natural languages are transformational and have rules that operate on abstract, as opposed to explicit surface, structures; that all human languages make use of cycles of transformations working on successively more inclusive structures within sentences; and he has suggested that nouns, verbs, and adjectives are likely to prove universal deep-syntactic categories of human languages, and that at least one constraint on grammatical rules, which *prohibits transformations that move material in or out of various conjunctive structures,* is probably universal. (Leiber, 1975, pp. 133–134, italics added)

This theory is not about performance—what we actually say—but about recurrent abstract patterns in what we say and how patterns relate to one another. The theory claims that there are kernel forms for sentences, transformations (such as relating verb tense and voice), and ordering (Shapiro, 1992, p. 205). This means that fundamentally, the structure of natural language (as characterized by grammars, descriptions of patterns) has some aspect of its origin in meaning-independent processes. Put another way, the theory argues that words have roles, which are conceptualizations that are not grounded in the meaning of the words or sentences per se, but in the compositional structure of the utterances. The underlying neural construction process becomes evident in certain constructions that do not occur (emphasized in the preceding quote). The ensuing discussion and the next chapter develop these ideas in detail.

Chomsky's theory was given special credence when it was determined that transformational grammars could be formulated as augmented transition networks (ATNs), a computational representation allowing conditionality and recursion, aspects of *generativity* required to produce both the patterns and open nature of human language. The arguments against the simpler FSA representation directly parallel the limits of simple recursive networks (section 3.2). Further, the ATN formulation fits the idea of holding details active (ATNs allow arguments, bound variables); by categorization of sequences (naming and invoking an ATN), the ATN formulation also allows recursive generation on multiple levels of abstraction.[2]

---

[2]The requirement to create unlimited sets of utterances by combining words and phrases according to a fixed set of rules has been termed *generativity*—"the general ability to form multipart representations from canonical parts" (Corballis, 1989, cited in Donald, 1991, p. 71).

Chomsky's view is controversial—and perhaps misunderstood[3]—because he claimed that some of the patterns of grammar are not learned from the patterns of spoken language, but based on the mechanism of conceptualization itself. In the opposing view, patterns have their origin only in meaningful expressions, that is, patterns are (only) representations of experienced expressions. This view was summarized by Langacker (1986) in his theory of *cognitive grammar*:

> Grammar is not a distinct level of linguistic representation, but reduces instead to the structuring and symbolization of conceptual content . . . .
>
> Lexicon, morphology, and syntax form a continuum of symbolic units, divided only arbitrarily into separate "components"—it is ultimately as pointless to analyze grammatical units without reference to their semantic value as to write a dictionary which omits the meanings of its lexical units. (pp. 1–2)

Opposing Langacker's view might at first appear to place Chomsky with Piaget, suggesting that transformational patterns are general mechanisms, independent of content, with a physiological basis. But, as we see, Chomsky explicitly rejected Piaget's theory as being too general in attempting to cover all kinds of learning. The spectrum of opinion therefore can be arranged as follows:

> general, uniform learning principles (Piaget) ⇔
> meaning-general, linguistic mechanism (Chomsky) ⇔
> conceptual patterns (Langacker et al.)

Langacker's (1986) claim was that linguistic structure is not autonomous or meaning-general—and specifically not a reflection of an inherited "grammar organ"—but conceptually constructed as a generalization of actual utterances:

> The term conceptualization is interpreted quite broadly: it encompasses novel conception as well as fixed concepts; sensory, kinesthetic, and emotive experience; recognition of immediate context (social, physical, linguistic); etc. (p. 3)

This definition is intended to avoid the notion that concepts are descriptions, such as the frames in cognitive models:

---

[3]For example, Lieberman (1998) said, "Chomsky claims that human beings do not really learn the rules of syntax. He instead proposes that we come equipped at birth with a 'language organ' that specifies all the rules of syntax of all human languages" (p. 10). Lieberman failed to distinguish between neural constraints on the form of grammar (the essence of Chomsky's interest), regularities in speaking, and a grammarian's description of syntactic patterns.

My advice to all researchers: When a reputable scientist appears to make claims that are patently absurd, consider that the absurdity is in your interpretation of the claims. Critics of situated cognition made the same mistake in interpreting the claim that behavior is not strictly driven by representations (meaning descriptions of goals and plans) to be a claim that there were no representations in the brain at all (e.g., Sandberg and Wielinga, 1991). Of course, it is also possible that I misread Lieberman.

Specifically rejected is the idea that a semantic structure reduces to a bundle of
features or semantic markers (cf. Katz & Fodor, 1963). Rejected as well is the
notion that all meanings are described directly in terms of semantic primitives. (p. 4)

By this view, grammar and lexicon are on a continuum of conceptualization.
In claiming also that the units are "symbolized," Langacker (1986) wanted to
show that no additional kinds of structures are required. All linguistic patterns
derive from:

(i) semantic, phonological, and symbolic structures that occur overtly in linguistic
expressions; (ii) structures that are schematic for those in (i); and (iii) categorizing
relationships involving the structures in (i) and (ii). (p. 20)

The effect is to

...rule out arbitrary descriptive devices, that is, those with no direct grounding in
phonetic or semantic reality . . . [such as] syntactic "dummies" . . . contentless
"features" . . . and the derivation of overt structures from abstract, "underlying"
structures of a substantially different character . . . e.g., the derivation of passives
from actives. (p. 20)

Thus, Langacker supported the view that speaking is not a process of
subconsciously manipulating other descriptions; internal representing is not in a
language of pattern names and qualifiers. This is the same argument used
against arbitrary frame-slot models of slips (section 6.2).

Langacker's (1986) sketch for how expressions become integrated and
composed fits the perspective of neural map activation and composition:

The present framework does not posit phrase trees of the sort familiar from
transformational studies, nor does it rely on phrase-structure configuration for the
definition of grammatical relations. Constituency is simply the sequence in which
component symbolic structures are progressively assembled into more and more
elaborate composite expressions. (pp. 34–35)

Rather than positing intermediate representations of patterns, Langacker's
cognitive grammar is a mechanism that generates new coordinations from
previous ones, involving multiple levels of generalization, sequencing, and
categorization. Addressing the content of these compositions, Chomsky and
Piaget claimed that the patterns are not all conventional or cultural, but have a
basis in physiological constraints.

The value of the neural activation perspective is in reifying and relating these
two dimensions of organizers: On the one hand, relationships conceptually
constructed in the past are organizing new utterances—previous sequences are
being reactivated, generalized, and are operating on different levels of
abstraction. On the other hand, the kinds of conceptual constructions that are
possible *de novo* are determined by the process of perceptual categorization,
sequencing, reactivating sequences, categorizing sequences (conceptualizing),
and constructively composing sequences on different levels. That is, the
mechanism for creating any sequence at all is captured by transformational
grammar. Some content arises from the mechanism itself. This is not such a

complicated idea, except for the emotionally charged controversy over the idea that language is somehow genetically constrained. The trick is to elucidate the sense in which what we can mean, the content of language, is therefore bounded by neural processes.

More direct examination of Chomsky's claims is helpful. We can summarize the theory according to several principles:

- Linguistic ability reflects an evolutionary development of the brain and its physical properties, not merely an individual's accumulated learning:

It is clear why the view that all knowledge derives solely from the senses by elementary operations of association and "generalization" should have had much appeal in the context of eighteenth-century struggles for scientific naturalism. However, there is surely no reason today for taking seriously a position that attributes a complex human achievement entirely to months (or at most years) of experience, rather than to millions of years of evolution or to principles of neural organization that may be even more deeply grounded in physical law. (Chomsky, 1965, p. 58)

- Linguistic ability reflects a specialization of biological function, just as in other physical processes:

No one believes that the human embryo learns to grow arms rather than wings . . . . It seems to me not unlikely that much of our knowledge of the nature and behavior of objects in our physical environment is rooted in principles of mental structure that we may think of on the analogy of physical systems such as the visual or circulatory system. These "mental organs"—which need not, of course, be isolable in a particular neural region—develop in a specific way on the basis of our biological endowment and provide the basis for substantial parts of our knowledge. (Chomsky, 1981, p. 6)

- A proper understanding of semantics requires understanding conceptualization, which involves much more than sensorimotor coordination, but is not itself linguistic:

The conceptual system involves the principles that enter into naming, categorization, and other cognitive functions. It is no doubt involved in many aspects of perception, thought, and expression beyond language. The structure of the conceptual system may involve principles that have little to do with the language faculty in a narrower sense of the word, although their effects will of course appear in the use of language, given the interaction of these systems . . . . Much of what we think of as semantics of natural language is more properly understood, I believe, in terms of the structure of conceptual systems that are not strictly speaking part of language although they interact with the language faculty in the use and understanding of language. It should be possible in principle for the conceptual system to be intact and functioning even although the computational and representational aspects of grammatical competence are impaired or even destroyed. (Chomsky, 1981, p. 11)

- ▪ Linguistic syntax is produced by a device or mechanism that is general across human languages:

Syntactic investigation of a given language has as its goal the construction of a grammar that can be viewed as a device of some sort for producing the sentences of the language under analysis. More generally, linguists must be concerned with the problem of determining the fundamental underlying properties of successful grammars. The ultimate outcome of these investigations should be a theory of linguistic structure in which the descriptive devices utilized in particular grammars are presented and studied abstractly, with no specific reference to particular languages. (Chomsky, 1957, p. 11)

This study can be thought as a analogous to human physiology. Indeed, it is a kind of "abstract physiology," seeking to determine the fundamental properties that are somehow realized in the brain. (Chomsky, 1981, p. 13)

- ▪ The rules of syntax are not arbitrary descriptions of patterns, but restricted to certain structural characteristics of phrases:

The theory of transformational grammar is, in effect, a theory of structure-dependent rules. It stipulates a certain format for possible rules: they may involve analysis into successive phrases, but the notion "first occurrence of *is*," although very simple intuitively, is inexpressible in this format . . . . All known rules are, in fact, structure dependent in the technical sense. (Chomsky, 1981, pp. 16–17)

In these remarks, Chomsky appeared not to distinguish between structured processes that embody rules (by virtue of being restricted patterns) and a body of explicit rules that have an existence apart from actual speaking (as in descriptive cognitive models). Indeed, he appeared to accept uncritically the notion of a stored-rule mechanism:

Certain properties of grammatical competence are coming to be reasonably well understood, I believe. These systems provide various types of abstract representation for the sentences of a language: in terms of sounds, words, phrases, abstract syntactic structures, networks of semantic relations, and the like. They are based on principles of computation that generate, relate, and associate these various representations . . . ultimately represented in some way now unknown in the physical mechanisms of the brain. If this line of thinking is correct, then our knowledge of language is not properly construed as a capacity to do such and such, but rather as a system of rules and principles that enter into such a capacity. (Chomsky, 1981, p. 7)

Like Langacker, I have argued that we must take pains to distinguish between an abstract representation that *describes* patterns as a set of rules and principles (as in conventional cognitive models) and a *mechanism*, as suggested by consideration of neural activation, in which the patterns are embodied in coordinated sequences of behavior. The success of descriptive models suggests that some "sequences," occurring as temporally ordered neural map activations, may correspond to linguistic phrases. However, the examples analyzed in Part II suggest an integration with multimodal attention and physical coordination that a word-based model cannot adequately explain. (Recall especially the errors and transformations examined in chapter 6.)

Chomsky's focus on a mental organ and mental physiology is precisely the level of organization I have sought to explore. The lesson we can draw from Chomsky's objection to Piaget is not to become enamored by the idea that everything is based on principles of sensorimotor coordination: We cannot reduce all aspects of learning to uniform principles in all animals. Insofar as we conjecture that the processes of categorization, sequencing, and generalization are uniformly occurring in, say, normal adult humans, the claim of universality may be more warranted. But we must acknowledge that categorization of sequences, broadly termed *conceptualization*, involves additional aspects of coordination in people, including:

- Holding active a focus detail to include it in a reconceptualization.
- Correlating multiple focus details.
- Rearranging sequences to break out of merely serial, habitual ordering.
- Shifting flexibly between "top down" and "bottom up" organizers.
- Naming conceptualizations and then coordinating relations of names (as in speaking).

I could of course go much further to characterize other aspects of conceptualization that distinguish cognition from mere perceptual categorization, conditioned association, and serial learning. In doing so, building especially on aspects of transformational grammar, we would be sketching the properties of a neural processing *system* that Chomsky identified with a mental organ. Chomsky's (1981) summary of this quest is worth emphasizing:

> Across a spectrum of opinion ranging from Skinner to Piaget, it is assumed that there are certain general principles of learning or development that apply uniformly in all domains. The idea that the principles [of transformational grammar] . . . are the same as those operative in the development of sensorimotor constructions is about as plausible as the suggestion that the visual system and the circulatory system are determined by the same genetic instructions. Even within the system of language we find differentiation of subsystems with their own special properties: syntactic rules and phonological rules, for example, are of quite different sorts. The concept of uniform development of cognitive structures can be maintained, I believe, only if we abstract away from their detailed character, thus disregarding the crucial facts to be explained. (p. 21)

As a biologically grounded scientist, Chomsky might have taken for granted the underlying processes of self-regulation, equilibration, assimilation, and accommodation that Piaget sought to elucidate. Thus, he de-emphasized what cognitive science has yet to appropriately acknowledge in theories of learning. According to Chomsky, there may be relations to sensorimotor coordination in the language mechanism, but a sensorimotor theory of learning is too general to explain the details of transformational grammar. Proponents of situated cognition, especially Lakoff and Searle, have sought to bring sensorimotor processes into the theory of linguistic conceptualization. Somewhat unfairly, Chomsky interpreted them as making the opposite mistake of Piaget by explaining behavior patterns in terms of communicative function.

Again, Chomsky's (1981) interest was somewhere in the middle: To understand assimilation, for example, in terms of the *evolution* of different kinds of schemas, not just their development in an individual's conceptualizing: "functional explanation is nature at the level of evolutionary development, not ontogenesis" (p. 20). Indeed, it is this commitment to the human neurological structure that Chomsky ultimately insisted on, claiming like Edelman that some biological processes have evolved that distinguish humans from other primates and enable language learning: "Study of the products of mind can give some insight into these innate structures and principles, which determine what we might think of as 'the human essence,' in the cognitive domain" (p. 13).

In conclusion, there is value in all of these perspectives, relating sensorimotor experience, generalized speech patterns, and neural mechanism. A neural perspective is useful because it points in the direction of a mechanism consisting of patterns developed in experience, assembled out of self-organizing neurological processes, not words and descriptive rules.[4]

9.3 BERWICK'S APPEAL TO CONNECTIONISM

Berwick, a cognitive scientist, sought to relate the insights of grammar theory to computational architectures. In particular, he explained how "modern linguistic theory" of Chomsky's generative grammar is consistent with the connectionist approach. Considering this argument allows us to more specifically relate transformational grammar to a neural perspective. This establishes background for a more detailed analysis of the relation of grammar to categorization and sequence construction in the next chapter.

Berwick's (1983) summary of modern linguistic theory recapitulates the argument against a mechanism based on descriptions that mediate all action: parse trees are not explicitly built, the units of information are associated with individual words, and surface structure is the product of many constraints acting in parallel (p. 385). The idea of abstract rules *describing classes* of words and how they interact is replaced by a mechanism by which words interact to produce sequences by ordering and thematic constraints. Hence syntax and semantics are effectively integrated. The phrase structure rules of early transformational theory are reinterpreted as being an observer's descriptive abstractions of a set of sentences, not part of the mechanism itself.

---

[4]The debate about the relation of a grammatical description to the mechanism of speech and thinking has often brought out points I make here. See especially Demopoulos and Matthews (1981), Stabler (1983), and Chomsky (1980). Stich's (1980) commentary in particular addresses the issue of internal representation of a linguist's grammar.

In classic phrase structure theory, syntax rules, such as "Vt ->
V_{t3}—<T><AP>Nanim," are literally manipulated by mental operations (p. 391).
But there was no evidence that the language generation steps in the human mind
worked precisely as the rules required. Furthermore, the computational
processes were overly complex because phrase structure rules combined "two
distinct kinds of constraints: (1) the relative order of Nouns and Verbs in
English; and (2) the required thematic arguments of verbs" (p. 390). For
example, the fragment of the rule just cited indicates that a certain kind of
transitive verb (V_{t3}) requires an animate object Noun (Nanim), exemplified by
the verb *frightens* in the phrase *frightens John*. How is ordering information
(which syntax rules embody) and type constraints (called *features*) actually
categorized and related in neural structures?

The general gist of Chomsky's (1975) solution is to associate all the
constraints with words themselves:

> The categorical properties of words like boy or frighten were to be encoded as an
> unordered set of finitely-valued features associated with that word. For instance, boy
> could have the features, [+N, +Count, +Common, +Animate, +Human], describing
> it as a Noun, a Count Noun (one can say *two boys*), Animate, etc . . . . Words
> become in effect "complex symbols," feature bundles that may be inserted into the
> proper places by a hierarchical tree structure. The tree structure itself is generated by
> phrase structure rule with simple node names—just S, NP, VP, and so forth. Thus,
> there are two kinds of knowledge, kept distinct: (1) knowledge about the basic tree
> structure of sentences, expressed in terms of rewrite rules e.g., that in English, a
> single sentence consists of a Noun Phrase followed by a Verb Phrase; and (2)
> knowledge about the categorization of words, expressed in terms of complex
> symbols, e.g., that boy is a Noun, Animate, Human. (p. 392)

For example, Fig. 9.1 shows a representation for a phrase structure rule in
which a verb is indicated as having an animate object, as in the full sentence,
"Sincerity frightens John." *Nanim* (corresponding to the word *John*) is a feature
that "percolates to a higher node to carry out a compatibility check" (Berwick,
1983, p. 393).[5]

The right side of Fig. 9.1 shows a neural activation trace analysis, in which Vt
is a conceptualization of a kind of verb phrase, as indicated by following a
subject in a sentence sequence and coupling to certain qualifying details,
especially an animate noun object. Most important, this activation perspective
shifts from talking about "on the left" or "on the right" of the verb to kinds of
activation. Viewing the object as a qualifier makes clear that the verb plus object
constitutes a unit (a verb phrase) and that the kind of qualifier determines the
kind of noun phrase (here, a V_{t3}). Alternative ways of depicting role relations
possible (as, e.g., one might want to represent that the object follows the verb),

---

[5]My previous presentation of this example (Clancey, 1998, p. 185) is confused; I
mistakenly interpreted *Nanim* to refer to the "Not animate" word, *sincerity*.

but this simplification—a sentence in English is a subject followed by a verb—will turn out to be useful in the many other examples I analyze in the next chapter.[6]

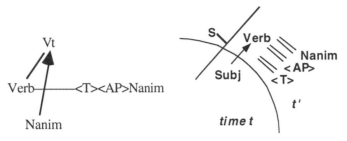

Fig. 9.1. Combined phrase structure and feature representation of a kind of transitive verb (left), with neural activation trace representation (right). Verb is part of a Sentence (S) sequence having coupled qualifiers (optional determiner <T>, optional adjective phrase <AP>, and animate Noun object). (Left diagram from Berwick, 1983, p. 393. Copyright ©1983. Reprinted by permission of Lawrence Erlbaum Associates, Inc.).

The shift from rules plus features to simply features of words was appropriately summarized by Berwick (1983) as a shift to understanding language processing in terms of constraints:

Note that we have taken the first step away from a system of *rules* to a system of *constraints*. The lexical entry for a verb simply specifies *what* the context around that verb must be. It does not say that there is a "rule" that acts as a computational unit (that is a rule that must be "followed" in some direct sense) during language processing. Rather, it says that, whatever the actual computational process involved, the final outcome must be a sequence of elements that obeys the constraints. It is this distinction between *following a rule* and *obeying constraints* that frees modern transformational theory from the burden of a literal computational interpretation of a system of rules. (p. 394).

Nevertheless, note that Berwick still spoke in terms of encoded information and lexical entries as if there is a dictionary in the brain. A strict neural interpretation is that the constraints are activation relations between categorizations of words and sequences. Furthermore, alternative patterns exist as categorized sequences of different kinds. For example, rather than requiring a *Nanim* feature to be tagged onto a Vt categorization, as in the percolation view (left side of Fig. 9.1), it is inherent in some linguistic behavior sequences that

---

[6]In particular, in languages that do not have a hierarchical phrase structure, such as Arabic, which allow ordering such as verb → subject → object, it may be possible that two categories are both coupled and in a sequence, such that an object follows the subject, but the verb is also coupled to its object to form a verb phrase.

the verb is qualified by an object that is categorized as noun and animate.[7] In saying "Sincerity frightens John" we are reactivating a sequence of a certain kind. This of course fits Langacker's view that grammatical knowledge is the history of utterances itself.

Unfortunately, the idea that linguistic knowledge is centered around words—which is tantamount to saying that linguistic relations are centered around word categories—moved somewhat too far in de-emphasizing the inherently sequential aspect of language and the process of composing sequences as units. Hence, we talk about "lexical entries" in which all sequencing information is "encoded" in a description of a word. My analysis (left side of Fig. 9.1) is an attempt to reconcile these views, viewing utterances as sequences of categories, whereby words are categorized in many ways simultaneously (the "features"). Rather than a compatibility check by which the verb causes the animate feature of the object to be checked (the computational approach in interpreting such diagrams), the word *John* activates the categories noun and animate and this combined categorization "object-noun-animate" is coupled to the verb *frightens*. This combined coupling is categorized as V_{t3}, which is activated by an abstract-subject, and so on. The operations are activation of categorizations by coupling and sequence, not assembling and checking.

One reason for showing the qualifiers (<T>, <AP>, and Nanim) as coupled to the verb is to emphasize that a verb phrase not just a verb followed by an object, but is rooted in—has activation relations with—the verb. This follows Chomsky's X-bar theory of 1970, paraphrased by Berwick (1983):

> A Verb Phrase *must* be expanded with a verbal "Head"—that is what it means to be a Verb Phrase. Similarly, a Noun Phrase is always expanded as . . . N. In short, every phrase of type "X" is grounded on a word of type X. Phrases, then, are merely projections of lexical items . . . . There is no specific phrase structure rule needed to describe the required constraints. (p. 396)

But the relation between the phrase categorization and the root is even more general—the ordering is the same for all kinds of phrases.

> Chomsky observed that not only does every phrase of type X have an X-based root, but also that the order of arguments of each phrase is fixed across all phrase types. For instance, in English, Verb Phrases are headed by Verbs, followed by optional Noun Phrases, Prepositional Phrases, and Sentential Phrases. Prepositional Phrases are headed by Prepositions, and are also followed by phrases of the same type. Similarly for Adjectival Phrases. That is, once we have fixed the phrasal order XP->X NP PP, it is fixed for all phrasal types. (Berwick, 1983, p. 396)

---

[7]This interpretation fits Small's theory, on which Berwick (1983) drew, that a thematic argument such as a kind of noun phrase is a "concept structure," which is a "grouping of words" (p. 410). The difference is that we replace "encodings in a dictionary" by categorizations of process sequences.

This linguistic pattern suggests that a general sequencing "coordinator" is learned and applied systematically whenever speaking a given language. A conceptualization that orders sequences within a phrase applies to all kinds of phrases:

> Thus, so-called "X-bar theory" radically restricts the class of permitted base structures; and conditions on rules as well as "output conditions" on surface structure and "logical form" have permitted a substantial reduction in the class of possible transformations, perhaps approaching the limit of a single rule, "Move A," where A is an arbitrary category. (Chomsky, 1980, p. 46)

Only one kind of sequence categorization, which Chomsky characterizes as the rule, "Move A," is applying throughout. The rule is "applied" as constraints operating in parallel, as mentioned by Berwick, involving activations in sequence and the formation of new phrase conceptualizations in accord with previous phrase conceptualizations. This suggests that learning a new kind of phrase conceptualization is generalizing an existing one, for example, reactivating the categorization XP as the sequence X $\rightarrow$ NP $\rightarrow$ PP (where here "$\rightarrow$" denotes a sequential activation). Or perhaps better, to allow for the fact that kinds of phrases (e.g., noun, sentential) are not necessarily learned separately, learning phrase ordering in a given language involves conceptualizing what ordering means in that language, which according to X-bar theory is one categorization, not many.

Like Langacker, Bickhard (1995) rejected the idea that comprehension is a process of encoding grammatical descriptions about propositions (utterances). He argued, as I have here, that the apparent patterns in Universal Grammar can be explained as emerging from relatively simple neural mechanisms by which behavior is functionally organized:

> The structure that is taken as a structure of propositional encodings is not that at all, but is instead a structure of functionally organized action. Constraints on such structures, in turn—constraints on grammars—emerge as intrinsic constraints on that functional organization. (p. 541)

In summary, the constraints of transformational grammar are revealed as being processes of sequential activation and recategorization of sequences, not stored dictionary entries as in a descriptive cognitive model. These observations fit Berwick's theoretical claims in relating modern transformational grammar to connectionism, and they further support the conceptual coordination perspective. In the following chapter, I will pursue the grammatical data further, building on evidence that people have difficulty understanding sentences that programs can parse. But first it is useful to examine yet another metaphor for understanding a system of constraints, namely the idea of a "soup of strings" developed by Kauffman.

9.4 KAUFFMAN'S AUTOCATALYTIC SYMBOL STRINGS

Activation trace diagrams are of course abstractions, representing some still unknown neurological system. Chaos models of perceptual categorization (such as Freeman's [1991] model of olfaction) suggest that anything similar to a discrete manufacturing model—with a kind of conveyor belt working memory for assembling products—is probably a gross simplification of how categories form and compose in time. We need new metaphors, new ways of understanding complex systems, for understanding the parallel, self-organizing properties of the brain. Kauffman (1993) is one of the scientists reaching for such a new synthesis, explicating the nature of self-organizing systems by generalizing molecular and biological processes:

> The generalization of autocatalytic polymer systems is based on the realization that polymers can be regarded as strings of symbols. For example, a protein is a string of 20 kinds of amino acids. The catalytic and other chemical rules governing the ways enzymes catalyze ligation and cleavage among proteins can be thought of as a kind of *grammar*. In this grammar, strings of symbols act on strings of symbols to yield strings of symbols. An autocatalytic set is a type of *collective identity operator* in this space of symbol strings, an operator which produces at least itself. (p. 369)

Playing the game of general systems theory, Kauffman (1993) applied his model broadly to not only molecular interactions in an organism, but "goods and services in an economy, and perhaps even conceptual elements in a cognitive web or mythic elements in a cultural system" (p. 369). That is, Kauffman developed "models of functional integration, transformation, and coevolution" (p. 369) by analyzing complex systems in terms of "the *kinds of compositional sets* of symbol strings that emerge in systems in which strings act on strings to produce strings" (p. 369, italics added).

Kauffman's (1993) contribution is to provide a mechanism—not just the language of transformation and integration of Piaget and Chomsky—that avoids the stored and interpreted descriptive rules approach. The key idea is to

> define grammars of substitutions plus ligation and cleavage operations, but require that strings contain "enzymatic sites" such that the strings themselves are carriers of the grammatical operators. Thus, if the grammar specifies that string ab is replaced by string cddcde, then an enzyme string with an ab enzymatic site would search target strings for a matching ab site and, if found, substitute cddcde in the target string at that site. (p. 383)

Such a grammar "could make definite choices about precedence order in which rules are applied and in which depth of recursive substitution or other actions at one site are pursued" (p. 383). As stated, polymer and protein formation processes provide the model for such an embodied grammar: The patterns are in the previously constructed structures and how they can physically relate, not in separate templates or descriptive rules.

Now, the power of this model is that we can view a *coordinated neural map sequence* as a string. We must keep in mind that the elements (by hypothesis, global maps subsuming each other and simpler classification couples; Fig. 3.1) are temporally ordered, and hence do not necessarily all exist at one time, as a whole, in contrast with a data structure, in which a string like *aabbcde* is stored and present at one time. Again, the nodes in activation trace diagrams are not like tokens in a descriptive cognitive model.

Next, we can view the collection of previously constructed, coordinated sequences as a set of strings. The mechanism by which strings are created through reactivation, new sequencing, generalization of categorizations, composition (top-down) and new conceptualization (bottom-up), and so on, can be thought of as a kind of grammar. Thus, during sequence formation—specifically during conceptualization—sets of strings operate on sets of strings to yield a new string. *Enzymatic sites* are category couplings—categories that simultaneously and mutually activate each other (e.g., the relation of a class to an instance).

A neural activation sequence would thus embody its own relations of allowable substitution, recursion, ordering, and so on, by the classification couples and global mappings of which it is constituted. These categorizations themselves would provide for their own generalization, substitution, and so on, while reorderings (such as shifting from passive to active tense) would be embodied by another sequence of global mappings, which would categorize active components differently. This embodied grammar mechanism fits Kauffman's (1993) views:

> Unlike AI models, although, where the couplings among the elementary processes are defined by external criteria, the coupling in grammar string models is defined internally by the grammatical rules which determine how strings generate one another. (p. 394)

So again, we have two kinds of organizing constraints: The set of previously active strings embody the grammar at the conceptual level, and the way in which strings are assembled—based on the activation and self-organizing mechanism of classification couples and global maps, including especially sequencing, coupling, and composing—means that basic transformational characteristics of the grammar are embodied in every string itself. That is, every neural organization embodies both its history in other organizations, as well as its own formative mechanism. This is another way of saying that the grammar is not a separate description or process (which the phrase *internal grammar rules* might suggest), but inherent in the processes being coordinated themselves.

The set of strings previously constructed and open for activation and inclusion in a new composition at any time constitutes a grammar that maps to itself. That is, the set constitutes a "collective identity operator" in the sense that it constructed itself. This clearly fits Maturana's (1975) view that the nervous system is "structurally closed"—new structures are determined by those that previously existed. Bateson (1979) referred to this property by saying that the system is "tautological" (p. 87)—all existing relations are logically based on each other. By Kauffman's (1993) analogy to molecular biology, the set of strings is "autocatalytic"—its forms provide the conditions for maintaining its functional organization: "The transformations mediated by symbol strings on one another *are* the functional couplings among the symbol strings" (p. 403).

Like Chomsky, Kauffman sought a biological answer to the question of how complex order could develop so quickly in a child. However, he extended the analysis beyond the individual's conceptualizing and speaking capability to the evolutionary process itself. Rather than placing the mechanism solely in the competitive behavioral interactions of the world or in stored explicit instructions or templates of a genetic code, Kauffman, like Chomsky, sought to understand how a highly structured system, such as the brain, might have its own laws of assembly and integration. Hence, order does not merely derive from random mutation and selection, but by finite internal structures (at any one time) operating on themselves in a way to generate an infinite, but self-consistent set of structures. This theory is based both on the developmental constraints of biological structures and general laws of self-organization.

Such a shift in perspective suggests that the often-mentioned analogy between DNA and symbol processing[8] not only ignores the evolutionary problem (how did the programs get created?), but places too much emphasis on independently existing frames or scripts that dictate what happens when. Kauffman's analysis provides an intriguing mechanism that is at once self-organizing and consisting of ordering patterns. Consistent with this shift from the view that strings encode real world relations, consider that less than 1% of DNA codes directly for protein. DNA's role is more dynamic, "making 'meta-statements'—statements about statements—which are on a higher logical level and may not evolve, as time goes on, in the same way that statements evolve" (Campbell, 1982, p. 132). Blending Kauffman's and Edelman's models, we may refer to transformational processes of competitive selection. Such processes develop organization on multiple levels without describing structures or supervising how they are built. That is, forms can be abstract, but also embodied in concrete, functional processes. Descriptive cognitive models treat this distinction by separating learning (abstraction) from doing and storing models and instructions for later instantiation. This is a reasonable view of how written scientific models and textbooks get created and used, but is a poor characterization of biological processes and development.

My elaboration of Kauffman's theories, in many respects speculative and sketchy, suggests that a student of cognitive processes seeking to understand conceptual coordination would do well to adopt a broad perspective on the

---

[8]See Hofstadter (1985) for discussion.

nature of neural mechanisms.[9] The analysis so far has departed greatly from the modeling approach based on stored descriptions, making contact with sensorimotor coordination, perceptual generalization, and nondescriptive conceptualization. At the same time, I have sought to remain in contact with the fundamental interest of cognitive science in grammars, analogical reasoning, and conceptual learning. We find important bridging notions by examining the experience of coordination in next–next–next learning, impasses, and slips. And now we find that our still new and tentative understanding of neuronal group selection might be better framed in terms of autocatalytic sets of ordered strings. But Kauffman's analogy with molecular strings cannot be directly applied, for the elements of a coordinated neural sequence are not static symbols, but stable, temporal relations between processes. We shift from a model of memory based on stored and manipulated substance to one based on processing relations. The descriptive symbols in cognitive models are better viewed in mechanistic terms as always generalized activation relations between categories. Viewing categories in isolation ignores the temporal functions of categorizing (sequence, coupling, composition).

This stage in the analysis is just a small plateau on a large research mountain. My intent is to establish that this mountain is the one we should be climbing, and to provide an analysis grounded in the description of existing computer programs and human experience that gets us out of the deep ravine that placed too much emphasis on words, descriptive knowledge, control procedures, and formal problem solving.

---

[9]As indicated by Berwick's analysis, these issues are indeed now prevalent in the natural language research community. See for example Lehnert (1991), which is reviewed by D. E. Rose (1993), and other book reviews in *Artificial Intelligence, 62*(1).

10

Comprehension Difficulties Related to "Interference in Short-Term Memory"

A language, then, is not a system of rules, but a set of specifications for parameters in an invariant system of principles of Universal Grammar (UG); and traditional grammatical constructions are perhaps best regarded as taxonomic epiphenomena.

—Noam Chomsky, *The Minimalist Program*, 1995, p. 129

In cognitive psychology, certain difficulties of comprehending and remembering are explained in terms of *interference* between elements (such as words) that have been copied and located in a working memory. The title of this chapter comes from an article by R. Lewis (1996) based on this idea.[1] Lewis' paper presents a variety of sentences that people have difficulty comprehending. Using these examples, R. Lewis developed a model of natural language comprehension (NL-Soar) that explains the comprehension in terms of interference effects. Apparently, the inability to coordinate multiple noun phrases (more than two or three) is caused by an inability to hold fixed a greater number of references while other parts of the sentences are being processed and related.

Applying the same examples, I develop in this chapter a constrained form of activation trace diagrams that is consistent with the Universal Grammar and explains the effects of phrase embedding and movement in neural terms. The two or three limit on comprehension results from an inability to reuse a category in the same way within one sentence. By categorizing their functional (semantic-syntactic) relations and holding active these anchor categories for later inclusion in the utterance, multiple uses of a syntactic category are possible. These ideas of reuse and anchoring were introduced in the discussion of computational

---

[1] See also Pinker (1994, pp. 203–207) for an introduction to this phenomenon.

memory architectures (Fig. 2.6) and slips (Fig. 6.6). Here the phenomena are established by a wealth of data, and the value of the neural activation perspective is fully realized.

10.1   THE INTERFERENCE PROBLEM

In his discussion of interference effects in short-term memory, R. Lewis gave the following examples of comprehension difficulties.[2] This sentence with two noun phrases (NPs) is acceptable:

>   (S1)   The dog that the girl scared ran away.

While this sentence, with three embedded NPs, is incomprehensible:

>   (S2)   The cat that the bird that the mouse chased scared ran away.

S2 is an example of double center-embedding, but the pattern is not clear. Other forms of center-embeddings, involving subject relatives and propositions, are acceptable, although awkward:

>   (S3)   That the food that John ordered tasted good pleased him.

And right-branching appears to be significantly less bounded:

>   (S4)   The mouse chased a bird that scared a cat that ran away.

R. Lewis (1996) concluded, "The basic result is that center embedding is always more difficult than right branching, which can carry the same amount of content, but exhibits no severe limits on depth of embedding" (p. 95).

A related problem, discussed by Berwick (1983) concerns "movement" of NPs. Both of the following statements are acceptable:

>   (S5)   I believe that Mary likes Bill.

>   (S6)   Whom do I believe that Mary likes?

But introduction of the embedded NP, "the claim that," makes the sentence unacceptable:

>   (S7)   Whom do I believe the claim that Mary likes?

For Berwick, this suggested a "locality principle"—"*Who* cannot be moved across more than one sentence boundary" (p. 406). However, we can understand sentences in which *whom* appears to move arbitrarily far:

>   (S8)   Whom does John think that Mary said she saw Tom go to the
>   store with?

---

[2]From R. L. Lewis (1995) This section was written with significant assistance from Rick Lewis, whose questions and counterexamples were crucial for developing the initial ideas into a more elaborate, substantial theory.

Explanations of these observations focus on the limitations of short-term (working) memory, which may be stated in terms of *categorical structure* ("each relation in working memory indexes at most two nodes"; R. Lewis & Lehman, 1994, p. 14) or *activation interference* (Church's [1982] closure principle, "only the two most recent nodes of the same category may be kept open at any time" [R.L. Lewis & Lehman, 1994, p. 24]). Similarly, the evidence may be explained in terms of a limited stack mechanism (items aside held during the parse) or a processing limitation on recursion. I re-examine these claims here, applying a neural activation analysis to distinguish the various cases and to reformulate the limitations in terms of the mechanism by which neural maps compose to form a conceptualization of sentence meaning.[3]

10.2   EXAMPLE OF NOTATION FOR ACCEPTABLE SENTENCES

Examples of center-embedded subject relatives are interesting because no model currently accounts for why some are unacceptable and others are easy (R. Lewis, 1996). I use activation trace diagrams to show why subject relatives with center-embedded NPs are unacceptable. The following was predicted by NL-Soar as unacceptable, but is comprehensible:

> (S9)   "The book that the man who hired me wrote deals with politics."

In applying the activation trace analysis to represent the *process* of sentence comprehension, I have simplified the notation for categorical sequences and introduced the notion of an *anchor*. As shown in Fig. 10.1 and Fig. 10.3, the "T bar" for representing a categorized sequence (Fig. 1.6) and the arrow on the diagonal representing sequential activation of maps are combined. The arrow is, as before, always to the right. An arrow is added to show the order of incorporation of a qualifying *detail* (a word or phrase) in a higher-order categorized sequence (e.g., "politics" qualifies "deals with"; the arrow indicates that the order is "deals with" followed by "politics"). Phrases are incorporated by an arrow indicating activation from the head of the phrase sequence ("the book" is the head of the phrase sequence "the book deals with"). This change to the notation facilitates representing embedded sequences. For example, "the book → deals with" is a categorized sequence, but it is constructed with an intervening (embedded) phrase: "the book"—"that the man who hired me wrote"—"deals with politics."

---

[3]Except where noted, the examples come from R. L. Lewis (1996). I have replaced "who" by "whom" where appropriate, and made other changes, such as using "believe" instead of "think" for consistency.

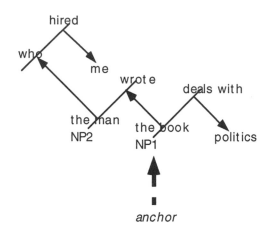

Fig. 10.1. Activation trace representation of S9 "The book that the man who hired me wrote deals with politics." Arrows indicate temporal order of activation. Anchor indicates the first noun phrase, which is held active.

The diagram notation I am developing here is not a parse tree; rather it shows the neural composition process. For contrast, consider how the deep structure[4] might be diagrammed (Fig. 10.2). The arrow indicates a transformational operation that moves an NP (the book) to where it is heard in the sentence. The deep structure diagram represents underlying grammatical roles, which are manifest in the sentence's surface structure. Grammatical, phrase relations are to be contrasted with the *temporal relations* of how words and roles are activated and composed in an utterance. Thus, Fig. 10.1 shows that "the book" is held active as a higher-order sequence is constructed for which "the book" is a detail. The deep structure shows "that the man who hired me wrote" as qualifying "the book." In subsequent analysis, we see how the ideas of temporal sequence and coupled details developed through other examples (Part II) complement the deep structure analysis such that the idea of "movement" is not necessary and is indeed shown to be the wrong metaphor.

---

[4]This is similar to the notation used by Pinker (1994, p. 122).

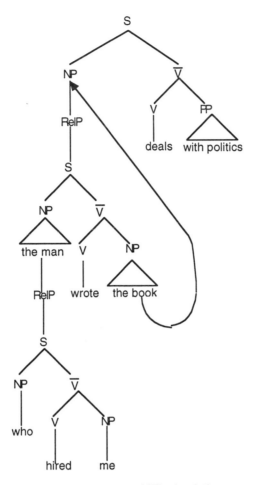

Fig. 10.2. Diagram of deep structure of "The book the man who hired me wrote deals with politics."

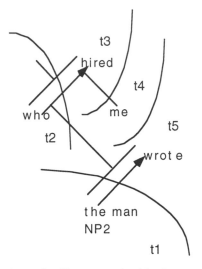

Fig. 10.3. Activation trace for "the man who hired me wrote" using original notation. Five constructions are shown in order numbered as time t1, t2, and so on (compare with simplified version shown in Fig. 10.1).

The second change to the activation trace notation being introduced here is the presence of anchors. The anchor is always the first NP or relative pronoun (whom, that) in the utterance. In S9, the first NP categorization ("the book") is held active as an anchor. Throughout, we find the pattern that the NP categorization can be reused in comprehending the utterance, as long as the anchor becomes incorporated in the subsequent composition ("the man who hired me wrote"). Then comprehension may continue from the anchor ("deals with politics"). An anchor holds active a categorization mapping (so-called short-term or working memory) so effectively the syntactic categorization (NP) may be reactivated (reused) in the same sentence construction. I call this *the rule of anchored-composition.*

I stress than an anchor is not stored in a separate buffer off to the side (a special data structure), but is a categorizing (neural) process that is held active so it may be incorporated later in another composition. Notice especially my phrasing—*the* NP categorization—for there is only one such neural map, a physical structure, available. In the diagrams I have used so far (e.g., Fig. 7.3) an anchor is shown as a detail on the right side. Unlike the examples analyzed in Part II, representations of grammatical structure necessarily involve several levels of categorized sequences (corresponding to subject–verb relations), each with their own details in lower-order sequences. An anchor is therefore a special detail denoted by an arrow and a label.

By use of an anchor, center-embedding is possible: Intervening words may appear that are composed on other levels before the sequence that the anchor begins is completed (as illustrated by S9). In particular, notice that *that* in "that the man" signifies *a higher, subsuming composition,* as does *who.* More conventionally, these words are shown as modifiers of an NP, hanging *below* it in a parse tree, rather than being higher. As we go through the examples, I discuss other principles of neural activation suggested by this analytic perspective and how the principles relate to Universal Grammar. I also present counterexamples and extensions to this introductory analysis.

Besides center embedding, S9 illustrates a second pattern that will occur throughout these examples. *A semantic categorization* (e.g., "the book" and "the man") may play two roles, but they must be different. For example, "the book" is the object of "wrote" and the subject of "deals with." This rule explains why some subject relatives with double NPs are acceptable and others are not.

For example, S10 is incomprehensible because an NP categorization (the man) plays the *same role twice in* a given sentence. To do this, it must be active in two ways at the same time.

> (S10)   The boy that the man that hired the woman yesterday hated cried.

A simplification works (see Fig. 10.4):

> (S10')   The boy that the man hated cried.

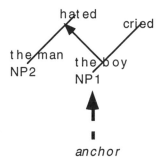

Fig. 10.4. S10' "The boy that the man hated cried."

S10 requires "the man" to play the role of subject in two ways simultaneously: "The man hired" and "The man hated." The repeated role can be shown as an invalid composition of sequences (Fig. 10.5). This construction is invalid because a given node "the man" cannot be the head of two NP sequences at the same time. More generally, a given semantic categorization can only appear once in a given composition. To be included in two different ways (playing two different roles), "the man" would have to be subsumed within a higher composition (exemplified by the double role "the boy" plays in S10' or that "the book" plays in S9). "The man" plays the role of subject twice in S10, but plays two different roles in S9 (subject of "wrote" and qualifier of "who," which is the subject of the phrase "who hired").

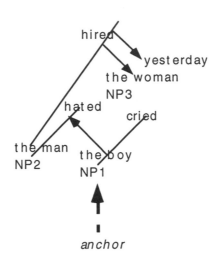

Fig. 10.5. Invalid composition, S10 "The boy that the man that hired the woman yesterday hated cried."

According to R. Lewis (1996), NL-Soar wrongly predicts that S10 is acceptable unless the parsing strategy were changed so "specifiers trigger creation of their heads" (p. 101)—which is to say that how categories activate each other is important. Furthermore, the use of an anchor is equivalent to the claim that the comprehension process is not strictly bottom up. I conclude that self-embedding of NPs is not the critical difference in comprehensibility. Rather, the issue is reuse of an open syntactic category (multiple NPs) or multiple, conflicting syntactic categorization of a semantic category (repeated role of an NP).

To restate the hypothesis (which I subsequently illustrate with other examples): These diagrams describe mental representations, which are *physical constructions created in time*. During the sentence comprehension process, neural structures are physically activated and composed by categorization coupling and sequencing relations. More specifically, semantic categorizations (such as "man") are being syntactically categorized during comprehension according to their role. Thus "man" can be categorized as qualifier/detail as well as subject. This means that multiple (syntactic) categorizations are possible of a single (semantic) categorization—multiple roles. Equivalently, a semantic categorization ("man") may syntactically relate within a given construction in different ways (qualifier and subject). However, a given syntactic relation (e.g., "subject"), may not be applied to a single semantic categorization ("man") twice in the same sentence construction.

In this analysis, I am looking at the surface structure (the actual words) and assigning roles played in the phrases. "The man" qualifies "who" and is also the subject of "wrote." That is two roles. But in S10, "the man" is the subject of "the man hired" and "the man hated" (as shown by Fig. 10.5). This is an impossible construction. The human brain's neural activation process cannot produce such a physical composition by the comprehension process alone.

Significantly, we may look at Fig. 10.5 and engage in a different kind of conceptual coordination process by trying to comprehend the diagram. Or we may restate the sentence by simply changing the second *that* to *who*:

> (S10'') "The boy that the man who hired the woman yesterday hated cried."

Rather than heading two sequences as subject, "the man" plays two roles as in S9, subject and qualifier.

To summarize the theory so far: If a semantic categorization plays the same role twice or more, the utterance will be unacceptable. Put another way: The comprehension construction process can categorize a categorization multiple ways, but not in the same way (e.g., as subject) in two different ways. In some sense, to do otherwise is illogical. You cannot say that X is a subject in Way 1 and also in Way 2. If X is a subject in the utterance, it must be a subject in a particular, singular way.

This logical restriction is a *physical* limitation related to composition of physical structures. You cannot have a ball at the top of a pyramid while it is also at the top of a cube. A ball can only be sitting on top of one structure. Of course, structures can be composed (e.g., a ball on top of a pyramid on top of a cube). This recursiveness of mention is accomplished in language by virtue of words like "that" and "who." These words (strictly speaking, their conceptual categorizations) are actually playing the other subject or object roles. The relation between "who" and "the man" is one of the roles that "the man" plays, as *qualifier* of an NP. The relation between "hates" and "the man" is another role that "the man" plays, as *subject* of another NP.

The pattern and construction process I have described so far correctly predicts the comprehensibility of (S11) and (S12) as well (Fig. 10.6 and Fig. 10.7). These are triple-subject sentences, which NL-Soar predicts should be difficult, but which are easier to understand than S10 (R. Lewis, 1996). The neural activation structure of these sentences is identical.

> (S11) The reporter everyone I met trusts had predicted that Thieu would resign in the spring.

Notice the different ways in which details may qualify a higher-order sequence: an adverb of the verb, adjective of the subject or object, or embedded proposition ("the reporter predicted").

> (S12) Isn't it true that example sentences that people you know produce are more likely to be accepted?

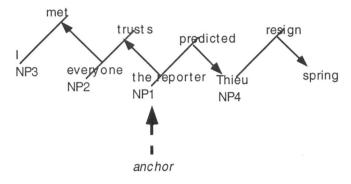

Fig. 10.6. S11 "The reporter everyone I met trusts had predicted that Thieu would resign in the spring."

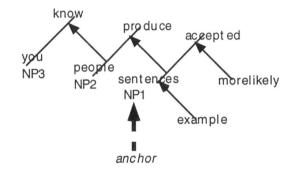

Fig. 10.7. S12 "Isn't it true that example sentences that people you know produce are more likely to be accepted?"

("Isn't it true that" is an invitation to comprehend a sentence, which could precede every declarative sentence to make it an interrogative, so I have omitted it.)

As noted by R. Lewis (1996),

[These sentences are] counterexamples of the claim that double center-embedded relative clauses are always difficult in English . . . . [They] fit the general prediction of the interference hypothesis that making the constituents more distinct or similar in some way should help processing. (p. 103)

The distinctions, so to speak, are that one categorization may be held as an anchor and any NP may play multiple roles (the difference between S10 and S10'). Lewis concluded that in the NL-Soar theory, "something may be missing in the way that the H/D [Heads/Dependents] set has formalized similarity" (p. 103). Besides the notion of anchor and multiple roles, NL-Soar is missing the effect of encapsulation in the composition process. For a sequence of center-embedded NP categorizations to be acceptable (e.g., S11 and S12), the higher-order clauses must be complete prior to encountering the verb for the anchor.

But we are not out of the woods yet. Even with NP1 held aside, how can there be two more NPs (in S11 and S12)? S2 shows that three NPs are not acceptable. The idea of "closing off" is too weak, for it predicts that S2 should be acceptable. What is the difference between S2 and these acceptable examples of (apparent) double center-embedding? Is there a related limitation that makes "two" a magic number, as in Church's (1982) principle that "only the two most recent nodes of the same category may be kept open at any time" (Lewis & Lehman, 1994, p. 24)? Or is the limitation a product of the role assignment, anchoring, and recursion processes? To explain the differences between S2 and S11 and S12, we must consider the nature of propositional embedding and how sentential recursion allows another form of holding aside.

10.3   EMBEDDED PROPOSITIONS

I approach the issue of embedded proposition in terms of the "movement" of NPs, an issue raised by Berwick (1983) and transformation theory in general. Consider first the acceptable, right-branching S5. Here the proposition "Mary likes Bill" is represented as a qualifier of the statement, "I believe." To show that the entire phrase is the qualifier (and not just "Mary"), the arrow coming from the sequence "Mary likes Bill" is centered on the sequence (Fig. 10.8). This is the representation I use for embedded propositions. Note that S5 has the same structure as:

(S5')   Mary, I believe, likes whom?

in which "Mary" is an anchor and the order of the NPs is swapped ("Mary" is NP1 and "I" is NP2).

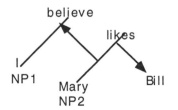

Fig. 10.8. S5 "I believe that Mary likes Bill"

Now consider the center-embedded S6 in Fig. 10.9. (Note how these sentences are easier to understand if "that" is included: "Whom do I believe that Mary likes?" Words like *that* and *whom* mark embedding and apparently trigger compositional processes in our comprehension.)

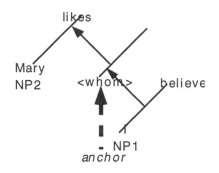

Fig. 10.9. S6 "Whom do I believe that Mary likes?"

Here "I believe" qualifies "whom," which is an anchor. Thus "whom" is held open, qualified as "the whom I believe" (marked by "do") and then becomes the object of "Mary likes." "Whom" is placed in brackets to indicate that it is an interrogative (an unspecified noun) and may be bound to other nouns in the sentence.

But is the notation being used inconsistently? Why does "I believe" hang off as a detail qualifying "whom" in S6, whereas Mary hangs off as a detail qualifying "I believe" in S5'? To repeat, activation trace diagrams are not conventional parse structures. They represent syntactic relationships within a coordinated serial production process. Thus, S5' has the equivalent representation of "I believe Mary likes Bill" because in both cases the serial production of "Mary likes Bill" is right-branching, a proposition that qualifies "I believe." But in S6 "I believe" functions as a qualifier of "whom." As this example makes clear, the notation represents the qualifying relations within the constraints of serial production, not a conventional syntactic parse tree, which is temporally independent.

Note also that (S5'') "I believe Mary likes whom?"[5] has the same compositional structure as S5' (Fig. 10.10). However, the order in which the words are said is different, therefore the activation order is different. Because the order changes to right-branching in S5'', an anchor is no longer required. Given that we grasp the same meaning, the compositional structure appears to be a more important indication of the meaning than the order in which the words appear, fitting the conventional view of grammatical structure. That is, the roles the words play is what matters, not how the phrases are embedded. Nevertheless, the point of the neural activation analysis is that ordering in the utterance (the form of the surface expression) will affect whether the utterance is comprehensible.

---

[5]This is an example of an "echo-question" (Jackendoff, 1994, p. 76) — "Beth ate WHAT for breakfast?!" The *wh*-interrogative (e.g., *what*) appears in a right-branching utterance, so an anchor is not required

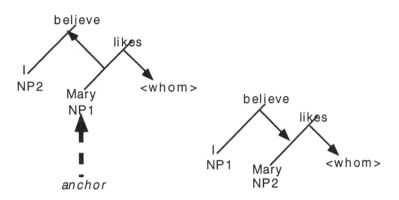

Fig. 10.10. Center-embedded S5' "Mary, I believe, likes whom?" compared to right-branching S5" "I believe Mary likes whom?" for which an anchor is not required.

At the end of this section, I provide a neural explanation of why a single compositional structure can represent two kinds of utterances, namely the right-branching $head_1$-$tail_1$–$head_2$-$tail_2$ . . . or center-embedding $head_1$-$head_2$- . . . –$tail_1$-$tail_2$- . . . (with optional inclusion of qualifiers as "I believe" in S6 and "more likely" in S12 or optional appending of a right-branching statement after center-embedding as in S11). Indeed, it should not be surprising that in a neural process explanation, which after all is based on a simple set of mechanisms, utterances having quite different conventional parse representations would be based on the same internal categorizations (i.e., have the same activation trace representation), although the relations will be activated (constructed) in a different order. In effect, I am claiming that grammatical deep structure must refer to neural operations, not just phrase structure patterns in utterances.

As another example, according to the activation trace analysis, S7 is unacceptable because the phrase "the claim" marks this as an embedded sentence (Fig. 10.11). In general, embedded sentences are acceptable, but here the head of the sequence is ambiguous. An attempt is made to construct a combination of S5 and S6.

The result is like a mobius strip or a box labeled on both ends "open other end." Does the sentence begin "Whom do I believe" or does it begin "I believe the claim that . . ."? In the first case, "I believe" qualifies "whom"; in the second case, "Mary likes whom" qualifies "I believe." "Whom" cannot play the role of qualifying "I believe" and be qualified by it at the same time. This is obvious in the neural compositional representation, where the dashed line shows a loop that is invalid. S6 is an acceptable restatement that follows the pattern of closed-off center-embedding (Fig. 10.9).

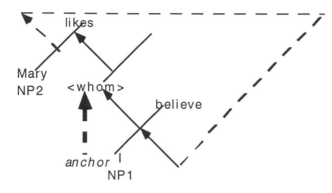

Fig. 10.11. S7 "Whom do I believe the claim that Mary likes?" (unacceptable).

Berwick (1983) argued that S8 is different because "*who* is passed along from sentence to sentence in these cases where the intermediate sentence might have legitimately held a *who*" (p. 407). The problem with S7 is that "the claim that" or "it seems certain that" cannot contain *who* (p. 407). I claim that "who" in S8 is not passed along, but *held active* as an anchor (Fig. 10.12). Berwick argued against this "memory store method," what he called "a hold cell," because there is no limitation on how long it can be held, and it could allow parsing the unacceptable S7. However, as my analysis shows, there is another explanation for example S7 (an ambiguous reference), and there are other examples in which an anchor appears to be necessary, such as S8.

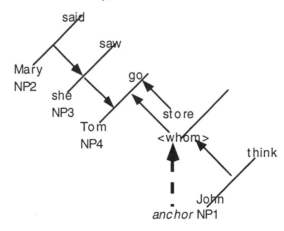

Fig. 10.12. S8 "Whom does John think that Mary said she saw Tom go to the store with?" (embedded right branch).

As an anchor, "whom" is held in stasis while a higher-order construction, the right-branching, embedded proposition "Mary said she saw Tom go to the store" is composed. Once again, the rule of anchored composition holds: The anchor is subsumed (incorporated) as a detail in an intervening (embedded) composition.[6] (Two details qualify "go"—"with whom" and "to the store.")

Right branching (as within S8) allows "closing off" categorizations that center-embedding requires holding active. The three subjects (Mary, she, Tom) are not buffered. Instead, each NP is left behind in the composition at a higher level (just as happens when the verbs are encountered in embedded relative clauses). Each syntactic categorization is incorporated in the overall construction (by relating it to semantic categorizations) before another reuse is required. For example, "Mary said . . ." is incorporated before we encounter "she." In general, comprehending occurs in our sequential behavior, rather than creating a data structure that we hold in mind. We move through the meaning, rather than holding a result as a parse tree.

In conclusion, neural comprehension processes need not actually "move" NPs around. Berwick's (1983) locality principle should be considered as a constraint on process reconstruction; the characterization "moving around" incorrectly focuses on the serial order of the surface structure that is the manifestation of a compositional process. Furthermore, the neural activation analysis is consistent with Langacker's (1986) analysis, in which abstract syntactic relations, such as sentence and NP are treated as *conceptual* relations. However, the strict conventional distinction between structure and content does hold in the sense that comprehension can be understood as a process of assigning syntactic roles to semantic categories.

The examples of unacceptable sentences do not concern center-embedding or the number of times a category appears per se, but the limitations in how active (syntactic and semantic) categories are used. That is, the examples reveal a limitation in our ability to coordinate multiple conceptualizations to construct a new conceptualization. Specifically, the activation and sequencing composition process imposes the constraint that a given syntactic (NP or sentential) categorization may only be active in one sequence at a time, but may be incorporated multiple times by virtue of an anchor and closing off sequences. These closed-off sequences are always compositionally at a higher-level, whether the structure is center-embedding or right-branching (illustrated further later). Also, a semantic categorization (e.g., given NP) may play a syntactic role in only one way (e.g., be a subject once)—fitting the conventional ideas that syntactic categorization is a "way of viewing" an utterance and comprehension is a process of assigning possible roles in unique ways.

The locality principle of phrase structure theory is merely structural, based on *proximity*. The conceptual coordination theory I am developing seeks constraints in terms of *activation* (and holding or closing off activation) of composed

---

[6]A good introduction to this phenomenon with similar examples appears in Jackendoff, (1994, pp. 77–80).

physical processes. The constructed meaning of an utterance constitutes a global mapping between previously existing categorizations, now reactivated, sequenced, and composed, with syntactic roles relating semantic categorizations.

I elaborate on the neural aspects of this theory in the following section. First I would like to illustrate further the issue of NP "movement" from the neural activation perspective and another aspect of "reuse" of syntactic categories.

In particular, the acceptability of S8 invites us to revisit the unacceptable sentential center- embedding in S2. What is the difference? First let us look at the notation for S1 (Fig. 10.13).

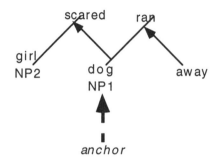

Fig. 10.13. S1 "The dog that the girl scared ran away."

This fits the examples examined so far. The notation for S2 would therefore be as shown in Fig. 10.14.

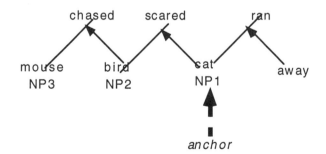

Fig. 10.14. S2 "The cat that the bird that the mouse chased scared ran away" (apparently valid compositional structure, but incomprehensible, cf. Fig. 10.7).

Unlike S7, this sentence can be "parsed" as in the activation trace notation, and indeed it is structurally identical to the acceptable S12 (Fig. 10.7). So why cannot such a composition (S2) be constructed by the human comprehension process?

Up to this point, I have claimed that a theory based on syntactic categories and counts is insufficient. I have illustrated that the limitation is not nesting or depth per se, but reuse of an open syntactic categorization in a different phrase sequence. For example, a sentence must have one head (S7) and a given NP categorization can only be the head of one phrase sequence (shown by various examples). Similarly, a semantic category may only play a given role once in a sentence (S10). But this is the same activation rule: An "open" semantic categorization may not be used in different phrase sequences. Up to this point, the compositional structure of the notation has been sufficient to explain acceptability. S2 reveals that something is missing. The problem is with how we define NP.

To explain why S2 is unacceptable, R. Lewis (1996) began by observing that "to compose propositions (as in relative or complement clause), two clauses must often be held simultaneously in working memory" (p. 8). Thus, the "number of nodes that each relation may index" is assumed to be at least two. If the number is only two, then S2 will not be acceptable, for the notation shows that NP has three open indexes—the anchor, NP2, and NP3. The limit cannot be simply two, for S11 and S12 are acceptable.

Obviously, S1 shows that reuse of a syntactic categorization is possible. I have explained this in terms of an anchor. My hypothesis is that the limit should be stated not as "two places" or "two nodes," but as a constructive process of composing neural maps (i.e., conceptualizations), such that composing occurs with one level of recursion. That is, during comprehension we can "hold onto" the first use of a syntactic categorization (e.g., NP1 in S1), allowing reuse of that categorization in a higher-level construct—insofar as the higher construct is "closed off" before we return to the lower (original) construct. We see this closing off occurring in center-embedding examples S8, S9, S11, S10', and S12. But why then is S2 difficult to understand?

Strikingly, in S11 and S12, NP2 is not categorizing a particular noun (e.g., *the bird*) but a *collective noun* (*everyone, people*). Furthermore, NP3 is not categorizing a particular noun but a personal pronoun (*I, you*). One explanation is that the acceptable reuse of NP as the head of a sequence (i.e., subject) depends on the occurrence of different nominative categories. *Everyone* and *people* are not merely nouns, like *cat* or *Mary*, but are functioning as variables, like the pronouns, *whom* or *that*. Indeed, substituting the collective nouns by regular nouns produces unacceptable variations of S11, similar to S2:

(S11') Jack that Mary that Kathy met trusts predicted that Thieu would resign in the spring.

(S11'') The reporter that the publisher that the editor met trusts predicted that Thieu would resign in the spring.

But notice what happens when we substitute "whom" for "that":

(S11''') Jack whom Mary that Kathy met trusts predicted that Thieu would resign in the spring.

(S11^{iv}) The reporter whom the publisher that the editor met trusts predicted that Thieu would resign in the spring.

Although obviously awkward, these variations are less confusing.

Strikingly, "reporter everyone I" (S11) and "sentences people you" (S12) do not require intervening pronouns (*that* or *whom*), while obviously "Jack Mary Kathy" and "cat bird mouse" are unacceptable. The serialization permitted of pronouns and collective nouns (as in "everyone I met") suggests that

<collective object> <pronoun subject> <verb>

is a familiar conceptual unit in English, which is comprehended as one chunk (e.g., as if "everyone-I-met" were a single word[7]).

Or perhaps S11 is acceptable because "the reporter" is treated as if it were followed by "whom":

(S11^{v}) The reporter (whom) everyone I met trusts had predicted that Thieu would resign in the Spring.

The structure is now like S6 and S8, with "whom" marking an embedded sentence. But introducing implicit words is a highly problematical way of explaining comprehension, especially because different words need to be posited for different examples (in S12 "example sentences" is implicitly followed by "that," not "whom"). Perhaps encountering a second NP recursion begins automatically, so the first NP becomes an anchor by default, even without a subsequent "that" or "whom." Perhaps the pattern of acceptability is explained by a combination of kinds of NP categorizations and sentence recursion. Thus, a second categorization is permissible by virtue of the anchoring during recursion and the subsequent NPs are not really the same—some are collective nouns, others are pronouns.

This hypothesis appears to be substantiated by the following acceptable (although still awkward) variations:

(S11^{vi}) The reporter whom the publisher I met trusts predicted that Thieu would resign in the spring.

---

[7]Indeed, combination of pronouns before the verb, as in "everyone I met," is common in other languages. For example, in French one might say, "*Je vous en donne*," whereas in English we would prefer the ordering "I give you some." Some pronoun patterns, such as "*Il y a*" (literally, "It there has") although apparently grammatically complex, are so useful they are easily understood, so the grammarian calls them "idioms." Collingwood (1938) reminded us that these are not exceptions, but rather indicate how language really works: It is inherently conceptual and functional, and not reducible to syntactic relations.

(S11^{vii}) The reporter the bull you saw gored had predicted that Thieu would resign in the Spring.

(S11^{viii}) Nobody people I met trust had predicted that Thieu would resign in the Spring.

(S2') The cat whom the bird I chased scared ran away.

These expressions are more understandable because the first occurrence of a kind of NP categorization is anchored and is only reused once; the third NP is another kind of NP categorization. Thus, the term *NP categorization* is too general, as is *subject*, to explain the data. "NP categorization" is the observer's characterization. The comprehender must be categorizing the subjects more specifically: collective NP, pronoun NP, proper NP, and so on.

Finally, it is possible that S2 is confusing because it is semantically unusual—typically cats chase birds and mice. But even a more familiar sentence with this syntax is confusing:

(S2'') The child that the mouse that the cat chased scared ran away.

Here, by association, we get a glimmer of what must be intended (e.g., the child is scared by a mouse). We must conclude that comprehension is not an all or nothing process. The very idea that there are "proper" syntactic styles and informal usage indicates that difficulty is a matter of degree. This is most obvious by the use of punctuation (or indeed context) that resolves many confusions. I present these other "dimensions" involved in comprehension in the following section, where I elaborate on the idea of recursion and multiple anchors.

10.4   DOUBLE ANCHORING IN RECURSIVE SENTENCES

The idea that composing occurs with one level of recursion is quite similar to some very early ideas proposed in a paper by G. Miller and Isard (1964). They proposed a kind of subroutine architecture that could only hold onto one other level while recurring.[8] The basic problem with this kind of approach, and other similar approaches that limit to two sentences (Kimball's principle of two sentences), is the set of center-embedded structures in English (and other languages) that are acceptable despite their double center-embedding of sentences, such as S3 and S13.

(S13) What the woman that Frank married enjoys best is smoked salmon.

---

[8]This observation and the criticism of my analysis comes from R. Lewis. See also the discussion of a single temporary state in progressive deepening (section 5.5).

S3 (Fig. 10.15) is truly different from the examples analyzed so far. Here the anchor is an embedded sentence itself, not just an NP. This embedded sentence is effectively the subject of the containing sentence.

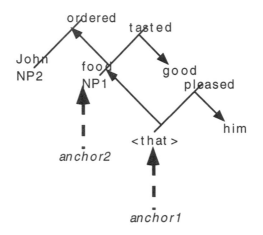

Fig. 10.15. S3 "That the food that John ordered tasted good pleased him."

Notice how this is different from the other examples, such as S12, in which the anchor is the subject of a subsequent verb. However, in accord with the rule of anchored comprehension composition, in comprehending the embedded sentence "Food John ordered tasted good," a second anchor must be operating. This allows the NP categorization to be reused. Note that the first anchor is a sentence categorization (indicated in the diagram by making <that> the anchor), the second is an NP categorization (a subject). Note also that it is not necessary to postulate that "food" and "John" are different kinds of NP categorizations (as I required to explain S11 and S12). The sentence, "That Mary John married cooked well pleased him." is equally acceptable (although we prefer to follow "Mary" by "whom").

As might be obvious to the reader by now, the restriction on reuse does not apply to simple conjunctions, as in "Matthew, Mark, Luke, and John went to the store." The restriction, as the sentential embedding now reveals, is on *composing an active NP categorization in a different phrase sequence*. Effectively, an anchor holds active a sentence (S13) or the head of a sentence (S1, etc.). This suggests that the construction difficulty involves holding multiple phrase sequences active (and hence why right branching, which closes sequences in order, is easy). Thus, as shown in the analysis of S11 and S12 (vs. S2), each kind of NP categorization allows holding open another sequence (where in S11 there are three kinds of NPs).

Building on this idea, it appears that S13 (Fig. 10.16) has two anchors: A relative pronoun (*what*) and a regular NP ("the woman"). Also, in the processing the first anchor (*what*) is bound to a subsequent particular noun (*salmon*). That is, the construction process not only incorporates the relative pronoun anchor in embedded ("higher") phrases, but effectively binds it to an NP. The compositional process is also the same as before—up through the subsuming subjects and back down through their verbs (e.g., Fig. 10.6). The anchoring of NP1 ("the woman") allows the subsequent categorization NP2 ("Frank"). (An argument could be made that "smoked salmon," like "example sentences" in S12, is a single conceptual unit so it could appear as a single NP term.)

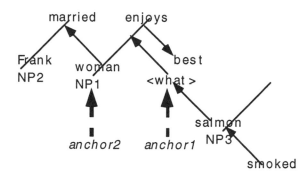

Fig. 10.16. S13 "What the woman that Frank married enjoys best is smoked salmon."

S3 and S13, as well as S8 (sequential embedded propositions) and S4 (right branching), illustrate what can be done with different kinds of anchors. S3 is especially interesting because the comprehension process holds onto an entire proposition. In all the other examples, the anchor is a pronoun or NP playing the role of an object and/or a subject. In S3 the anchor is a relative pronoun ("that") that designates a *proposition* playing the additional role of a subject. (I have otherwise dropped "that" when it is stemming directly from an existing sequence.) Analysis shows that multiple anchors are possible (S3, S11), but each must be a different syntactic category. Thus, S2 is incomprehensible because it requires two subject anchors (for "the cat" and "the bird"). S12 requires a relative pronoun object anchor ("what") and a noun object anchor ("the woman"). S3 has a propositional clause anchor ("that . . .") and a noun object anchor ("the food"). Three anchors are also possible, as in S12' (Fig. 10.17).

To repeat and elaborate the theory so far, the limit is not two sentences or two of anything per se in the surface structure. The limitation is how categorizations are employed in a given construction:

(P1)   A semantic categorization can play multiple syntactic roles, but not the same role twice in an active construction. That is, a semantic categorization appears once in an activation trace diagram.

(P2)   A syntactic categorization may "index" multiple semantic categorizations, but may only be active once at a given time.

(P3)   The use of an anchor allows a syntactic categorization to be "open" as *the head of a sequence* twice at a given time. But in physical terms the anchor is holding a categorization mapping between semantic and syntactic categories; the neural processes representing the syntactic categorization are actually released (recall the discussion in chapter 2 about "types" being incorporated, rather than "instances" that are copies of types).

(P4)   Meaning construction (comprehension) is a sequential behavior, not holding a parse tree or "moving" items in a data structure.

(P5)   Two general kinds of anchors are possible, one holding an embedded sentence and another holding a relative pronoun or NP within it. Anchors serve as "stacks" that allow one level of recursion, in the computational sense that the stack may be "popped" and compositional processing returns to the previously anchored element. A higher-order construction must be closed off before returning to an anchored categorization.

(P6)   Multiple anchors may appear in one utterance, but each must be a different semantic–syntactic relation (e.g., embedded proposition, relative pronoun object, noun object, noun subject).

(P7)   Multiple conceptual dimensions ("distinctions") are operating simultaneously, including different kinds of NP categorizations, and conceptual organizers also include rhythm, stress, and visualization. These dimensions allow and facilitate reactivation and composition of multiple object and event references during the comprehension construction process.

I recognize that "qualifier" is a nonstandard syntactic category. But that is the point of the activation trace analysis: The number of structural relationships in a neural construction is far simpler than the number of syntactic categories in a grammarian's catalog. On the other hand, the use of the single NP categorization in conventional grammars overly abstracts the conceptualization processes at work. There are evidently multiple kinds of NP categorizations and anchors that may be active at a single time.

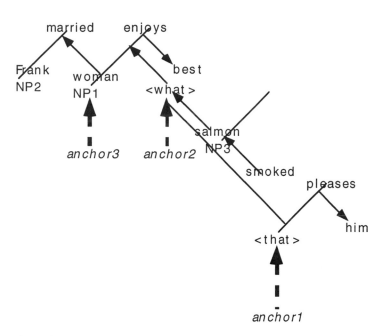

Fig. 10.17. S12' "That what the woman Frank married enjoys best is smoked salmon pleases him."

10.5   PERMISSIBLE SYNTACTIC RELATIONS

By further analysis of restrictions in relative clauses, the idea of "qualifier" and multiple anchors can be further reduced to simpler compositional restrictions. For example, the unacceptable S14 shows how other kinds of categorizations besides NPs may be reactivated and hence are limited in their usage (Fig. 10.18).

(S14)   Fred is easy for the woman whom the man who hired me married to please.

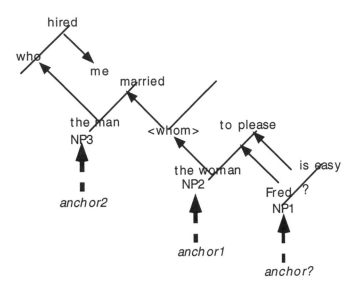

Fig. 10.18. S14 "Fred is easy for the woman whom the man who hired me married to please" (invalid composition, requiring two noun object anchors due to ambiguous opening role of "Fred"—subject or indirect object?).

The sentence varies from the examples we have seen by apparently using NP1 as a subject in an opening sequence ("Fred is easy") before the center-embedding occurs. (I show "the woman" as being a detail qualifying "whom.") The problem with S14 is the apparent requirement for two NP-subject anchors ("Fred" and "the woman"). A reordering is (barely) acceptable because it makes clear that "Fred" is an indirect object before the next NP is encountered (which in S14 forces anchoring "Fred"):

> (S14') "Fred is easy to please for the woman whom the man who hired me married."

Making "the woman" the unambiguous subject to be anchored helps a great deal:

> (S14'') "The woman whom the man who hired me married easily pleases Fred."

The pattern of all the other center-embedding examples is the same: Multiple relative clauses are possible only when the open NP (subject) can be anchored (e.g., "the woman").

In general an embedded relative clause is acceptable (Fig. 10.19):

> (S15) "I called the guy who smashed my car a rotten driver" (Church, 1982, p. 34)

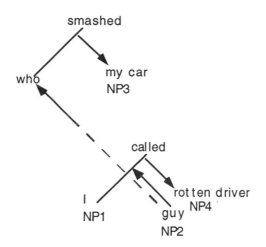

Fig. 10.19. S15 "I called the guy who smashed my car a rotten driver."

Here "guy" is a qualifier of "I called" (indirect object) and the complement of the relative pronoun "who."

Comparison of S14 and S15 (and its also acceptable variation, "Fred called the woman who smashed his car a rotten driver") suggests again that the problem with S14 lies with the anchored NPs ("Fred . . . ," "woman . . . ," "man . . . ."). This is evident by examining the following acceptable variations:

(S14''') Fred is easy for the woman who smashes his car to love.

(S14^{iv}) Fred is waiting for the woman whom the man who hired me married.

S14''' works because "Fred" can be anchored ("the man" is omitted). S14^{iv} works because the embedded clause "for the woman" right branches off as an object (so the sequence headed by "Fred" is completed before the next NP "the woman" is encountered).

Removing the anchor on "the man" by deleting "who hired me," we find some semantic ambiguity concerning the reference of "the man," but the syntax is comprehensible:

(S14^{v}) Fred is easy for the woman whom the man married to please.

Making "the man" more concrete, we have the more acceptable:

(S14^{vi}) Fred is easy for the woman whom the boss married to please.

My analysis may be contrasted with that of R. Lewis (1996) and others, who explain S14 in terms of the triple "for the woman," "whom . . . ," and "who," as requiring three open NP heads. I claim that the limitation on comprehension is not a prohibition on reuse, number of reuses, number of NPs, center-embedding, or amount of center-embedding per se. The issue is the "stacking" limitation of *not being able to hold more than one instance of a categorization open at a time.* S14 is unacceptable because it requires the categorization of "NP-object" to be active as an anchor more than once ("Fred" and "the woman whom"). Note that this is a complex semantic–syntactic *relation*, not a single NP classification in isolation. This illustrates my broader claim that all conceptual categorizations are physical relations constructed between other categorizations.

Strikingly, adding punctuation helps, indicating again the role of rhythmic and visual processes in conceptual coordination. The lexical (written) notation does not capture all the information that speakers employ. For example, commas provide grouping information about what is modifying what:

> (S14[vii]) Fred is easy for the woman, whom the man who hired me married, to please.

When we scan S14[vii] we may hesitate, but finding the commas, we can visually associate "for the woman" and "to please," such that this sequence may be held and the embedded clauses parsed. But now of course we are coordinating on multiple dimensions, relying on the image before us to hold the meaning (similar to the referential process in sending two messages, chapter 4). The visible text, "the woman," becomes a reference object, as discussed by Bamberger and Schön (1983).

Punctuation and use of a relative pronoun also helps S2:

> (S2''') The cat, whom the bird that the mouse chased scared, ran away.

But the sentence remains unacceptable because it requires two subject NP anchors, "the cat" and "the bird." That is, the reactivation required by NP3 requires anchoring NP2, violating Principle P6. Note that the constructions "pronoun-whom" and "noun-whom" anchor on the NP head, not on "whom" (Fig. 10.20).

To complete this analysis, I make a few general comments about activation trace diagrams. First, the notation used in representing the comprehension of S15 is equivalent to a construction on two planes (Fig. 10.21). This diagram reminds us that relating the activation trace analysis to neural processes, the mechanisms of qualification, anchors, and composition in general may be realized as multidimensional physical structures, not just lists or binary trees in a plane.

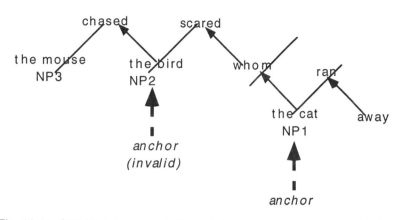

Fig. 10.20. S2''' "The cat, whom the bird that the mouse chased scared, ran away" (invalid composition requiring two NP-subject anchors).

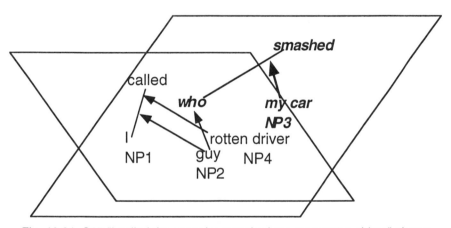

Fig. 10.21. S15 "I called the guy who smashed my car a rotten driver" shown as two sequences in different planes.

Second, the overall syntactic patterns of the examples can be summarized as three diagrams showing how a subject of one phrase may be a complement of a relative pronoun (Fig. 10.22) or an direct or indirect object (Fig. 10.23) of a higher-order sequence.

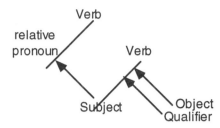

Fig. 10.22. Subject (head of sequence) becomes qualifier of center-embedded phrase (higher-order sequence). Examples. S9 and S14.

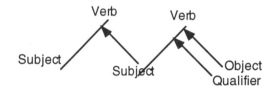

Fig. 10.23. Subject of phrase becomes object of higher-order sequence (either center-embedded with anchors or right-branched). Examples. S1, S2, S3, S5, S6, S8, S9, S10', S11, S12.

A composition itself may also qualify a higher-order composition as a proposition (what is believed, said, seen, and so on; Fig. 10.24).

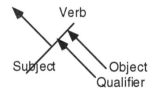

Fig. 10.24. Embedded proposition (sequence as whole). Examples. S6 and S8.

Here "qualifier" can be another proposition, an adverb, or an indirect object. The three constructions shown here can be composed. For example, an object may be the subject of another phrase, the complement of a relative pronoun, and so on. (Note how S6, S8, and S9 are listed as examples multiple times.) To repeat a key point: An embedded clause is constructed as a higher-order sequence.

In the Universal Grammar a noun plus modifier forms an NP and an NP plus verb forms a verb phrase (Jackendoff, 1994). The preceding diagrams are based on a subject–verb link; that is, a verb phrase (VP) sequence. Indeed, all the activation links are necessarily binary—one categorization activates another.

Besides the obligatory subject → verb sequence, the subject or verb may be optionally qualified:

- An adjective modifies the subject NP (S13 "smoked salmon").
- An object modifies the VP (S9, "wrote the book").
- An indirect object modifies the VP (S15, "called the guy").
- An adverb modifies the VP (S12 "more likely to be accepted").

Thus, the three kinds of neural activation relations—sequential, coupling, and compositional (categorized sequence)—are used to construct, respectively, the basic subject–verb phrase, qualifiers, and clauses (either embedded or right-branched).

I have glossed over many details of syntactic structure, of course, especially connectives such as *and* that may involve transitive (nonbinary) categorizations. But if my overall hypotheses about conceptual coordination are right, then I would expect the three kinds of activation relations to account for all syntactic structure. In this respect, it is interesting that the three *physical* relations somehow fit our intuitive sense of grammatical form: sequence corresponds to the subject–verb order (in English), coupling corresponds to modification of some categorization, and categorization of sequences corresponds to hierarchical composition of clauses.

10.6   NEURAL PROCESSES INTERPRETATION OF "TWO NODE" LIMITATION

Rather than saying that human memory is unable to keep in mind only two or three similar chunks at the same time, the sentence comprehension data can be more parsimoniously explained in terms of reusing (reactivating and relating) categorizations within a new composition. The number is two (period) because the first use is held and the others are composed as details in a construct by a process that allows the categorization to be reactivated. Effectively, the composition process encapsulates the categorization by relating (mapping) to another categorization. Thus, the physical construction is composed of such relational categorizations, allowing the types to be used multiple times. Furthermore, constructing a semantic structure requires that semantic categorizations are incorporated uniquely with respect to syntactic relations. That is, a given semantic category (word or phrase in surface structure) has only one relation to a given syntactic category or role. For example, a given noun can be a subject only once in the sentence (S10). This is a complex way of saying what the diagrams show more simply.

In a neural activation analysis, center-embedding has a simple structure (Fig. 10.25).

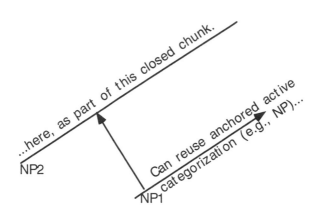

Fig. 10.25. The structure of center-embedding composition.

In this notation, center-embedded clauses compose upward, from right to left (Fig. 10.26), corresponding to a anchoring process that enables making an NP a qualifier of a larger composition.

Fig. 10.26. Composition of center-embedded clauses.

In center-embedding, NPs are encountered first, followed by verbs, which then "pop" the stack from left to right (evident in all the preceding examples). That is, the serial order of production for center-embedding is up through head nodes (NPs) and back down through tails and qualifiers (with an optional right-branching phrase appended on the end).

Right-branching sentences (e.g., S4) move forward to produce an identical compositional structure, but encounter the NPs in sequential, left to right order (Fig. 10.27). That is, the traversal completely constructs each sequence before moving to another sequence (the only kind of serial production shown in the diagrams of Part II).

The resultant forms of Fig. 10.25 and Fig. 10.27 are identical. In both cases the higher sequence incorporating a detail is completed before the detail is used in a second role as the sentence goes forward. The difference is that in embedded clauses (Fig. 10.25) the detail is encountered first and then embedded in a higher context. In the purely sequential case, the NPs appear in order from higher scope to lower (Fig. 10.27).

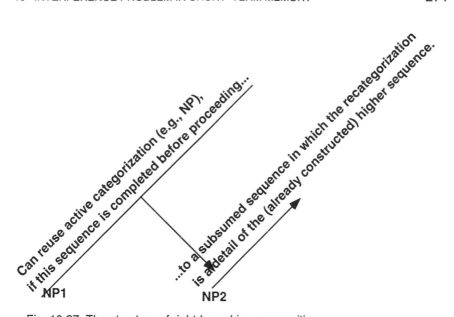

Fig. 10.27. The structure of right-branching composition.

The sequence does not exist as a data structure, but as activation in time. Anchoring is a means of holding a categorization active; this is apparently done by *categorization of reference.*[9] Put another way, a given categorization is only active once at a given time. The apparent "keeping a second NP open" is really two processes:

- Attention holding onto (keeping active) the first (NP) activation as a semantic–syntactic relation, a categorization constituting an anchor.
- "Recursive" reuse of a previously open syntactic categorization, such that the second use of the categorization is a detail in the first (Fig. 10.27) or the second creates a sequence that contains the first (Fig. 10.25).

By showing how syntactic structure and the composition process interact, the activation analysis teases apart multiple methods by which categorizations may be reused. This reveals that some examples may be explained by multiple mechanisms. For example, S5, "Mary, I believe, likes Bill," is acceptable because "Mary" and "I" are different kinds of NPs (the anchoring of "Mary" is not the necessary factor). But "Mary John believes likes Bill" is acceptable only because the first NP is anchored and so can be reused. Perhaps unexpectedly, S8 is acceptable, despite having two NPs that are not anchored (Tom and Mary), because the embedded proposition is right-branching ("Mary said she saw Tom go").

---

[9]See Clancey (1997c), chapters 12 and 13.

Lewis, 1996, p. 106), I have claimed that a categorization (the relation) can only be active in one "instantiation" at a time. It can be reactivated, but cannot be held as two activations simultaneously. This makes sense because a categorization is a particular neural structure (although generalized and hence physically changed on each reactivation). A neural structure can only be active or not. It cannot be copied and used in two different ways (e.g., to relate or bind different details) at the same time.

The basic idea is that a neural structure is active or not, and not copied and reused arbitrarily, might underlie the limitations that R. Lewis and others have labeled *interference*.[10] In fact, we can view the concept of interference as a theoretical placeholder, a term prevalent in descriptive cognitive models, which can be fleshed out by a theory of neural processes that gives rise to the effects. This illustrates the value of working at the descriptive (or symbolic) level and then moving to a theory of neural implementation.

The idea of being active or not is basic to any theory involving neural maps. From this perspective, comprehension must be a process of constructing a composition of neural maps (categorizations). Physical structures in the composition are active at some point in time to be included. This is tantamount to a token being included in a symbol structure. The difference is that the tokens are living processes; they are activated *in line* within a system that is doing something (i.e., comprehending is a physical activity) and they are generalized (re-related to other categorizations) by virtue of being incorporated in a composition that is active and functioning for the organism. Activation occurs by virtue of how categorizations have been activated in the past; that is, by virtue of how they have functioned together. (See related discussion of multiple, concurrent activations in chapter 2.3 especially the discussion of multiple drafts.) Also, tokens are copied, but categorizations must be released and

---

[10]Lehnert (1991) argues similarly that a lateral inhibition network can explain the "no-crossing branches rule" for relating propositional phrases to their modifier. For example, according to this rule the sentence "The man saw the woman with binoculars in a green dress" is right branching, and "with binoculars" modifies "the woman." But the semantic constraint that relates seeing to binoculars provides another, preferred interpretation, which violates the no crossing rule: The first sequence "the man saw" is qualified by "with binoculars" after constructing "the woman in a green dress." Lehnert's system, CIRCUS, uses numeric time stamps to represent these activation relations, thus using local information rather than a global parse tree to construct an interpretation. This approach shows again how a distance metric (e.g., between "the man" and "with binoculars") can be replaced by an activation relation. From the perspective of activation trace diagrams, CIRCUS's stored numeric value represents not a time interval per se but a physical structure with a weakening connection. The difficulty of crossing branches here is actually the difficulty of relating a new structure during right branching to an otherwise completed sequence. The example shows, as Lehnert suggests, that the comprehension process can best be modeled as a relaxation between conflicting physical constraints.

reactivated (as in right-branching) or encapsulated by an anchoring relation to be used multiple times in one utterance. Finally, in a neural theory the tokens are *categorizations*, which are constructed in their own ecology of functional, tautological relations, not an arbitrary alphabet of symbols.

From a conventional standpoint, this theory articulates "where the symbols come from." The claim is that all categorizations are constructed by coupling, sequencing, and categorizing sequences of other categorizations—and these are the symbols of conventional symbolic analysis. Once again, these symbols cannot be arbitrarily copied, stored, and arranged as in conventional programs (except through the conscious actions of a person doing symbol manipulation), but are activated in the ways described to form higher-order compositions and hence new categorizations.

The idea of not copying falls out from the basic constraints of a biological system based on activation: All the brain can do is activate categories by coupling, sequencing, and composing them. One interesting way around copying is categorization in multiple modalities, which effectively re-represents a relation by creating a corresponding category. For example, you can clap your hands while you sing a song to interactively represent the beat. You can visualize a relation you have just described, and then hold the image. In general, the visualization–body conception–verbalization triad provides an important way to hold, project, and coordinate multiple temporal and spatial relations (the essential point of Gardner's [1985] "multiple intelligences"). Here the idea of analogical representation has a different twist and important implication for creativity (e.g., analogical reasoning by *painting*, chapter 7).

What is meant by recursion and reuse in this theory? *Recursive reuse* means that a syntactic categorization may be incorporated in multiple sequences within a hierarchical construction. With respect to a conventional parse tree, in a neural construction a given node (categorization) has multiple relation-links, but each link from a given node must be different. The neural compositional process is recursive; it builds a higher (subsuming) level or delves back down to subsumed sequences to supply the verbs, and so on. Anchoring allows a single-level stack for NP and sentence categorizations. Composing is a sequential process and may itself be conceptually coordinated (the idea that syntactic composition is learned, although it rests directly on neural processes of composition and sequencing).

How does the anchoring process work? Attention holding is a means of working around the fundamental limitation on multiple use of a map at one time. The anchoring process does not literally keep a categorization active, but rather categorizes its semantic–syntactic relation, such that the resulting category functions in the same way. For example, in S9 NP can be reused by virtue of creating an anchor relation, "the book—NP," which can later function as the object of "wrote." The activation on NP is released and reactivated in forming the relation "the man—NP." In programming, the formation of a semantic–syntactic category is like saving a pointer or "handle" to a data structure. Once again, in conceptual coordination, the anchoring process is not a "refreshing" or feedback relation that holds a categorization active, but use of a composed semantic-syntactic relation. If my analysis is correct, all the grammatical analyses that have puzzled over how NPs could be moved or reused were mistaken—the functional unit being incorporated in the composition is a semantic–syntactic relation (e.g., "the book—NP"), not a syntactic unit in isolation (NP).

Nevertheless, during the anchoring process a categorization is being held active (in a kind of stasis) so that it may be incorporated later in an ongoing construction. The ability to hold a category active (what has conventionally been called a *state*) is central to what Edelman (1992) called *secondary consciousness*. Holding a categorization active is the basis of being able to compare categorizations, indeed, to categorically relate categorizations at all (a "deliberate" process). For example, holding active a categorization of a sequence, and coordinating behavior with respect to it, may be the basic mechanism for goal-directed behavior in animals without language. Relating categorizations semantically and syntactically provides a significantly different conceptual coordination capability that is the foundation of rationality. For example, when we say, "X causes Y" we must be able to hold both X and Y active and then incorporate them in a subsuming (conceptual) categorization of causal relation, in which X is subject, Y is object, and *causes* is the linking relation (Fig. 10.28). In general, constructing mental models (Johnson-Laird, 1983) involves a combination of such grammatical constructions coupled to representations in other modalities, especially images.

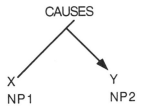

Fig. 10.28. Understanding causality requires coordinating semantic-syntactic relations.

The capability to hold categories active and relate them is the basis of conceptual learning, but it has been taken for granted in most descriptive cognitive models. Our modeling languages have taken for granted the qualification, sequencing, substitution, composition, use of variables, and so on. that distinguishes human conceptualization from that of other animals. NL-Soar research is starting to discover that there are strict limits and a model cannot presuppose the power of arbitrary programming languages. Some limits on conceptual understanding, such as the ability to coordinate the relations between two or more objects or events, are grounded in neural limitations during the comprehension process.

This observation has fascinating implications for how a computer might be able to do better than people (at least people who do not have computers to use!). That is, it is becoming clear that our consciousness (mental representation creation capability) is limited in ways that are not logically required and that are easy to avoid in computer architectures. The flip side is that we do not appreciate fully what the brain's architecture can do and haven't replicated it yet. So we have improvements in hand (tools) the power of which we do not understand. These tools are built on a computational architecture with limitations relative to the brain that we do not understand. As stated in this book's opening section, until we appreciate the differences between computational architectures and neural processes, we cannot possibly have a secure, scientific foundation for building more capable machines; that is, for accomplishing the goals of AI. Nor can we claim to understand naturally occurring, biological cognition without relating it to computational mechanisms.

My approach is precisely as advocated by Newell, Simon, and Lewis: "attempting to explain a range of empirical phenomena with a small set of independently motivated architectural mechanisms and principles and their associated constants" (R. Lewis, personal communication, 1996). The neural activation analysis I have presented assumes that such syntactic judgments can be made out of context. However, it must be remembered that everyday comprehension operates with additional contextual information and other mechanisms, such as visualization, gestures, and external representations. For example, in reading the acceptable S8, I still had to repeat it several times. I replaced the original "who" by "whom," and rephrased it as: "Mary said she saw Tom go to the store with whom?" I visualized the scene of "Tom going into the store." This scene is part of my understanding (the reference of) "what Mary saw." Is "whom saw with" a conceptual schema that I am using to comprehend this sentence? Indeed, over thinking about S14 for several years in preparing this chapter, I surely know what it is intended to say.

In short, it is difficult to talk about "constraints of short-term memory" without considering: multimodal aspects of comprehension (e.g., visualizing the meaning) and conceptually grasping the meaning as a familiar kind of event (Langacker's [1986] theory). We should be suspicious about theories that view comprehension as a purely verbal phenomenon that does not depend partially on context, rhythm, stress, visualization, and past experience with the expressions themselves. That is, theories of grammar comprehension cannot be separated from a theory of mental models. In some respects, this is the claim of Polk and Newell's (1995) theory of verbal reasoning, and under certain interpretations, Skinner's (1957) view of speaking as a behavior.

To summarize this important chapter: A theory is required that explains why center-embedding is always more difficult than right-branching. Previous theories have lacked clear psychological motivation for the "posited structure of short-term memory (stacks, lookahead buffers, etc.), or how the structure should be limited" (R. Lewis, 1996, p. 95).

My hypothesis is that the interference effect and limits on short-term memory result from the mechanism by which conceptualizations activate and compose to form new constructions. The diagrams I use to explain the data suggest that a relatively simple coupling, sequencing, and composing process explains the limits observed. I reformulated the idea of similarity-based interference in terms of how a syntactic categorization can be reused or a semantic categorization related syntactically as an anchor. These are two sides of the same coin, but reveal how the composition is coordinated: Syntactic roles appear multiple times, but semantic categorizations appear only once.

When linguistic observations are reformulated by a neural activation analysis, we find the kind of mechanism that Chomsky argued for—a physiological process that structures conceptual content. The limitations on reuse show further that the procedural languages take for granted what neural processing cannot do directly (a practically unlimited stack) or in other respects does with amazing facility (creating compositional structure). However, it remains true that this analysis is still a gross abstraction of an unknown activation and coordination mechanism.

11

Stored Descriptive-
Schemas Revisited

To do something thinking what one is doing is, according to this legend, always to do two things; namely, to consider certain appropriate propositions, or prescriptions, and to put into practice what these propositions or prescriptions enjoin. It is to do a bit of theory and then to do a bit of practice.

—Gilbert Ryle, *The Concept of Mind*, 1949, p. 29.

Having seen how the conceptual coordination perspective explains patterns of memory and comprehension, we are now in a good position to reconsider the conventional stored descriptions view of memory. In many respects, the descriptive cognitive modeling approach goes well beyond Bartlett's theories; important insights need to be preserved and restated, even although the foundational assumptions about storing, matching, and copying are inaccurate.[1] I begin by considering the logicists' position, showing how it fails to explain how new conceptualizations are possible. I then reexamine Schank's model of episodic memory in some detail, reconsidering how past and present experience are related in storytelling. Next, I consider Feigenbaum and Simon's model of memory, called EPAM (Elementary Perceiver and Memorizer), which can be reformulated to support the conceptual coordination perspective.

Throughout, I am exploring Ryle's idea that everyday behavior (practice) does not consist of following descriptions of how to behave or how the world works (theory). If memory consists at a neural level of something other than stored descriptions—what Ryle called *propositions* and *prescriptions*—then we must find a way to re-relate such descriptions to memory and behavior. The reconsideration in this chapter focuses on the nature of novel behavior, the process of describing experience, and the conceptual control of sequence learning.

---

[1]For an evaluative survey of descriptive models of memory, see Clancey (1997c), chapter 3.

11.1   LOGICAL NOVELTY

The stored description view of reasoning draws a distinction between inductive and deductive formations of new ideas. In *deduction,* particular ideas are inferred from general descriptions (the way a medical expert system produces a patient-specific model from a general model of disease processes). In *induction,* new generalizations are inferred from a body of described examples (the way a program analyzing mass spectrometry data finds patterns between spectral lines and molecular configurations). However, describing the world *always* has inductive aspects, involving perceptual recategorizations and reconceptualizations (cf. the role of storytelling by the paintbrush inventors; section 7.6). As Vygotsky (1934) put it, "every thought is a generalization" (p. p. 217). Reconciling these two positions is important if we are to understand how new statements relate to old ones, and in what sense novel descriptions are possible.

In my interpretation of Bartlett's theory of memory, a conceptualization is regeneralized every time it is brought into the main stream of interest (represented by the diagonal of activation trace diagrams, Fig. 8.2). In contrast, descriptive cognitive models assume that concepts are *instantiated*—reused as if they were rigid structures that are merely retrieved and rotely interpreted like recipes or blueprints (Fig. 1.4). But we must distinguish between the *notations* we use (such as an alphabet), the *expressions* using such notations, and the *conceptualized meaning* descriptions express.

For example, one AI theory, based on the logic programming paradigm of storing propositions in memory, attempts to define learning exclusively in terms of the novelty of descriptions in a database: "A central process in any learning experience is the incorporation of a new fact into an existing theory" (Greiner & Genesereth, 1983). Greiner and Genesereth spoke about "any learning activity," as if to include human learning, and proceeded to provide a completely machine-oriented, mathematical analysis, without any evidence about what people do. In their work, "an existing theory" refers to a descriptive, mathematical c1onstruct, a collection of propositions with variables. Knowledge ("an existing theory") is a set of propositions with an interpretation—a mapping relating the terms and predicates to the world. By this view, the act of perceiving—creating new details in our experience—is separable from the processes of making sense, including creating novel descriptions.

But we saw in the paintbrush inventors example (chapter 7) how feature creation and reconceptualization are coupled; consequently their interaction plays a key role in theory development. To paraphrase Schön (1987), learning begins in determining what the facts are. Incorporation of previous descriptions involves reconceptualization. Based on his work with children, Piaget (1970) concluded, "In each act of understanding, some degree of invention is involved" (p. 77).

Everything we do is at some neural-categorical level new. But if every conceptualization is a recategorization, why doesn't every moment feel novel?

Why isn't every novel recategorization a novel *experience*? In some sense, unless we are feeling *dèjá vu*, all life does have a new character. But smooth recoordination is the norm; usually no disjuncture is felt. The chair I am seeing now is part of a fresh momentary experience. Yet I recognize the chair because I have owned it for a quarter-century. By contrast, in a slip (chapter 5) a disjuncture occurs and not only is the moment new, it is confusing. This is novelty of the conceptual form, "I do not know what is happening to me now." In between is the experience, say, of seeing a new chair and describing the nature of the recognition as, "This is a chair (but) unlike any I have seen before." In many respects, this is the kind of "logical novelty" Greiner and Genesereth (1983) were studying—although without the perceptual basis for making such conceptual abstractions.

Because logical novelty is based on coordinating perceptual recategorization and reconceptualization, it is inherently a historical and therefore *experiential* phenomenon. A theory of novelty in human understanding must include a notion of time. Specifically, without the ability to hold active and reflect on the main stream of interest, everything would appear new. Sacks (1987) described a patient, Jimmie, "stuck in a constantly changing, meaningless moment" (p. 29). He could understand what he was told and engage in complex activities. But if distracted or required to pursue a line of reasoning for more than few minutes, he forgot what he was doing. His whole sense of what he was doing had to be constantly reconstructed from a bottom-up categorization of features. For example, when asked the time of year, "he would immediately look around for some clue . . . and would work out the time of year, roughly, by looking through a window" (p. 27). Significantly, if there were distracting stimuli, Jimmie would pick up a different main stream of interest, abandoning what he had been doing.

So there are two temporal aspects to novelty—the experiential and the descriptive. First, all experience involves recoordinations of perceptual and conceptual categorizations. The ease of recategorizing past experience to construct what is before us now gives a primary sense of novelty. Second, the degree of novelty may be *articulated*—literally, "broken into jointed parts"—in descriptive comparisons of the past and present. Logical novelty characterizes only the descriptive product and not the experiential basis for describing. Descriptions of logical novelty appear to adequately characterize how present and past experience are related because recurrent, higher-order conceptualizations order and organize our particular thoughts.

A theory of novelty must distinguish between novelty of an *artifact* (especially a description, such as a musical score) and novelty of an *experience* (e.g., our hearing of the piece). The song may be novel as a written description, but be a poor copy of another familiar piece. The emotional, experiential novelty is of course the distinction important to evaluating art. When creativity is viewed just in terms of rules for manipulating symbols (as in the laws of logic), it may appear as a puzzle that new songs can be created from a given set of scales and notes or that a new book can be written, when all the words are known in advance (Morris, 1991, p. 47). "New" is viewed in terms of the arrangements of the symbols, not what they mean or evoke. By flattening conceptualization, meaning, and statements to sets of descriptions, Greiner and Genesereth (1983) were able to precisely define the meaning of novelty. But in so doing, they ignored the original problem, which was to understand the novelty of meaning.

11.2   SCHANK'S FAILURE-DRIVEN MODEL OF MEMORY

Schank's theories of human memory formed the basis of a generation of programs for reading and writing stories. The approach, known as *case-based reasoning*, claims that memory is organized around specific experiences that are generalized over time. On the surface, this is compatible with a neural activation perspective. However, Schank meant that *descriptions of experience* are stored in a structured repository, not that processes are reactivated:

> Information about how memory structures are ordinarily linked in frequently occurring combinations, is held in a memory organization packet [MOP] . . . .

> As a memory structure, the role of a MOP is to provide *a place to store new inputs*. As a processing structure, the role of a MOP is to provide expectations that enable prediction of future inputs or inference of implicit events on the basis of previously encountered, structurally similar, events . . . .

> Any number of different MOPs may be applicable at one time . . . . At least two MOPs are relevant to processing, memory, and understanding of what a visit to a doctor's office entails. They are: M-PROFESSIONAL OFFICE VISIT and M-CONTRACT . . . . (Schank, 1982, p. 83, italics added)

MOPs are generalizations with a purpose that transcends the scenes (settings) to which they apply and the scripts abstracting specific experience:

> Scenes hold memories. Scenes are general structures that describe how and where a particular set of actions take places. WAITING ROOM or AIRPORT RENT-A-CAR COUNTER are possible scenes . . . .

> Scripts...embody specific predictions connected to the more general scene that dominates them. Thus, an individual might have a *$DOCTOR JONES' WAITING ROOM* script that differs in some way from the more general WAITING ROOM scene . . . . Scripts can also hold memories that are organized around expectation failures within that script. (Schank, 1982, p. 84)

A MOP represents what a social scientist calls an *activity* (e.g., professional office visit), with associated descriptions of the *scene* (place, objects, roles), and a chronological *script* of events that occur.

Schank's insights include that memory is continually evolving (dynamic), that performance failures are associated with generalizations, that generalization occurs by including an episode in a previous generalization, and that a path of learning junctures constitutes a script for an activity. These observations are consistent with the generalization process in Bartlett's theory.

However, as we follow through Schank's questions and theory, we find the conventional idea that remembering is retrieving descriptions and *reasoning* subconsciously. Schank (1980) began with the observation that "Reminding is simply the bringing to mind of highly relevant memories" (p. 268). He framed his inquiry in terms of two questions:

- "How do we go about finding what is stored in memory?"
- "Why is this phenomenon available consciously when so many other processing phenomenon are not?"

These questions embody the fundamental assumption (and fallacy) of the stored descriptive schema approach, namely that remembering is a process of matching labeled indexes (finding what is stored) and that conscious experience is merely a matter of *availability* of certain processes to awareness. Again, the architecture of conventional computer programs is taken for granted (Fig. 3.5), and what consciousness accomplishes is never articulated or explained. The operations of consciousness—holding multiple categories active, categorizing categories *as being ideas* (the reification of thought), and comparatively categorizing ideas—are the very capabilities that history telling and reasoning require. Again, the idea of processing is viewed uniformly in MOPs—in Russell's terms, it is "turtles all the way down"—making no distinction between subconscious neural categorizing and cycles of perceiving and acting over time that construct, hold active, and relate multiple ideas (cf. Fig. 7.2).

Schank's (1980) model of failure-driven memory was an attempt to explain why we are reminded of previous failures. For example, in a restaurant, you might be reminded of the time that you were asked to pay before eating. This earlier experience was unexpected, and hence was an anticipation failure. The special case of paying first is stored in the script of what happens at a restaurant. Now, in the process of eating at a restaurant another time, this possibility is usefully remembered: "We are reminded of this experience because the structures we are using to process this new experience are the same structures we are using to organize memory" (p. 267).

According to this theory, remembering is retrieving a past experience at a relevant juncture in current experience:

> Every deviation from standard script is stored . . . . Such discriminations must be done at processing time since one cannot know beforehand what relevant similarities might be for future inputs . . . deviation serves as beginning of a reminding experience. (Schank, 1980, p. 271)

Schank's theory of memory requires that descriptions of every deviation from expectation must be stored. But now, he must explain why we are not reminded of all these details every time in the future. His model conjectures that details of a *subscene* are collected into a new kind of *episode*, so we are reminded of a kind of encounter, rather than the details of past experience. Necessarily, some processing must occur during the original experience as well, to anticipate what details might be useful in the future and to form these abstracted packages (called MOPs).

The problem is that this theory relegates descriptive generalization to the past and makes remembering a comparison of present and past descriptions. To the extent that we do experience and recollect failures, Schank's theory is revealing, but it misrepresents the nature of a failure experience, and hence misrepresents where the descriptions of the past experience come from.

At the core, Schank's theory of memory is based only on manipulation of descriptions. In effect, he equated experience with descriptions, just as most conventional theories equate concepts with descriptions. A theoretical conflict therefore arises between the relation of experience, expectation, and relevance. Schank's view is that we *retrieve* descriptions of past failures. In contrast, Bartlett's theory postulates that a remembering episode occurs because of a conceptual coordination failure, occurring now in present experience.

Remembering is not merely the idle retrieval of a past related experience, but the conscious, deliberate attempt to handle a problem occurring now. Remembering has a functional role in sustaining activity—our sense of place and norms for behaving, our comprehension of some task domain, and our naming and manipulating objects in our world—all aspects of our constructed private and public *persona*. Remembering is not merely coincidental "reminding"—a similar experience coming to mind—although that is a necessary process that must always be occurring at the neural level as categories are forming from past coordinations. Indeed, there may have been a similar failure in the past that we can now draw on, but the description of the past is being generated now—not retrieved.

Consequently, relevance need not be strictly *anticipated* (facts prestored for future use). A story is generated from conceptualizations and perceptual categorizations, not from stored descriptions of these. The breakdown in ongoing reperception and reconceptualization—attempts to competently behave by generalizing past coordinations of WIDN— provokes the remembering process (cf. Fig. 8.2). As I indicated in the critique of Soar (section 2.2.2), "episodic memory" is a capability to recoordinate and reenact previous ways of seeing, conceiving, and talking—not a stored body of descriptions of the world or how we behaved (literally, a script).

According to Bartlett (1932/1977, p. 196, 206, 208, 214), the "phenomenon of reminding" is "available consciously" because articulating experience to "turn around on past schemata" is the very essence of consciousness, its function. Schank (1981) suggested instead that we are continuously making subconscious hypotheses, predictions, and notations of failure—as if all these aspects of reasoning could occur *inside* the very mechanism that makes them possible. This is of course the homunculus bugaboo that inevitably creeps into any theory of cognition that makes words the material substance of knowledge and verbal reasoning the process of all coordination. In some sense, Schank (1981) was correct that failure instigates a memory "notation" (p. 44). However, his theory fails to distinguish the different modalities of experience and their relation to verbal phenomena. The reduction of memories to descriptions makes remembering like database retrieval—"producing a maximally relevant memory" (p. 43). Accordingly, the neural aspect is not distinguished from the protracted, conscious, storytelling phenomena of making a tentative claim and reflecting on its meaning in activity. The essential work of coordinating what we say to what we experience is never acknowledged because the very nature of speaking is misconstrued.

Insights and confusions are so mixed in Schank's account, a few tables and diagrams are required to compare his model to Bartlett's. Table 11.1 summarizes the points I have made so far: Remembering is a process of describing experience based on a mechanism of perception, conception, and coordination that produces—but is not constituted from—descriptions. Remembering occurs because of an impasse or "failure" that is occurring now. A rationalized description of this experience may be generated and subsequently remembered—and it is this aspect that Schank overemphasized. Even when a past failure is recollected, the story is not merely retrieved and recited, but reconstructed by two steps:

Table 11.1

Comparison of Memory Organization Packets Model to a Neural Interpretation of Bartlett's Theory of Remembering

Aspects of Remembering	Schank (MOPS)	Neural Interpretation of Bartlett
Why we remember	Because it is useful to do so	A juncture or impasse occurs in coordinated sensorimotor activity
Nature of memory "store"	Stored descriptions of past incidents and their generalizations organized by exceptions (failures)	Previous neural coordinations, prone to reactivate and work together in the same way
Role of language	The mind is continually processing descriptive structures (linguistic expressions) subconsciously, which controls all conscious behavior	Speaking is a conscious behavior only; behaving can occur without language.
Nature of reasoning	The mind is always hypothesizing, predicting, and comparing descriptive generalizations subconsciously	Rationalization, descriptive representation of WIDN (or "what I was doing then"), "knits together" (neurally coordinates) past and present experience

- Reactivating past processes of verbal conceptualization.
- Generalizing these categorizations and sequences by incorporating present details (images, events, terminology) and past details in possibly new ways.

The overall storytelling episode is itself conceptually coordinated by present viewpoints in the current setting (such as to emphasize a different aspect, or to reframe the failure experience in a humorous way).

Schank's theory of failure-driven memory incorporated several important insights, which significantly improved the psychological theory of human learning:

- Human memory is continually evolving (it changes with every experience).
- Expectation failures are associated with generalizations of experience.
- Generalization occurs by including a new episode in a previous generalization.
- When the generalization is reincorporated in a story (a remembering event), we will tend to recollect the detail out of which it was constructed (e.g., a public gaffe that provoked an impasse).
- A path of learning "junctures" constitutes a script for an activity.

In view of Bartlett's empirical studies and my analyses, Schank's theory could be improved as followed :

- Human memory is not a place where theoretical descriptions of the experienced world and behavior are literally stored.
- Speaking is not assembling internally predescribed story fragments, but comprehending and articulating, which involves conceiving verbally and coordinating different modalities of conception (image, sound, posture, etc.). Speaking is (re)constructing verbal conceptions, not *translating* them.
- In human coordination, generalizing occurs with every step of behavior; impasses and recoordinations may occur without a full-blown experience of failure and need to tell a story (cf. Schön's reflection-in-action).
- An unpleasurable emotion, coupled with considerable confusion about WIDN could account for why a failure experience is reasoned about and later reexperienced.
- The relation between the detail and the generalization is dialectic—the meaning of the generalization is not strictly separable from the meaning of the detail that was incorporated to form it (explaining why included details are activated when the generalization is reactivated and composed in later experience).
- There is no such thing as "the" restaurant script; different people in a restaurant are conceiving of their activity in different ways, depending on

their roles. The problem of interpersonal coordination is in reconciling different ways of seeing and organizing behavior—they are not following the same script.

A few subtle differences between the theories deserve special attention:

MOPs Claim 1: Detecting a failure is detecting that an expectation fails to materialize—that is, assumptions, expectations, justifications are previously stored statements that are brought out later, when an explanation is required.

But such articulations are constructed on the spot, when we are trying to make sense, as theoretical reflections on our behavior (e.g., "Oh, I see, I usually pay after eating"). Such theories did not necessarily exist before, and in particular were not required internally to generate our behavior.

Episodic memory includes the capacity to *articulate the history* of what you thought you were doing (a kind of descriptive modeling) and hold that generalization up against the detail that instigated the impasse (e.g., "pay first"; this restates the analysis of chapter 7). Also, you can project the future by telling the story of what normally happens next—assumptions and expectations are consciously created and experienced by reimagining the past flow of experience, not by retrieving internally hidden descriptions.

MOPs Claim 2: "When we detect a failure of an action to conform to our expectations, we remember that failure. In a sense, we are attempting to jot it down for next time, so that we won't fail that way again" (Schank, , 1981, p. 44).

But incorporation of episodic details in our conceptual coordination is ongoing and has nothing specifically to do with failures. We do not *record a description* of the failure, we *conceptualize* the situation when we form a satisfying new generalization of WIDN. We do not index or retrieve the description in memory at a later time, we reactivate the conceptualization of the situation. Schön made the same point in criticizing the "historical revisionism" of stored descriptive schema models of analogy (cf. Table 7.2).

MOPs Claim 3: Reminding occurs because a subsequent expectation failure reminds us of the failure in the past.

But reactivation of past ways of seeing and interacting is always occurring. Reminding about a past unusual situation may occur because of the emotional aspect of that categorization ("Once I forgot to pay"), not because we necessarily need the information now to deal with an expectation failure.

We are conceiving a current situation in a way similar to how we have conceived situations in the past. Subsequent speaking is not a rote recital of what we learned by the previous failure (although it can chain together the same details), but a new generalization, a new way of viewing the previous experience. Theorizing occurs now, in the story telling activity. We say that the experience has recurred, but really the past way of correlating experience has been adapted to the particulars of what we are doing.

In conclusion, a theory of reminding must account for what conscious storytelling is accomplishing that subconscious recoordination alone cannot. Schank's general observations are sound and significantly distinguish his work from the approach of Greiner and Genesereth (plus countless others), which makes little attempt to relate to human experience. But because the MOPs theory is based on storage, indexing, and literal reapplication of pattern descriptions, almost every detail is incompatible with the process of learning Bartlett empirically discovered and described more than half a century ago.

11.3   FEIGENBAUM AND SIMON'S EPAM

EPAM is a simulation model of human verbal learning from the early 1960s created by Feigenbaum and Simon (1984). The program learns to recognize words, word associations, and properties associated with them. For example, the program can learn to recognize words like Wine and the association Cat–Dog. The model is of special interest to our discussion for several reasons. First, Feigenbaum and Simon provided a review 20 years after their original work, showing how the approach has withstood extensive evaluation and is superior to other approaches. Second, the model emphasizes serial learning, which is central to a theory of conceptual coordination.

A detailed examination of EPAM shows that it incorporates a model of conceptualization, including categorizing sequences of perceptual categorizations, detecting recurrent sequences, and controlling attention for noticing features of new inputs. In this respect, EPAM is a model of *active perceptual remembering*. EPAM is a useful abstraction of how memory works. Using the conceptual coordination perspective, we can reformulate the model in terms of dynamic construction of active processes versus storing programs and symbols in a tree. My analysis makes the following points:

- *Recognition is reactivation* rather than "testing" (comparison). Elements may be partially activated and hence partially matched.
- Categorizing of input sequences may occur even as words are not recognized.
- Recursiveness involves reactivation and reincorporation of sequences rather than redundant storage.
- A control structure involves conceptualization of feature patterns in the input and how to look at the visual field.
- A *noticing strategy* is necessarily integrated with representations of words (hence adaptive ordering should not have been left out of EPAM-III).

As we found in the analysis of analogy and other memory models, EPAM folds processes that can only be conscious—which are indeed the very function of consciousness—into the subconscious storage and matching machinery. Thus, the nature and corresponding functions of internal processes and consciousness are not appropriately attributed or understood. In the following sections, I explain what and how EPAM learns, bringing out how the noticing strategy models conscious action and uses the nature of recursive recognition to reveal additional aspects of neural activation.

11.3.1 What EPAM Learns

EPAM accepts inputs such as "SGX" and sorts them using an n-ary (multiple branched) tree of tests, stored images, and pointers to properties (Fig. 11.1). The terminal nodes of the tree are effectively primitive tests, where the full image to be recognized is stored: "The image is a memory structure that has a unique internal symbolic name" (Feigenbaum and Simon, 1984, p. 308) called a token, such as "SGX," which "is needed to indicate the presence of the object in its various contexts" (p. 308). The preceding branches in the discrimination tree test features of the image:

> According to the EPAM theory, when information is received by the sensory organs...it initially undergoes an encoding process usually referred to as *feature extraction*. The stimulus is then *recognized* on the basis of the features that have been encoded by the feature extraction process, and a symbol is stored in *short-term memory* that "points to" or accesses the relevant information in *semantic long-term memory*.

> EPAM must be visualized as sandwiched between a sensory-perceptual front-end that detects features and a semantic back end that accumulates and stores, in associative fashion, information about the things that have been discriminated . . . .

> In short, we think of the semantic long-term memory as the "encyclopedia" in which most of the knowledge acquired by the learning system is stored; the discrimination net as the "index" to this "encyclopedia," a recognition memory; and the short-term memory as a small working memory needed by learning processes. (pp. 306–307)

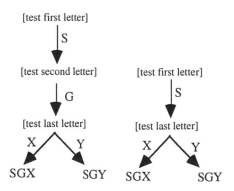

Fig. 11.1. Two possible discrimination trees for recognizing the inputs "SGX" and "SGY."

Elsewhere, Newell and Simon (1972) indicated,

> [This encyclopedia] contains various aspects of the meaning of the word—e.g., its spelling, pronunciation, synonyms, visual representations of its referent, etc. Thus a recognition process makes the word into a symbol." (p. 34)

The index reflects the history of stimuli and "can be highly redundant, with many paths leading to the same terminal node" (Feigenbaum and Simon, 1984, p. 325). This model of a front-end recognizer and a back-end encyclopedia fundamentally distinguishes between the "representation for identifying a pattern and for storing knowledge about its properties" (p. 323). EPAM models what we might view as the perceptual aspect of cognition, concerned with features that are learned, but not integral in themselves to a reasoning process:

> We do not believe that there is any contemporary dispute that the first stages of sensation and perception are essentially parallel in operation. The retina and the cochlea are most obviously parallel devices that extract a panoply of basic features from incoming stimuli. EPAM is a proposed model of what happens to those features once extracted, and how they are used for the recognition of objects. (p. 329)

In neural terms (chapter 3), EPAM's features are perceptual categorizations, such as the letters of the alphabet. The tests are perceptual categorizations of *parts* of objects in the world, such as the first letter of a word. Categories such as *letter* and *word* are clearly not part of the visual system, but higher-order categories. As Feigenbaum and Simon (1984) note, their model does not consider how objects such as letters and words are detected and their features learned: "The feature extraction process is not modeled, nor is the whole structure of schemas and associations in long-term memory" (p. 307). As they indicate, the tests (and control structure for attempting tests in different orders) are

> substantially specialized to a particular set of stimulus materials . . . . When EPAM was used in the context of two-dimensional visual perception (chess perception), it had to be provided with an appropriate noticing mechanism (PERCEIVER) to control its attention to parts of the stimulus. (p. 334)

Thus, the learning of what constitutes a stimulus, tests referring to parts of stimuli, features of stimuli corresponding to these parts, and preferences for ordering tests are not part of the EPAM model. EPAM therefore models an "expert's" already-formed recognition process, not the process by which a new ontology of objects, tests, and features is learned (such as when the paintbrush inventors first see and conceive bristle-spaces as channels). Viewing the front end, recognition, and semantic back end processing as serial stages may be valid when the front end and semantic back end are already organized and relatively stable. This does not refute the descriptive adequacy of the model, but does question whether EPAM is a good model of human verbal learning, as claimed, because a child usually learns to recognize letters and sounds at the same time he or she is learning to read words. (Consider also the adult experience of perceptual–conceptual interaction in learning new sounds in a foreign language, section 5.6.)

11.3.2 How EPAM learns

EPAM learns when recognition failures occur:

> EPAM typically learns (expands the discrimination net) as the result of confusing an unknown stimulus with one previously learned. It recognizes its mistake because of the redundant information...that is stored at the terminal node to which it has (erroneously) sorted the new stimulus. By comparing the novel stimulus with the incomplete image of the familiar stimulus, it discovers a feature that will discriminate between them, and inserts precisely *this* feature into the net. (Feigenbaum and Simon, 1984, p. 324)

EPAM has multiple strategies for recognizing new words. First, EPAM attempts to recognize the entire word. The word will be tested and sorted, possibly resulting in misidentification (i.e., the word sorts to an existing, different word, such as Wone sorting to Wine). "Only after recognition in the word net fails does the strategy shift to attending to individual letters" (Feigenbaum and Simon, 1984, p. 327). The program's control structure for ordering tests is based on the "anchor point of assumption" of starting with the first letter, shifting to the last, and then moving to other letters (or back to the first): "The noticing order postulated in EPAM-I and EPAM-II is under strategic control, and can be altered by the subject under particular circumstances or as a result of experimental instructions" (p. 324).

For example, given a stream of heterogeneous three-letter syllables and an initial strategy of discriminating on the basis of the first letter, if the experimenter changed the input "so all first letters are the same, EPAM II would rapidly shift its attention to looking directly at third-letters for discriminating differences" (p. 311). That is, the model implies awareness of repeated failure or repeated similarity of stimulus items (e.g., all are now ending in the same letter). This noticing and strategy-shifting mechanism is of course more sophisticated than perceptual categorization alone allows. The mechanism is not only learning sequences, but *detecting patterns in its learning process*, such as, "fruitless search for first-letter differences" and "attention to third-letter no longer paid off" (p. 311). Such conceptual induction is itself complex and is indeed the focus of much machine learning research.

In short, EPAM models not just learning serial order of stimuli, but serially ordering testing itself, a form of conceptualization. This is most clear when Feigenbaum and Simon contrast their model with parallel-distributed systems:

> [PANDEMONIUM] does not deal with the strategies of attention or noticing order, but deals impartially with all of the stimulus information that is presented to it . . . . Real-world stimuli have orderly structure, and one pays an enormous penalty for parallelism that ignores that structure. (p. 331)

Strategies of attention are alternative conceptualizations about the kind of input being processed and *how to look* at the input. That is, they are aspects of sensorimotor coordination, not merely perceptual categorizations or sequences of such categorizations. An EPAM learner is sophisticated, indeed, if shifts of attention are brought about by experimental instructions. This is a machine that can understand language, and not just store verbal associations in an encyclopedic memory. As in Schank's MOPs model of remembering, we find in EPAM both a model of categorization (low-level memory) and a model of a *subject*, a conscious agent.

Evaluating EPAM is therefore a complex problem. Holding aside the issue of how the features are learned, we are still left with the word learning process itself. This process is not merely mechanically building a tree of features, but involves active consideration of how well the current tree-building process is working and application of previously learned strategies for building trees. Such strategic reasoning involves—in EPAM as well as people—*describing* methods, their results, and making *inferences* about described alternatives.

One way to approach this issue is to hold aside the visual problems posed by EPAM's application to chess perception and focus on the sequence learning of words. Seriality of features clearly dominates here, and the strategies of anchoring on the first or last letters might reflect properties of a more basic segmentation process, as I discussed in the modeling of slips (section 6.2). Feigenbaum and Simon's (1984) data support this view:

> Seriality in EPAM's noticing process accounts for the empirical phenomena of the serial position curve, as well as for the fact, observed both from the tip-of-the-tongue phenomenon and from spelling errors, that words are discriminated largely on the basis of their first and last letters, and with little attention to those near the middle. (p. 329)[2]

In contrast, ways of looking at a chess board, involving rows, relations between pieces of different types, and so forth, may reflect more the spatial configurations of chess moves than internal aspects of serial ordering.

In any event, Feigenbaum and Simon's (1984) description suggests that the learner is conceptualizing about the learning experience. The "learner's strategy in familiarization of material" suggests an active coordination process that goes well beyond rote remembering of next–next–next sequences. Strategy shifts suggest a reconceptualization of how to remember or make sense in an experimental setting—which is most obvious when the learner is comprehending the experimenter's instructions. This conceptualization is a categorization of the sequences being presented, and it constitutes a way of coordinating behavior that includes *how to look* at the sensory field.

Ironically, despite an attempt to focus on a slice of cognition sandwiched between perception and meaning, EPAM's operation presupposes an ability to observe and conceive its progress, weigh adequacy of an approach, and

---

[2]See also the "*Je connais . . . Place de Cathedral*" example in chapter 6.

discretely shift to an alternative coordination. This is not a mere recognition or indexing system, but a coordinated learning process that itself presupposes conceptualization and reasoning. As we saw in the paintbrush inventor examples and as Feigenbaum and Simon's (1984) choice of what to include in EPAM nicely illustrates, conscious aspects of theorizing and perceptual categorization cannot be easily separated from recognition learning. We must consider how people conceive how to look and how to remember. The noticing mechanism of EPAM, especially in chess perception, is not necessarily a built-in process, but a learned conceptual coordination. Knowing how to look is a kind of knowledge, too.

11.3.3 Recursiveness Suggests Conceptualization

Another approach for understanding EPAM is to focus on the recursive recognition process and hierarchical storage. Feigenbaum and Simon state that EPAM "build[s] up its stimulus units into recursive structures of hierarchically organized chunks" (p. 317). The recursiveness is important because chunks (words) may appear in multiple, different associations (e.g., Cat–Dog and Cat–Lion). Allowing chunks to be treated as subobjects that are themselves recognized by the network removes "duplication of clusters of subtests when the same substructures reappeared in different contexts as components of larger structures" (p. 314).

For example, Cat is a subobject in the input Cat–Dog. After learning the pair, the net will indicate that a subobject test on Cat occurs at a particular place. Processing of the original Cat–Dog object is suspended to process the subobject "Cat." This occurs by recursively reexamining the discrimination network from the root. Thus, there are perhaps multiple "'open decisions' in suspense awaiting the completion of further subpart recognitions" (p. 309).

Such a recursive control structure relates to neural activation in several ways. First, in EPAM sequences are uniquely represented, as a neural map interpretation suggests (cf. the representation of typing "book" in Fig. 6.6). Rather than representing Cat as a discrimination tree testing the first letter, and so on, we might represent it as a sequence of perceptual categorizations (Fig. 11.2). For simplification, we can show the letters as being on the diagonal itself (right side of the figure).

By this analysis, the letters are perceptual categorizations and words are sequences of such categorizations; that is, a sequence of activations of perceptual categorizations *over time*. A chunk is a categorization of a sequence (Fig. 11.3).

It is essential to the EPAM model that not all letters of a word need to be noticed to recognize the word. With repeated exposure to the same stimulus, the FAMILIARIZATION module will detect and store more properties. In particular, a distinction is drawn between recognizing an image "CAT" and being able to spell the word Cat. Here we are considering what happens when "CAT" becomes recognized as a subobject; that is, it is treated as having component parts that are themselves primitives.

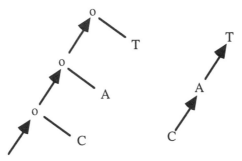

Fig. 11.2. Neural activation representation of "Cat" stimulus. Letters shown as categories coupled as details in a sequence; right side shows a simpler representation of the same activation relations.

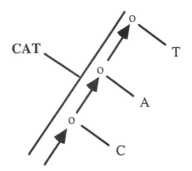

Fig. 11.3. A *chunk* represented as a categorized sequence of perceptual categorizations.

In this respect, reactivating the sequence C → A → T (Fig. 11.3) is a way of reusing structures, and avoiding redundant encoding. Hence, the idea of a recursive, hierarchical network is fully consistent with a neural activation mechanism (as indeed it better be!). But rather than viewing the features as stored in a tree, we view the discrimination network as a collection of neural categorizing processes that are *sequentially activated* and *composed* during the recognition process. We can represent what the subject knows as a tree (e.g., Fig. 11.1), but the learning process involves direct activation of perceptual categorizations and categorizations of sequences, not storing the names of features (tokens). Specifically, the sequence Cat–Dog would be represented as a temporal activation of two chunks (Fig. 11.4).

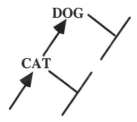

Fig. 11.4. Neural activation representation of sequence Cat–Dog, consisting of two "subobjects," each of which is a categorization of a sequence of letters (details omitted, refer to Fig. 11.3).

Again, partial learning of spelling and *noticing* of features of an image would need to be worked out in a neural model that reformulates EPAM. For the moment, consider that this representation (Fig. 11.4) has the advantage of showing serial recognition as serial reactivation of categorizations ("extracted" features). Such a neural model leaves open to what extent recognition is top-down (as EPAM assumes in attempting to match a subobject, such as "Cat," as a single test), or whether it mixes top-down and bottom-up components. In particular, the neural activation approach has the advantage of removing the serial ordering of stages EPAM imposes between perceptual learning (feature extraction) and categorical learning (recognizing a word). Recognition of a chunk would occur by the neural activation of the sequence it categorizes, and then any sequences containing the chunk would become (partially) activated. In terms of the diagram (Fig. 11.4), activation could flow from the right side (bottom-up), from the left, or in some combination. The recursive aspect does not require a stack and interpreter to suspend operation, but is modeled as multiple sequences and categories vying for activation.

One consequence of recursive recognition is that "Learning is forced to the highest possible levels of the existing tree before any new subtrees will be added . . . . Net growth is biased toward breadth, not depth" (Feigenbaum and Simon, 1984, p. 310). For example, if we assume that the learner can detect recurrent properties of inputs and conceptualize different strategies for attention and detection, as in EPAM, then initial sequences might also be categorized. For example, Fig. 11.5 shows how a reflective learner would categorize an initial sequence "CA," thus conceiving "I am processing sequences that start with 'CA'." Again, this is a categorization of WIDN.

In Fig. 11.5, I show first the notation for a chunk, C–A. To keep the notation readable, I again use a notation developed for grammatical analysis in the previous chapter to show how such a chunk might be *specialized* in multiple sequences. In effect, the sequences C–A–R and C–A–T are kinds of CA sequences—C–A qualified by different details, R and T.

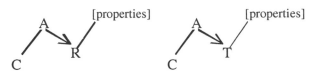

Fig. 11.5. A neural activation representation of categorized sequence, CA, having two specializations, CAR and CAT, each with associated properties.

The interpretation of Fig. 11.5 is as follows: Repetition of the sequence C–A, accompanied by repeated failures because the initial tests are not discriminating, leads to categorizing or chunking the sequence C → A as a unit. (Holding such a sequence active is assumed by the EPAM model, which suspends processing and shifts to a discrimination phase when images wrongly map to each other.) Next, subsequent inputs are (initially) viewed as kinds of C → A sequences, and because these are three-letter sequences, the *strategy of attention* is to examine the last letter. The learning of a specialization of CA is directly parallel to the conceptualization that CA is *a kind of sequence.* Now the processing is clearly top-down as a higher-order categorization (C → A) is held active. Finally, I show the properties as following the A and T in sequence, suggesting that the associations of the encyclopedia could be just a sequence of categorizations (i.e., a memorized list).

The conceptualization "I am processing CA sequences now," is a context or organizing process for looking at the subsequent inputs. As I show in more detail in the next chapter, such a categorization resembles subgoaling, where C → A is a higher problem space and specializations or instances are included within it. In terms of the problem space terminology, when an impasse repeatedly occurs at the third letter in the recognition process, a subspace is formed. Depending on the nature of the third letter, the subspace indicates how processing should proceed (if R continue in one way, if T continue in another). In goal hierarchies of descriptive models, C → A would be named as a procedure or task and the test between R versus T would appear as a predicate in a rule at the higher (C → A) problem space.

Although I have only sketched how EPAM might be reformulated as hierarchical categorization of neural sequences, it should be clear enough that a discrimination tree of "tests" (Fig. 11.1) is only one way of visualizing the recognition process. I have claimed that there is a great advantage to modeling serial learning as reactivation of categorizations. This explanation does not require assuming there is a separate interpreter to traverse the discrimination network, but instead integrates perceptual categorization and conceptual coordination for looking at the stimulus. There are no tests per se because there is no matching—only an activation promoted by ongoing perceptual categorization and reactivation of neural maps in a sequence.

There are many more details to be worked out: How are multiple (suspended) sequences coordinated at an impasse? What is the neural process by which conceptualization and qualification of conceptualization occurs (Fig. 11.5)? Furthermore, as the discussion of the experimenter's instructions suggests, the learner must have some way of conceiving and hence participating in such a learning interaction: There is no root node in everyday life; there must be some way of starting up a certain kind of coordination and restricting attention to some conception of WIDN.

Newell and Simon (1972) emphasized that the complexity of EPAM's operation is determined by the content of the program stored in the net, not the interpreter. Hence, the population of words to be recognized and the discrimination program are inseparable. This fits a neural analysis very well. Furthermore, Newell and Simon left open the possibility that in an information processing system, the interpreter "is a complete mechanism that produces the effective behavior" (as I view a neural process memory) rather than being a "true interpreter that follows a program" (as in EPAM). They ironically add that "if the interpreter is simply a mechanism that produces a sequence of behaviors, then of course we have no way of describing its internal structure in information processing terms" (p. 36). My use of information processing notations and language—with a neural interpretation—to describe conceptualization would appear to belie this claim (or fear). The shift is that, unlike Newell and Simon, I do not view such an information processing system as *equivalent* to what the brain is capable of doing. An information-processing cognitive model only grossly describes the categorizing and their subsumption and temporal relations.

To summarize, a conceptual coordination reformulation calls attention to different aspects of EPAM:

- Explains why the noticing strategy is integrated with representations of words (hence why adaptive ordering should not have been left out of EPAM-III). Categorizing of input sequences may occur even as words are not recognized.
- Views recursiveness as reactivation of multiple sequences and inclusion of perceptual categories (instances) within a conceptualization of a sequence (type), satisfying the need to avoid redundant storage. (In the example, T and R might be both partially activated rather than being "tested.")
- Views a control structure as conceptualization of feature patterns in the input and how to look at the visual field. Rather than a separate processor for controlling learning, this is a person's conscious conceptualization of the activity (cf. discussion of pragmatic context; section 7.5).

In general, a conceptual coordination perspective focuses on the dynamics by which categorization occurs and controls behavior, rather than viewing knowledge as a static, descriptive net "index" that resides in a memory and is "read off" by an interpreter. In EPAM and Schank's MOPs, remembering (recognizing) and learning are appropriately viewed as a single process. However, in people the learning process is a coordination of and constituted by active processes that are also representing *what needs to be learned*. Like MOPs, EPAM captures many of the patterns of human learning, but attempts to separate out both the simpler and more complex stages of cognition (perception and reasoning)—and these are then unwittingly folded back into subconscious processing.

In people, describing and manipulating descriptions is a conscious process. The higher-order aspects of storytelling and organizing learning cannot be built into a memory module. Similarly, categorizing and coordinating are the operations of schemas themselves, not stored descriptions of them. Describing occurs in conscious behavior, not as subconscious comparison and editing of textual models. There is an internal mechanism—a neural categorizing and sequencing process. Without addressing these as different representational functions, the rationalizing and strategizing of remembering that both MOPs and EPAM build into the lowest levels cannot be explained.

12

Problem-Space
Models Revisited

We think that the grammarian, when he takes a discourse and divides it into parts, is finding out the truth about it, and that when he lays down rules for the relations between these parts he is telling us how people's minds work when they speak. This is very far from being the truth. A grammarian is not a kind of scientist studying the actual structure of language; he is a kind of butcher, converting it from organic tissue into marketable and edible joints. Language as it lives and grows no more consists of verbs, nouns, and so forth than animals as they live and grow consist of forehands, gammons, rump-steaks, and other joints.

—R. G. Collingwood, *The Principles of Art,* 1938, p. 257.

In this chapter I apply the conceptual coordination perspective on memory and learning to models of reasoning, or symbolic information processing. In considering models of remembering in Soar (section 2.2.2), MOPs (section 11.2), and EPAM (section 11.3), I have already show that knowledge is frequently represented hierarchically in descriptive cognitive models. Correspondingly, problem-solving architectures, which model human reasoning, contain one or more hierarchies of problem types and solution methods. These hierarchies provide a means of focusing attention and ordering reasoning steps. For example, the hierarchy of infectious diseases in a medical disease taxonomy would constitute a *problem space* for focusing on particular diagnoses. The contained subtree of bacterial infections constitutes a more specific problem space. Similarly, diagnostic methods, such as procedures for gathering information, forming hypotheses, and discriminating hypotheses, may be organized into hierarchies of *problem-solving operators.* This chapter concerns how such hierarchies are structured and related in descriptive cognitive models and what, if anything, this reveals about conceptual coordination at the neural level.[1]

---

[1]This chapter is revised from "Perceptual Recategorization versus Grammatical Task Models—Relating Neomycin, Soar, and Neural Darwinism," Presented at International Conference on Computers in Education (ICCE '93) December 15–17, 1993, Taiwan.

Extending the perspective of studying Caitlin in the pool (chapter 5) and slips (chapter 6), my underlying question is: How can people conceptualize and perform procedures before they have a language for *rationalizing* what they do? We find that the descriptions of patterns in problem-solving models often go beyond what a typical person can say about the reasoning process, just as a natural language grammar goes beyond what someone who has not learned grammar in school can say about speaking. Are these simply the patterns in a scientist's analysis of problem solving? If they correspond to structured processes in the brain, how are such hierarchical conceptualizations formed? I have suggested throughout this book that procedures may form by categorizing sequences of simpler categorizations. But how do multiple conceptual hierarchies become coordinated, as problem-solving models suggest?

In the analysis that follows, I show that each problem-space level in these models corresponds to a way of categorizing the problem situation, and hence learning complex problem-solving procedures is a form of *coordination between conceptual and perceptual categorizations:*

- A problem-solving operator (e.g., "group and differentiate hypotheses") describes a *categorized sequence* of behavior.
- Each problem-solving operator strictly applies to just one descriptive level in the model of the situation being understood (e.g., in medical diagnosis these levels may include: the patient, the most general competing hypotheses about what is happening to the patient, a particular hypothesis, or a particular finding relevant to that hypothesis).
- Two kinds of learning can be distinguished, one deliberate (categorizing of operator sequences at a given level) and the other automatic ("chunking" of habitual paths across levels).
- Applying the neural activation perspective suggests that problem spaces may be learned as categorizations of operator sequences, in which each operator is a conceptualization of WIDN and each operator in a sequence has the same kind of operand (focus details are the of the same type).

The second point means that the grain size of operators strictly corresponds to levels of abstraction in how the world is viewed. The final point means that categorizations of the situation (what is problematic in the world) impose distinctions on the categorization of problem solving methods (what questions to ask and how to relate evidence to actions). The two hierarchies of categorizations are thereby coupled and form a *conceptual system* ("what to do when"). Suppose that the structure of problem-solving models, which I have already outlined, is not just an artifact of how scientists describe the world, but reflects analogous patterning in the brain. Then a closer look at these models, with an eye toward neural processes, reveals (as these conclusions suggest) how conceptual systems form by coordinating different kinds of organizers (different kinds of categorization hierarchies).

My exposition has several parts:

- Describe how world situation and operator models are related, a pattern often implicit in problem-solving architectures. I do this by recasting "knowledge-based" problem solving models in terms of the Soar architecture.
- Show that in general knowledge bases are idealizations that often constitute new scientific models of phenomena in the world, and thus go beyond what individual experts knew before the model-building activity.
- Show that, nevertheless, models of problem-solving strategies do have a good fit to human behavior, and constitute a kind of "grammatical analysis" of reasoning patterns—descriptions that reveal underlying, nonverbal processes of conceptual coordination.
- Show how models of the world situation and operators are related, such that new ways of viewing the world and new operators arise together.
- Argue that operators thus originate in a conceptual coordination process that develops the "grammar" of problem solving by relating ways of seeing to ways of acting.

12.1 STUDYING DESCRIPTIVE MODELS OF PROBLEM SOLVING

The Neomycin model of diagnosis (Clancey, 1988, 1992) is an idealized description of how experienced physicians reason. The architecture consists of a domain model (a disease taxonomy, or the medical knowledge base) and a diagnostic procedure (a hierarchy of procedures called *tasks;* Fig. 12.1). The Neomycin architecture was designed to enable description of recurrent sequences of physician behavior, specifically to provide a source of strategic advice for students. The diagnostic procedure models how a physician formulates the next question when gathering information about a patient. Specifically, as a psychological model, the diagnostic procedure models shifts of attention in constructing a model of the patient (the "situation-specific model"; see also Fig. 12.3). In this section, I briefly recount how the diagnostic procedure was formulated and in what sense it constitutes a grammar.

12.1.1 Problem-Solving Grammars

Rules in a descriptive cognitive model are usually stated with variables. For example, in a typical medical expert system, such as Mycin, rules refer to "the patient" instead of a particular person. Descriptive models are therefore general, just like a set of numeric equations: One rule covers many specific situations. Therefore, a fixed set of rules can be used to diagnose an indefinite number of patients. A descriptive model of a reasoning process can be therefore be used, as I will show in this chapter, as a kind of grammar to abstract and explain the surface events of problem-solving behavior over time. I will discuss how *problem-solving grammars* are related to language grammars, how such process models are created by knowledge engineers, and what the knowledge acquisition process reveals about human knowledge.

Neomycin clearly illustrates the nature of problem-solving grammars because its architecture was designed to separate the medical knowledge from the diagnostic procedure. Specifically, Neomycin is a rationalized reconstruction of Mycin; it explicitly describes patterns that are implicit in Mycin's rules. For example, in examining Mycin's rule set with an instructional application in mind, I discovered many recurrent orderings of clauses in rules. For example, whenever a rule mentioned "the patient has had neurosurgery," the immediately preceding clause would say, "the patient has had surgery." Dozens of such patterns were generalized to form a new, more general *metarule*, "If a type of finding is not present, then the specific subtypes are not present." I then added statements like "Neurosurgery is a subtype of surgery" to the medical domain model.

In general, there are many implicit patterns in Mycin's rules (and in other descriptive models) because hierarchies, preferences, and procedural sequences are often represented as orderings in lists, "(A B)", which mean "do or check A before B." By using metarules, an instructional program can present the domain model and diagnostic procedure more clearly. The associated student-modeling program can also more precisely explain differences between Mycin and a student's problem solving in terms of variations of their disease models or their diagnostic process.

Fig. 12.1 shows Neomycin's procedure for carrying on a diagnostic interview. Each node of the graph corresponds to a set of ordered metarules that specify how to carry out a particular task. For example, one of the rules for the task Test-Hypothesis indicates that rules relating the hypothesis to symptoms it causes should be applied. This leads to asking further questions about the patient (Findout).

Such a procedure is general because there are no medical terms in the network. The same procedure has been applied to mechanical engineering (diagnosing the cause of faults in iron cast in sand molds) by creating a new domain model expressed in the same *relational language* used by Neomycin: "causal enabling condition," "subtype," "symptom caused by a disorder," and so on. Thus, we have found that, to a certain useful degree, biological and mechanical engineering systems can be represented by a common language of causality and subtype and manipulated by a common procedure for generating and discriminating between hypotheses.

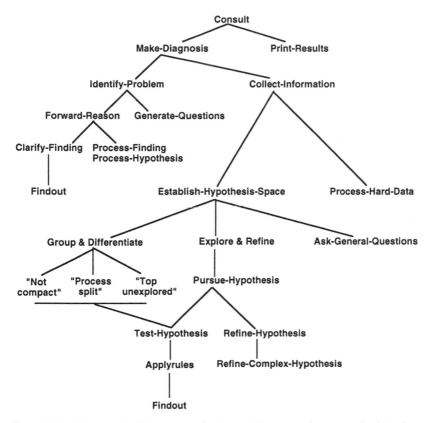

Fig. 12.1. Neomycin hierarchy of diagnostic procedures, called tasks. Procedural patterns in Mycin's rules were generalized to describe this abstract model of the diagnostic process, a strategy model.

With the domain model separated from the diagnostic procedure, Neomycin's architecture makes clear how knowledge-based programs work: The reasoning process is modeled by a procedure that applies a general model to facts and constraints in some problem-solving situation to derive a situation-specific model (SSM; Fig. 12.2). The SSM constitutes a plan, a design, a diagnosis, and so forth, or a sequence of these. The general domain model is to the SSM as a population of patients is to a single patient in a point in time. Thus, the diagnostic procedure in Neomycin is more generally called an *inference procedure* to make clear that in general the procedure may involve other kinds of model construction purposes, such as planning, design, auditing, prediction, and so on.

Different knowledge-based programs emphasize different modeling issues, such as the uncertain nature of the data, ways of posting and contrasting multiple SSMs, ways of making the inference procedure more efficient, how statistics can be incorporated in the general model, and so on. Even although the program modules are not always explicitly so described, every knowledge-based program works by the model construction process shown in Fig. 12.2. In effect, the general domain model is a kind of map. The problem-solving procedure applies the map to make a situation-specific solution that is a copy and reconfiguration of nodes and paths in the general model.

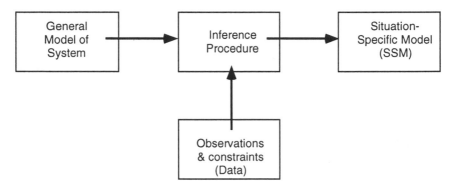

Fig. 12.2. The model construction view of inference. An inference procedure is a program for gathering information about the behavior of some system in the world and the environment (data) to make assertions about the system producing this behavior (the task called "diagnosis"), the system that could produce this behavior (the tasks called "design" and "control"), or how a system will behave ("prediction").

An SSM is a graph constrained to have a certain form (Fig. 12.3). The graph is not an arbitrary network, but *a representation of processes,* constructed for a purpose. In particular, the graph is a model used by a program. For example, consider the form this graph takes for medical diagnosis. Each node of the graph represents an aspect of a disease process. In an SSM concerned with infectious processes, different levels of abstraction indicate the location, duration, and agent causing the infection. According to the Neomycin general model, the description "Viral-Meningitis" need not be elaborated into causes of viral meningitis, because all subtypes have the same therapy (orange juice, aspirin, and rest). If Neomycin's purpose were scientific description rather than medical therapy, we would represent what causes viral-meningitis. Hence, the adequacy of Neomycin's domain model is evaluated with respect to the discriminations the program must make between therapy alternatives. This is the idea of *heuristic classification* (Clancey, 1985), in which classification models are chained in a sequence of steps: Patient → disease → therapy. Distinctions at each step constrain modeling alternatives at the next.

Fig. 12.3 also illustrates how the subprocedures of Neomycin's diagnostic procedure, called *tasks*, are operators that examine and modify links in the SSM. The SSM is inspected by the operators during reasoning, such that the partial state of the SSM drives the inference process. The operators search and relate the general model and SSM according to the current incomplete form of the SSM. This is somewhat like copying a shopping list from a recipe book, in which the recipe is a general model and the shopping list is a SSM, a plan for the next step of acquiring ingredients. One may either scan the recipe or scan the shopping list when trying to think of other things to buy. In constructing a diagnostic SSM, Neomycin looks up relations between diseases and symptoms to postulate disease processes that might be occurring in this patient. This process is driven by gaps the program detects in the SSM. For example, referring to Fig. 12.3, might seizures be caused by the same disease causing the fever, stiff neck, and headache?

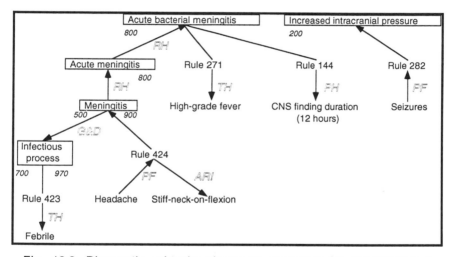

Fig. 12.3. Diagnostic subtasks shown as operators for constructing a situation-specific model (arrows indicate the order in which nodes were linked; Refine Hypothesis (RH) grew a link upward from meningitis to the more specific hypothesis, Acute-meningitis; Process Finding (PF) links symptoms to the diseases that cause them). (From Clancey, 1992, p. 27; reprinted with permission.).

By working bottom up from symptoms and top down from disease hypotheses, Neomycin's reasoning procedure constructs a description of processes in the patient's body that are causing a specific patient's complaints. For example, information about a headache triggered Rule 424, which caused a question about stiff-neck-on-flexion to be asked and meningitis to be hypothesized (subtasks process-finding abbreviated PF in Fig. 12.3, and applyrule! abbreviated AR!). The procedure Group-And-Differentiate (G&D) looked for support for meningitis by considering categorical evidence (for infection process, a more general process description). Ideally, a diagnostic SSM is just one tree, containing all the abnormal findings.

We are now ready to relate Neomycin's architecture to Soar. Soar is probably the most well-known model of human learning—"a symbolic architecture for intelligence that integrates basic mechanisms for problem solving, use of knowledge, learning, and perceptual-motor behavior" (Cho, Rosenbloom, & Dolan, 1991, p. 673; see also Laird & Rosenbloom, 1990). By bringing Soar and Neomycin together, specifically relating NL-Soar's model of comprehension to Neomycin's model of diagnosis, we can understand better the architecture of descriptive models. This comparison has two steps:

1. Show how Neomycin's task hierarchy (Fig. 12.1) relates to Soar's problem spaces and operators.
2. Show how the grain size of Soar subgoals strictly corresponds to levels of abstraction of the SSM (by showing how NL-Soar fits the model construction view of inference (Fig. 12.3)).

We find that Neomycin is a simplification of Soar, but there are fascinating parallels in how diagnosis and comprehension are modeled in these two architectures.

12.1.2 Model Construction in Natural Language Understanding Programs

NL-Soar, the natural language understanding program introduced in chapter 10, illustrates the generality of the SSM idea. NL-Soar was developed by Lehman and her colleagues at Carnegie-Mellon University in the late 1980s. The objective of NL-Soar research was to incorporate a natural language capability in Soar's problem-solving architecture. The idea explored in NL-Soar is that a general procedure can interpret the meaning of an utterance by incorporating information about the context in which the utterance is made. This includes specific information about problems the program and speaker might be working on and general models about the world.

NL-Soar produces an SSM that the developers called an *annotated model* (Lehman, Lewis, & Newell, 1991, p. 2). An annotated model includes the model of the utterance (a parse structure) and the model of the situation in the world (including current and desired states; Fig. 12.4). The annotated model chains together data structures in Soar's working memory to show how problem-solving plans, states of the world, and the meaning of utterances are related. This chaining of models graphically shows that Soar programs accomplish a form of model manipulation, which I have claimed is characteristic of knowledge-based programs, whether they be expert systems or programs like NL-Soar intended to model human cognition.

Simply put, in the NL-Soar model *comprehension is viewed as parsing*, in which syntactic and domain-specific descriptions are combined. A strict one-to-one mapping exists between input words and nodes in the annotated parse, which represents the structure of the utterance. This parse is then mapped by *reference links* to the situation model, which describes the meaning of the utterance in terms of the present context (see Fig. 12.4).

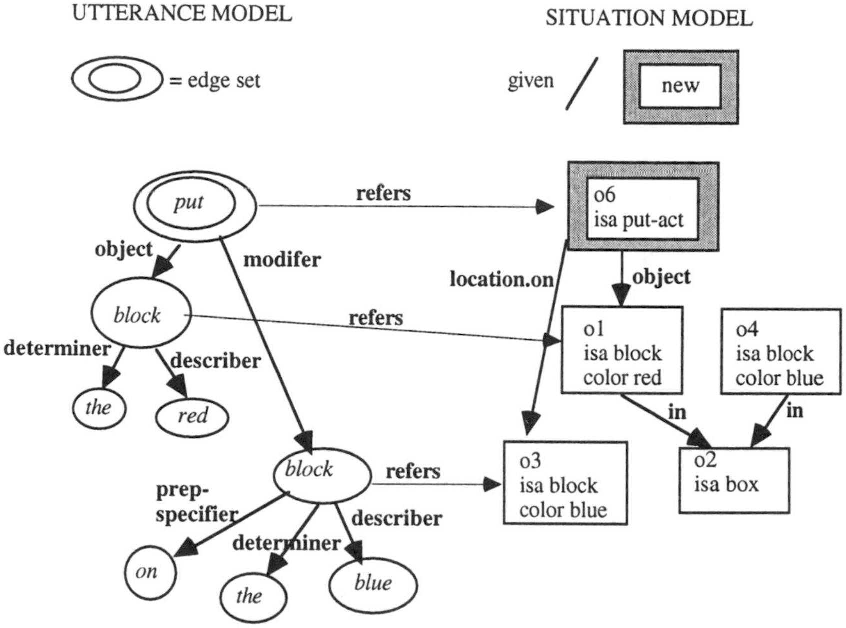

Fig. 12.4. NL-Soar's situation-specific models of utterance and world context corresponding to comprehension of the sentence, "*Put the red block on the blue block.*" (Adapted from Lehman et al. [1991], p. 10; reprinted with permission.).

The mapping here is similar to what occurs in instructional programs or expert systems, in which the user makes an inquiry or request, which is mapped onto the program's model of the problem being discussed. For example, this mapping occurs in Mycin's explanation program when the user asks questions such as, "Did you consider the patient's fever when concluding about the meningitis?" In this case, a model of the user's utterance indicates what kind of question is posed (how were specific data used?) and the subject–object relations of the question (fever, meningitis). This utterance model is related to both the model of the patient (the situation model in NL-Soar) and the representation of the diagnostic process carried out by the program.

Thus, in Mycin's explanation system three processes are related in comprehending a statement about the problem-solving process: the user's inquiry, the program's diagnostic reasoning, and disease processes occurring in the patient. We can show the three process models graphically as:

INQUIRY PROCESS —(about)→
DIAGNOSTIC PROCESS —(about)→
DISEASE PROCESS.

The chained parses (process models) refer to each other, as shown by the "refers" link in Fig. 12.4. The "put-act" node in NL-Soar's SITUATION models indicates how an action of the problem-solving agent relates to the world. Similarly, Neomycin's SSM (Fig. 12.3) shows how the diagnostic process relates to disease processes.[2] That is, the SSM combines a description of the agent's actions and a description of the world being acted on.

This chaining of process of descriptions (domain ⇔ problem solving ⇔ explanation) is characteristic of many programs, even although research publications emphasize the program's knowledge and representations as if they were uniform or not structured in this way. This practice of referring to knowledge instead of models of processes has obscured how descriptive cognitive models of complex problem solving chain *qualitative models of processes*. For example, Lehman and her colleagues note that the "situation" model data structure was only made explicit in Soar in 1988. Before this time, it was simply called *working memory*. The articulated design of Neomycin (shown in the previous figures) and the introduction of modeling terminology in NL-Soar (Fig. 12.4) shows that a model of natural language comprehension at a certain level constructs and manipulates models using graphs, just like a medical expert system. Indeed, stronger relations exist between models of language understanding and models of problem solving, as I show by more precisely relating the Soar and Neomycin architectures.

12.1.3 Relating Soar and Neomycin Terminology

Relating Soar and Neomycin requires understanding how the term *impasse* is used in Soar and the nature of chunking. Aside from these two processes, the architectures are essentially isomorphic. However, the effort required to show this is daunting; the reader may find the detail overwhelming. Nevertheless, relating and synthesizing descriptive cognitive models is necessary if we are to articulate conceptual patterns that might be explained in neural terms. A terminological tower of Babel is partially responsible for cognitive psychology

---

[2]The parsing process is more complicated because the student modeling programs maintain both an idealized expert's view (i.e., what Neomycin would believe and do) and a model of the student's view.

becoming stalled in the 1980s and the prevalent uncertainty that connections can be found to the neural level.

In this case, we are helped by the work of Washington and Rosenbloom (1988/1993), which partially reformulated Neomycin in Soar's terms in a program called Neomycin-Soar. We begin with some basic terminology:

- A Neomycin subtask is called a *goal* in Soar.
- Neomycin's metarules correspond to *operators* for accomplishing a goal.
- Soar's *working memory* corresponds to the SSM (called a "situation model" in NL-Soar).

The first terminological hurdle is the use of the term *operator* in Neomycin-Soar to refer to aspects of the disease model. This association exists nowhere else in the medical AI literature; in the medical AI community, *operator* is used to refer exclusively to diagnostic subtasks, such as G&D. However, in Soar search is treated uniformly—both the domain space and the diagnostic procedure space are represented as a hierarchy of operators. Thus, in Neomycin-Soar, "infection" is an operator, too.

The second terminological hurdle is that the production rules themselves—both domain rules and diagnostic metarules—are called operators in Neomycin-Soar. In Neomycin, we called the subtasks operators and viewed the metarules as *implementations* of them. In effect, we labeled the nodes of the diagnostic strategy (Fig. 12.1) as operators; Soar researchers labeled the links below each node as operators. Table 12.1 summarizes these two perspectives.[3]

The third terminological hurdle is understanding that each level in Neomycin's task hierarchy corresponds to a problem space in Soar. This correspondence eluded me for more than a decade, because I thought of search as occurring only in the domain space, viewing the diagnostic taxonomy as a hierarchy of problem spaces. (Indeed, the task Establish-Hypothesis-Space was originally named "establish-problem-space," following Newell's terminology.) Rather than viewing both the domain and subtask hierarchies as being a hierarchy of problem spaces, I viewed the problem space as being on the domain side, consisting of the entire disease taxonomy, and viewed the operators as being on the diagnostic procedure side.[4] By separating Soar terminology in this way, I failed to realize that Soar operators hierarchically relate problem spaces.

---

[3]This mismatch between terminology and visualization is typical of multidisciplinary cross-talk. See Clancey (1993) for additional examples.

[4]This is how the terms were generally used in medical AI research (e.g., see Pople, 1982). The Neomycin-Soar effort uncovered many of the connections between the two programs I am summarizing here. However, the relation between the SSM and the levels of the problem space hierarchy has not been noted elsewhere, to the best of my knowledge.

Table 12.1

Relation of Neomycin and Soar Terminology

Neomycin Terminology	*Soar Terminology*
Domain hypothesis	Domain goal
Domain rule	Domain operator
Premise and action of the rule, plus properties of domain rule and domain findings indicating whether the rule is an antecedent rule, trigger rule, historical versus laboratory data, certainty factor	"productions implementing the operator"
A hierarchical level in the disease taxonomy	Domain problem space
Diagnostic subtask	Diagnostic goal
Metarule	Diagnostic operator
Premise of the metarule	"production implementing the operator"
Subtasks: group-and-differentiate, establish-hypothesis-space, pursue-hypothesis, refine-hypothesis, find-out	Generation problem spaces
Subtasks: test-hypothesis	Selection problem spaces (not implemented in Neomycin-Soar)

The interpretation of Neomycin's diagnostic procedure in terms of problem spaces and operators is shown in Fig. 12.5 (subtasks are nodes in Fig. 12.1). In Neomycin, higher-level metarules determine which subtasks to apply; in Soar, productions in LTM determine preference for competing operators.[5]

Unlike in Neomycin, Soar's productions are fired in parallel, so any production that matches elements in working memory will fire, a process called *recognition*. When Soar cannot proceed by recognition alone, an impasse

---

[5]An initial mapping between Neomycin and Soar is provided by the Neomycin-Soar program (Washington & Rosenbloom, 1988/1993). However, they did not explicate the shift in terminology required to understand the relation between these cognitive models. When Washington and Rosenbloom said, "The basic steps of the subprocedures map onto more problem-space operators" (p. 680), they meant that the metarules (the steps) of subtasks (subprocedures) are problem space operators. Furthermore, "the subprocedure control maps onto additional operator selection knowledge (encoded as productions)" (p. 680) means that the premises of metarules are used for selecting which operator at a given level (i.e., which metarule) to apply.

occurs. That is, direct matching of the SSM to productions in LTM does not yield an action to follow (a domain rule to apply, assertion to add to the SSM, or finding to request from the user), so the program must deliberate what to do next In effect, this is the process in Neomycin of invoking a subtask to carry out a higher task (e.g., invoking Test-Hypothesis to carry out Pursue-Hypothesis)—that is, moving into another problem space. In Soar this explicit invocation may not be necessary, due to the result of prior chunking, which assembles and stores recurrent paths through the problem space hierarchy.

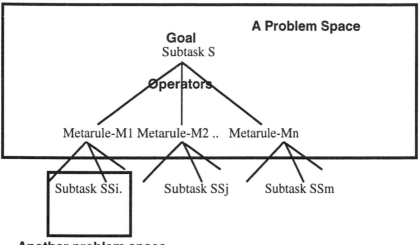

Fig. 12.5. Relation of Soar terminology to Neomycin's inference procedure. A Soar problem space consists of goals and operators. A Soar goal is a subtask; the operators are metarules. Metarules invoke subtasks corresponding to other problem spaces.

To implement chunking in Neomycin, each time the program reaches a primitive task, which places an element in the SSM, we would bundle together the line of reasoning through the subtasks to create a new production rule. This rule would necessarily compose the general model and the diagnostic procedure into a domain-specific rule. The rule would be placed into LTM. Subsequently, when encountering a similar situation, Neomycin could go directly to this low-level operation in a single step (assuming that the precondition matching occurs in parallel). Hence, the fundamental difference between Neomycin and Soar is the idea of chunking. Neomycin maintains a separation of domain model and diagnostic procedure. Soar continuously composes them, saving the path and variable bindings in new rules.

12.1.4 Problem Spaces in NL-Soar and Neomycin

Consideration of NL-Soar's problem spaces allows us to see that the correspondence between the two programs is not only structural, but based on a direct relation between how comprehension and diagnosis are modeled.

The problem space levels of NL-Soar (Figure 6) correspond to the familiar levels of natural language processing:

- Comprehension
- Language (surface structure of utterances, including statements in situation models)
- Constraints (semantic and syntactic relations in the general model)
- Semantics (facts in the general world model, which they call "knowledge").

(Syntactic problems can cause impasses in the constraints problem space, but there is no lower problem space for resolving them.) Again, if productions exist at a given level for accomplishing a goal, then no subgoaling (movement into a lower problem space) is necessary. After subgoaling occurs, a new production is composed (with variable bindings generalized) in the chunking process. This effectively moves syntactic, semantic, and pragmatic aspects of the model into the higher problem spaces. As a result of this integration of diverse perspectives into new production rules, in some cases comprehension can proceed at the top level in one "decision cycle" without subgoaling: "Chunking results in increased efficiency in each problem space in the hierarchy by transforming search in lower problem spaces into direct operator implementation in the higher space under similar circumstances" (Lehman et al., 1991, p. 14).

We can reformulate Neomycin's subtask hierarchy in terms of NL-Soar's problem spaces and operators. Fig. 12.6 suggests that we partition the subtask hierarchy (Fig. 12.1) into problem space levels (names on the left side of Fig. 12.6), and explicate the different aspects of the general (domain) model and SSM that are brought to bear at each level. Also, we will show groups of metarules (subtasks) as labeled operators connecting states (shown as circles in Fig. 12.6). In this adaptation (Fig. 12.7), I have simply mapped Neomycin's subtask hierarchy into the problem space representation of NL-Soar, working bottom up from the subtask Pursue-Hypothesis. To make an analogy between diagnostic "story understanding" and natural language comprehension, I have only slightly modified the NL-Soar terminology of Figure 6. The key parts of the mapping are:

- "Word" is replaced by "finding."
- "Utterance" is replaced by "findings."
- "Lexical" is replaced by "domain."
- "Syntactic and semantic" is replaced by "subtype and causal."
- "Pragmatic knowledge" corresponds to the situation-specific model.
- "General world knowledge" corresponds to the general domain model.

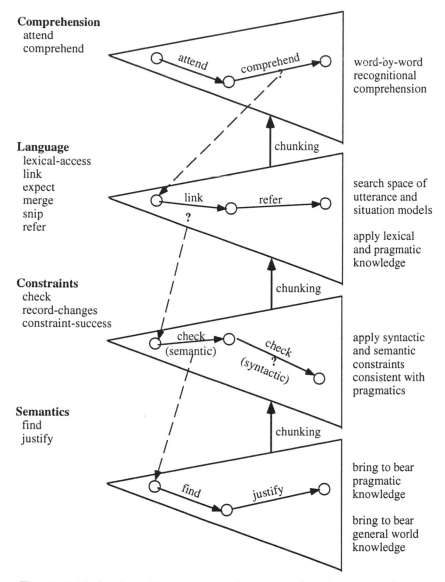

Fig. 12.6. NL-Soar's problem spaces and operators (from Lehman et al., 1991, p. 12; reprinted with permission).

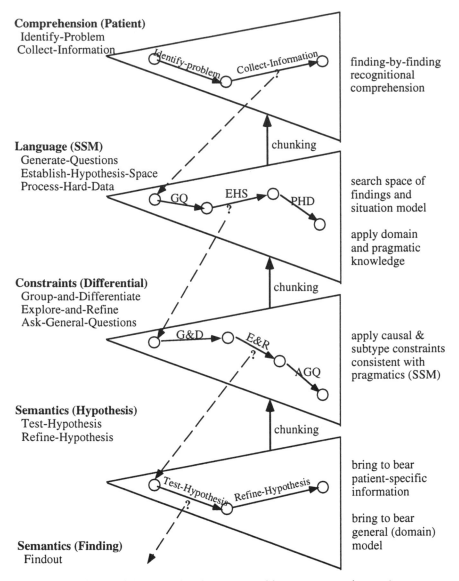

Fig. 12.7. Neomycin's subtasks shown as problem spaces and operators.

There is of course no chunking in Neomycin, but the form of the diagram of NL-Soar is maintained to show how chunking could be implemented to allow recognition at higher levels and hence avoid invocation of lower tasks (subgoaling).

Ordering of metarules is shown as an ordering of operators (and hence states) within each problem space. For example, Establish-Hypothesis-Space (EHS) is implemented as a set of ordered metarules, corresponding to G&D, Explore-and-Refine (E&R), and Process-Hard-Data. These are states in the process of constructing a well-formed SSM (called the *differential* in medical diagnosis, when referring to the list of top-level, most-specific disease hypotheses). A *procedural sequence* is first and foremost a concatenation of operators in a problem space. Thus, in reformulating Neomycin's task hierarchy in problem space terms, I have shown in general how a hierarchical procedure relates to the operator–problem space architecture of Soar.

A curious and important result of this analysis is shown by the parenthetical terms on the left side. Each problem space level is concerned with a different grain-size in the diagnostic story comprehension process, corresponding to the patient, the SSM, the differential (top level of the SSM), a hypothesis, and a finding. Moving downward, an impasse is resolved by adopting a new focus that is contained within (more specific than) the focus of the current problem space, as follows:

- We start by characterizing the patient in general terms (age, sex, etc.) and the originating complaint. The result is an initial set of hypothesis, represented in the SSM.
- Focus now shifts to the form of the SSM, gathering more information if there are no initial hypotheses (i.e., Generate-Questions), constructing a disease model based on history and physical signs, and ending by gathering laboratory information to support or refute the disease model.
- The third hypothesis space examines relations between the most specific hypotheses in the SSM (i.e., the differential), selecting hypotheses to be compared, generalized, or refined. An attempt is made at the end to throw new hypotheses into the pot by asking general questions that have not been considered so far.[6]
- The fourth problem space focuses on hypotheses, which are supported or discarded by comparing the general domain model and patient information.
- Finally, the lowest problem space (not detailed here) focuses on findings, making inferences on the basis of subtype and definitional information.[7]

---

[6]In particular, E&R is implemented as a set of preference rules for selecting a hypothesis to focus upon. The subtask invoked by these metarules is always Pursue-Hypothesis, which is omitted in Fig. 12.1, because it is simply a shorthand name for two subtasks (Test and Refine).

[7]The story is somewhat more complicated. The operator Identify-problem is itself concerned with relating findings in the initial patient information (analogous to the utterance being parsed by NL-Soar). Hence, the same constraints brought to bear when comparing or testing hypotheses is considered directly here, but in the opposite direction, proceeding from findings to hypotheses, rather than hypotheses to findings. This subtask, not shown in Fig. 12.7, which we call Forward-Reason, is invoked whenever new

From the perspective of learning, the broad pattern by which *each problem space focuses on a finer aspect of the story being constructed* is quite striking.[8] In effect, this structure leads us to conjecture that the process by which operators are learned directly parallels a process of *envisioning* the story at different grain sizes: the patient, the SSM, the differential, a hypothesis, and a finding. That is, impasse resolution involves moving to a lower grain size of analysis; chunking involves packaging this analysis into a single production at a broader context. Each problem space considers the story being constructed in terms of internal structure, involving components and relations not occurring a level higher. For example, to resolve an impasse in EHS, we examine the SSM to determine whether more general hypotheses have been considered (i.e., the "Group" part of G&D). To resolve an impasse in E&R, we examine the most specific hypotheses in the SSM (the differential) to select a single hypothesis to pursue (i.e., to test and refine). To resolve an impasse in Test-Hypothesis, we select a single finding to pursue (i.e., to rule out, generalize, or infer by definition).

After making some further general observations about the nature of Neomycin and grammatical models, we will be ready to consider learning in more detail.

12.2   FROM SPEAKING TO GRAMMARS AND THEORIES OF SPEAKING

The skeptical reader might be wondering at this point whether all these patterns are like epicycles—in finding interesting patterns in NL-Soar and Neomycin, are we merely describing models people created, rather than how categories are related in human understanding? Of course, if patterns in models replicate preexisting patterns in the modeler's understanding there may be no problem. However, we have striking evidence that the modeling process itself changes human understanding, rather than merely dumping "knowledge" into computer

---

findings are entered into the SSM. In effect, this subtask corresponds to the immediate matching that always occurs on every cycle in Soar, as new elements in the working memory (SSM) are related to productions in long-term memory. That is, we don't need a representation for Forward-Reason in Fig. 12.7; although it is implemented as an operator in Neomycin (for purposes of explanation to the user), such processing is part of the Soar architecture.

The same observation holds for the subtask Apply-Rule. subtask Findout is represented in   Fig. 12.7 as a pointer to another problem space. Findout is actually invoked by operators at every level (Clarify-Finding within Identify-Problem; the subtasks Generate-Question and Ask-General-Question; the Differentiate part of Group-and-Differentiate; and of course Test-Hypothesis)

[8]Hobbs (1985) pointed out the nature of granularity in relation to theories:

> When we move from one level of a hierarchy to the level below, we are moving from a coarse-grained local theory to a more fine-grained local theory, and the axioms that specify the decomposition of coarse-grained predicates into fine-grained ones constitute the articulation between the two theories. (p. 434)

format. In this section, I argue that indeed the domain modeling effort is likely to advance scientific understanding (of say, medicine) beyond what experts know. Domain models created by a knowledge acquisition process (e.g., the disease taxonomy of Neomycin) should be viewed as artifacts, as tools, rather than models of what people previously knew. On the other hand, the grammatical form of inference procedures does appear to capture preexisting patterns in the comprehension process.

12.2.1 Reconsidering the "Knowledge Acquisition" Process

In effect, we are asking, What is the relation of descriptions in cognitive models to conceptualizations and memory? What is the relation of a knowledge base to the mechanism inside the brain that produces similar behavior in an expert? Is a knowledge engineer merely writing down descriptions of structures stored in the head that generate the expert's speaking behaviors? Or do the described patterns abstract expert behavior over time, which is generated by other means? How does comprehending a newly formalized rule change an expert's behavior? In what way does it become part of the mechanism? These questions are illustrated by Fig. 12.8.

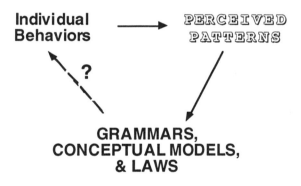

Fig. 12.8. What is the relation of a descriptive model of grammar rules, concept networks, and inference heuristics—abstracted from patterns in human behavior—to the memory–coordination–reasoning mechanism of the human brain?

Domain-specific situation–action rules, such as "If the patient is less than 7 years old, do not prescribe tetracycline," describe what experts most directly know—*how to behave.* However, when we study and decompose these rules into conceptual and procedural abstractions (such as occurred when we restructured Mycin for use in teaching), we are creating descriptions that go well beyond what experts can articulate without our help. Knowledge engineers, with the help of human experts, invent new models and new ways of talking.

Building on the ideas presented by Winograd and Flores (1986), I reconsidered how Mycin related to human knowledge and presented the following summary at the 1986 Banff Knowledge Acquisition Workshop. I was greeted by everything from wide-eyed amusement to adamant disagreement. Today I believe that such claims are generally accepted (e.g., see Wilson, 1995). The fact that such ideas were *ever* not obvious indicates the ubiquity of the "knowledge = descriptions stored in human memory" idea in the community of researchers developing expert systems, natural language programs, and instructional systems. Here is what we find when we compare knowledge bases to what experts know:

- *Symptom–disease or disease–therapy associations may be learned by rote, without understanding their scientific basis.* Just because an association can be explained, this does not mean that every person applying that association learned it by *compiling* it from explanatory concepts and relations. For example, even although the tetracycline rule can be broken down into an explanatory chain of concepts and relations (indicating how chelation binding of molecules produces discolorations in growing teeth), I memorized and applied this rule in conversations about patients without having first learned about the underlying physiological processes. In the AI literature of the 1980s, however, superficial associations were often referred to as "compiled knowledge," as if this were a property of the statement itself, as opposed to the history of the individual learning it.

- *If experts have principled subtype and causal networks encoded in memory, such networks are not structured according to the same principles used in scientific modeling.* When creating descriptive models of physical and biological systems, particularly simulation models, knowledge engineers make distinctions for the sake of formal consistency. For example, the physicians' term *intracranial-mass-lesion* combined a *cause* (the process of a mass growing), an *effect* (the mass-substance produced), and a *location* (intracranial). Thus, in a descriptive model of human knowledge, intracranial-tumor is both a subtype (tumor is a kind of mass) and a cause (growth of a tumor lesions or cuts brain tissue) of an intracranial-mass-lesion. In contrast, a principled scientific model requires distinguishing between kinds of substances and processes causing changes to substances. The physicians' understanding of the disease that they called intracranial-mass-lesion did not distinguish between process and substance.

- Reconfiguring Mycin for teaching in creating Neomycin, we had the choice of modeling how the expert talked or modeling disease processes scientifically. With the aim of formalizing medical science in a model for teaching, we chose to create a scientifically proper model, not merely one that replicated how physicians talked. This kind of "cleaning up" is a large part of the work of developing "model-based" expert systems; that is, expert systems in which the general domain model, such as a disease taxonomy, is formulated explicitly, apart from the diagnostic procedures (Fig. 12.2).

- Constructing descriptive models to be manipulated by computer programs enforces a discipline one does not necessarily find in everyday speech or even textbooks. Hence, the 1970s view that knowledge bases are merely extractions of what people already know and building models is *acquiring* knowledge is false. The knowledge representation languages of AI began as ways of modeling how people talk and reason, but became new, principled ways of formalizing processes in the world, with terminology and simulation methods that have no necessary relation to the human reasoning that inspired their construction. The "extract knowledge from experts" viewpoint actually sells short the scientific work of knowledge engineers and the accomplishment of AI in creating very general, descriptive modeling languages.

- *The terms in a model are not fixed in meaning, but open to reinterpretation and reuse according to convenience and changing conventions.* For example, the formal term Significant in Mycin originally meant "evidence of organisms on a culture," and later was generalized to mean "evidence of an infection requiring therapy." What started as a model of expert ways of speaking became the research group's model—an artifact of our own construction, use, and interpretation, which was adapted for convenience to subsume other disease processes and kinds of evidence.[9]

- *Expert behavior can be regular without knowledge that a pattern exists or knowledge of why a pattern exists.* For example, we found that physicians tended to gather evidence for exposure to an infectious disease as the first question for every disease. We abstracted this pattern, and physicians were able to rationalize the more general rule when it was presented to them. Just as people spoke grammatically before there were linguists, experts in the field may develop consistent orderings and procedures without knowledge engineers to write down their diagnostic strategies (cf. Collingwood's (1938) remark at the beginning of this chapter). This suggests that conceptualization of "what to do" may develop tacitly. Are the regularizing processes that produce grammatical speaking at work in learning the associations and procedures that we later describe in problem-solving grammars?

- *Even when experts articulate general procedures that describe their habitual practice, they may be unable to articulate a generative*

---

[9]For related discussion and elaboration, see Clancey (1997c), chapter 2.

justification for these procedures. For example, the idea of generalizing diagnostic questions (e.g., asking about medications when a particular drug is of interest) is justified by a combination of constraints:

- The mathematical constraint that a hierarchy can be pruned by eliminating nodes closer to the root.
- The *social-activity constraint* of minimizing the number of questions asked of a patient or nurse to keep the consultation interview short.
- The *world (patient population) constraint* that the specific item of interest is generally not present (e.g., if most patients received antibiotics, we would *increase* the number of questions by first asking if the given patient was receiving medications).

The justification for the diagnostic procedure refers to the environment in which the problem solving occurs and the *form* of the general model being applied. Experts can talk in such terms, but certainly mathematical considerations of search lie in the domain of the knowledge-engineer theorist, not the physician.

If we accepted the view that "knowledge = descriptions," a physician's explanations in knowledge acquisition sessions would be acts of *retrieving* and *restating*. But all the evidence suggests that the physician, working with a knowledge engineer, is constructing new descriptions of the world and behavior—that is, giving names to concepts, reifying the context in which decisions are made, weaving causal stories, and theorizing for the first time. Thus, a proper consideration of the knowledge acquisition process requires viewing it as a process of invention (chapter 7). As Schön (1979) said, we engage in "historical revisionism" when we suppose that explanations (including expectations and assumptions) were necessarily described and used for guidance prior to their articulation. But we commonly say "I must have assumed that . . ." regardless of whether we actually thought of the thing before. In this respect, it is important to realize that describing and theorizing about knowledge has a causal effect *toward the future*, as a means of organizing behavior. Thus, an interactive, historical view of learning would interpret Fig. 12.8 as cycles, and especially consider how verbalization is coordinated with other modalities of conceptualization in the process of creating representational artifacts.

In modeling human knowledge—even in describing our own reasoning—we do not always distinguish between a description of a prior *conceptualization* and a description actually articulated in the past and reflected on. We might say, "I did not actually say that, but I must have been thinking it." Such a statement may be a fair model of our conception, but again does not acknowledge how actually having a description in hand may change what we do. We play fast and loose with how concepts and words are related. Sometimes by *thought* we do mean a formulation in words: "If I had thought of that, I might not have done it." In the first case, we take an assumption to be something subconsciously entertained; in the second, "thinking about something" is a conscious experience. Just as folk psychology makes no distinction here, the descriptive cognitive modeling approach often conflates subconscious processing with articulating and using models.

But a critique of descriptive cognitive modeling can go much further. For example, Neomycin's rules are a gross simplification even for the routine professional activity of diagnosing a patient. For instance, they do not describe how the physician gets information by using instruments, how gaps in medical knowledge are filled by making a phone call to a pharmacist; or how a patient's attitude biases what evidence, diseases, and therapies are considered. That is, the Neomycin diagnostic procedure poorly characterizes the dynamic aspects of reasoning in an everyday environment (Cicourel, 1990)—what we called *pragmatics* in the analysis of analogy formation (chapter 7). Furthermore, we find that Neomycin combines heuristics for information gathering with a theory of attention and memory, which Soar models tend to make explicit (Cicourel, 1987; Robins, 1990).

The relation between descriptive models and human behavior was questioned earlier in the 20th century by psychologists, philosophers, and social scientists, long before scientists formulated such models as computer simulations. Consider for example the remarks by Collingwood (1938) cited at the opening of this chapter, claiming that the linguists at the time were "intellectualizing" language, making speaking appear as a carrier of ideas rather than an action, an emotional expression. This does not deny the theoretical value of the grammatical categories, or even their accuracy as abstractions of neural processes, as I demonstrated in chapter 10. But the linguist's methodology of breaking phrases into words atomizes the subject's understanding, just as the knowledge engineer's breaking expert's statements into a classification of terms and principled explanatory causal arguments asserts that a scientific model must be the "real knowledge" driving intelligent action. Indeed, the separation of domain model and inference procedure (Fig. 12.2) directly applies the semantics–syntax distinction to complex problem solving.

Collingwood (1938) claimed that the categorization of everyday speech must involve some arbitrariness, in which some units will not come apart. We observed this when we examined the physician's use of the term intracranial-mass-lesion. We subsequently lost respect for his thinking, suspecting that, indeed, his knowledge was not *principled*, and was therefore less useful for our endeavor. Similarly, the linguist is forced to treat some phrases as single words, violating the principles of formalization:

> [A] coagulation of several words into a single whole, quite different from the sum of the words that compose it in their recognized grammatical relations to each other, is called an "idiom."

> [A]ll the grammarian has done by calling them idioms is to admit that his own grammatical science cannot cope with them, and that people who use them have

spoken intelligibly, when according to him, what they say should be meaningless. (p. 258)

In abstracting patterns from behavior and focusing especially on what people say, words become the focus of the cognitive modeling analysis and the larger conceptualizations of role, identity as a person, and a day's activities are replaced by technical goals, stored models, and tasks. The role of language in expressing human authority, personal caring, or independent thinking is replaced by a view of activity as creating SSMs by which we describe the world scientifically and always deliberate before acting. Thus, even expert reasoning is intellectualized. Today we call this view of knowledge *rationalism* (Winograd and Flores, 1986; Schön, 1987; Varela, 1995).

Basic questions about human conceptualization and the different modes of thought become lost as descriptions are viewed as the ultimate means and product of cognition, and the relation between descriptions becomes the focus of analysis:

> Language is an activity; it is expressing oneself, or speaking. But this activity is not what the grammarian analyses. He analyses a product of this activity, "speech" or "discourse" not in the sense of a speaking or a discoursing, but in the sense of something brought into existence by that activity. (Collingwood, 1938, p. 254)

Collingwood's philosophy was developed further in Wittgenstein's (1953/1958) functional view of meaning (language games), Searle's (1969) speech act theory, and more recently in Lakoff's (1987) developmental theory of metaphor and Clark and Schaefer's (1989) study of conversational action. Thus, modern linguistics raises questions about both the mechanism of thought and the content of descriptive models. From the perspective of content, social scientists reveal how the diagnostic strategy of Neomycin captures very little about the activity of a medical clinic, and hence provides only a narrow view of what a physician knows (Robins, 1990).

Nevertheless, just as syntactic patterns describing human utterances and capabilities to comprehend sentence fit behavior, experimental evidence suggests that the kinds of patterns described in Neomycin's diagnostic procedure have psychological validity (Clancey, 1988). Indeed, our ability to explain complex syntactic rules in simpler neural terms (chapter 10) supports the claim that these descriptions, although not driving human behavior directly, do capture properties of conceptual mechanisms, and are not just the tidy diagrams of a people trying to make the world appear simple and understandable. In the following section I argue that the experimental evidence and the success of grammar analyses suggests that we take these patterns seriously and find some way to reconcile Collingwood's warnings with the evident structure of human behavior.

12.2.2 Using Knowledge Bases to "Parse" Human Behavior

The relationship between language grammars and knowledge bases has not been widely recognized as the essence of the descriptive cognitive modeling methodology. The pattern is revealed when models of comprehension are presented in terms of a specific world of objects and relations, as in NL-Soar (Fig. 12.4), and when problem solving is described in terms of *model construction operators*, as in Neomycin (Fig. 12.7). Such comparisons reveal how descriptive cognitive models of comprehending a sentence, diagnosing symptoms, planning procedures, scheduling errands, designing buildings, auditing spreadsheets, and so on, are analogous. All explain human behavior in terms of stored descriptions of the world and stored model construction procedures. The "grammatical" form of the model construction process is obvious when such programs are used for parsing human behavior, as I now explain.

As I mentioned, Neomycin was originally developed to facilitate explanation and student modeling in an instructional program. Neomycin's diagnostic procedure constitutes a grammar for the diagnostic process: The diagnostic procedure is abstracted and separated from the lexicon of diseases and their relations. As described earlier, this was accomplished by using variables, rather than domain terms, in the rules for how to carry on a diagnosis, directly analogous to using variables like "noun" and "verb" in natural language grammars, rather than specific words. For example, in the rule "If a type of finding is not present, then the specific subtypes are not present," *finding* is a variable. *Neurosurgery* is a particular finding in the lexicon (usually called the domain model; Fig. 12.2). Relations, such as *type*, serve to classify the terms of the domain model in the same manner that a natural language lexicon classifies words (e.g., passive verb, demonstrative pronoun), determining how grammar rules control the assembly of terms into sentences.

Put another way, the grammatical form of Neomycin and its use for instruction assumes that learning to diagnose multiple patients is like learning to use a grammar rule in analogous situations. For example, speakers of English must remember that the object noun of a sentence must be in the accusative case and that *whom* is an accusative noun. So we say, "Whom did you see?" Similarly, speakers of the language of medical diagnosis must remember that a follow-up question about a disease finding refers to the quality of the symptom and that *headache-duration* and *headache-location* characterize the quality of a headache. So after learning that the patient has a headache, we ask, "When did it begin? Where does it hurt?" Thus, "quality of a symptom" classifies *headache-duration* in the way "accusative noun" classifies *whom*—both are implicit, generalized relations in discourse patterns. Neomycin's metarules characterize patterns at the sense making and storytelling level; natural language grammar rules characterize patterns at the sentence level.

Most theories of instruction are based on the idea that a student abstracts from given examples, so *general procedures* are learned from discussion of specific patients. Once the student can talk about the diagnostic procedure itself, he or she can then refer to it for guidance. For example, a student may realize that a follow-up question may be appropriate, but not know what aspects of a rash, for example, one commonly asks about: "I know I might now ask about the qualities of a rash, but I do not know any." The most general procedures (such as "ask general questions" and "explore and refine") order what findings and disease hypotheses will be considered at various stages in a dialogue about a particular patient. In this respect, Neomycin's diagnostic procedure serves as a higher-order description of the entire consultative interview.

In natural language research that focuses on turn-taking, object reference, explanatory logic, and so on, the overall form of a protracted dialogue is called a *discourse grammar.* Hence, a physician carrying on an interview coordinates both the form and topic of the conversation by rules of English, as well as rules for gathering information and constructing a coherent model of the patient. Neomycin's model assumes that the discourse is a monologue (not mixed initiative) and focuses only on the logic of model construction. However, instructional programs built from Neomycin include and are driven by models of how to carry on a mixed-initiative interaction with the student. Again, my point is that descriptive cognitive models represent all aspects—language, diagnosis, and disease processes—in similar ways.[10]

The grammatical form of Neomycin's diagnostic procedure is evident in its generative nature: By the use of variables, an indefinite number of disease models may be constructed, producing the parse structure of the SSM (Fig. 12.3). Student modeling programs turn this around, using Neomycin's diagnostic procedure as a grammar for recognizing the student's strategy and inferring the SSM implicit in the student's problem solving actions. For example, consider the following sequence of questions, asked by a student in the course of diagnosing a patient:

    1) HAS THE PATIENT HAD A CHEST XRAY?
        No
    2) DOES HE HAVE A RASH?
        No
    3) HAS HE UNDERGONE SPLENECTOMY?
        No

---

[10]An early form of this idea was Brown, Burton, and de Kleer's (1982) semantic grammar for understanding student questions and requests in their Sophie instructional program. Sophie used a relational network modeling an electronic circuit to parse a student's questions about the behavior of the circuit. The student might ask the program, "What is the voltage of transistor T3?" The qualitative model would indicate that voltage is an attribute of a transistor and map this question to an internal template, "What is the value of the attribute A of the object O?" This parsed form would then be used to examine the current model of the simulated circuit.

4) HAS HE EXPERIENCED A RECENT PENETRATING HEADTRAUMA?
   Yes
5) ARE THERE SIGNS OF NECK TRAUMA?
   Yes

From the student's intermediate hypotheses and other explanations about how he or she is developing a causal understanding, a program can produce a parse structure that fits this sequence of questions (Fig. 12.9). Instead of parsing a sequence of words (as in NL-Soar), the program parses a *sequence of statements*. Neomycin's diagnostic strategy grammar (Fig. 12.1) classifies the question types asked by a physician and shows the logic by which they are ordered. Just as the choice of phrasing in natural language depends on the context in which you are speaking, the choice of which domain inference to consider depends on the focus of attention (which is by definition part of the SSM). Like a discourse grammar, the strategy rules determine the subject or focus of attention of each subsequent statement.[11]

Even although I have focused mainly on how the modeling program uses Neomycin's diagnostic procedure like a grammar, we can also view the diagnostic process itself as being a kind of comprehension, such that producing the SSM is itself a parsing process. In particular, a model of the medical diagnostic process is a model of comprehension, in the sense that diagnosis is constructing a causal story about a patient. The facts about the patient are either provided or elicited; they constitute the surface structure to be "parsed" (Fig. 12.3). The resulting SSM portrays the "deep structure" of processes occurring in the body. The story must fit the available information to the general disease models at a level of detail useful for prescribing therapy. As indicated above, the domain model corresponds to a lexicon or vocabulary. The diagnostic procedure corresponds to a *story construction process*. Indeed, Fig. 12.3 and Fig. 12.9 are duals—used to drive a dialogue with a patient, the procedure creates a causal story of disease processes; used to parse a dialogue with a patent, the procedure can be interpreted to reconstruct a causal story of reasoning processes.

---

[11]Similar grammars have been developed for modeling conversational discourse, illustrated by the transition network of Guidon. Two student modeling programs were developed that use Neomycin's diagnostic procedures to parse student behavior. Image (London & Clancey, 1982) focused on the problem of generating advice for the student as he was diagnosing a patient. This work emphasized that inferring the student's hypotheses was central to understanding what he was doing. Odysseus (Wilkins, Clancey, & Buchanan, 1986) examined more precisely the mathematical properties of parsing as a search problem; it generates alternative parses that it maintains and reexamines in the course of the dialogue with the student.

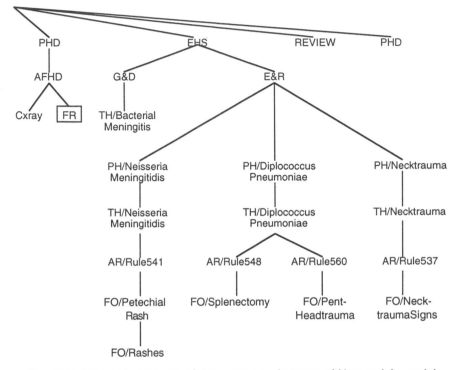

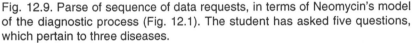

Fig. 12.9. Parse of sequence of data requests, in terms of Neomycin's model of the diagnostic process (Fig. 12.1). The student has asked five questions, which pertain to three diseases.

Thus, by constructing models to explain how hidden processes are producing surface behavior, Neomycin, NL-Soar, and student modeling programs are all comprehending. Each parsing process maps the surface structure of a complex system (its appearance or behavior) to a grammar. The grammar consists of operators that perform compositional transformations on a general model comprised of a lexicon and set of relations, producing a SSM (Fig. 12.3 and Fig. 12.4). Model construction procedures for designing, planning, auditing, predicting, and so on, can be formalized in a similar way (Clancey, 1992).[12] All of these inference procedures, although they construct and interpret models for

---

[12] The idea that problem-solving strategies can be formulated like the rules in a language grammar is a recurrent theme in AI research. For example, in the mid-1970s representations of a student's reasoning in computer programming were described in terms of *planning grammars* (M. L. Miller, 1982). A program interpreting the student's work might infer that the student is applying the plan of "decomposing subgoals and applying a repetition operator." (Such an abstract plan might also apply to scheduling errands, assigning jobs to a staff of workers, or a designing a computer chip.) Plans are thus identified with strategies for constructing and using models.

different purposes with different kinds of data, can be formalized as grammars, such that the relation of the procedures, general model, and SSM is explicit (Fig. 12.2).

When formalized as a problem-solving grammar, models enable the explanation and recognition capabilities illustrated by Neomycin (e.g., Fig. 12.3 and Fig. 12.8 were produced by computer programs). But just as language grammars must have some relation to how people speak and understand speech, problem-solving grammars must have a relation to how people actually focus attention and create an SSM. Specifically, the comparison of Neomycin, NL-Soar, and student modeling suggests principles by which conceptual coordination involves language, such that problem solving is a kind of comprehension process. The process components include:

- A domain model (including a lexicon or vocabulary) describing the general properties of objects and processes, organized by subtypes, parts, and causal relations (e.g., the general domain model of Neomycin).
- A syntax for structuring utterances (e.g., syntactic constraints in NL-Soar; question templates in Neomycin).
- A problem-solving model (e.g., the diagnostic procedure of Neomycin)
- A parsing process for mapping between utterances to an agent actions and belief model (SSM; e.g., NL-Soar plus a student modeling program).

The grammatical form of problem-solving knowledge is most clear in cognitive models designed to observe human behavior and automatically create an explanation of what the person is doing, such as protocol analysis programs. Not all program architectures are constructed as systematically (according to the distinctions in Fig. 12.2) and can be used in this way. Nevertheless, formulating models in terms of grammars serves as a kind of landmark for articulating the accomplishments of the descriptive cognitive modeling approach. The idea of problem-solving grammars makes explicit how studies of knowledge in cognitive science focus on *how descriptive models of the world* are represented, manipulated, and learned. For the rest of this chapter we assume that diagnostic operators in Neomycin correspond to conceptualizations in physician's understanding and focus specifically on how they are learned.

12.3   LEARNING NEW OPERATORS
AND PROBLEM SPACES

The definition of problem-solving operators suggests that problem-solving operators (the grammar rules) coordinate the perception of the problem being solved (the SSM in working memory) with previously constructed descriptive models of the world (the semantics or knowledge base). To summarize the terminology so far:

- *Operators* are categorizations of sequences (conceptualized coordinations) with a common kind of focus, constituting a problem space.
- A *problem space hierarchy* is a composition of categorized sequences.
- Specifically, *chunking in Soar* constructs a sequence across levels (a line of reasoning).

We find that two kinds of sequences are learned: *laterally*, within a problem space (within a triangle in Fig. 12.7) and *longitudinally* (across problem spaces, corresponding to Soar's chunks, productions in LTM). These two forms of sequence learning correspond to how problem spaces form and how they get instantiated and composed by practice into units that may be directly "recognized." The first form of sequence learning involves conceptualization (of new operators), and the second is an automatic process called the *practice effect*, an aspect of habit formation (cf. the comparison of Caitlin to the water shrews; chapter 5).

It is perhaps easy to see how chunking produces a situation-specific production, essentially traversing an existing composition of operators and problem spaces (from top to bottom in Fig. 12.7). But how does categorization produce a new problem space? In Soar's terms, a new problem space would be formed when a special kind of impasse occurs: Not only is there no practiced chunk to apply; there is no existing set of operators to "traverse" to construct a new path. New kinds of sequences are required; a new goal must be *conceived*.

In general, understanding how problem spaces are formed involves understanding how talking about a situation leads to physical recoordination. For example, it is obvious that the knowledge engineers' conceptualization of the diagnostic process (represented by Fig. 12.1) involved a complex process of naming, history telling, causal theorizing, and so on—the full mechanism of what we have called descriptive modeling. A physician does not strive for such a coherent description, but clearly engages in related conversations in medical school and when reflecting on past problems.

But I have in mind here a simpler, more fundamental, aspect of the learning mechanism, a process operating without instruction or deliberate reflection. As I have emphasized, based on the relation between operators, general model, and SSM in Neomycin and NL-Soar, the conceptualization of a sequence of operators (a new problem space) occurs when the operators all *focus on the same kind of operand*. Referring to Fig. 3.2, this suggests that a sequence of global mappings might be more likely to be held active and categorized as a sequence if the focus details (e.g., classification couples 1 and 2) are reactivating the same categorization. That is, if the details (foci) of the two operators are perceived as similar, sequencing by different higher-order maps (as shown in Fig. 3.2) could be viewed as a unit. In effect, I am turning the diagram upside down: The notation shows a new categorization as a "T bar" above the sequence, but the pattern suggests that in some sense the sequence is first held "from below" by the recurrent operand categorization (e.g., hypothesis, finding).

The result is a sequence of activations of different conceptualizations with similar foci, corresponding to a problem space, a new goal-oriented procedure. By continued composition, a goal hierarchy of operators will be constructed (Fig. 12.7), each viewing the SSM at a specific grain size. Simultaneously, situation-specific sequences (Soar's chunks) will be constructed, cutting across levels of this hierarchy.

Put another way, *perceptual segmentation* of working memory or the environment activates alternative actions and hence the basis for categorizing new sequences. Hence, it is not just what is in working memory that drives reasoning, but "how we are seeing," our *manner of looking at trouble* (cf. the paintbrush inventors). Even when using a descriptive model, we refer to "looking up" and "looking down," as in searching a disease hierarchy. Bamberger (1991) discussed how this segmentation occurs in hearing music in new ways. Similarly, Lakoff's (1987) and Johnson's (1987) analyses of metaphors indicates that new conceptualizations are tied to perceptual-motor experience.

Referring to Neomycin, we can see that defining new operators (metarules) tends to require defining a new domain relation:

new problem space ← new focus grain size
(subtask)

|

(metarule)
new domain relation ← **new operator**

I had long ago observed the new-operator–new-relation pattern. Indeed, more generally we found that for every interpretive procedure we designed (diagnosis, explanation, student modeling, teaching) we needed to make new distinctions in the domain model. However, it is only now visible, through the reformulation in terms of Soar's architecture, that problem spaces (the subtask hierarchy, Fig. 12.1) conform to the focus grain size for viewing the problem. This was perhaps not apparent because the focus grainsizes are relatively fixed, few in number, and quite general. Specifically, the grain size levels— "system," SSM, differential, hypothesis, finding—would characterize the diagnostic process in any electromechanical or biological domain. The domain relations—aspects of causality and subtype, such as "necessary causal-enabling condition" (e.g., contact with infectious agent) and "observable specification of symptom" (e.g., the duration and location of a symptom)—are equally general ways of characterizing any physical process. Thus, learning either new problem spaces or new operators would be a relatively rare event for even a novice; most of the effort is in understanding the complex function and behavior of the system being diagnosed (or designed, audited, controlled, etc.). That is, the student is busy learning causal-temporal-spatial facts, not new kinds of relations.

In NL-Soar there is seamless representation and structuring of patterns and operators from the linguistic utterance level to the domain representations (Fig. 12.6). At every level there are productions and feature mapping, chunking, and search. How does this bottom out? The researchers acknowledge that perhaps the most fundamental learning problem remains to be addressed. In the final paragraph of their report, Lehman et al. (1991)said, "We have not solved the genesis problem (*Where does the knowledge in the lower problem spaces come from*?) . . . ." (p. 39; emphasis in original). In admitting that the descriptive approach cannot explain where the lower problem spaces come from, the descriptive modeler is admitting that the nature of problem spaces has itself been inadequately explained.

In the analysis given here, I have suggested that reasoning is a conceptual coordination process. Three classifications are related:

types of things in the model of the situation (SSM)
⇔ types of operators
⇔ types of things in the world (general model)

That is, ways of conceiving a problematic situation are coordinated with general ways of conceiving the world by means of modeling operators that transform descriptions of the situation in a way that is useful for taking action. Bickhard (1995) called this a *relationally-structured representation*. The classifications serve as functional constraints in problem solving (cf. left side of Fig. 12.6 and Fig. 12.7). Problem spaces constitute a functional differentiation of views. In terms of the SSM, the diagnostic operators are graph transformations, applying to a specific grain size for viewing the graph. Differentiation corresponds to the process of "subgoaling" when an impasse occurs in a given problem space. In Bickhard's terms, the problem space is a *functional generator*, not a fixed, stored procedure. By this view, generating and recognizing (parsing) are processes of representing, but not necessarily describing.

Obviously, a great deal more needs to be said about the Soar model and neural-level models.[13] For example, NL-Soar uses a "snip" operator to undo a link in the SSM, as a simple form of backtracking. In general, felt-path sequences are one-way (recall the story of Caitlin and the water shrews; chapter 5), and perhaps we cannot arbitrarily move around within a procedure either (note the highway directions in Fig. 12.7). But the very nature of the procedure is that it enables flexible coordination of the views of disease processes (through domain relations) and the views of the problematic situation (through focus grain size of operators). Nevertheless, backtracking cannot be arbitrary, but is

---

[13]Neuro-Soar (Cho, Rosenbloom, & Dolan, 1991) is an initial "connectionist" implementation of Soar's production memory and binding process. But impasse detection, subgoaling, and learning were omitted. Our analysis of NL-Soar relative to TNGS suggests that efforts to develop new functional architectures should begin with categorization and attempt to show how subgoals are conceptualized.

constrained by the process of anchoring and activation at the neural level (as discussed in chapter 10).

This analysis has direct implications for instructional design. For example, in developing Guidon-Manage (Rodolitz & Clancey, 1989), we were concerned with teaching the diagnostic procedure of Neomycin. Now it is evident that learning new operators should be grounded in an understanding of the conceptual levels of the SSM (Fig. 12.7). The examples we have examined suggest that not knowing where or how to look (what grain size is meaningful) could be a significant source of ambiguity in interpreting lesson materials. By leaving out the problems and resources of perceptual recategorization, the Soar model fails to account for why certain kinds of repetition occur (e.g., the duck–rabbit example, Fig. 1.11; sending two messages, Fig. 4.4), slips (Fig. 6.4), and the role of figure–ground shifts in reconceptualization (Fig. 7.3). Learning is not just getting faster or being told new terms and definitions. The recoordination mechanism I have sketched here makes *the management of views* central in reasoning.

In showing how Neomycin and Soar have basically the same architecture, and then in relating the problem space hierarchy to conceptual coordination, we have considerably tightened up the value of the chunking and problem space architecture in modeling human learning. Note the difficulty in getting this far: relating different terminology (Table 12.1), reformulating control hierarchies as recurrent behavior sequences, realizing that recurrent sequences can emerge by interacting with a given environment over time, viewing goals not as names or procedures but as categorized sequences, and so forth. Nevertheless, as shown in this chapter, patterns may be found in descriptive models (Mycin, Neomycin, and Soar) that yield more than the initial theories claim about memory and learning.

Table 12.2 summarizes how different problem-solving models may be related. As a knowledge-level model, Soar describes cognitive processes in terms of behavioral and conceptual patterns. Problem space models, like diSessa's (1993) p-prims constitute an ontology (a taxonomic description) of transformations that occur in sense making. Rather than calling the lowest level the symbol level, as Newell (1990) did in the unified theories of cognition framework, a conceptual coordination perspective seeks to explain how symbols are created from nondescriptive biological constituents. I call this the *symbol-creating level*. From this perspective all descriptive cognitive models are knowledge-level models of cognition. The symbol-creating level does not exist in these theories.

The levels in Table 12.2 are descriptions of processes: The knowledge level is a description of knowledge or capability, oriented around goals and beliefs, driven by the theory of rationality that knowledge can be inferred from goals and actions. The symbol-creating level is a description of an architecture, oriented around neural maps, driven by the theory of conceptual coordination that knowledge is constructed by processes of activation, sequencing, and composition. Both parts of the table are of course only partial models. We cannot build a human-equivalent mechanism yet. But the table serves as a way of acknowledging what we have described so far and how these descriptions (of strategies, conceptualization, and learning in general) will be further explained by a theory of neuropsychological function.

Table 12.2

Relation of Knowledge-Level Models to Symbol-Creating Models

Cognitive Processes Being Described	Mechanistic Constructs in Models	
Behavioral routines: Phrases (story schemas) Sense-making	Strategies, grammars	
Transactional and conceptual schemas: Ontology	P-prims, operators	
		Knowledge level
		Symbol-creating level
Sense-making architecture: Comprehension, practice	Chunking, impasses coordination	
Categorization mechanism: Differentiation and correlation between sensorimotor maps	Classification couples, global maps	

The analysis given here suggests that problem spaces are not merely *applied* when an impasse occurs, but *dynamically reconstructed* by activating previous coordinating processes. This suggests that insofar as the perceptual categorizations are stable, the operators and hence subgoal conceptualization will be stable. But insofar as the problem solver is seeing a problem in a new way—*reconceptualizing the grain size and focus relations*—the nature of a problem space will change. It is this ability to coordinate new kinds of similarities and sequences of sensorimotor experience as novel, nonverbal conceptualizations that is missing in descriptive cognitive models.

In short, descriptive cognitive models can provide evidence for neural mechanisms once the models are reformulated to show how *conceptual hierarchies* (operators and domain models) relate to *perceptual categories* (the views of the problem situation). This chapter accomplishes such a reformulation for two well-known architectures, Neomycin and Soar, by relating them to each other.

As we have seen elsewhere, applying the conceptual coordination perspective yields unexpected results. In particular, the points I make here about grain size and learning of operators provide evidence for a neural model of conceptualization: A sequence of coordinated processes can be held active in memory and categorized as being a "type" (a problem space) when attention is focused at a common level of detail throughout the sequence (in problem space terms, the operators refer to the same level of description in working memory). Higher-order consciousness provides the capability to hold a sequence active in this way, such that behavior sequences become conceptualized procedures.

13

Conclusions: The Nature and Role of Consciousness

I think what kept psychology from continuing to develop steadily along these lines was its stubborn antiphilosophical stance that kept it isolated from currents of thought in its neighboring disciplines in the human sciences. Rather than finding common cause with our neighbors in defining such central ideas as "mind" or "Self," we in psychology preferred to rely upon standardized research paradigms to "define" our "own" concepts . . . . In time, these methods become proprietary, as it were, and come rigidly to define the phenomenon in question.

—Jerome Bruner, *Acts of Meaning*, 1990, p. 101.

I have pursued three fundamental theories in this book that break with the dominant assumptions of cognitive science over most of its history:

- *Concepts are not simply words or word networks in the brain,* but higher-order categories (categorizations of categorizations) in different modalities (visual, verbal, auditory, postural, etc.), related synchronously and sequentially in time.
- *Conceptual memory is inherently reconstructive,* involving reactivation of categories in ways they have worked together before, both compositionally and temporally, involving processes of generalization, coupling, repetition, and substitution.
- *Human consciousness involves aspects of conceptual coordination that most procedural programming languages provide for free, rendering them invisible,* and thus the accomplishments of the brain are by and large unexamined, taken for granted, unappreciated, or whisked away as epiphenomenal and unnecessary.

My overall thesis has been that a theory of intelligence based on stored descriptions of the world and behavior (knowledge models) that takes formulation of such models (diagnoses, interpretations, situation assessment,

333

plans) to be the mechanism of thought confuses the mechanism of thought with its products and outward appearance. The conscious work of reasoning has been wrongly placed at the core of the processing unit. Consequently the process memory capabilities of the brain necessary for conceptualization remain largely unquestioned, and thus have never been engineered in an AI machine.

My interest throughout this book has been architectural; specifically, to describe the process mechanisms by which behavior is sequenced and composed. Following Bartlett's lead, I began by assuming that learning and memory should be viewed as the dynamic construction of coordinated sequences from *previous coordinations*. That is, *physical structures* are reactivated and reused in accord with how they categorically and temporally worked together in the past. This analysis describes what neural processes accomplish (e.g., coupling, categorized sequences, subsumption, composition) through activation relations alone. The activation approach, *which forbids either copying or multiple simultaneous "use" of a single categorization*, strongly constrains the roles categorizations can play in a given construction (as evidenced in grammars), as well as enabling flexibility and variation (as evidenced in slips).

In this concluding chapter, I briefly summarize what I have shown in this book, discuss some lessons about terminology, and indicate how the study of consciousness might now be more fruitfully pursued.

13.1   WHAT THE EXAMPLES SHOWED

By analyzing how categorizations are activated and related in time, the analyses in this book have built on and improved a variety of related theories, ranging from animal navigation to grammatical speaking and problem solving:

- Patterns of generalization, repetition, and extension in sequence learning, including especially interactive behaviors in physical space, constitute *dynamic reconstruction of behavior strings*. Progressive deepening represented by problem-behavior graphs can be better explained and extended by a neural analysis that reformulates the use of anchors, landmarks, and "adding a piece on the end" as aspects of learning physical coordinations (and not just search in a problem space).

- Slips in speaking and writing, previously enumerated in more than a dozen types, can be explained in terms of *two basic neural activation substitution and composition processes*.

- *Analogical reasoning* in deliberately creative situations (e.g., trying to invent something), *may be understood as a physical coordination process* (and not just the symbolic calculus in manipulating descriptive models of the world). Thus, both the mechanism of "seeing as" and the origin of new ideas are better understood.

- *Causal reasoning is placed within a larger framework of story construction*, as a means of coordinating experience in time:

- Naming, framing, and storytelling provide verbal means of handling surprises (conceptual discoordination) and, in general, repairing the always developing and expanding understanding of WIDN.
- Causal explanation is functionally part of the construction of the self (not ever just an impersonal, disembodied inferential process).
- "Satisficing" in explanation and behavior is thus understood in terms of *social conceptualization* by an actor (regarding place, interactive role, choreography).

- *Natural language comprehension capabilities and limitations may be understood in terms of activation of categories* as opposed to the size of working memory buffer or "moving" strings in a symbolic expression. Strictly speaking, there are no capabilities for copying, storage, or multiple use of categories during a single sentence comprehension (see section 10.4 for a full list of principles):

  - An anchor holds active a syntactic categorization (e.g., NP), so effectively the categorization may be reactivated and reincorporated (reused) in the same sentence construction.
  - A semantic categorization (e.g., "the book") may play two syntactic roles, but they must be different (e.g., subject and indirect object).

- *Problem-solving operators originate in a conceptual coordination process* that develops a "grammar" of problem spaces by relating ways of seeing and speaking to ways of acting; that is, one conceptual system (ways of seeing or talking about a problem) imposes a space of distinctions that "controls" another conceptual system (model construction operators).

Descriptive cognitive models (symbolic models) only roughly explain the nature of verbal memory and learning. Although conventional stored program models can replicate many of the phenomena I have considered, they do not parsimoniously explain the phenomena, they merely mimic them. I emphasize that pattern replication by use of taxonomies and stored procedures was an important step in cognitive science. But such models show only how verbal expressions, once formed, may be logically related. *How categorization, sequencing, composition, and comparison are possible at all is not explained.* The operations taken to be especially fundamental in cognitive psychology—association, analogy, and generalization—must be understood as constructing categories from simpler activation relations, rather than creating categories by manipulating existing categories. At heart, the problem is that the nature of objects, relations, time, and memory in conventional computer programming is not the same as what neural processes construct, and thus modeling languages have too often been assumed to be isomorphic to operations in the brain.

For a theory of cognition to be explanatory, it must elucidate patterns in terms of fundamental processes that are neurobiologically grounded, explain why all animals do not have the same capabilities, and elucidate how such capabilities evolved. Subsequent sections consider what we have learned about these fundamental processes of memory and learning.

13.2   THE PROPER INTERPRETATION OF ACTIVATION TRACE DIAGRAMS

Like the logicians of AI, I have employed a mathematician's hypothesis that all the phenomenological examples and all the models are broadly pointing in the direction of something simple in the mental organizing process, accounting for the patterns cognitive science has previously described in scripts, strategy rules, concept hierarchies, and problem spaces. Unlike the logicians' approach, which has sought to base cognition on a descriptive calculus, I have looked instead for a neurobiological (and hence inherently temporal and physical) process that corresponds to the basic operations of programming languages: sequences and compositions of sequences. Accordingly, I have attempted to account for a broad variety of behaviors and experiences by the ideas of categorization (forming a unit) and sequencing (ordering units).

Probably the most important hypothesis is that *sequences are categorized.* That is, experience in time is segmented so that it is discretized and made into a substitutable unit, providing the basis for intentionality, logical comparison, naming, and causal-grammatical distinctions (subject, object, etc.). But to move beyond practiced repetition to awareness of having a goal, reentrancy is required (Fig. 3.2), allowing the agent to hold a categorization active and work with it, to categorize activity over time, to perceive and hence to be *aware* of WIDN.

The nodes on the diagonal of the diagrams I have presented are not reactivated states, goals, or merely symbols. The emphasis is on flow and change, not defined moments or events—there is no result or end being matched against (except in a person's conscious reasoning). Nor does composition of categories imply top-down control. Instead, qualifications and higher-order categorizations are based on coupling, a simultaneous, mutual-activation process that is neither serial (one thing following another) nor parallel (two independently created things coming together at a later time). The presence of a categorization that was previously constructed does not imply retrieval, copying, or instantiation (as in conventional computer programs), but reactivation and hence generalization—a recoordination.

It bears repeating that a given activation trace diagram is not a representation of a data structure inside the brain, but a diagram showing the order in which neural processes occurred and influenced each other. The notation represents different temporal periods, not a structure that has been assembled or something stored in LTM. The diagram is more like a *historical timeline* showing physical relationships, rather than a knowledge structure.

There is no buffer (such as working memory) where each act is predescribed or assembled into a plan. Instead, neural organizations coordinating perception and action become hierarchically recomposed (this is especially clear in the analysis of slips and analogical reasoning). Conceptions of activities that scope WIDN on different grain sizes of attention, involving different focus details, become and remain active simultaneously. The relationship of these levels is of coordination broadly speaking, including physical coordination in its usual sense. However, in computational terms, the more appropriate relation is not procedural invocation, but *subsumption*—the levels are mutually active and relate to one another.

As another example, the experience of musical memory may be contrasted with activation trace diagrams. Music is composed of perceived notes of course, but replete with contrasts and changes in loudness, rhythm, and harmony. Music is most of all experienced as a flow, like meaning comprehension in sentence understanding (chapter 10). Accordingly, activation trace diagrams must not be viewed as a chain of packets or box cars, but more like a river flowing. Rather than a structure built up (a parse tree) or even a moving entity containing structures (a train), activation trace diagrams depict a course of transformations in time, punctuated and segmented by perceptual and conceptual categorizations.

In short, the diagrams in this book are *psychological analyses of experience*, not a mechanism itself. Some of the key characteristics I have illustrated, which constitute a theory of conceptual coordination, include:

- The coordination theory is *architectural*, that is, it is a domain-general description of how categorization processes are structured in time and physically with respect to one another.
- Categorizations may be *conceptual, but nonverbal* (e.g., sending a second message, extending a felt path, slips, seeing-as). Verbal articulation involves describing such conceptual relations (images, orderings, values); that is, creating a linguistic model of the world and behavior.
- Descriptive operations and investigations are the province of the conscious person, not the neural architecture. The processes of matching, comparing, and inferring that are central to problem-solving models depend on previously unexamined and inadequately explained neural categorization processes of reactivation, generalization, sequencing, composition, and coordination across conceptual systems, which I have described here.

The neural processes we are discovering constitute a theoretical basis for building a new kind of machine with the capabilities of naturally occurring animal intelligence. This was the original aim of AI, but now the focus is broadened to include physical coordination and conceptualization without language.

The key distinction between neurobiological processes and the conventional view of machinery is that functional parts in neural systems are not fixed—they have form and are formed only when the system is operating. Forms and their interactions depend on how parts of the system have worked together in the past—this is *a memory based on physical interaction and spatial-temporal relation,* as opposed to a memory based on description. The very idea of "storage" is meaningless for such processes; by conjecture, they are never merely reused, but always generalized in each recoordination. The reorderings and substitutions of slips reveal these subconscious characteristics of *sequence generalization.*

Put another way, concepts are not static objects, but temporally constrained, coordinated physical processes. The manner in which understanding and skills develop as modular, co-operating, but independent processes is visible in the nature of analogical reasoning, multimodal coordination, slips, inventiveness, and so on.

Most important, these neural processes are not subcognitive in the way silicon is merely an implementation of a computational process. Rather, the self-organizing nature of these processes has a pervasive affect on behavior and cognitive experience. Specifically, aspects of sequencing, substitution, generalization, and composition are manifest in conceptual understanding, speaking, and reasoning. Some of the basic neural constructive operations produce behavior such as starting at the beginning when impassed, adding a step on the end, and repeating a step by qualifying it with different, correlated perceptual details. That is, previously unexplained (or taken for granted) phenomena can be understood in terms of how neural processes activate in time as physical structures.

With this improved theory of cognition, we have the basis for not only building more capable machines, but understanding individual differences so we can better treat dysfunctions and eventually build machines that exceed the creative capability of people. My hunch is that what neurally distinguishes da Vinci, Bach, or Einstein from the rest of us is an enhanced capability to construct a scene or sequence that coordinates multiple conceptual systems (e.g., describing an image) and the capability to hold active a complex conceptual composition (e.g., a musical form).

In this respect, I must emphasize that the diagrams used in this book, although valuable for coarsely representing the phenomenology of cognition, imperfectly describe multimodal (multidimensional) coordinations and must be assumed to grossly abstract the spatial and temporal properties of the neural mechanism.

13.3   HOW CONVENTIONAL COGNITIVE MODELS NEED TO BE REVISED

For the reader's convenience and to tie together the themes, I list here by broad category some of the findings that contrast with conventional problem solving claims.

13.3.1 Goals and Intentionality

Procedures are dynamically developed and ordered, not merely retrieved and re-executed. Learning occurs during this recoordination process. An LTM of production rules models "steps" and allows for dynamic sequencing, but the conventional computational binding process (instantiating variables) does not properly articulate the interaction of coupling of perceptual categorizations to scenes and reactivation biases (leading to repetition):

- Goal-driven behavior, in its simplest form, is based on categorization of previous sequences; reconstructed later these categorizations constitute intentional activities.
- Chunking is not only an effect of repetition operating across levels as emphasized in Soar (path optimizing), but categorizing a sequence within a level to create a problem space (path finding).
- The conceptual operators in a given problem space all categorize "the situation" (WIDN) at the same grain size. The formation of problem spaces as categorized sequences of operators depends on holding the sequence active, and this is enabled by the common level of detail they operate upon.

Chunking of verbal conceptualizations in Soar fits the practice effect of physical skills because verbal conceptualization is a physical coordination. Perceptual chunking of scenes is another modality of conceptualization. The term chunking has been applied in cognitive psychology without always observing that different kinds of conceptualization are involved (sequences and scenes). Categorizing involves different kinds of units and modalities, of which simultaneous and sequential relations must be distinguished. These are not to be equated with *descriptions of scenes* and *descriptions of actions*.

By categorizing, we always mean categorizing in time. The term *interactive* emphasizes that categories are processes, "actively doing something all the time" (Bartlett, 1932/1977, p. 200). When we say *conceptual process*, we mean activation of neural structures in time based on different ways of categorizing sequence and simultaneity inherent in their previous activations or in the ongoing flow. These temporal relations give rise to different kinds of mental organizers or conceptualizing processes: scenes, physical skills (composed sequences), rhythm (dance), gesture (e.g., salutes), melody, verbalization (organized by phonetics, phrase, argument, and discourse), and activity (roles, choreography of participation in a social process).

13.3.2 Learning

Understanding must involve learning (as in MOPs). All coordinated behavior involves learning as every act involves an internal adjustment to how processes work together. Consequently, these relations are reinforced and biased to repeat. Conceiving and behaving are not in the role of input and output, goals and actions in the traditional linear sense of one process controlling another, but of codependent processes. For example, speaking involves simultaneously understanding what one is saying and what one wants to say; that is, conceiving meaning and intent occurs *as the speaking occurs*. In point of fact, our computational mechanisms do not work this way. Traditionally, the alternative to linear or serial behavior is called parallel. But it amounts to the same thing: independent processes, parts of the brain whose outputs are only rolled up and put together later. There is another kind of distinction, not just serial versus parallel, but synchronous versus simultaneous.

At the first order, I now make no distinction between memory, learning and coordinating. The control regime of symbolic models, such as Neomycin's strategy rules, is but a snapshot of temporal-sequential conceptualizing: reactivating, generalizing, and recoordinating behavior sequences (whether occurring as outward movement or private imagination). In this respect, knowledge is constructed as processes in-line and integrated with sensorimotor circuits. Cognition is *situated* because perception, conception, and action are physically coupled.

13.3.3 Where Do The Lower Level Problem Spaces Come From?

If we take the higher-level problem spaces to be verbal, as in models of human reasoning, then the lower level problem spaces are categorizations of different modalities: perceptual details, scenes, sequences. But it is a mistake to view verbal conceptualization as being at the top; other organizers in other modalities may be used for organizing sense-making (exemplified by the patients studied by Sacks, 1987).

Although models like NL-Soar do not preclude other organizing modalities, descriptive cognitive models inherently operate as if the only organizers are verbal descriptions of the world and behavior; they are consequently poor explanations of musical experience, dance, or "optimal flow" (Csikszentmihalyi, 1988). Further, analysis of dysfunctions and unusual experience (e.g., see Cytowic, 1993) reveals that interactions are occurring "side by side" in multiple modalities of categorizing operating together—a violation of the near decomposability (causal modularity) on which the descriptive modeling approach relies.

Descriptive cognitive models leave out both the origin of categorizations in sensorimotor experience and the nature of problem solving as multimodal conceptual coordination. Such models view conceptualization one-dimensionally as manipulations of descriptions in a defined verbal space. For example, studies of geometry and physics view pictures as a set of implicit descriptions (Larkin & Simon, 1987). In contrast, Schön's (1979) study of inventors reveals how drawings and other artifacts are reinterpreted within the process of framing the problem to be solved—involving a dialectic (simultaneous) and feedback relation between visual and verbal conceptualization, perceptual recategorization (seeing the drawings in new ways), and theorizing.

13.3.4 Categories and Grounding

Grounding of categorization—traditionally formulated in linguistic theory as our capability to relate names and meaning—develops as conceptual coordination of *multiple modalities* of categorization. Meaning is not a thing such as a stored description, but a *dynamic relation* between different ways of conceiving: verbal, visual, rhythmic, and so on.

The adaptability (or openness) of verbal conceptualizing follows from the adaptability of perceptual categorizing because conceptualizing is a kind of categorizing. Automatic, neural-level recombinations of categorizing (e.g., the experience of seeing-as and slips) are operating simultaneously with conceptual coordinations developed in the knowledge of the agent (e.g., the logic of explaining, proceeding from naming to history telling to causal ordering).

Human behavior is not determined by a calculus of descriptions of the world and how behavior should appear (even the deep structures of grammar). Rather, human behavior is bound by the mechanism of conceptualization operating with previous constructions: substituting, eliding, seeing as, repeating as a generalization, identifying, negating, ordering in time, chunking as a sequence, and so on. Allowing for reinterpretation in time (over seconds or many days), conceptualizations have an "open texture" that makes recoordination of goals and plans virtually unrestricted (Wittgenstein, 1953/1958; Kolenda, 1964). Nevertheless, conceptual change is sometimes painfully slow and confusing, as well as socially discordant.

13.3.5 Representational Terminology

The meaning of the terms *intelligence, knowledge,* and *learning* has become almost too general to use; they are neither things nor separate processes that need to be included in a model of cognition (cf. the lists of what early cognitive science ignored; e.g., Norman, 1980). It is obviously useful to call other animals intelligent, and there is no reason to exclude this term from descriptions of computers. But calling a rule in an expert system "a piece of knowledge" should be avoided.

The term *symbol*, previously used almost exclusively to refer to human artifacts, such as words and other notations, should be viewed in terms of functional, *categorizing processes* in a *symbol system.*[1]

The focus on "representations" in the philosophy of AI was largely a great distraction because it never considered broadly the different points of view. Arguments about meaning and reference focused almost exclusively on *correspondence between things* instead of the functional formation of coordinating processes. Because of the focus on mathematical and scientific reasoning, the investigation in the AI community took for granted mechanisms of reifying the world into objects and referential categorization (e.g., "images represent objects"; Johnson-Laird, 1983, p. 147). Few of the arguments about representation questioned how conceptualization of object, subject, and causal relations develop (let alone evolved; see Donald, 1991, 1993, 1994). The main reason for progress in the past decade has been recognizing the relevance of the data from child psychology (Thelen & Smith, 1994), neurobiology (Edelman, 1992), and animal cognition (Cheney & Seyfarth, 1992) for reformulating the fundamental questions about memory and learning.

Meaning is best viewed as an experience, a kind of coordination. Tacit knowledge is a conceptualization, not necessarily verbal and certainly not more text. The term *latent* should be avoided because it suggests an existing description or an organizer that has been suppressed. We should distinguish instead between tacit conceptualizations and conscious experience (what the agent is perceiving and feeling).

Cognition is situated in different ways: *behaviorally choreographed* in a place and time (e.g., the contextual, interactive process of learning by doing), *structurally configured* as categorization relations, and *functionally social,* as forms (patterns and means) of participation. By this reformulation, cognition is not only physically and temporally situated ("knowledge is in the environment"), but conceptually situated as a tacit understanding of WIDN. In people, this conceptualization is pervasively social in content; this is the essential psychological implication of the theory of situated action (Lave & Wenger, 1991; Suchman, 1987).

13.3.6 Subsymbolic

Rather than using terms like *subsymbolic* or *subconceptual,* which are common in connectionist theorizing, I view the architectural process being described here

---

[1] I compare the developmental and operational differences of natural and artifactual symbol systems in Clancey (1997c), chapter 13.

as *symbol creating* (cf. Table 12.2). The problem with "sub X" talk is that it appears to leave behind the higher-order processes (rather than account for them) or reduces the lower-order processes to being components, a substrate, or a mere "implementation." My interest as a cognitive scientist in the study of neural activation is only in terms of what it reveals about higher-order "psychological" behavior and experience. For this reason, I find Edelman's (1987, 1992) TNGS to be particularly satisfying. TNGS describes lower-level structures whose very existence (as activated, grouped entities) depends on their functionality in a coordinated feedback system (classification couples).

Indeed, the good aspect of research couched in terms of sub X processes is the attempt to make a distinction between nonverbal and verbal categorization. Such theories break away from the idea that a learning mechanism must necessarily consist of parameterized descriptions (named objects, with properties that have named values). Thus, talk about sub X processes is often an attempt to find out what underlies human language and consciousness. The term *subconceptual* misses the point, for conceptualization is what we need to understand (the researcher often means "concepts that are not words"). *Subsymbolic* is perhaps more innocuous, but too often regresses to studying how symbolic expressions can be stored in something like a hash table.

I especially resist relegating conceptual knowledge to a symbolic level and subconceptual knowledge to a connectionist, subsymbolic level.[2] The conceptual coordination analysis suggests instead that an intermediate level of description is required if we are to understand the *varieties of categorization*. This level must relate both to conceptual, symbolic experience and neural, subconscious processes. I conclude that rather than talk about sub X we need simply to talk about categorization (as a neural process).

13.3.7 Behavior or Experience?

I have finessed and sometimes stepped awkwardly around the words *behavior* and *experience*. What happens next in a sequence, the next behavior or the next experience? Philosophically, experience connotes awareness, which by my analysis involves the categorization WIDN. Insofar as higher-order categorization as I have defined it is conceptual, there is an implicit claim that all animals conceptually coordinating behavior are experiencing (aware of) what they are doing. Therefore it does not matter which word is used when we are analyzing conceptually coordinated behavior; all such behaviors are experiences. That is, the events we have described are part of what is normally called *intentional*.

---

[2]Compare to the idea of meshing two modules in a hybrid system (Sun, 1996).

Of course, the resultant behavior is not always deliberate (e.g., slips) and need not involve language (e.g., the perceptual experiences presented in chapter 1). And the patterns themselves, such as repetitions or progressive deepening, are often not noticed and by the very theory presented here, they occur without requiring planning or reasoning. That is to say that the mechanism causing the patterns does not require models of the world or behavior. This includes the whole variety of phenomena considered: sending two messages in succession, Caitlin's explorations in the pool, typing slips, forming the initial analogy between paintbrushes and pumps, grammatical speaking, and so on.

Other researchers use the word *experience* to refer to anything the organism did (whether a subconsciously ordered behavior or a conscious thought), as in the episodic knowledge modeled by Soar (section 2.2.2). I do not endorse this usage for, like most of descriptive cognitive modeling, it potentially confuses the observer's descriptions with the subject's cognitive mechanism and elides conscious and subconscious processes.

13.4   UNDERSTANDING PATTERNS IN SELF-ORGANIZING MECHANISMS

The focus on categorization as a neural process replaces the idea of control dictated by a descriptive schema by the notion of *mental organizers*. Higher-order categorizations, such as conceptualizations of activities, are competing and operating simultaneously with lower-level perceptual and motor processes in different modalities. Slips, and a variety of dysfunctional phenomena analyzed by others (e.g., split brain experiences; Bogen & Bogen, 1983; Bradshaw & Nettleton, 1981; Cytowic, 1993; Puccetti, 1981; Sacks, 1987, 1990), suggest that multiple organizers in the brain (e.g., verbal and visual organizers) can be modular and yet operating together in ways the serial versus parallel dichotomy has not captured. One modality, such as vision, may be "idling," while a verbal, "hypnoidal" attention dominates; yet on recollection the different modalities are coupled (such that reconstructing the image reactivates the verbal thoughts).

To understand the brain, I suggest that we conceive neural processes as constituting *a new kind of machine*. As I have indicated, one distinction that appears central is that components are not fixed, but continuously adapted and reconfigured to work together. By hypothesis, selection and generalization are always operating in categorizing and sequencing, not just in our conceptualizations of ideas. This process is indeterminate, in the sense that serialization and composition can occur without *choice*. The situated action argument that behavior is not strictly planned applies specifically to this "within the moment" coordination. Behavior is not only improvised in cycles of conscious perceiving and redirecting, but *multiply determined*. Our speech (and hence our descriptive cognitive models) linearize in time what is simultaneous and codetermined in the mind.

The theoretical difficulty in understanding self-organizing processes is perhaps most evident in arguments about the built-in (innate) versus learned aspects of language (section 9.2). The regular ("grammatical") form of language is constrained by and reflects how neural processes are sequenced and composed. But constructed compositions later reactivate and become part of the architecture that constrains new formations. Hence two kinds of constraints are operating simultaneously. The "language machine" is *both* within a certain architectural system (innate) *and* virtual (learned). Transformational grammar characterizes *patterns that perform*. Performance occurs as organizing and selecting, which can be viewed in the language of programming as instantiation, binding, substitution, sequencing, proceduralization, and so on. Hence, neural processes have computational form, but are simultaneously creating this form as they are created by past manifestations of it.

Besides the structural changes to categorizations as they are reactivated, coordination (knowledge) processes only exist when they are functioning; they are formed within and as coordinations in time. A dynamic perspective emphasizes the role of *motion in time*; knowledge is viewed as choreography-in-action. A schema is a coordinating process that is inherently related to changes in perception and timing of movements, not an inert description or entry in a database.

Well-known observations in language and memory (such as noun phrase reference and slips) can be understood *temporally* as sequential reactivations and inclusions of processes instead of only *spatially* as "proximal" relations in surface structure. Slips are detected by awareness of novel conceptualization, not a separate system that looks at or compares descriptions of behavior and expectations. In contrast, stored memory models (such as Schank's MOPs) construe reminding as retrieving a past experience alone, leaving out the impasse and repair occurring as the reminding process itself. Although MOPs scripts concern interactive behavior over time, learning is viewed as modifying a conceptual hierarchy, instead of a more fundamental process of reactivating and recombining *behavior sequences*. EPAM is a good model of active perceptual categorization, but it implicitly incorporates a coordinated learning process that presupposes conceptualization of and reasoning about environmental patterns.

Understanding the self-organizing nature of neural processes requires resolving the either–or view of structure and process. For example, symbols are not fixed patterns (a strict structure view). But we must not dismiss the idea that processes are discretely structured and recombined by throwing out the idea of tokens and symbols altogether. A both–and view (i.e., both structures and processes) suggests that structures are always adapted, not immutable; but their *stability as recurrent processes* fits the "category as a thing" view. Thus, we can view scenes and phrase conceptualizations as being recurrent neural processes and hence recurrent structures with relations that are reconfigured in time. As Bartlett (1932/1977) said, the associationist view has its place, especially in language where details such as words obviously recur.

13.5   CONSCIOUSNESS AS HIGHER-ORDER CONCEPTUAL COORDINATION

The study of consciousness has become an important part of cognitive science (Dennett, 1992; Edelman, 1992; Hameroff, Kaszniak, & Scott, 1996). Many researchers now believe that notions such as intentionality and reference are fundamental to understanding how people pursue goals and relate objects and events in the world. For example, animals lacking intentionality (very likely insects and reptiles) or people with dysfunctions (such as autism) are unable to flexibly coordinate their behavior (Baron-Cohen, 1995; Sacks, 1990). Rather than only modeling the complex problem solving behavior of a specialist such as a physician, physicist, chess player, or a student learning algebra, cognitive scientists are now considering the greater variety of cognitive phenomena as they occur in people and nature.

For example, a conventional, descriptive cognitive model would generally take for granted that 7 ± 2 categorizations can be held in working memory and related. But how is this neurally possible? Evidence suggests that not all animals, or even all mammals, have such a capability (Edelman, 1992; Griffin, 1984, 1992; Walker, 1985). Descriptive cognitive models assume that a complex template, such as a script describing a common sequence of events in a restaurant, can be held active as a whole, at one moment, and used to guide behavior. This makes all sequential behavior appear to be a form of reasoning (i.e., referring to the template as if it were a user manual and deducing what to do next).

But suppose that an animal is not capable of holding active and relating a sequence of categorizations. Could a categorization of a scene—simultaneous activation of multiple categorizations—nevertheless offer a means of coordinating behavior? Are such processes perhaps active in people, despite their having other linguistic means to conceptually coordinate their behavior?

On the other hand, if we start with an overly complex mechanism, as I argue has been the case in most cognitive modeling, we will miss the variety of mechanisms present in the brain for organizing behavior, fail to understand how complex organizations are actually learned, and in general have a poor foundation for understanding how the capabilities of animals have evolved and how cognition develops in children. (This is an ironic conclusion, given my disdain for the emphasis on rats and pigeons in my experience of early 1970s psychology.) The analysis of navigation learning by children and animals in chapter 5 distinguished between processes of "rote" path learning, categorizing sequences, and being able to hold active, categorize, and order multiple sequences. Most descriptive cognitive models take these coordinations for granted in how knowledge structures are applied.

For example, carrying out the progressive deepening exploration depicted by problem behavior graphs (Fig. 5.3) to design tasks (including games, such as cryptarithmetic puzzles) requires a capability to compare and evaluate symbolic artifacts for closeness to an imagined end state. In this respect, detecting food or comparing directional heading back to a home location is quite different from the comparing alternative world states or situation descriptions (such as chess board positions).

Besides evaluative comparison of states, progressive deepening requires the ability to return to earlier states. As noted in the discussion of short-term memory in section 5.5, return to a previously constructed state follows from the Newell and Simon (1972) model of a landmark memory, *"stored in terms of the way it differs from the base position*, which is under continual surveillance" (p. 720). Newell and Simon recognized that such constraints are required for a computational model to be a theory of cognition. From my programmer's computational perspective building expert systems in the late 1970s, such limitations appeared arbitrary and unnecessary. In contrast, my entire approach in this book has been to find such constraints in the phenomenology of coordinated experience and to explain such limits or patterns in neural terms (i.e., the idea of anchors in language comprehension; chapter 10). Indeed, this is a good example of how symbolic theory provides a suggestive specification for what the neural level is accomplishing: Detecting and remembering a difference relationship is precisely how EPAM stores sequences; it is the basis for remembering anything at all in Schank's failure-driven model of memory. From the neural activation perspective, it fits the idea that a new categorization is always a relational distinction, with respect to a previously constructed categorization. Thus, the "architecture of cognition" is revealed not to be so general as an arbitrary production rule memory, but a neural coordination "machine" with certain capacities for coupling, sequencing, and composing categories. It is then, with such a subconscious mechanism, that the conscious problem solving studied by most of cognitive science occurs.

One useful starting point for understanding how consciousness is partly learned and partly an architectural facility is shown in the summary of how ideas developed in the example of inventing a synthetic paintbrush (Table 7.2). I suggested that categories build on one another, from types (things in the world), to an order of types (distinctions about location, size, or alignment), and causal relations between types (how one property influences another). A few points are worth highlighting:

- Higher-order categorizations relate (conceptually structure) lower-order categorizations.
- Relations are themselves learned categorizations; for example, the ideas of causality and containment.
- Modern developmental theory argues that higher-order relations develop from and remain grounded in body experience (e.g., the idea of physical containment of geometric figures may not only be defined, but understood as a physical experience, Johnson, 1987; Lakoff, 1987, 1995).

- In theorizing, the developmental order is recapitulated in processes of objectifying, naming, history telling, and modeling (e.g., explaining, planning, and designing).
- Verbal terminology and descriptions are always, often tacitly, related to nonverbal conceptualizations in other sensory-physical modalities, especially visual, but including tactile, auditory, and posture.
- Conceptual, nonverbal understanding includes temporal relations of rhythm, frequency, attack (e.g., abruptness of onset), and so on, and these are in turn coupled to emotional experience.

Now from here, we can move in two directions—downward to the mechanisms of how categorizations are held active and related, such that reference and self-image are possible; and upward to the social content of conceptualizations, such that identity and social norms pervade all human thought (including subconscious aspects of conceptualization and deliberation). Thus, there is a dual aspect in conceptualizing the self: categorizing *internal activity* (multimodal categorizing in time) and *interactive role* (functional identity in time). Indeed, the present understanding of intentionality, from studies of primates and autistic children especially, indicates that the ability to coordinate these multiple categorizations across modalities is what enables consciousness as we know it in human beings (Clancey, 1997a; in press; in preparation). Levels of increasingly higher-order categorizations constitute a conceptual system of beliefs, awareness of beliefs, models of other agents, and symbolic artifactual models.

For example, the evidence suggests that a distinction can be drawn between *first-order intentionality* provided by basic conceptualization (such as the conceptualization of "mother-offspring" in vervets; Cheney & Seyfarth, 1992) and *second-order intentionality* (attributing beliefs or desires to the self or another animal). That is, a distinction is drawn between having beliefs and having the categorization of "the belief that . . . ." More complex yet is the *referential categorization* that a belief is an attribution, that it is an idea, that it might be wrong, and so forth. My claim is that these are all learned categorizations—matters of conceptual content—but they require a conceptual coordination mechanism that allows, first, *categorizing a categorization* (a composition), and second, *relating categorizations that are not temporally simultaneous or sequential*. That is, one must be able to hold two categorizations in stasis, as it were, and then physically combine them. This is clearly different from coupling and sequential activation and appears to be something vervets cannot do. Finally, building on referential categorization, an object may be viewed as having a referential interpretation; that is, the object is symbolic of something else (e.g., a photograph). Interestingly enough, gorillas have this capability, which suggests that they have referential categorizations and are thus capable of deception, as several studies now attest (Cheney & Seyfarth, 1992; Gordon, 1995).

Symbolic reference requires a triadic conceptual coordination, relating the conceptualization (e.g., the idea of a table), the symbolic form (the word *table*), and the referent (a particular table in the world or being mentioned in a story; Fig. 13.1). That is, the conceptualization that a symbol stands for a referent (e.g., a word refers to something in the world) involves two other categorizations of "symbolizing" and "refers to." In effect, five categorizations are being coordinated to construct the "stands for" relation. Viewed mathematically, it is possible that a neural mechanism that can construct a binary relation (Concept refers to Referent) may be operating on itself to produce a triadic relation. But it may also be the case that in the case of symbolic meaning the coordination is cross-modal, the relation of sound or image is conveyed by pointing, or simply that a sound is standing for an image. Autism may result in part from an inability to form cross-modal coordinations (Baron-Cohen, 1995), suggesting that the neural process for constructing symbolic meaning requires an additional kind of categorization mechanism. Beyond this, recent anthropological studies (Shreeve, 1995) suggest that language and conceptual coordination alone are not sufficient for developing a symbolic system, such as written language. The tens of thousands of years of apparent relative stasis in *Homo sapiens* tool building suggest that the very idea of design as meaningful variation in artifacts was a cultural invention that required eons to develop. For example, there may have been a cultural bias to throw away variations in tools as mistakes. But when clans from different areas encountered each other, they discovered systematic variations in the other group's tools, which when encountered out in the wild were recognized as standing for the presence of the other group.

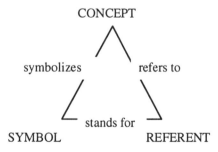

Fig. 13.1. The meaning triangle. (Adapted from CONCEPTUAL STRUCTURES, Sowa, 1984, Figure 1.4, p. 11. Copyright ©1984 Addison Wesley Longman. Reprinted by permission of Addison Wesley Longman.).

Although my interest in this book is primarily to elucidate simple ideas about categorization in time, the last points stress again that such a study necessarily returns us to the fact that animals with higher-order consciousness (at the referential level at least) are engaged in a process of sustaining a self-image relative to a group identity. Even in apparently very simple coordinations, ongoing conceptualization of WIDN accounts for certain aspects of *why repetition occurs* (as an active process of extending capability), *why certain behaviors are errors at all* (by an internal feedback process related to WIDN), and *how in general discordant categorizations can be brought together and creatively reconceived* (by the ability to hold categorizations active and relate them with respect to the conception of WIDN). That is, one cannot understand the patterning of behavior from a neural perspective alone, but must consider the content of categorizations—how they are being related in time by higher-order conceptualizations of the self and activities.

As I showed in (Clancey, 1997c), although one may attempt to separate out issues of social identity and social setting to understand mechanistic phenomena of memory, perception and learning, the broader issues always have an important part to play. The reason is that conscious beings are never just subjects or neural machines, but always subjective participants, playing a role and making their behavior part of their understanding of what they are supposed to be doing and what they conceive is happening to them. In the final analysis, one cannot easily separate the human conception of self and basic processes of coordination from each other.

13.6   NEXT STEPS FOR COGNITIVE
AND SOCIAL SCIENCE

In this section I present some threads for elaborating the interactive-coordination process model and then highlight the implications for cognitive neuropsychology and the social sciences. Fig. 13.2 provides one way of ordering these questions, associating different kinds of explanations with different levels of description. The diagram highlights that I have not presented a neural network model, but rather articulated architectural specifications based on the phenomenology of human experience, descriptive cognitive models, and neurobiology (cf. the introduction to chapter 3). The levels of analysis may be reformulated by relating previous cognitive modeling assumptions about storage, copying, and reuse of descriptions to the constraints of neural activation and categorization. For example, in the previous section I showed how the evolution of language might be related to the ability to conceptually coordinate two other coordinations across sensory modalities. In this section I list areas for further research suggested by the overall framework of Fig. 13.2, focusing first on neural theories and then on cognitive and social theories.

13.6.1 Questions About Neural Activation and
Categorization Processes

What is the neural evidence for the claim that segmenting experience into events and activities is a kind of categorizing ("a categorized sequence")? Does reentrancy between neuronal groups, as claimed in the TNGS, also occur between global maps? Is reproduction of neuronal populations happening at the map level? Does the Darwinism metaphor not fit here? How are multiple categorizations held active?

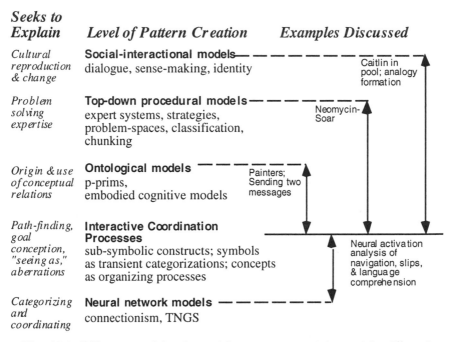

Fig. 13.2. Different models of mental processes seek to explain different phenomena (left column) by describing patterns at different levels: social, procedural, conceptual, perceptual-motor coordination, and neural (middle column). The neural activation perspective bridges knowledge-level models of problem solving and learning (above) with neural network models (below). Arrows (right column) indicate broad relations between levels illustrated by examples discussed in this book.

What kind of coordinating process allows imagination of past experience? For example, how is it possible to reactivate a sequence of images on a path without actually causing the animal to move? Is this the same mechanism that allows dreaming, such that dreaming is the more fundamental, evolved capability? What happens to the sensorimotor systems when I visualize rotating an object? (Calvin: "Thoughts are actions that haven't happened yet.")

The binding idea of computation (cf. Fig. 3.5) needs to be related to neural processes. Is a form of coupling involved in generalizing a previous categorization to new details, and does this constitute the instantiation process of descriptive cognitive models? Can the classification coupling of TNGS be extended to show how multiple categorizations are simultaneously active in a "scene"?

How are individual differences, summarized by Gardner's (1985) theory of multiple intelligences, accountable by different ways of coordinating the specialized areas of the brain? Does the study of unusual ability reveal why "the blend of intelligences in an intact individual," allowing different kinds of conceptualization, is necessary for "the solving of problems and the creation of products of significance" (p. xiii)?

Is emotional attitude a quality of all categorization, as Bartlett's analysis and TNGS suggests? As emotions become conceptualized, how does this allow transcending their influence on behavior? Is this simply a process of forming a higher-order, encapsulating categorization that conceptually coordinates the situation, the emotion, and the reaction?

How are neural processes always developing together, becoming coordinated and correlated, without losing their ability to be recombined in new ways as discrete units? The stability of categorization within a sequence is somehow maintained, despite the fact that every conceptualization is always incorporated in some train of thought. How do grammatical and semantic categorical systems retain their apparently distinct character, despite the fact that they are always operating together? Is essential work of dreaming to relax such constraints across conceptual modalities that have formed during the day ("unlearning")?

How do the conceptual and neurophysiological constraints on seeing-as interact? (For example, puns are conceptually disallowed transformations.) What is happening when we pause in thought: Is there a real competition of specific alternatives or are we just waiting for quiescence, for *some*, single process to take shape?

Speaking and comprehending are obviously central: How do they occur together as we talk? In the study of self-explanation and comprehending instructions, can we detect momentary tacit, multimodal conceptualizations in an individual's experience?

Can we use the conceptual coordination perspective to reformulate models of how children learn to count? Can we reformulate models of mathematical learning to incorporate nonverbal conceptual coordination? Can stories about the use of imagery in scientific invention be broken down to reveal how scenes and kinesthetic conceptions are recoordinated with descriptions?

Can we now go back to the interviews from which Neomycin was abstracted to reinterpret the side remarks that we viewed as noise originally, finding in them evidence of the physician's categorizing flexibility that Neomycin does not have? Can ergonomic design for complex systems like airplanes and manufacturing plants be reformulated in terms of the *conception of activities*, so that we may relate better relate an operator's conception of organizational roles to reasoning and action?

13.6.2 Implications for Cognitive and Social Psychology

Historically, individual and social cognition have been treated separately except by the early advocates of situated cognition, such as Dewey, Bartlett, Mead, and Bateson. Our opportunity is to reformulate the nature of cognitive development in individuals and groups, appreciating the diversity of individuals, the discord of groups, and the tacit coordinating processes ("knowledge") that smooth everyday interaction.

A social view of cognition leads us to investigate how people create, modify, and use representations (e.g., slides for a talk, architectural drawings, texts, expert systems) in their visible behavior. Because descriptions are consciously created and interpreted, the manipulations we observe reveal the interactive nature of *representing*. New studies are reexamining how representations are created and used from this perspective—just as to learn about carpentry, we must watch how a carpenter uses tools and assembles materials (Agre, 1997, Bamberger & Schön, 1983; Clancey, 1994b; Star & Greisemer, 1989).

Recalling many years studying medical reasoning, I cannot imagine pursuing such investigations today without involving a social scientist tuned to the organizational setting. Reasoning is framed by the agent's conception of the group's activity: Some of Neomycin's strategy rules are descriptions of patterns in group dynamics. However, the regularities in social systems (e.g., the doctor–nurse–receptionist–spouse–patient encounter) are not based on *descriptions of the patterns*—the community of practice is a higher-order, self-organizing system, with behaviors and capabilities that transcend any individual's knowledge or control:

> A group is maintained by its activity . . . the social group possesses a certain trend of development . . . . This trend need not be, and in the majority of cases it certainly is not, present in the mind, or fully represented in the behaviour, of any individual member of the group. (Bartlett, 1932/1977, p. 275)

Schank and Abelson's (1977) script language might serve well to describe social patterns. But there is no single "restaurant script," as Schank suggested. Human actors have different viewpoints and roles, which may collide and conflict. The work of a business office may be locally coherent and even well articulated. But practice may also be fraught with discoordination, waste, and misalliance. Just as psychologists idealized the omniscience and uniform nature of individual knowledge (the objective view), social scientists eager to elevate our attention to the group sometimes overcompensated in idealizing the harmony and interactive fluidity of social settings (Hughes, Randall, & Shapiro, 1991). Ironically, the cognitive psychologist's individual perspective of a "shared" script and shared knowledge was reinforced. The social scientist's view that behavior is emergent and interactively coordinated seems odd to the psychologist who responds, "No, behavior is coherent because members of the group have the same grammars, strategy rules, and scripts stored in their brain."

A different view of how the brain works—conceptions are not stored descriptions—suggests a new understanding of social processes. This suggests that explanations of behavior in everyday life must take into account *how the conceptualization of activity develops and is sustained.* Groundbreaking research by Lave, Suchman, Wynn, and many others (Greenbaum & Kyng, 1991) now reveals the *work* of sustaining a categorized, ordered view of the world:

> The person who works with information deals with an "object" that is more difficult to define and capture than information flow charts would have us imagine. These show "information" in little blocks or triangles moving along arrows to encounter specific transformations and directions along the diagram. In reality, it seems, all along the arrows, as well as at the nodes, that there are people helping this block to be what it needs to be—to name it, put it under the heading where it will be seen as a recognizable variant, deciding whether to leave it in or take it out, whom to convey it to . . . . A more traditional approach would treat both the information and the functions as if they were permanently defined, always recognizable entities. (Wynn, 1991, p. 56-7)

This new social psychology requires a both–and approach—both the social sciences and psychology. Even although the social sciences are a source for many insights within the theory of situated cognition, neural and perceptual theories are nevertheless essential. The social sciences alone cannot explain why habits develop or how looking and conceiving interact, or even account for the effects of practice. Rather than treating the brain like a black box, the social sciences would do well to consider the biological origins and limits of human thought.

A social science that ignores the individual psyche cannot claim to be speaking for the human side of everyday life. Social accounts focusing on the group too often ignore the origins of leadership and pride (preferring to see them as the construction of the group), overlooking individual contributions and unique capabilities. Yet the descriptive cognitive modeling approach has been as bad, not in denying the individual memory and skills of course, but in ignoring individual personality, conflicts, and pleasures. The study of human cognition would suggest that we are exclusively goal-oriented, task-performing machines. There is little place for sitting out on the patio enjoying the view; all human action is theoretically framed as a means toward some survival or business objective. By an analysis where conversation is conveying information, it is perhaps no surprise that the very notion of activity, of being in an interactive, meaningful role that has no specific output or product is almost completely missing from cognitive psychology. Indeed, the few forays into the study of emotion suggest that drive, despondency, and enthusiasm are colorings or ratings ("my happiness is 6 on a scale of 10"), rather than conceptual organizers.[3]

---

[3]See Iran-Nejad (1984, 1990) for an affective, self-regulating model of memory.

A reading of social sciences sometimes suggests that motivation, humor, pride, and curiosity exist in thin air. What are their biological bases? Although much can be gained by viewing motivation in the context of social participation (e.g., "learning is becoming a member of a community of practice"), little place is allowed for inborn differences. Perhaps the present-day political climate is too freshly scarred by racial, gender, and ethnic partitioning. Nevertheless, it remains the responsibility of scientists to help identify the biological origins of differences in temperament and preferences for expression.[4]

Most of psychology and sociology proceeds as if there are no human or even animal characteristics in behavior, when every grandmother knows how a child is more like one family line than another. Psychology and sociology proceed as if an individual's emotion, drives, and attitudes were all plastic and subject to every external influence (according to S. J. Gould, 1987: "a reductionist, one-way theory about the grafting of information from environment upon organism," p. 50). A theory of *appreciation* (again a pursuit of Dewey) requires distinguishing between conceptual coordination abilities, which may vary between individuals, and a social policy of equal opportunity. Although we are quick to allow that anatomical variations constrain our sports aspirations (or all swimmers would be just as good at playing football), many AI researchers view the newborn's brain like a computer processor off the assembly line. Geschwind's observations ring clear:

> Once you start looking methodically you realise very quickly that brains differ from person to person, just like hair colour, height, the pattern of the facial bones and the proteins in the blood. Therefore, we have every reason to believe that not all brains are going to respond in the same way. (quoted in J. Miller, 1983, p. 129)

Although we may perhaps all learn to draw, individual differences lead some of us to tool over the piano, some to dance, some to take up photography, others to write of imaginary castles in the air, and so on. And these are not exclusively matters of nurture or mere "preference." Referring to discoordinations of neural dysfunction, Geschwind suggested that "disunity is present in normals, although we have overlooked it" (J. Miller, 1983, p. 125). An appreciation of such variation and proclivities may help prevent us from shoehorning children into a verbally dominated pedagogy and perhaps facilitate enjoying other forms of intelligence. For a society moving in the direction of more leisure and more choice in lifestyle, it is none too soon to recognize the forms creativity may take. A related investigation, as Bateson (1972) and Griffin (1984; 1992) promoted, is to view animal cognition in its own terms. This exploration, too, requires a more pluralistic account of cognitive difference.

With the imbalances of our past studies and the blindness between the disciplines in mind, I proceed to my final topic: How did we get into this mess?

---

[4]A notable example is Kagan (1994).

Does the parochial separation of disciplines reflect the conceptual isolations of
the individual mind?

13.7   COORDINATING CONCEPTUAL SPACES
ACROSS DISCIPLINES

Bateson lived and worked not 5 miles from the "Mycin trailer" where we
schemed over rules and control structures in the 1970s. Yet I did not hear about
the man until 5 or 6 years after he died. Today, he stands in my mind as a pillar
for all the ideas in this book, a personality who synthesized cybernetics and
anthropology, whose interests ranged over the feedback mechanisms of
thermostats, the verb-centered conceptualization of dolphins, the double bind of
unhappy families, and what the patterns on the back of a crab's shell reveal
about the structure of ideas.

The presence of Bateson in Palo Alto during the Mycin project and my
ignorance of him looms in my mind as a great clue about the development of
modern science and perhaps the nature of conceptual modularization in the
individual mind. But we must not be simplistic: The isolation of our
communities was not symmetric. Although no one came to me until 1987
saying, "You must read about Bateson," Bateson knew about us and wrote
clearly about the limitations of the symbolic approach. Furthermore, cognitive
science journals published papers before 1980 that I never saw, such as those
Bransford et al. (1977) and Jenkins (1974), which experimentally critiqued the
stored description view.

Apparently the cause of theoretical isolation today is not geographic or even
so much along the boundaries of disciplines, but conceptual, in our own ability
to work with a variant idea. Probably the greatest enforcer of the descriptive
worldview was the lack of an architectural alternative, another model that would
do as well or even identify missed data. We said that the descriptive calculus
("symbolic") approach was "the only game in town," and what we meant is that
this scientific *activity*, this game, was the only one we knew how to play. We
identified a form of intelligent behavior (ranging from puzzles to engineering
design and medicine) and then formulated a model representing the objects and
relations of a general model and transformation rules to create SSMs (chapter
12). No one came forward with a better way to do medical diagnosis or
manufacturing process control. The philosophical criticisms of course appeared
anachronistic and ignorant of what had been accomplished. In this respect, one
cannot discount the effect of the arrogant enthusiasm of AI researchers (which I
knew very well) in presenting a closed society that discouraged outsiders from
seeking the stage.

On the other hand, a community cannot explore every viewpoint thoroughly at
once. If the fundamental arguments had been allowed to take hold early on (say
in the 1950s), qualitative modeling might never have been developed. Adopting
S. J. Gould's (1987) view of progress, we should not view too harshly the

inventive eddies of science or the serendipity of discovering chemistry when we so stupidly tried to turn lead into gold. The architectural approach of computational modeling may now be brought to bear on neurobiology (as the activation trace notation attests). The social conception of activity may transform task models of reasoning. Qualitative modeling might be used to represent social networks, and so on.

Now we are doing the work of relating our points of view. There was some advantage in parallel, distributed, noncoordinated development of the cognitive, neurobiological, and social sciences. Such walling off is locally useful within a community (we pursued frames and rules on the two sides of the United States in the early 1970s) and the isolation of our disciplines may prove equally useful as cognitive science now reveals the individual point of view for anthropology and sociology.

Within the individual mind, categorizations are never isolated and arbitrarily reconfigurable, but always experienced and interpreted within activities. Logically, there is freedom and openness in getting from here to there. But conceptual coordinations are always transformations of paths already taken. The freedom of reason is in possibility; practice takes time. The conceptual isolation within and between communities occurs every day (and indeed partially originates) in our own thought. Someone points out that Ron Goldman who works in the cubicle next to you is also the name of a famous person—now why didn't you think of that? If we cannot recognize a name in another context, how can we expect complex concepts and entire fields of inquiry to find themselves and become coordinated? The both–and view helps again: We wondered earlier how conceptualizations retain their identity in use. Now we are wondering why they appear to be so isolated!

In practice we are always drawing boundaries, segmenting, and sorting our ideas and activities into piles. Conceptualizations are integrated in action, but isolated relative to activities.[5] Activities are separated by times and places, language, tools, and methods. Conceptual separation across social boundaries makes the experience of novelty possible (Bartlett, 1932/1977; Star & Greisemer, 1989). Everyone knows that the real scientific action lies in crossing communities of practice: That is where conflicts and borrowings are realized. Yet without the boundaries there would be nothing to share, nothing new to learn. Bateson knew about expert systems, but it is probably just as well that we did not know about him. He was in a synthesizing, boundary-crossing mode; we were establishing the perspectives that needed to be reconciled.

---

[5]Indeed, according to one theory (Mithen, 1996, pp. 162–163), the real difficulty in the cultural development of cognition was to integrate the conceptual domains of natural history (e.g., animal tracking), social intelligence (e.g., intentional communication in teaching children), and technical intelligence (e.g., producing arrows and clothing) to develop the idea of symbolic artifacts for communication.

13.8   ARE THERE PRINCIPLES FOR FACILITATING INTERDISCIPLINARY RESEARCH?

It is very fine to say that cognitive science needed its own space to grow, but the fact remains that a small forest was felled publishing mostly fruitless papers on the frame problem, the nature of symbols, and the like. In retrospect, those debates appear somewhat narrowly conceived. The internecine scrambles over "scruffy" and "neat" forms of description in AI appear like turf battles isolated down near the 10-yard line, with the players blind to the whole field behind them. Can we learn anything from our inability to understand criticisms of the symbolic approach? Are there any general heuristics for reframing difficult questions so we can more quickly involve other disciplines and tools?

The self-limitation of the descriptive cognitive modeling approach appears to be particularly difficult, like a box of its own making. The discreteness of language and the apparent discreteness of other process–structures in the world (trees, rocks, people) and especially of our artifacts (cars, pens, books) led us to believe that structures in our head were similarly articulated and located as separately stored or reconstructible modules, facts, procedures, and associations. Not only did we lack an alternative architecture, but the very nature of description itself reinforced the objective conceptions of thing and knowledge. Our ability to stably recognize, comprehend, and talk about things was identified with knowledge. The multimodal aspects of conceptualizing got lost by confusion between the map and the territory. Because the models performed (Aaron [McCorduck, 1991] produces drawings, Mycin (Buchanan & Shortliffe, 1984) gives medical advice), and because speaking and instructions do change human behavior, it was difficult to conceive that text played a different role in human learning than in computer programs. Much was written about the propositional form of imagery, for example, but again no one could say what images were, if not descriptions. Surely there was no screen and inner eye. Wasn't it obvious? Concepts must be things; processes create things. All this was reinforced by the visualization of semantic networks in graphic diagrams: Here are concepts, right here on paper, and now in the computer.

Like any science, cognitive psychology mostly ignored what it could not appropriately consider: dreaming, visualization, song,[6] dance, gesture. As Rosenfield (1988, 1992) showed and Sacks (1987, 1990) lamented against, models of neural dysfunction were boxed in by the same storage, descriptive view of memory. The result, as perhaps for any science, is that the experiments *defined* the phenomenon of interest: word problems, puzzles, math, electronics, medicine, things you learn in school. Cohen's work on Aaron (McCorduck, 1991) is exciting precisely because he confronted the dilemma of applying the descriptive mechanism to art, an activity that is profoundly visual and emotional. Although the perceptual aspect of chess playing was identified early

---

[6]But see Rubin, Wallace, & Houston (1993).

on, the idea of perceptual chunks was assimilated theoretically in verbal-sequential terms, so again a chess position must be *encoded* as "seven plus or minus two" chunks in short-term memory (Newell and Simon, 1972, p. 780). The idea that a scene is a *different kind of chunk* than a phone number or an operator sequence (and not composed of descriptive units) was difficult to conceive. Because the information processing system is only operating on symbols, by definition, the visual perception of a chess position must be "represented internally by a single symbol," too (p. 793).

Despite understanding the difficulties of the enterprise, I cannot be sympathetic to the logical mistakes I was drawn into. The errors that matter are not the particular explanations and models we developed in creating the first expert systems or knowledge-based tutoring programs, but the kind of scientific theory we sought, and especially our idea of what a mechanism could be. We repeatedly engaged in false dichotomies and either–or thinking. It seems that every time we said, "It must be X or it must be Y," we would have done well to ask, "How could it be both X and Y?" What kind of symbol processing mechanism could be both stable and yet reconstructed? Both serial and parallel? Both a memory and a processor? Both physical and cognitive? Both organized and organizing? Both reused and not stored? Although there is no promise that such riddles would not just add to the confusion (consider the mystery of saying, "A knowledge base is a representation of knowledge, not knowledge itself"), at least we should have tried such reformulations and might have invented something different.

S. J. Gould's (1987) analysis also suggests that our idea of system levels was too dominated by metaphors of space, communication, and control. We viewed the relation between levels as mappings, like the relation between an abstract specification and a machine, or the translation from one language to another. We did not understand the way in which a system might be operating at different levels, without requiring that higher levels be *descriptions* (such as instructions) that are implemented by simpler mechanisms. We viewed lower levels as simply carrying out the details of a higher level's responsibilities or functions (whether by a translation process as in program compilation into machine code or by an interactive monitoring and controlling process of prioritizing goals and choosing among alternative problem solving methods, or knowledge sources).

However, organizing need not be either a process of implementation or control. Although social systems and even the brain may be "nearly decomposable" as Simon (1969/1981) suggested, the interactions between the layers may be *historically composed* in a parallel way that the later *decomposition into parts* in our analysis misconstrues. In particular, the time scale of the construction must be considered. Thermal diffusion across rooms of a building (p. 211) presumably operates very differently than conceptualization of a sentence. Buildings and knowledge may be hierarchically constructed, but the processes—the kinds of mechanisms—required are wildly different. We should question models that attempt to view biological systems *spatially* (as in stored-structure models of LTM) and strive instead for models of mechanism that emphasize dynamic flow and recoordination (Thelen & Smith, 1994).

Similarly, coming from the other direction, cognitive modeling has been fundamentally ahistorical, lacking both a perspective of how representing evolved from nonrepresentational means and how knowledge develops within a community. Again, the objective view of science suggests that change is progressive, so knowledge bases are steadily accumulating and approaching truth about the world. Many researchers reflected on how a child's capability to learn exceeded that of expert systems, but few (at first) realized the contradiction that machine learning required huge numbers of examples or an already existing set of stored theories and descriptions. This tension properly formulated might have broadened AI to include a stream of research focusing on child development, rather than making the one or two papers referring to Piaget stick out like sore thumbs.

In this vein, it is perplexing that such a new science would have such a narrow view of scholarship. Why did not the early AI textbooks open with a historical review of the study of intelligence, knowledge, and memory? Why did their reviews begin with chess and block-stacking robots, rather than Dewey? Why didn't the arguments in the most esoteric journals cite the debate between Dewey and Russell or Bartlett's struggle against associationism? The founders of AI (for example, Simon, Newell, and Minsky) who were raised in other disciplines knew this work (*Human Problem Solving* [Newell & Simon, 1972] is noteworthy for its historical survey), but their students and subsequent students became less and less familiar with the approaches in psychology, systems theory, and cybernetics that spawned the field. My memory of learning my discipline is of having to contain my personal interests within public activities: On the one hand, I viewed my personal interest in Polanyi and Freud as relevant to the study of cognition, but not something I could publicly write about. On the other hand, I was paid to design expert systems, and the ideas about strategy rules and clinical parameters were intoxicating. There was much to build and write about already. The practice of conceptualizing is constrained by activities—but still, the related-work chapter of a dissertation in cognitive science should not begin with 1970.

Vera and Simon (1993) warned about "the tail of philosophy wagging the dog of cognitive science" (p. 132), but their argument appears to be as much a lack of appreciation for the philosophical method as a fear of talk over action. In this respect, the descriptive cognitive modeling view has been boxed in by its own theory of the nature of knowledge, fact, and theorizing. How theories change is inadequately modeled by the descriptive approach (cf. chapter 7), and the management of cognitive science itself has suffered from that. Scientific progress is not only processing experimental data, but also reperceiving what needs to be explained. Data are not just present in the world and ready to be observed. The conception of activity changes what we see and are permitted to talk about.

I feel deep gratitude to those researchers who had the spark and wit to break open the discourse dominated by formalism and description and focus back on the study of people: I think especially of Schank's work on reminding, Norman's curiosity about our slips and problems with doorknobs, Minsky's concern with the brain, and Newell's realization that knowledge bases were descriptions. But this book would not have been possible without the courage of Winograd and Flores (1986) to strike out against the dominant paradigm in *Understanding Computers and Cognition: A New Foundation for Design*, written more than a decade ago. Focusing on the difference between cognitive models and people, Winograd and Flores reconceived expert systems as tools for human inquiry. I have endorsed this shift; but I also ask, if these theories are incomplete, then how does the brain work? Winograd and Flores' philosophical groundwork suggested what limits to question in analyzing descriptive cognitive models, what answers to seek in simulation models of neurobiology, and what human experience to value in understanding the function of conceptualization in organizing activity.

A clear vision, distinguishing between human capabilities and computer models, will yield many new ideas for using computers in everyday life, new psychological and social theories, and new approaches for building robots. To attain this, we must study existing computer models and be open to observing and *saying* what people actually do and experience. Unlike physicists or plant biologists, cognitive scientists have the advantage of being able to hold the best theories up against personal experience and ask, "What more is there to life than what this program can do?"

References

American Heritage Electronic Dictionary. (1992). Boston, MA: Houghton Mifflin.

Agre, P. (1997). *Computation and human experience.* New York: Cambridge University Press.

Anderson, J. R. (1980). *Cognitive psychology and its implications.* San Francisco: W. H. Freeman.

Anderson, J. R. (1990). *Cognitive psychology and its implications, Third edition.* San Francisco: W. H. Freeman.

Anderson, J. R., & Bower, G. H. (1980). *Human associative memory: A brief edition.* Hillsdale, NJ: Lawrence Erlbaum Associates. (Original work published 1973)

Arbib, M. A. (1981). Visuomotor coordination: From neural nets to schema theory. *Cognition and Brain Theory, 4*(1), 23–39.

Bamberger, J. (1991). *The mind behind the musical ear.* Cambridge, MA: Harvard University Press.

Bamberger, J., & Schön, D. A. (1979). *The figural formal transaction: A parable of generative metaphor.* (DSRE Working paper No. 1). MIT Division for Study and Research in Education.

Bamberger, J., & Schön, D. A. (1991). Learning as reflective conversation with materials. In F. Steier (Ed.), *Research and reflexivity* . London: Save.

Bannon, L. (1991). From human factors to human actors: The role of psychology and human-computer interaction studies in system design. In J. Greenbaum & M. Kyng (Eds.), *Design at Work* (pp. 25–44). Hillsdale, NJ: Lawrence Erlbaum Associates.

Baron-Cohen, S. (1995). *Mindblindness.* Cambridge, MA: MIT Press.

Barresi, J., & Moore, C. (1996). Intentional relations and social understanding. *Behavioral and Brain Sciences, 19*(1), 17.

Bartlett, F. C. (1958). *Thinking.* New York: Basic Books.

Bartlett, F. C. (1977). *Remembering: A study in experimental and social psychology*(Reprint ed.). Cambridge, UK: Cambridge University Press. (Original work published 1932)

Bateson, G. (1972). *Steps to an ecology of mind*. New York: Ballentine.

Bateson, G. (1979). *Mind and nature: A necessary unity*. New York: Bantam.

Beer, R. D. (1995). A dynamical systems perspective on agent-environment interaction. *Artificial Intelligence Journal, 72*, 173–175.

Berwick, R. C. (1983). Transformational grammar and artificial intelligence: A contemporary view. *Cognition & Brain Theory, 6*(4), 383–416.

Bickhard, M. H. (1995). Intrinsic constraints on language: Grammar and hermeneutics. *Journal of Pragmatics, 23*, 541–554.

Bickhard, M. H., & Richie, D. M. (1983). *On the nature of representation: A case study of James Gibson's theory of perception*. New York: Praeger.

Boesch, C. (1991). Teaching among wild chimpanzees. *Animal Behavior, 41*, 530–532.

Bogen, J. E., & Bogen, G. M. (1983). Hemispheric specialization and cerebral duality. *Behavioral and Brain Sciences, 6*(3), 517–533.

Bradshaw, J. L., & Nettleton, N. C. (1981). The nature of hemispheric specialization In man. *Behavioral and Brain Sciences, 4*(1), 51–92.

Braitenberg, V., Heck, D., & Sultan, F. (1997). The detection and generation of sequences as a key to cerebellar function: Experiments and theory. *Behavioral and Brain Sciences, 20*(2), 229–277.

Bransford, J. D., McCarrell, N. S., Franks, J. J., & Nitsch, K. E. (1977). Toward unexplaining memory. In R. E. Shaw & J. D. Bransford (Eds.), *Perceiving, acting, and knowing: Toward an ecological psychology* (pp. 431–466). Hillsdale, NJ: Lawrence Erlbaum Associates.

Brooks, R. A. (1991). How to build complete creatures rather than isolated cognitive simulators. In K. VanLehn (Ed.), *Architectures for intelligence: The 22nd Carnegie Mellon symposium on cognition* (pp. 225–240). Hillsdale, NJ: Lawrence Erlbaum Associates.

Brown, J. S., Burton, R. R., & De Kleer, J. (1982). Pedagogical, natural language, and knowledge engineering techniques in SOPHIE I, II, and III. In D. Sleeman & J. S. Brown (Eds.), *Intelligent tutoring systems* (pp. 227–282). London: Academic Press.

Bruner, J. (1990). *Acts of meaning*. Cambridge, MA: Harvard University Press.

Bruner, J. S., Goodnow, J. J., & Austin, G. A. (1956). *A study of thinking*. New York: Wiley.

Buchanan, B. G., & Shortliffe, E. H. (Eds.). (1984). *Rule-based expert systems: The MYCIN experiments of the Heuristic Programming Project*. Reading, MA: Addison-Wesley.

Calvin, W. H. (1994). The emergence of intelligence. *Scientific American,* *271*(4), 100–108.

Campbell, J. (1982). *Grammatical man: Information, entropy, language, and life.* New York: Simon & Schuster.

Chalmers, D. J., French, R. M., & Hofstadter, D. R. (1992). High-level perception, representation, and analogy: A critique of artificial intelligence methodology. *Journal of Experimental and Theoretical Artificial Intelligence, 4*(3), 185–212.

Chase, W. G., Ericsson, K. A., & Faloon, S. (1980). *Acquisition of a memory skill.* (Tech. Rep. No. NR157-430). Carnegie-Mellon University.

Cheney, D. L., & Seyfarth, R. M. (1992). Precis of *How monkeys see the world. Behavioral and Brain Sciences, 15*(1), 135–182.

Chi, M. T., de Leeuw, N., Chiu, M. H., & LaVancher, C. (1994). Eliciting self-explanations improves understanding. *Cognitive Science, 18*, 439–477.

Cho, B., Rosenbloom, P. S., & Dolan, C. P. (1991). Neuro-Soar: A neural network architecture for goal-oriented behavior. In *Proceedings of the Thirteenth Annual Conference of the Cognitive Science Society* (pp. 673–677). Hillsdale, NJ: Lawrence Erlbaum Associates.

Chomsky, N. (1957). *Syntactic structures.* The Hague, The Netherlands: Mouton.

Chomsky, N. (1965). *Aspects of a theory of syntax.* Cambridge, MA: MIT Press.

Chomsky, N. (1975). *The logical structure of linguistic theory.* New York: Plenum.

Chomsky, N. (1980). Rules and representations. *Behavioral and Brain Sciences, 3*(1), 1–15.

Chomsky, N. (1981). A naturalistic approach to language and cognition. *Cognition and Brain Theory, 4*(1), 3–22.

Chomsky, N. (1995). *The minimalist program.* Cambridge, MA: MIT Press.

Church, K. W. (1982). *On memory limitations in natural language processing.* Unpublished doctoral dissertation, Indiana University.

Churchland, P. S., & Ramachandran, V. S. (1993). Filling in: Why Dennett is wrong. In B. Dahlbom (Ed.), *Dennett and his critics* (pp. 28–52). Oxford, UK: Blackwell.

Cicourel, A. V. (1987). Cognitive and organizational aspects of medical diagnostic reasoning. *Discourse Processes, 10*, 347–467.

Cicourel, A. V. (1990). The integration of distributed knowledge in collaborative medical diagnosis. In J. Galegher, R. E. Kraut, & C. Egido (Eds.), *Intellectual teamwork* (pp. 221–242). Hillsdale, NJ: Lawrence Erlbaum Associates.

Clancey, W. J. (1985). Heuristic classification. *Artificial Intelligence, 27*, 289–350.

Clancey, W. J. (1988). Acquiring, representing, and evaluating a competence model of diagnosis. In M. Chi, R. Glaser, & M. Farr (Eds.), *The nature of expertise* (pp. 343–418). Hillsdale, NJ: Lawrence Erlbaum Associates.

Clancey, W. J. (1992). Model construction operators. *Artificial Intelligence, 53*(1), 1–124.

Clancey, W. J. (1993). Notes on heuristic classification. *Artificial Intelligence, 59*(1–2), 191–196.

Clancey, W. J. (1994). Situated cognition: How representations are created and given meaning. In R. Lewis & P. Mendelsohn (Eds.), *Lessons from learning* (pp. 231–242). Amsterdam: North-Holland.

Clancey, W. J. (1997a). Conceptual coordination: Abstraction without description. *International Journal of Educational Research, 27*(1), 5–19.

Clancey, W. J. (1997b). The conceptual nature of knowledge, situations, and activity. In P. Feltovich, K. Ford, & R. Hoffman (Eds.), *Expertise in context* (pp. 247–291). Cambridge, MA: MIT Press.

Clancey, W. J. (1997c). *Situated cognition: On human knowledge and computer representations.* New York: Cambridge University Press.

Clancey, W. J. (1998). Interactive coordination processes: How the brain accomplishes what we take for granted in computer languages—and then does it better. In Z. Pylyshyn (Ed.), *Constraining cognitive theories: Issues and opinions* (pp. 165–190). Stamford, CT: Ablex.

Clancey, W. J. (in preparation). *Review of Chalmers' "The Conscious Mind."*

Clancey, W. J. (in press). You are conscious when you dream. *Why: Questions in Science.*

Clark, H. H., & Schaefer, E. F. (1989). Contributing to discourse. *Cognitive Science, 13*, 259–294.

Cleeremans, A. (1993). *Mechanisms of implicit learning.* Cambridge, MA: MIT Press.

Cleeremans, A., & McClelland, J. L. (1991). Learning the structure of event sequences. *Journal of Experimental Psychology: General, 120*, 235–253.

Collingwood, R. G. (1938). *The principles of art*. London: Oxford University Press.

Compton, P., & Jansen, R. (1990). A philosophical basis for knowledge acquisition. *Knowledge Acquisition, 2*, 241–257.

Corballis, M. C. (1989). Laterality and human evolution. *Psychological Review, 96*, 492–505.

Cottrell, G. W., & Tsung, F. (1989). Learning simple arithmetic procedures. In *Proceedings of the Eleventh Annual Conference of the Cognitive Science Society* (pp. 58–65). Hillsdale, NJ: Lawrence Erlbaum Associates.

Cowan, J. D., & Sharp, D. H. (1988). Neural nets and artificial intelligence. In S. R. Graubard (Ed.), *The artificial intelligence debate: False starts, real foundations* (pp. 85–121). Cambridge, MA: MIT Press.

Csikszentmihalyi, M., & Csikszentmihalyi, I. S. (1988). *Optimal experience: Psychological studies of flow in consciousness*. Cambridge, UK: Cambridge University Press.

Cummins, F. (1993). Representation of temporal patterns in recurrent networks. In *15th Annual Conference of the Cognitive Science Society* (pp. 377–381). Hillsdale, NJ: Lawrence Erlbaum Associates.

Cytowic, R. E. (1993). *The man who tasted shapes*. New York: Putnam's.

Damasio, A. R. (1994). *Descartes' error: Emotion, reason, and the human brain*. New York: Putnam's.

Damasio, A. R., & Damasio, H. (1992). Brain language. *Scientific American, 267*(3), 89–95.

de Groot, A. D. (1965). *Thought and choice in chess*. The Hague, The Netherlands: Mouton.

Dell, G. S., Juliano, C., & Govindejee, A. (1993). Structure and content in language production: A theory of frame constraints in phonological speech errors. *Cognitive Science, 17*(2), 149–195.

Demopoulos, W., & Matthews, R. J. (1981). On the hypothesis that grammars are mentally represented. *Behavioral and Brain Sciences, 6*(3), 405–406.

Dennett, D. (1992). *Consciousness explained*. Boston: Little, Brown.

Dennett, D., & Kinsbourne, M. (1992). Time and the observer: The where and when of consciousness in the brain. *Behavioral and Brain Sciences, 15*(2), 183–247.

Dennett, D. (1993). Back from the drawing board. In B. Dahlbom (Ed.), *Dennett and his critics* (pp. 203–235). Oxford, UK: Blackwell.

Dewey, J. (1929). *Character and events.* New York: Holt.

Dewey, J. (1938). *Logic: The theory of inquiry.* New York: Holt.

Dewey, J. (1939). Experience, knowledge, and value: A rejoinder. In P. A. Schilpp (Ed.), *The philosophy of John Dewey* (pp. 517–608). Evanston, IL: Northwestern University.

Dewey, J. (1981a). The child and the curriculum. In J. J. McDermott (Ed.), *The philosophy of John Dewey* (pp. 511–523). Chicago: University of Chicago Press. (Original work published in 1902)

Dewey, J. (1981b). The reflex arc concept in psychology. In J. J. McDermott (Ed.), *The philosophy of John Dewey* (pp. 136–148). Chicago: University of Chicago Press. (Original work published in 1896)

diSessa, A. A. (1993). Toward an epistemology of physics. *Cognition and Instruction, 10,* 105–225.

Donald, M. (1991). *Origins of the modern mind: Three stages in the evolution of culture and cognition.* Cambridge, MA: Harvard University Press.

Donald, M. (1993). Precis of *Origins of the modern mind: Three stages in the evolution of cultures and cognition. Behavioral and Brain Sciences, 16*(4), 737–791.

Donald, M. (1994). Computation: Part of the problem of creativity. *Behavioral and Brain Sciences, 17*(3), 537–538.

Drescher, G. L. (1991). *Made-up minds.* Cambridge, MA: MIT Press.

Edelman, G. M. (1987). *Neural Darwinism: The theory of neuronal group selection.* New York: Basic Books.

Edelman, G. M. (1992). *Bright air, brilliant fire: On the matter of the mind.* New York: Basic Books.

Elman, J. L. (1989). Structured representations and connectionist models. In *Proceedings of the Eleventh Annual Conference of the Cognitive Science Society* (pp. 17–23). Hillsdale, NJ: Lawrence Erlbaum Associates.

Elman, J. L. (1991). Distributed representations, simple recurrent networks, and grammatical structure. *Machine Learning, 7*(2/3), 195–225.

Falkenhainer, B. (1988). *Learning from physical analogies: A study in analogy and the explanation process.* Ph.D. dissertation, University of Illinois at Urbana-Champaign.

Falkenhainer, B., Forbus, K. D., & Gentner, D. (1990). The structure mapping engine. *Artificial Intelligence, 41,* 1–63.

Feigenbaum, E. A., & Simon, H. A. (1984). EPAM-like models of recognition and learning. *Cognitive Science, 8*(4), 305–336.

Fodor, J. A., & Pylyshyn, Z. W. (1988). Connectionism and cognitive architecture: a critical analysis. In S. Pinker & J. Mehler (Eds.), *Connections and symbols* (pp. 3–71). Cambridge, MA: Bradford Books, MIT Press.

Forbus, K., Gentner, D., Markman, A. B., & Ferguson, R. W. (1998). Analogy looks just like high level perception: why a domain-general approach to analogical mapping is right. *Journal of Experimental and Theoretical Artificial Intelligence, 10*(2), 231–257.

Forgy, C. L. (1979). *On the efficient implementation of production systems.* Unpublished doctoral dissertation, Carnegie Mellon University.

Freeman, W. J. (1991). The physiology of perception. *Scientific American, 264*(2), 78–87.

French, R. M. (1997). Selective memory loss in aphasics: An insight from pseudo-recurrent connectionist networks. In J. Bullinaria, G. Houghton, & D. Glasspool (Eds.), *Connectionist Representations: Proceedings of the fourth Neural Computation and Psychology Workshop* (pp. 183–195). New York: Springer-Verlag.

Gallistel, C. R. (1981). Precis of Gallistel's *The organization of action:* A new synthesis. *Behavioral and Brain Sciences, 4*(4), 609–650.

Gardner, H. (1985). *Frames of mind: The theory of multiple intelligences.* New York: Basic Books.

Genesereth, M. R. (1983). An overview of metalevel architecture. In *Proceedings of the National Conference on Artificial Intelligence* (pp. 119–123). Los Altos: Morgan Kaufmann.

Genesereth, M. R., & Nilsson, N. (1987). *Logical foundations of artificial intelligence.* Los Altos: Morgan Kaufmann.

Gentner, D. R. (1981a). *Evidence against a central control model of timing in typing.* (Tech. Rep. No. Chip 108). University of California.

Gentner, D. R. (1981b). *Skilled finger movements in typing.* (Tech. Rep. No. CHIP 104). University of California.

Gentner, D. R. (1982). *The development of typewriting skill.* (Tech. Rep. No. Chip 114). University of California.

Gibson, J. J. (1966). *The senses considered as perceptual systems.* Boston: Houghton Mifflin.

Glenberg, A. M. (1997). What memory is for. *Behavioral and Brain Sciences,* *20*(1), 1–55.

Goffman, E. (1959). *Presentation of self in everyday life.* New York: Anchor.

Gordon, W. (1995). Koko and videos. *Gorilla—Journal of the Gorilla Foundation, 19*(Winter), 6–7.

Gould, J. L., & Gould, C. G. (1994). *The animal mind.* New York: Scientific American Library.

Gould, S. J. (1987). *An urchin in the storm.* New York: Norton.

Greenbaum, J., & Kyng, M. (1991). *Design at work: Cooperative design of computer systems.* Hillsdale, NJ: Lawrence Erlbaum Associates.

Greeno, J. (1995). Understanding concepts in activity. In C. A. Weaver III, S. Mannes, & C. R. Fletcher (Eds.), *Discourse comprehension: Essays in honor of Walter Kintsch* (pp. 65–96). Hillsdale, NJ: Lawrence Erlbaum Associates.

Gregory, R. L. (1970). *The intelligent eye.* New York: McGraw-Hill.

Greiner, R., & Genesereth, M. R. (1983). What's new? A semantic definition of novelty. In *Proceedings of the Eighth International Joint Conference on Artificial Intelligence* (pp. 450–454). Los Altos: Morgan Kaufmann.

Griffin, D. R. (1984). *Animal thinking.* Cambridge, MA: Harvard University Press.

Griffin, D. R. (1992). *Animal minds.* Chicago: University of Chicago Press.

Grossberg, S. (1982). *Studies of mind and brain.* Dordrecht, Holland: D. Reidel.

Grudin, J. T. (1982). *Central control of timing in skilled typing.* (ONR Rep. No. 8202). Center for Human Information Processing, University of California.

Hall, E. T. (1982). *The hidden dimension.* New York: Anchor. (Original work published in 1966)

Hameroff, S. R., Kaszniak, A. W., & Scott, A. C. (Eds.). (1996). *Toward a science of consciousness: The first Tucson discussions and debates.* Cambridge, MA: MIT Press.

Hanson, S. J., & Burr, D. J. (1990). What connectionist models learn: Learning and representation in connectionist networks. *Behavioral and Brain Sciences, 13*(3), 471–518.

Hebb, D. O. (1949). *The organization of behavior: A neuropsychological theory.* New York: Wiley.

Heinrich, B. (1993). A birdbrain nevermore: When put to the test, ravens display insight. *Natural History, 102*(10, October), 50–58.

Hetherington, P. A., & Shapiro, M. L. (1993). A simple network model simulates hippocampal place fields: II. Computing goal-directed trajectories and memory fields. *Behavioral Neuroscience, 107*(3), 434–443.

Hobbs, J. R. (1985). Granularity. In *Proceedings of the Ninth International Joint Conference on Artificial Intelligence* (pp. 432–435). Los Altos: Morgan Kaufmann.

Hofstadter, D. R. (1985). *Metamagical themas.* New York: Basic Books.

Hofstadter, D. R. (1993). *How could a copycat ever be creative?* (Tech. Rep. No. 72). Center for Research on Concepts & Cognition, Indiana University.

Hofstadter, D. R. (1995a). *Fluid concepts and creative analogies: Computer models of the fundamental mechanisms of thought.* New York: Basic Books.

Hofstadter, D. R. (1995b). A review of *Mental leaps: Analogy in creative thought. AI Magazine, 16*(3), 75–80.

Holyoak, K., & Thagard, P. (1994). *Mental leaps: Analogy in creative thought.* Cambridge, MA: MIT Press.

Hughes, J., Randall, D., & Shapiro, D. (1991). CSCW: Discipline or paradigm? A sociological perspective. In *Proceedings of the Second European Conference on Computer-Supported Cooperative Work* (pp. 309–323). Amsterdam, The Netherlands.

Hull, C. L. (1935). The mechanism of the assembly of behavior segments in novel combinations suitable for problem solution. *The Psychological Review, 42*(3), 219–245.

Hutchins, E. (1995). *Cognition in the wild.* Cambridge, MA: MIT Press.

Iran-Nejad, A. (1984). Affect: A functional perspective. *Mind and Behavior, 5*(3), 279–310.

Iran-Nejad, A. (1990). Active and dynamic self-regulation of learning processes. *Review of Educational Research, 60*(4), 573–602.

Jackendoff, R. (1987). *Consciousness and the computational mind.* Cambridge, MA: MIT Press.

Jackendoff, R. (1994). *Patterns in the mind.* New York: Basic Books.

Jenkins, J. J. (1974). Remember that old theory of memory? Well, forget it! *American Psychologist,* (November), 785–795.

Johnson, M. (1987). *The body in the mind: The bodily basis of meaning, imagination, and reason.* Chicago: University of Chicago Press.

Johnson-Laird, P. N. (1983). *Mental models: Towards a cognitive science of language, inference, and consciousness.* Cambridge, MA: Harvard University Press.

Jordan, M. I. (1986). *Serial order: A parallel distributed processing approach.* (Tech. Rep. No. ICS 8606). University of California.

Kagan, J. (1994). *Galen's prophecy: Temperament in human nature.* New York: Basic Books.

Kant, E., & Newell, A. (1984). Problem solving techniques for the design of algorithms. *Information Processing & Management, 2020*(1–2), 97–118.

Katz, J. J., & Fodor, J. A. (1963). The structure of a semantic memory. *Language, 39,* 170–210.

Kauffman, S. (1993). *The origins of order: Self-organization and selection in evolution.* New York: Oxford University Press.

Kihlstrom, J. F. (1984). Conscious, subconscious, unconscious: A cognitive perspective. In K. S. Bowers & D. Meichenbaum (Eds.), *The Unconscious Reconsidered* (pp. 149–211). New York: Wiley.

Koestler, A. (1964). *The act of creation: A study of the conscious and unconscious in science and art.* New York: Dell.

Kolenda, K. (1964). *The freedom of reason.* San Antonio, TX: Principia Press of Trinity University.

Kolers, P. A. (1972). *Aspects of motion perception.* Oxford: Pergamon.

Kolodner, J. L. (1984). *Retrieval and organizational strategies in conceptual memory: A computer model.* Hillsdale, NJ: Lawrence Erlbaum Associates.

Kosslyn, S. M. (1980). *Image and mind.* Cambridge, MA: Harvard University Press.

Kotovsky, K., & Simon, H. A. (1973). Human acquisition of concepts for sequential patterns. In H. A. Simon (Ed.), *Models of thought, Volume 1* (pp. 263–291). New Haven, CT: Yale University Press.

Laird, J. E., & Rosenbloom, P. S. (1990). Integrating execution, planning, and learning in Soar for external environments. In *Proceedings of the Eighth National Conference on Artificial Intelligence* (pp. 1022–1029). Menlo Park, CA: AAAI Press.

Lakoff, G. (1987). *Women, fire, and dangerous things: What categories reveal about the mind.* Chicago: University of Chicago Press.

Lakoff, G. (1995). The neurocognitive self: Conceptual system research in the twenty-first century and the rethinking of what a person is. In R. L. Solso & D. W. Massaro (Eds.), *The Science of the Mind: 2001 and Beyond* (pp. 221–243). New York: Oxford University Press.

Langacker, R. W. (1986). An introduction to cognitive grammar. *Cognitive Science, 10*(1), 1–40.

Larkin, J. H., & Simon, H. A. (1987). Why a diagram is (sometimes) worth ten thousand words. *Cognitive Science, 11*(1), 65–100.

Lashley, K. S. (1951). The problem of serial order in behavior. In L. A. Jeffress (Ed.), *Cerebral mechanisms in behavior.* New York: Wiley.

Lave, J. (1988). *Cognition in practice.* Cambridge, MA: Cambridge University Press.

Lave, J., & Wenger, E. (1991). *Situated learning: Legitimate peripheral participation.* Cambridge, UK: Cambridge University Press.

Lee, K.-F. (1990). Context-dependent phonetic hidden Markov models for speaker-independent continuous speech recognition. In A. Waibel & K.-F. Lee (Eds.), *Readings in speech recognition* (pp. 347–364). Los Altos: Morgan Kaufmann.

Lehman, J. F., Lewis, R. L., & Newell, A. (1991). *Natural language comprehension.* (Tech. Rep. No. CMU-CS-91-117). Carnegie-Mellon University.

Lehnert, W. (1991). Symbolic/subsymbolic sentence analysis: Exploiting the best of two worlds. In J. A. Barnden & J. Pollack (Eds.), *Advances in connectionist and neural computation Theory* (pp. 135–164). Norwood, NJ: Ablex.

Leiber, J. (1975). *Noam Chomsky, a philosophic overview.* New York: St. Martin's.

Lewis, C. (1981). Skill in algebra. In J. R. Anderson (Ed.), *Cognitive skills and their acquisition* (pp. 85–110). Hillsdale, NJ: Lawrence Erlbaum Associates.

Lewis, R. L. (1995). *A theory of grammatical but unacceptable embeddings.* Unpublished manuscript. Carnegie-Mellon University.

Lewis, R. L. (1996). Interference in short-term memory: The magical number two (or three) in sentence processing. *Journal of Psycholinguistic Research, 25*(1), 93–115.

Lewis, R. L., & Lehman, J. F. (1994). *A theory of the computational architecture of sentence comprehension.* Unpublished manuscript. Carnegie-Mellon University.

Lieberman, P. (1998). *Eve spoke: Human language and human evolution.* New York: W.W. Norton.

Linde, C. (1993). *Life stories: The creation of coherence.* New York: Oxford University Press.

Loftus, E. F. (1979). *Eyewitness testimony.* Cambridge, MA: Harvard University Press.

London, B., & Clancey, W. J. (1982). Plan recognition strategies in student modeling: Prediction and description. In *Proceedings of the National Conference on Artificial Intelligence* (pp. 335–338). Pittsburgh, PA: AAAI.

Lorenz, K. (1952). *King Solomon's ring.* New York: Penguin Books.

Mandler, G. (1962). From association to structure. *Psychological Review, 69,* 415–427.

Maturana, H. R., & Varela, F. J. (1987). *The tree of knowledge: The biological roots of human understanding.* Boston: New Science Library.

Maturana, H. R. (1975). The organization of the living: A theory of the living organization. *International Journal of Man-Machine Systems, 7,* 313–332.

McCorduck, P. (1991). *Aaron's code: Meta-art, artificial intelligence, and the work of Harold Cohen.* New York: Freeman.

McLuhan, M. (1967). *The medium is the message: An inventory of effects.* New York: Bantam. (With Quintin Fiore and Jerome Angel.)

Medin, D. L., Goldstone, R. L., & Gentner, D. (1993). Respects for similarity. *Psychological Review, 100*(2), 254–278.

Miller, G. A. (1956). The magical number seven, plus or minus two: Some limits on our capacity for processing information. *Psychological Review, 63,* 81–97.

Miller, G. A., Galanter, E., & Pribram, K. H. (1960). *Plans and the structure of behavior.* New York: Holt, Rinehart, and Winston.

Miller, G. A., & Isard, S. (1964). Free recall of self-embedded English sentences. *Information and Control, 7,* 292–303.

Miller, J. (1983). *States of mind.* New York: Pantheon.

Miller, J. R., Polson, P. G., & Kintsch, W. (1984). Problems of methodology in cognitive science. In W. Kintsch, J. R. Miller, & P. Polson (Eds.), *Methods and tactics in cognitive science* (pp. 1–18). Hillsdale, NJ: Lawrence Erlbaum Associates.

Miller, M. L. (1982). A structured planning and debugging environment for elementary programming. In D. Sleeman & J. S. Brown (Eds.), *Intelligent tutoring systems* (pp. 119–136). London: Academic Press.

Minsky, M. (1977). Frame system theory. In P. N. Johnson-Laird & P. C. Wason (Eds.), *Thinking: Readings in cognitive science* (pp. 355–376). Cambridge, UK: Cambridge University Press.

Minsky, M. (1985). *The society of mind.* New York: Simon & Schuster.

Mitchell, M. (1993). *Analogy-making as perception.* Cambridge, MA: MIT Press.

Mitchell, M., & Hofstadter, D. R. (1990). The right concept at the right time: How concepts emerge as relevant in response to content-dependent pressures. In *Proceedings of the Twelfth Annual Conference of the Cognitive Science Society* (pp. 174–181). Hillsdale, NJ: Lawrence Erlbaum Associates.

Mithen, S. (1996). *The prehistory of the mind.* New York: Thames & Hudson.

Miyata, Y. (1989). A PDP model of sequence learning that exhibits the power law. In *Proceedings of the Eleventh Annual Conference of the Cognitive Science Society* (pp. 9–16). Hillsdale, NJ: Lawrence Erlbaum Associates.

Montague, P. R., & Sejnowski, T. J. (1994). The predictive brain: Temporal coincidence and temporal order in synaptic learning mechanisms. *Learning Memory, 1*(1), 1–33.

Morris, H. C. (1991). On the feasibility of computational artificial life--A reply to critics. In J.-A. Meyer & S. W. Wilson (Eds.), *From Animals to Animats: Proceedings of the First International Conference on Simulation of Adapted Behavior* (pp. 40–49). Cambridge, MA: MIT Press.

Morrison, C. T., & Dietrich, E. (1995). Structure-mapping vs. high-level perception: The mistaken fight over the explanation of analogy. In *Proceedings of the Seventeenth Annual Cognitive Science Conference* (pp. 678–682). Mahwah, NJ: Lawrence Erlbaum Associates.

Mozer, M. C. (1983). *Letter migration in word perception.* (ONR Rep. No. 8301). University of California.

Mozer, M. C. (1986). *Early parallel processing in reading: A connectionist approach.* (ICS Rep. No. 8611). Institute for Cognitive Science, University of California.

Murdock, B. B. (1995). Human memory in the twenty-first century. In R. L. Solso & D. W. Massaro (Eds.), *The science of the mind: 2001 and beyond* (pp. 109–122). New York: Oxford University Press.

Neisser, U. (1976). *Cognition and reality: Principles and implications of cognitive psychology.* New York: Freeman.

Newell, A. (1990). *Unified theories of cognition.* Cambridge, MA: Harvard University Press.

Newell, A., & Simon, H. A. (1972). *Human problem solving.* Englewood Cliffs, NJ: Prentice-Hall.

Norman, D. A. (1979). *Slips of the mind and an outline for a theory of action.* (CHIP Rep. No. 7905). University of California.

Norman, D. A. (1980). Twelve issues for cognitive science. *Cognitive Science, 4*(1), 1–32.

Norman, D. A. (1988). *The psychology of everyday things.* New York: Basic Books.

Ogden, C. K., & Richards, I. A. (1923). *The meaning of meaning*(8th ed). New York: Harcourt, Brace, & World.

Patterson, K. (1991). Learning by association: Two tributes to George Mandler. In W. Kessen, A. Ortony, & F. Craik (Eds.), *Memories, thoughts, and emotions: Essays in honor of George Mandler* (pp. 35–41). Hillsdale, NJ: Lawrence Erlbaum Associates.

Payne, S. J. (1993). Memory for mental models of spatial descriptions: An episodic-construction-trace hypothesis. *Memory and Cognition, 21*(5), 591–603.

Pessoa, L., Thompson, E., & Noë, A. (1998). Finding out about filling in: A guide to perceptual completion for visual science and the philosophy of perception. *Behavior and Brain Sciences, 21*(6), 723–802.

Pfeifer, R., Schreter, Z., Fogelman-Soulié, F., & Steels, L. (Eds.). (1989). *Connectionism in perspective.* Amsterdam: North-Holland.

Piaget, J. (1970). *Genetic epistemology.* New York: Norton.

Pinker, S. (1994). *The language instinct.* New York: HarperPerennial.

Pinker, S., & Prince, A. (1988). On language and connectionism: Analysis of a parallel distributed processing model of language acquisition. *Cognition, 28*, 73–193.

Polanyi, M. (1966). *The tacit dimension.* New York: Doubleday Anchor.

Polk, T. A., & Newell, A. (1995). Deduction as verbal reasoning. *Psychological Review, 102*(3), 533–566.

Pollack, J. B. (1990). Recursive distributed representations. *Artificial Intelligence, 46*(1–2), 77–105.

Pople, H. E. J. (1982). The development of clinical expertise in the computer. In P. Szolovits (Ed.), *Artificial intelligence in medicine* (pp. 79–117). Boulder, CO: Westview Press.

Pribram, K. H. (1971). *Languages of the brain: Experimental paradoxes and principles of neuropsychology.* Monterey, CA: Brooks/Cole.

Puccetti, R. (1981). The case for mental duality: Evidence from split-brain data and other considerations. *Behavioral and Brain Sciences, 4*(1), 93–124.

Pylyshyn, Z. W. (1984). *Computation and cognition: Toward a foundation for cognitive science.* Cambridge, MA: MIT Press.

Rabiner, L. R. (1990). A tutorial on hidden Markov models and selected applications in speech recognition. In A. Waibel & K.-F. Lee (Eds.), *Readings in speech recognition* (pp. 267–296). Los Altos: Morgan Kaufmann.

Reason, J. (1977). Skill and error in everyday life. In M. J. A. Howe (Ed.), *Adult learning: Psychological research and applications* (pp. 21–44). London: Wiley.

Reason, J. (1979). Actions not as planned: The price of automatization. In G. Underwood & R. Stevens (Eds.), *Aspects of consciousness, psychological issues* (pp. 67–89). London: Academic Press.

Reber, A. S. (1993). *Implicit learning and tacit knowledge.* New York, NY: Oxford University Press.

Robins, L. S. (1990). *"We haven't gotten Pneumonia, have you?": The Interactive effects of pronoun usage in physician-patient discourse.* Unpublished doctoral dissertation, University of Michigan.

Rodolitz, N. S., & Clancey, W. J. (1989). Guidon-Manage: Teaching the process of medical diagnosis. In D. Evans & V. Patel (Eds.), *Medical cognitive science* (pp. 313–348). Cambridge, MA: Bradford Books, MIT Press.

Rosch, E. (1978). Principles of categorization. In E. Rosch & B. B. Lloyd (Eds.), *Cognition and categorization* (pp. 27–48). Hillsdale, NJ: Lawrence Erlbaum Associates.

Roschelle, J., & Clancey, W. J. (1992). Learning as social and neural. *The Educational Psychologist, 27*(4), 435–453.

Rose, D. E. (1993). Advances in connectionist and neural computation theory, volume 1: High-level connectionist models. *Artificial Intelligence, 62*(1), 129–139.

Rose, S. (1994). *The making of memory: From molecules to mind.* New York: Doubleday.

Rosenbloom, P. S., Newell, A., & Laird, J. E. (1991). Toward the knowledge level in Soar: The role of the architecture in the use of knowledge. In K. VanLehn (Ed.), *Architectures for Intelligence: The Twenty-second Carnegie Mellon Symposium on Cognition* (pp. 75–111). Hillsdale, NJ: Lawrence Erlbaum Associates.

Rosenfield, I. (1988). *The invention of memory: A new view of the brain.* New York: Basic Books.

Rosenfield, I. (1992). *The strange, familiar, and forgotten.* New York: Vintage Books.

Rubin, D. C., Wallace, W. T., & Houston, B. C. (1993). The beginnings of expertise for ballads. *Cognitive Science, 17*(3), 29.

Rumelhart, D. E., & McClelland, J. L. (1986). On learning the past tenses of English verbs. In J. L. McClelland, D. E. Rumelhart, & the PDP Research Group (Eds.), *Parallel distributed processing: Explorations in the microstructure of cognition: Vol. 2. Psychological and biological models* (pp. 216–271). Cambridge, MA: Bradford Books, MIT Press.

Rumelhart, D. E., & Norman, D. A. (1981). *Simulating a skilled typist: A study of skilled cognitive-motor performance.* (CHIP Rep. No. 102). University of California.

Rumelhart, D. E., Smolensky, P., McClelland, J. L., & Hinton, G. E. (1986). Schemata and sequential thought processes in PDP models. In J. L. McClelland, D. E. Rumelhart, & the PDP Research Group (Eds.), *Parallel distributed processing: Explorations in the microstructure of cognition: Vol. 2. Psychological and biological models* (pp. 7–57). Cambridge, MA: Bradford Books, MIT Press.

Ryle, G. (1949). *The concept of mind.* New York: Barnes & Noble.

Sacks, O. (1987). *The man who mistook his wife for a hat.* New York: Harper & Row.

Sacks, O. (1990, November 22). Neurology and the soul. *The New York Review of Books,* pp. 44–50.

Sahakian, W. S. (1976). *Introduction to the psychology of learning.* Chicago: Rand McNally.

Sandberg, J. A. C., & Wielinga, B. J. (1991). How situated is cognition? In *Proceedings of the Twelfth International Conference on Artificial Intelligence* (pp. 341–346). San Mateo, CA: Morgan Kaufmann.

Schank, R. C. (1980). Language and memory. *Cognitive Science, 4*(3), 243–284.

Schank, R. C., & Abelson, R. P. (1977). *Scripts, plans, goals, and understanding.* Hillsdale, NJ: Lawrence Erlbaum Associates.

Schank, R. C. (1981). Failure-driven memory. *Cognition and Brain Theory, 4*(1), 41–60.

Schank, R. C. (1982). *Dynamic memory: A theory of reminding and learning in computers and people.* Hillsdale, NJ: Lawrence Erlbaum Associates.

Schank, R. C. (1986). *Explanation patterns.* Hillsdale, NJ: Lawrence Erlbaum Associates.

Schneider, W. (1999). Working memory in multi-level hybrid connectionist control architecture (CAP2). In A. Miyake & P. Shah (Eds.), *Models of working memory* (pp. 340–374). Cambridge, UK: Cambridge University Press.

Schön, D. A. (1979). Generative metaphor: A perspective on problem-setting in social polity. In A. Ortony (Ed.), *Metaphor and thought* (pp. 254–283). Cambridge, UK: Cambridge University Press.

Schön, D. A. (1987). *Educating the reflective practitioner.* San Francisco: Jossey-Bass.

Searle, J. R. (1969). *Speech acts.* Cambridge, UK: Cambridge University Press.

Sejnowski, T. J., & Rosenberg, C. R. (1990). NETtalk: a parallel network that learns to read aloud. *Cognitive Science, 14*, 179–211.

Servan-Schreiber, D., Cleeremans, A., & McClelland, J. L. (1988). *Encoding sequential structure in simple recurrent networks.* (Tech. Rep. No. CMU-CS-88-183). Carnegie Mellon University.

Servan-Schreiber, D., Cleeremans, A., & McClelland, J. L. (1991). Graded state machines: The representation of temporal contingencies in simple recurrent networks. *Machine Learning, 7*(2–3), 161–194.

Shannon, B. (1992). Are connectionist models cognitive? *Philosophical Psychology, 5*(3), 235–255.

Shapiro, S. C. (1992). *Encyclopedia of artificial intelligence.* New York: Wiley.

Shreeve, J. (1995). *The Neandertal enigma: Solving the mystery of modern human origins.* New York: Morrow.

Simon, H. A. (1981). *The sciences of the artificial (2nd ed.)*. Cambridge, MA: MIT Press. (Original work published in 1969)

Skinner, B. (1957). *Verbal behavior*. Englewood Cliffs, NJ: Prentice-Hall.

Smolensky, P. (1988). On the proper treatment of connectionism. *Behavioral and Brain Sciences, 11*, 1–23.

Smolensky, P., Miyata, Y., & Legendre, G. (1993). Distributed representation and parallel processing. In *Proceedings of the Fifteenth Annual Conference of the Cognitive Science Society* (pp. 759–764). Hillsdale, NJ: Lawrence Erlbaum Associates.

Sowa, J. F. (1984). *Conceptual structures: Information processing in mind and machine*. Reading, MA: Addison-Wesley.

Stabler, E. P. (1983). How are grammars represented? *Behavioral and Brain Sciences, 6*(3), 391–421.

Star, S. L., & Greisemer, J. R. (1989). Institutional ecology, "translations" and boundary objects: Amateurs and professionals in Berkeley's Museum of vertebrate zoology. *Social Studies of Science, 19*, 387–420.

Stich, S. P. (1980). What every speaker cognizes. *Behavioral and Brain Sciences, 3*(1), 39–40.

Suchman, L. A. (1987). *Plans and situated actions: The problem of human-machine communication*. Cambridge, UK: Cambridge University Press.

Sun, R. (1996). Hybrid connectionist-symbolic modules, A report from the IJCAI-95 Workshop on Connectionist-Symbolic Integration. *AI Magazine, 17*(2), 99–103.

Thelen, E., & Smith, L. B. (1994). *A dynamic systems approach to the development of cognition and action*. Cambridge, MA: MIT Press.

Tolman, E. C. (1948). Cognitive maps in rats and men. *Psychological Review, 55*(4), 189–208.

Tomasello, M., Kruger, A. C., & Ratner, H. H. (1993). Cultural learning. *Behavioral and Brain Sciences, 16*(3), 495–552.

Touretzky, D. (1988). A distributed connectionist production system. *Cognitive Science, 12*, 423–446.

Touretzky, D. (1990). Dynamic symbol structures. *Artificial Intelligence, 46*(1–2), 5–46.

van Gelder, T. J. (1990). Compositionality: A connectionist variation on a classical theme. *Cognitive Science, 14*, 355–384.

Varela, F. J. (1995). The re-enchantment of the concrete. In L. Steels & R. Brooks (Eds.), *The artificial life route to artificial intelligence* (pp. 11–22). Hillsdale, NJ: Lawrence Erlbaum Associates.

Vera, A., & Simon, H. (1993). Situated action: Reply to William J. Clancey. *Cognitive Science, 17*(1), 117–135.

Vygotsky, L. (1986). *Thought and language.* Cambridge, MA: MIT Press. (Original work published in 1934)

Walker, S. (1985). *Animal thought.* London: Routledge & Kegan Paul.

Wan, H. S., Touretzky, D. S., & Redish, A. D. (1994). Towards a computational theory of rat navigation. In M. C. Mozer (Ed.), *Proceedings of the 1993 Connectionist Models Summer School* (pp. 11–19). Hillsdale, NJ: Lawrence Erlbaum Associates.

Washington, R., & Rosenbloom, P. (1993). Neomycin-Soar: Applying problem solving and learning to diagnosis. In P. S. Rosenbloom, J. E. Laird, & A. Newell (Eds.), *The Soar papers* (pp. 674–687). Cambridge, MA: MIT Press. (Original work published in 1988)

Wenger, E. (1998). *Communities of practice: Learning, meaning, and identity.* Cambridge, UK: Cambridge University Press.

Wertheimer, M. (1961). Experimental studies on the seeing of motion. In T. Shipley (Ed.), *Classics in psychology* (pp. 1032–1089). New York: Philosophical Library. (Original work published in 1912)

Wertheimer, M. (1985). A Gestalt perspective on computer simulations of cognitive processes. *Computers in Human Behavior, 1*, 19–33.

White, S., & Siegel, A. (1984). Cognitive development in time and space. In B. Rogoff & J. Lave (Eds.), *Everyday cognition* (pp. 238–277). Cambridge, MA: Harvard University Press.

Wilden, A. (1987). *The rules are no game.* New York: Routledge & Kegan Paul.

Wilkins, D., Clancey, W. J., & Buchanan, B. G. (1986). An overview of the Odysseus learning apprentice. In T. M. Mitchell, J. G. Carbonell, & R. S. Michalski (Eds.), *Machine learning: A guide to current research* (pp. 369–373). New York: Academic Press.

Wilson, K. D. (1995). Letter to the editor. *AI Magazine, 16*(1), 4.

Winograd, T. (1972). *Understanding natural language.* New York: Academic Press.

Winograd, T., & Flores, F. (1986). *Understanding computers and cognition: A new foundation for design.* Norwood, NJ: Ablex.

Wittgenstein, L. (1958). *Philosophical investigations.* New York: Macmillan. (Original work published in 1953)

Wynn, E. (1991). Taking practice seriously. In J. Greenbaum & M. Kyng (Eds.), *Design at work: Cooperative design of computer systems* (pp. 45–64). Hillsdale, NJ: Lawrence Erlbaum Associates.

Zhang, J. (1997). The nature of external representations in problem solving. *Cognitive Science, 21*(2), 179–217.

Author Index

Subject Index

Activation. *See* Neural activation
Activation trace diagrams, 6, 337
  basic example, 6
  compared to FSAs and PBGs, 131
  natural language sentences, 243
  neural theory, 90
  painters' experience, 177
  theoretical interpretation, 336
  with double anchoring, 259
Activity, xvi, 280
  being a person, 111
  categorization of, 59, 336
  composed, 173
  context in analogy, 186
  deliberate, 173
  descriptive, 194
  exploring, 128
  generalization, 208
  internal vs. interactive, 348
  laboratory experiments, 138
  related to consciousness, 110
  related to perception and emotion, 205
  related to WIDN, 129, 135
  role of rationalization, 209, 215
  scientific, 356
  sequence of, 18
  situated, 212
  social aspect, 318, 353, 354
  speaking as, 320
Actor, 46
Analogical thought, 181
  in practice, 182
  theory of high-level perception, 145
Anchor, 135
  in recollection, 206

in sentence comprehension, 243
Associative memory, 40, 74
Attitude, 205, 352
Autism, 349
Awareness, 108

Back talk, 175
Base position, 135, 136
Behavior, 343
  grammatical analysis, 321
Binding, 137, 351
  composed, parallel, 141
Biological perspective, 8

Case-based reasoning, 280
Categorization, 31, 339, 341
  activity, 59
  anchoring, 105
  experience over time, 17
  flow, 23
  holding active, 105
  holding active one instance, 266
  in time, 30
  operating on itself, 348
  reference, 271, 348
  referential, 206
  semantic, 247
  sequences, 7, 10, 336
  theoretical issues, 350
  varieties of, 343
Causal
  models, 194
  reasoning, 334
Cerebellum, 74
Chunk, 7, 31, 292
  familiarity, 62
Chunking, 326, 339
CIRCUS, 272